BETWEEN THE LINES

BOOKS BY JOSEPH PARISI

The POETRY Anthology, 1912–1977:
*Sixty-five Years of America's
Most Distinguished Verse Magazine*
(edited with Daryl Hine)

Marianne Moore: The Art of a Modernist (editor)

"Voices & Visions" Viewer's Guide

"Poets in Person" Listener's Guide

100 Essential Modern Poems

BOOKS BY JOSEPH PARISI AND STEPHEN YOUNG

*Dear Editor: A History of POETRY in Letters
Part I: 1912–1962*

The POETRY Anthology, 1912–2002

BETWEEN THE LINES

A HISTORY OF *POETRY* IN LETTERS

Part II: 1962–2002

COMPILED AND EDITED BY
JOSEPH PARISI AND STEPHEN YOUNG

Introductions and Commentary by Joseph Parisi

IVAN R. DEE

Chicago 2006

Library of Congress Cataloging-in-Publication Data:
Between the lines : a history of Poetry in letters / edited by Joseph Parisi and Stephen
  Young.
    p. cm.
    "Part II, 1961–2002."
    Sequel to: Dear editor : a history of Poetry in letters, the first fifty years, 1912–1962.
    Includes index.
    ISBN-13: 978-1-56663-656-8 (cloth : acid-free paper)
    ISBN-10: 1-56663-656-6 (cloth : acid-free paper)
    1. Poetry (Chicago, Ill.) 2. Periodicals—Publishing—Illinois—Chicago—History—
20th century. 3. Rago, Henry, 1915–1969,—Correspondence. 4. Nims, John Frederick,
1913–1999,—Correspondence. 5. Hine, Daryl, 1936– ,—Correspondence. 6. Parisi,
Joseph, 1944—Correspondence. 7. Editors—United States—Correspondence. 8.
Literature publishing—Illinois—Chicago—History—20th century. 9. American
poetry—History and criticism. I. Parisi, Joseph, 1944– II. Young, Stephen, 1960–
III. Dear editor.
PS301.P623B48 2006
811'.5405—dc22   2005037532

Contents

List of Illustrations

Acknowledgments

Without the great generosity of the poets, heirs, and literary executors listed at the back, most of whom waived permissions fees, this book could not have been printed. Stephen Young and I are especially grateful to the widows, children, and other relatives of the past editors, as well as to former staff members, who verified facts and gave us vital information unrecorded except in their memories. To Juliet and Christina Rago and to Bonnie Larkin Nims, we are much beholden for their extraordinary kindness in providing us private correspondence, photographs, draft texts, articles, and other documents from their personal collections.

Most of the *Poetry* archives are preserved and divided between two libraries, at the University of Chicago (1912–1960) and Indiana University, Bloomington (1961–): original manuscripts, letters, financial records, proofs, and other editorial materials—more than 600,000 items in all. The results of our examinations of the documents from the first fifty years were published in *Dear Editor* in 2002. To the unfailingly supportive staff of Special Collections at Chicago's Regenstein Library, we remain grateful for making our research there not only expeditious but pleasant. To Alice Schreyer, Curator, we owe a large debt for arranging for us to peruse the correspondence files even while the department was closed for renovations.

We are greatly obliged to The Lilly Library at Indiana University for granting both of us Everett Helm Visiting Fellowships, which helped underwrite our several trips to Bloomington to study the post-1960 files. To then Director Lisa Browar and Curator Saundra Taylor, Rebecca Cape, Joel Silver, and the rest of the staff at the Lilly Library, our sincere thanks.

In the Newberry Library we examined several unindexed items rediscovered there by our colleague Aaron Fagan, including private correspondence and memoranda that proved essential in reconstructing the magazine's "middle years" following World War II. The Newberry also allowed us to read files from the Regenstein archives in its own Special Collections department. Curators Diana Haskell and Robert Karrow were particularly courteous in accommodating our requests, and Mr. Karrow brought to our attention little-known correspondence by W. C. Williams in the Library.

We further wish to remember here, warmly and with abiding gratitude, that the Newberry provided *Poetry* with the office space that was crucial in sustaining the magazine from 1987 to 2003.

Several former and present staff members also helped uncover important business records, photographs, press clippings, ephemera, and other materials in the archives retained in the *Poetry* offices. Especially to Damian Rogers and Aaron Fagan we extend our thanks, with much appreciation for their assistance and good cheer as we engaged in the long process of collecting data and documents for this chronicle. Jayne Marek's POETRY *Index 1912–1997* was indispensable in tracking publishing histories early in our research.

While this book and the history of the earlier decades in *Dear Editor* have been our personal projects, we are grateful to the former Modern Poetry Association and now the Poetry Foundation, publishers of *Poetry*, for allowing us to use various documents, including photographs, from their archives and to quote from material printed in the magazine. We have tried diligently to be accurate in transcribing the letters and recording facts in these chronicles; any errors in the texts are unintentional. All opinions are strictly those of this commentator. I have enjoyed happy rapport with many poets and readers during and after my tenure at *Poetry*, and I cherish their cordial relationships and good wishes then and since. For their warm friendship and abiding care over many years, especially during trying times, I owe a debt to Gilda and Henry Buchbinder that I can never repay; their loyalty and unwavering support provided encouragement without which this project might not have been completed.

Finally, I should like to thank the John Simon Guggenheim Memorial Foundation again for its award of a fellowship in 2000, which was of great assistance in undertaking the research for and writing *Dear Editor* as well as in completing the preliminary work on the present volume. To the Master and Fellows of Churchill College, Cambridge, I wish to express, however inadequately, my deep appreciation for their support, genial company, and personal kindness while I was in residence as a By-Fellow finishing the research and assaying first drafts for *Between the Lines* during the 2004 Michaelmas Term.

J. P.

Chicago
January 2006

A Note on the Text

In transcribing the letters from the originals in the archives, we have retained the spelling, punctuation, abbreviations, inconsistencies, and idiosyncratic usages of the individual authors, except in cases of obvious misspellings and typographical errors, which have been silently corrected. For various reasons, certain curious spellings and deliberate misspellings (usually for comic effect), solecisms, and other oddities have been retained; they are indicated with [sic].

All ellipses in the letters are editorial ones, unless indicated by [sic]; thus, . . . [sic] signifies the author's own ellipsis. As a general rule, words underlined in the original letters are printed in italics here; on occasion, titles of magazines and books in roman in the originals have been set in italics, to avoid possible confusion.

To save space, short editorial notations, such as proper names and the publication dates of poems printed in *Poetry*, have been inserted in square brackets within the text of the letters.

Prologue

When we began delving into *Poetry*'s past in 1998, Stephen Young and I could not know that a spectacular and truly inconceivable ending to our history of the magazine would be provided three years later. In fact it arrived exactly a month after we had handed in the manuscript of *Dear Editor*, our chronicle-in-letters of the first fifty years. With the upcoming ninetieth anniversary in mind, we originally had thought we would encompass all nine decades in one book. But the riches we uncovered in the archives, particularly the correspondence files, were so abundant, the poets' first-person accounts of their lives—the private struggles, professional rivalries, backstage maneuverings, quarrels, kindnesses, and other little-known facts of poetry publishing revealed in the letters—were so fascinating, instructive, and often humorous, it became clear that two volumes would be required to tell the tale properly. The second half of our history, covering the author-editor exchanges over the four decades since 1962, and the cultural transformations that defined those years, will unfold in the letters that follow, nearly all of them unpublished until now.

In our researches we read through all the *Poetry* archives, beginning with the voluminous editorial files preserved in the University of Chicago's Regenstein Library. That collection spans the years 1912 to the early sixties and includes letters, business records, and the original manuscripts of many now-classic poems, most of them marked up for the printers. We also perused the personal papers of the founding editor, Harriet Monroe. We then traveled several times to the Lilly Library at Indiana University in Bloomington to complete our traversal of the still more plentiful papers dating from the sixties housed there. Between times we examined collections at the Newberry Library, including caches of personal letters and confidential memos uncatalogued (and probably unopened) since they were deposited by people associated with the magazine many decades earlier.

What we read surprised, saddened, amused, and sometimes appalled us. Whether writing about their work, private lives, literary theories, peers, pet peeves, or events of the day, the poets spoke to *Poetry*'s editors over the decades with remarkable frankness. On many occasions as we leafed through rarely viewed folders, Stephen and I could not help but burst out laughing, to the annoyance of the scholars scanning less entertaining materials in the Special Collections reading rooms. In all, we perused almost 600,000 documents, from which we selected and copied more than 7,000 letters. From these we chose some 600 for *Dear Editor,* and the almost 500 missives from the last 40 years printed below. In each volume we have sought to show the intricate, intimate interaction between authors and editors as work is transmitted from artist to audience—the seldom-seen process behind the scenes and between the lines when original writing is submitted, evaluated, argued over, revised, and otherwise prepared for publication.

Our narratives of *Poetry*'s many years in both books are filled with self-portraits by brilliant, opinionated, sometimes troubled, but always highly individual poets, most of them well known, others not so famous but no less interesting. Viewed chronologically, the letters paint a vivid picture of the history of twentieth-century poetry, *from the inside,* as it was in the making. Unearthing long-forgotten minutes and business files, we also discovered the course of the magazine's long career was spiked by several crises. Indeed, the ups and downs of *Poetry*'s adventurous but penurious past could provide enough engrossing episodes, cliff-hangers, odd twists, and curious characters to generate several plays or novellas.

Yet no one could have foreseen the startling climax and unthinkable conclusion our story would have. In fact, if our account were fiction, its plot would be rejected as incredible, the dramatic arc of its action dismissed as an affront to Aristotelian rules of probability. But, as James Merrill once quipped, "Life is fiction in disguise." If further proof be needed, the following pages may supply it.

Since to many what transpired in 2002 seemed preposterous, let us begin, taking that word literally, with last things first.

BETWEEN THE LINES

CHAPTER I

Outrageous Fortune

When you do finally adopt my scale of criticism you will, yes, you actually will find a handful of very select readers who will be quite delighted. . . .

I want the files of this periodical to be prized and vendible in 1999. Quixotic of me! and very impractical?

—*Ezra Pound to Harriet Monroe, 10 March 1913*

1. An Anniversary and an Announcement

On Friday evening, 15 November 2002, two hundred people crowded into the Arts Club of Chicago to celebrate an occasion truly extraordinary in literary history: the ninetieth anniversary of the founding of *Poetry*. Publications devoted to verse are noted for their ambitious or quirky beginnings. They are also notorious for their quick demises. But since its slender inaugural number came off the press in October 1912, *Poetry* had never missed a monthly edition—1,080 issues, an achievement still unsurpassed—outliving dozens of early competitors that sprang up following its first success and thousands of other "little magazines" that came and went over nine decades. "There is nothing quite like it anywhere else," T. S. Eliot wrote in 1952 on the eve of the fortieth anniversary: "*Poetry* has had its imitators, but has so far survived them all. It is an American Institution."

Poetry had already become something of a legend well before Harriet Monroe, its intrepid founding editor, expired in 1936, high in the Andes on her way to Machu Picchu, at age seventy-five. Besides giving Eliot his professional debut in 1915 ("The Love Song of J. Alfred Prufrock"), in the journal's earliest years Monroe had printed, often for the first time, such future classic authors as Wallace Stevens ("Sunday Morning"), Ezra Pound ("In a Station of the Metro"), and Carl Sandburg ("Chicago") as well as Marianne Moore, William Carlos Williams, Robert Frost, Pound's protégé "H.D., *Imagiste*," and dozens of other then-unknown writers who upset the old English and Eastern American literary establishments with what came

Harriet Monroe in the twenties.

to be known (and condemned) as The New Poetry.

Ezra Pound's very enthusiastic response to her proposed "Magazine of Verse" so impressed Harriet Monroe that by return post she asked him to be her foreign editor. The prime mover and major impresario among the innovators, Pound was a brash, twenty-seven-year-old expatriate when he assured Monroe in his first letter from London in August 1912 that a poetry Renaissance ("our American Risorgimento," as he termed it) was "inevitable"—a prediction that proved true, and in fewer than five years. By then *Poetry* and its iconoclastic authors had changed not only the way poetry was written but the very conception of the art itself. After its revolutionary first decade, *Poetry* continued to present successive generations of "new poets" and played host to a number of later aesthetic movements. Long world famous—and for most aspiring poets still *the* place in which to appear in print—*Poetry* was by 2002 the largest of the literary magazines, with "very select readers" in every state of the Union and in forty-five countries around the globe.

Among the magazine's birthday guests at the Arts Club were many longtime sponsors and contributing poets from around the country, including the U.S. Poet Laureate, Billy Collins. The previous evening Collins had performed as the master of ceremonies and narrator at a special ninetieth-anniversary program in St. James Cathedral. With the poet Linda Gregerson and a group of Chicago actors, Collins took the overflow audience on a rapid and amusing tour of the history of *Poetry* and modern poetry by means of dramatic readings from the candid correspondence between the magazine's editors and notable authors.

Frequently tart and brutally honest, the letters were drawn from *Dear Editor*, our recently released history of *Poetry*'s first fifty years, with a few others now printed here for the first time. These exchanges documented the glory days of the Poetry Renaissance and *Poetry*'s central place in the emerging Modernist movement, with its many aesthetic debates, intense rivalries, and behind-the-scenes politicking. The editors' letters, the majority never before published, also revealed the largely unheralded generosity of

The Ninetieth Anniversary program in Chicago, 14 November 2002,
St. James Episcopal Cathedral: a dramatized reading of letters with
(l. to r.) Billy Collins, narrator; the actors Michael Nowak,
Kirsten D'Aurelio, and Jeff Palmer, and the poet Linda Gregerson.

Harriet Monroe and her successors to poets in doubt and distress. This secret history of moral support, monetary aid, "career counseling," and other
private assistance, perhaps as much as its literary coups, helped account for
Poetry's extraordinary success and longevity, not to mention the deep affection expressed by many poets it "discovered" and promoted.

Told in the words of the chief protagonists themselves, the chronicle also
offered reminders of how precarious the magazine's existence had been,
particularly during World War I and the Great Depression, throughout and
immediately after World War II, in the early fifties, and at points between and
afterward. As bad luck would have it, the most serious fiscal crises (including at least five near bankruptcies) came regularly on the eve of ten-year an-
niversaries. Although recent decades had been relatively stable financially,
several supporters at the Arts Club gala could remember the days when *Poetry*'s shoestring budget was stretched to the snapping point. Among them
were donors who had come to the rescue on more than one occasion, as
when the telephone company threatened to cut off service unless bills were
paid—immediately—and the printers warned they would stop the presses if
nine months of past-due invoices weren't settled forthwith.

Toward the end of the dinner, the formal part of the celebration began with tributes to those most faithful helpmates on the magazine's way to its ninety-year milestone. Among them were Ruth Horwich, a trustee for almost half a century, Mrs. Eleanor Wood Prince, Diana Prince, and other members of the Prince family. Beginning with the late J. Patrick Lannan, founder of the annual Poetry Day readings in 1955, the Lannan family were recognized for their concern for artists and support of *Poetry*, which now continued unto the third generation. Last to be acknowledged was Ruth Lilly, the magazine's perennial patroness in Indianapolis. Besides giving generously to *Poetry* for well over twenty years, she had established the annual Lilly Poetry Prize and Lilly Fellowships, awarded through the magazine since the eighties. As the last ripples of applause faded, few at the tables seemed to notice when champagne flutes were placed near the coffee cups.

Another clink on a water glass called the assembled to attention for a final, and literally breathtaking, announcement. Thanks to another munificent and truly unparalleled gift from Ruth Lilly—in fact the largest donation ever awarded to a literary journal or group—the future of *Poetry* was now guaranteed in perpetuity. I did not mention a specific sum for the bequest. (In fact, no one could say exactly how much it might eventually come to.) But I noted that, through Mrs. Lilly's newly established estate plan, regular contributions over the next thirty years would place the magazine's parent, the Modern Poetry Association (soon to be re-

A billionaire's ode to charity: $100 million to poetry journal

By James Warren
Tribune staff reporter

In the early 1970s, an unsolicited poem arrived in the Chicago office of Poetry, a small, influential but typically financially strapped literary magazine. It was from a Mrs. Guernsey Van Riper Jr. of Indianapolis.

Joe Parisi, the editor, thought it good but not up to the standards of a monthly known for running the works of titans of 20th Century poetry, including William Butler Yeats, W.H. Auden and Dylan Thomas.

Perhaps it was Parisi's handwritten rejection note. Or similar rejection notes he'd send over the years to the same wom-

an, whom he has to this day never met or even spoken with. But, along the way, Mrs. Van Riper grew to have affection for the publication, the kind that may change the state of poetry in America.

Van Riper, who later divorced and switched back to her maiden name of Ruth Lilly, is the last surviving great-grandchild of Col. Eli Lilly, founder of Eli Lilly and Co., the pharmaceutical giant. At 87, she is a very low-profile, ailing billionaire-philanthropist who will now alter the 700-square-foot world of the four-person magazine housed in the basement of Chicago's Newberry Library.

Lilly will stratospherically

Ruth Lilly will give $100 million to Poetry, a Chicago magazine that had sent back her poems.

increase her own previous donations to Poetry by giving it well in excess of $100 million over the next 30 years, with no strings attached. The stunning development, the result of a new estate plan approved by an Indianapolis court and confirmed by lawyers, was outlined, though not fully detailed, by Pa-

PLEASE SEE **POETRY**, PAGE 20

Breaking the news: the front page of *The Chicago Tribune*,
Sunday, 17 November 2002.

structured as the Poetry Foundation), among the foremost arts organizations in the world.

Uncomprehending, most people in the room greeted the news with stunned silence. In a lighter vein I added that it appeared that after almost half a century of Poetry Day benefits, this year's dinner might be the last, or at least the final one to be held as a fund-raiser. More silence and puzzled glances followed. But freed at last from a year-long pledge of secrecy, board members began telling guests at their tables that the Lilly bequest might well exceed $100 million. As corks began popping around the room, the audience burst into waves of tumultuous, window-rattling applause.

Ever the optimist, Harriet Monroe had harbored the unrealistic hope that her magazine might someday be permanently secure, an aspiration that remained unfulfilled at her death and a goal increasingly unreachable in the many hardscrabble years that followed. Now, thanks to another magnanimous woman, Miss Monroe's dream had actually come to pass. All present rose and raised their glasses to salute them both.

2. A Media Frenzy

News of the astounding gift first reached the public less than twenty-four hours after the private announcement at the Arts Club, on the front page of the Sunday *Chicago Tribune* dated 17 November, early editions of which hit the newsstands on Saturday afternoon. Under the headline "A Billionaire's Ode to Charity: $100 Million to Poetry Journal," deputy managing editor James Warren began his exclusive story by recounting that since the seventies a poet in Indianapolis had sent *Poetry* unsolicited pieces under her married name, Mrs. Guernsey Van Riper, Jr., and that I had returned the submissions with personal notes. As the reporter put it, her work was "good but not up to the standards of a monthly known for running the works of titans of 20th Century poetry, including William Butler Yeats, W. H. Auden and Dylan Thomas." Warren speculated that because of the courteous rejection letters, "Mrs. Van Riper grew to have affection for the publication, the kind that may now even change the state of poetry in America."

Ruth Lilly, again using her maiden name following a divorce, the story continued, was eighty-seven, "a very low-profile, ailing billionaire philanthropist," and the last surviving great-grandchild of Colonel Eli Lilly, founder of the giant pharmaceutical company bearing his name. Her gift, "well in excess of $100 million over the next 30 years," had no strings attached, Warren pointed out. In his brief account of the magazine's history, he remarked (correctly) that *Poetry* had often had "less than $100 in its till" yet managed never to miss an issue. Transporting the *Poetry* office (incorrectly) from its actual location on the second floor of the stack building to the basement of the Newberry Library, he added that the donation would "now alter the 700-square-foot world of the four-person magazine": a colossal understatement if ever one were uttered.

Ruth Lilly's attorney had assured Warren she "did not take personally" the rejections from *Poetry*. The article then briefly outlined how six charitable lead and remainder trusts would fund the bequest through yearly payments staggered over the next three decades. While declining to comment on the size of the bequest, Mrs. Lilly's attorney told the reporter he felt that the beneficiaries, if prudent and conservative, with "a good investment committee and controls," would have "the base they need." But he prefaced the statement with a caveat: "There are people who can snatch defeat from the jaws of victory."

Ink on the *Tribune* story was barely dry when the phones started ringing at our (closed) offices, filling all four voice-mailboxes. A persistent producer from a local television station reached me at home late Saturday afternoon to arrange an interview. I offered to come by the studio on Monday, but she said that that really wouldn't be necessary, as they had a mobile unit—in fact, it was on its way to my place that very moment. Within minutes a reporter with microphone in hand and a young man with lights and camera appeared at my door. After a genial half-hour they packed up their gear, but as he turned to leave, the cameraman left a business card on the hall table. It was embossed with the logo of a prominent Chicago real estate firm, and carried the name of a woman agent. Seeing my puzzlement, the cameraman explained: "That's my girl friend. She's in commercial properties. You're going to need new office space, aren't you?"

By Sunday morning the story had raced across the country, indeed around the globe, as the *Tribune* article was picked up by hundreds of papers. The Associated Press and other wire-service reports soon spread the word as well. From then on *Poetry*'s outrageous good fortune provoked growing torrents of responses in the press that made the cliché expression "media frenzy" seem not merely an example of "colorful" language.

On Monday morning pandemonium broke loose the moment we stepped into the office. Reporters who had tried to contact us since Saturday renewed their attempts, repeatedly. The staff was overwhelmed by incessantly ringing telephones. At 8:30 I had the *New York Times* at one ear and the *Los Angeles Times* at the other, with four other newspapers waiting for callbacks. Television stations wanted instant access, and some producers, fearful of missing the early news programs and unwilling to waste time making appointments, simply dispatched crews straight to the Newberry.

By Monday the *Tribune* story had been reprinted or paraphrased in hundreds of dailies across the country. A number of papers in major cities, notably the *Boston Globe* and the *Los Angeles Times*, had staff reporters or stringers call for phone interviews and prepared their own stories, with additional information or from different angles. The *Christian Science Monitor* issued *two* articles, both on Friday, November 22: one by the poet David Kirby in its on-line edition, and a long print article, "From rhymes to riches: Poetry's sudden gift," by Elizabeth Lund, who rushed in from Boston and spent an entire day conducting interviews. All the papers focused on the rags-to-riches aspect of the story, of course, but they also remarked on the politeness of *Poetry*'s editors and the fact that Ruth Lilly made her gift without conditions, indeed selflessly, since her poems had never been printed in the magazine.

In his piece in the Arts section of the *New York Times* on November 19, Stephen Kinzer reported on our prospective educational programs. In a refreshing departure, he then quoted the poet Richard Tillinghast on our current *literary* state: "I've got a very high opinion of Poetry magazine." He explained, "You can pick up an issue and see a very representative selection of what's going on in poetry." Kinzer's article also listed some of Ruth Lilly's other charitable gifts, including parks, libraries, and hospitals. "Unlike many philanthropists," he observed, "Ms. Lilly does not seek publicity." He then relayed my observations on how little acknowledgment sponsors of literature usually receive: "[Y]ou don't get a plaque for supporting poetry. You better get a reward in heaven, because you sure won't get one on earth." The *Times* article also furnished a quip from Billy Collins. "Poetry has always had the reputation as being the poor little match girl of the arts," said the Poet Laureate. "Well, the poor little match girl just hit the lottery."

In his report for the *Los Angeles Times*, titled "$100-Million Gift Is Pure Poetry to Magazine" and featured on the front page (also on November 19), Eric Slater recounted the major facts but added several "human interest" details. He began by revealing that as a child Ruth Lilly was driven to school by Pinkerton guards, using different routes each day, to elude "would-be kidnappers," and thus she "explored the world mostly through poetry." He noted that as an adult she published some of her poems, but under a pseudonym.

When Slater interviewed us, we had pointed out that editorial staff recalled her memorable name but did not know who Mrs. Van Riper was when she sent her manuscripts. I added that it would not have mattered, in any case, since *Poetry* policy had always been to treat *everyone* politely. In his article, reprinted in several other newspapers, Slater noted that over its many years the magazine had "published—and rejected—poems from virtually every giant of 20th century verse," including Robert Frost. It was our emphasis on the quality of poems, "their merit and not on who wrote them," I said, that may have inspired Mrs. Lilly's gift and her confidence in

THE NEW YORK TIMES **EDITORIALS/LETTERS** *WEDNESDAY, NOVEMBER 20, 2002*

The Gift of Poetry

Late last Friday Joseph Parisi, the editor of Poetry magazine, announced that Ruth Lilly, an aspiring poet and a granddaughter of Eli Lilly, had given the magazine $100 million. One imagines lots of things that might have made a difference to the state of poetry over the years, like someone handing Shelley updated weather advice as he left the dock, or talking Sylvia Plath into reconsidering at the last moment. But this bequest is pretty hard to beat.

It more or less frees Poetry, which is published by the Modern Poetry Association, from the kind of financial constraints that most magazines have to worry about. And it does so without ethical compromise, since the magazine has always rejected Ms. Lilly's poetry submissions in the past and will, no doubt, continue to judge them with its usual critical acuity.

One assumes that most people know that poets don't make a lot of money from publishing poems. If you're good enough to have a sonnet accepted and printed in Poetry, you make $2 a line, or $28 total. Making a sonnet is no accident, and making one

good enough to stand in the company of the poets that appear in Poetry is indeed the art of a lifetime, whereas $28 is about half the hourly rate of a decent auto mechanic. It is unlikely that Poetry will use Ms. Lilly's gift to raise rates to a level that will be more than honorific, though they will go up some. Instead the money will help increase the staff at the magazine, give it a new home and, most important, expand its programs designed to encourage the writing of poetry and enlarge its audience.

This was not Ms. Lilly's first gift to Poetry and the Modern Poetry Association. Her name adorns the Ruth Lilly Fellowships and the Ruth Lilly Poetry Prize, which amounts to $100,000 and was given this year to Lisel Mueller. At the moment the tendency is to gaze in wonder at the scale of Ms. Lilly's benefaction. But what will really matter, of course, is the effect her gift has over the years and years to come. Ms. Lilly, who is 87 and in ill health, may not have published her poems for posterity's benefit, but she has found a way to benefit posterity nonetheless.

Editorial on the gift to *Poetry, The New York Times,* 20 November 2002.

our judgment. Slater also mentioned the fact that authors often sent thank-you notes to the editors for their kind rejection letters.

Poetry's long tradition of courtesy to aspiring authors became the subject of the *Chicago Tribune*'s staff writer Eric Zorn in his regular column, published the same day. Noting the magazine's huge number of annual submissions, he remarked on the "personal touch" maintained by the editors since the founding in 1912. Whether in letters or simply a few sentences to the senders, I had told him, "we want them to feel that someone did read their stuff and did appreciate that they sent it." In his essay, Zorn reflected: "One moral of the story might be that you should always be considerate of others because you never know who might actually be an heir to staggering wealth inclined to toss some of the boodle your direction."

Most unusually—in fact, an occasion perhaps unprecedented on the subject of poetry in the newspaper's history—the *New York Times* the following day ran an editorial on the Lilly donation, entitled "The Gift of Poetry." "One imagines lots of things that might have made a difference to the state of poetry over the years, like someone handing Shelley updated weather advice as he left the dock. . . . But this bequest is pretty hard to beat," it began. Commenting briefly on our plans for the new endowment, the editorial concluded: "Ms. Lilly, who is 87 and in ill heath, may not have published her poems for posterity's benefit, but she has found a way to benefit posterity nonetheless."

Chicago Tribune

FOUNDED JUNE 10, 1847

SCOTT C. SMITH, *Publisher*   ANN MARIE LIPINSKI, *Editor*

R. BRUCE DOLD, *Editorial Page Editor*   JAMES O'SHEA, *Managing Editor*

GEORGE DE LAMA, *Deputy Managing Editor, News*   JAMES WARREN, *Deputy Managing Editor, Features*

N. DON WYCLIFF, *Public Editor*

EDITORIALS

Saying no gently pays off

Thank you no, Ruth Lilly.
Nice poems, but not for us.
So went the notes declining
again—and again—and again
her verse, her stanzas, her poems.

Poetry, the magazine, after all,
has published veritable giants
of verse in its 90 years.
Carl Sandburg, Dylan Thomas,
Yeats, Auden, Frost and Pound,

You understand, Ruth Lilly, they're
titans all. The top. The legends.
But Joe Parisi was gentle in declining
again—and again—and again—
her verse, her stanzas, her poems.

Poetry was poor, but proud to be
the oldest continuously published
literary magazine in America.
Staff of four, housed in Chicago and
dedicated to the art of the soul.

The art people turn to when their
hearts break or their spirits soar
or their nation weeps for the dead.
When people ache, they turn to poems
again—and again—and again.

Turns out, though, Ruth Lilly could write
poems and, well yes, checks too.
The heiress from Indianapolis
doesn't hold a grudge for being denied
again—and again—and again.

Ruth Lilly is writing Poetry's new chapter.
She proved it with a gift worth
$100 million, or more, to the magazine
that turned her down so many times.
Who could have imagined such a gift?

Decades from now, Ruth Lilly
will be revered by those who love poems
because Joe Parisi said no gently
again—and again—and again
to her verse, her stanzas, her poems.

Chicago Tribune editorial, 23 November 2002.

    This assessment of her altruistic generosity would be echoed many times throughout the media in the weeks to follow. In its own editorial, "Saying No Gently Pays Off," printed on 23 November, the *Chicago Tribune* sang the praises of Ruth Lilly and *Poetry*, with originality, through eight stanzas of clever verse. In ironic counterpoint, immediately across from the editorial the *Tribune* ran a letter to the editor from a suburban couple protesting the "Poetry windfall." They took exception to Mrs. Lilly's gift, on the (predictable) grounds that the money might be better spent to cure disease, protect the environment, even combat international terrorism; they recommended she disburse the rest of her fortune on these and similar causes to

help create a better world. Like other amateur and professional commenta-
tors quoted in the press, the naysayers obviously were unaware of Ruth
Lilly's longtime (and even more bountiful) support for nursing programs,
service organizations, and other worthy, nonliterary causes.

Coverage on radio and television, while briefer and thus less detailed,
reached more people. Within seconds of some broadcasts, listeners called
the office to order magazine subscriptions; by the end of the first week, almost two hundred new readers had signed up. A few days after stories aired,
the mail sacks grew noticeably heavier too, because of increased numbers
of poetry submissions.

In an interview for Chicago's WLS-TV, taped at his home outside New
York City, Billy Collins remarked, "Well, it is a staggering figure. It's an awful lot of zeroes for poetry. To paraphrase Calvin Trillin, most poets are used
to getting paid in the high two figures."

Interest in all those "zeroes" continued undiminished, as articles in
weekly magazines and other journals over the next several weeks attempted
a deeper analysis, with a wide range of opinions on the significance of the
gift. Paragraphs and full pages on the Lilly bequest appeared in *Time*,
Newsweek, *U. S. News & World Report*, *The New Yorker*, *The Nation*, *Barron's*,
and *Newsday*, among others. Foreign papers, including the *Irish Times*, the
[London] *Times Literary Supplement*, and *The Guardian*, as well as in publications from Greece and Germany to Australia and Japan. The *Financial
Times* printed a lengthy interview with the editor, complete with carica-
ture. The Paris-based *Libération* flew in a special envoy to interrogate us; the
resulting piece, liberally punctuated with Gallic sneers, bore the arch title
"Ruth Lilly aime les rimes riches."

These first waves of articles and broadcasts on local, network, and cable television and radio were followed by another flood of newspaper features and
editorials and letters to the editor, opinion pieces in literary and political journals, analyses and reader responses in e-magazines and on-line editions of major and more obscure publications around the world. Even *People* magazine,
ordinarily not interested in the relatively unpopular subject of poetry, ceded
space usually reserved for celebrity items to run a half-page story, with a large
picture. More surprising, a producer at Comedy Central called to request an
interview, perhaps a personal appearance, on "The Daily Show with Jon Stewart." (Although an admirer of the satiric news program and its exceedingly
sharp host, I regretfully declined, knowing the potential perils for interviewees
through their "creative" editing.) For several weeks more, journalists and
broadcasters continued to call while e-mail messages clogged our computers.

Rather testily, Peter Davison, the poetry editor for the *Atlantic Monthly*,
rhetorically asked the *Boston Globe*'s Fred Kaplan: "What does money have
to do with poetry? . . . What does this grant do for poetry as an art form?"

(Davison conceded that at least *Poetry* was "trying to get people to read poetry.") In his November 19th front-page article entitled "Her Rhyme and
Reason," Kaplan also quoted Billy Collins's further reflections: "I'm not
sure it will encourage people to read poetry. . . . But it does show poetry is
moving to a more robust condition in America. It's returning a bit closer
to the center of cultural life than it was 15 or 20 years ago."

During the first weeks of the blitz, it became increasingly difficult to accomplish regular editorial tasks in the office, for the endless interruptions.
After handling priority business at my desk, I took to slipping into the coffee shop around the corner, poems or page proofs in hand, to get some literary work done in relative peace. But even this refuge was not always safe.
At 7:30 one morning, as I was midway through my first cup of coffee
while reading manuscripts, I looked up and was startled to see a large
young man in a jogging suit staring at me through the window. Moments
later he stood before me breathing heavily. After confirming my identity,
he introduced himself as an associate at one of Chicago's larger financial
institutions (he just happened to have his card with him), and with a winning smile offered his services in "handling our portfolio." At least he
wasn't wearing a red "power" tie and suspenders, the favored uniform in
his field.

Besides the media barrage and the incessant solicitations from would-be
money managers, multiple inquiries and offers appeared from real estate
companies, and (of course) unnumbered hopeful private and organizational
supplicants for funds. But amid the multiple distractions and despite the increased workload and responsibilities, we realized that many others would
love to have such "problems." Having struggled to make ends meet for
decades, we appreciated fully the radical contrast in our circumstances.

Beyond the financial boon, we enjoyed intellectual and other intangible
benefits as a result of the bequest. We came to know and to learn from a
number of exceptionally bright people who were expert in law, finance,
philanthropy, and other fields we had limited contact with earlier. The
months after we were informed of the gift were hectic but stimulating, genuinely exciting and a challenge to our creativity, and we all recognized how
privileged we were to be engaged in an adventure that none of us could
have foreseen when we signed on to work for a little magazine.

Less happily, if perhaps inescapably, as the obsession with the monetary an-
gle continued unabated in the media, it presented a simplistic, distorted image of what poetry and *Poetry* (and arts organizations in general) are principally about. In his irascible response to the *Boston Globe* reporter, the rightly
indignant Peter Davison had tried to refocus on the critical distinction between material wealth and artistic worth. Similarly, we attempted repeatedly

to redirect attention to the idea that the true value of money should be measured in the good works it could foster.

To little avail: the enthralling news of the Lilly gift all but eclipsed the less sensational but still rather important ninety years of literary achievement that preceded it. Memory of the birthday celebration soon began to fade, and with it remembrance of the years of struggle and of the service and sacrifice of so many—generations of loyal contributing authors, faithful donors and readers, devoted editors and staff with low salaries or none—who had carried the magazine through to its unparalleled anniversary and unexpected prosperity.

Amid the lingering fascination with the passing strange story of sudden wealth, something of greater significance was in danger of becoming a mere sidebar: *Poetry*'s central role in the making of modern poetry as well as the poor, old American Institution's defining traditions of kindness, humane concern, and substantial support for literary artists.

CHAPTER II

The Lyre and Lucre:
Poetry's First Fifty Years

The Open Door will be the policy of the magazine—
may the great poet we are looking for never find it
shut, or half-shut, against his ample genius!

—*Harriet Monroe, 1912*

1. Mixed Motives

Lofty artistic ambitions were inextricably intertwined with the more mundane realities of publishing from the beginning. Harriet Monroe started out with a well-conceived financial scheme; but, pragmatic manager though she was, the editor's sympathy toward fellow poets often overruled the founder's business plan. Her stern manner in public masked the fact she was a soft touch in private, and her openhandedness hastened the depletion of her tight budgets. The Open Door was not just editorial policy; it was taken literally, and *Poetry*'s assistance to authors was far more various, subtle, and extensive than people knew.

Monroe's main motive in undertaking her "experiment," as she called it in her first appeals to potential backers and prospective authors in 1911 and '12, was to present "all kinds of verse," including longer, "more intimate and serious" works, and she promised to "read with special interest poems of modern significance"—that is, exactly the sort of material commercial magazines wouldn't print because it was unprofitable. Monroe also proposed to pay for it, generously. At ten dollars a page for poetry, the rate was four times the average daily salary a worker made in a "good" factory job at the time. Ninety years ago, when poetry truly "didn't pay," when there was no such thing as a career in the field, no creative writing majors or M.F.A.'s—when, in fact, contemporary literature was deemed unworthy of consideration in most English departments—*Poetry*'s checks unquestionably were a major attraction for many authors.

By the same token, since little was at stake professionally—academic advancement, fellowships and grants, major prizes, and other aspects of "pobiz," so called, became widely available only after poetry began to be institutionalized in the 1950s—authors perhaps felt freer to be outspoken. As we read through the files, Stephen Young and I were constantly amazed by the unvarnished opinions poets young and older shared with the staff, and occasionally taken aback by their acerbic tone. But the fact that poets could be so fearless reflected the open-mindedness and tolerance of Monroe and her successors as well. Even when they insulted her, Monroe seems not to have taken the remarks personally.

What she *did* take to heart was the poets' work, their artistic frustrations, and their practical needs, not least their requests for aid in hard times. Many who received their first paychecks for poems from *Poetry* or made their names through its pages maintained lifelong allegiance, particularly those who carried on through lean stretches thanks to the extra help that Monroe provided. In her prospectus she also proposed to offer large annual cash prizes, starting with a $250 award, in order to give poets the kind of lucrative acknowledgment painters and sculptors had long enjoyed. As an art critic for the *Chicago Tribune* and other papers, Monroe had keenly observed, and resented, the discrepancies in compensation between poetry and the other arts.

While she envied the Art Institute and other well-subsidized cultural institutions in the city, she recognized she would have to emulate them if her endeavor was to succeed. Not wealthy herself, Monroe convinced 108 friends and acquaintances among Chicago's financial and social leaders, their spouses, and other civic-minded "guarantors" to pledge fifty dollars each for five years. By that point, she naively believed, the enterprise would be self-sufficient. Monroe's faith was badly shaken when *Poetry* ran a deficit within its very first year. The editor had to accept that poetry would never pay its way, and that she (and her successors) needed to be as adept at fundraising as at making literary judgments. Scores of little magazines perished during Monroe's twenty-four-year tenure, and hundreds after, for want of fiscal wherewithal. Peter Davison asked, "What does money have to do with poetry?" *Plenty* was the answer we found in our researches, confirming what we already knew well from our own experience keeping the magazine and its educational programs running.

Through the decades, insistent base notes on the theme of financial insecurity played counterpoint to the higher leitmotifs of poetic invention, aesthetic revolution, and artistic success. The little-known fiscal facts we uncovered were not only enlightening about the economics of *Poetry*'s long endeavor but also offered intriguing psychological insights. Late and soon we found that cash, or rather the poets' attitudes toward it, provided an incisive index to character.

Oddly enough, it may be noted, money is the rarest of all topics in poetry itself. "Getting and spending" consume enormous amounts of human energy, as Wordsworth observed, but this central reality of the human condition is almost never mentioned in verse. Today virtually every other topic, no matter how intimate or once embarrassing, is treated explicitly in poetry—but not money, the last taboo. In their letters, however, poets are not at all reticent about discussing filthy lucre, or more often, their lack thereof. The *Poetry* archives are replete with grouses about, advice on, and requests for money, as well as thank-you letters for timely loans, prizes, and cash in emergencies. As it does with denizens of the workaday world, money seems to bring out the worst, seldom the best, but occasionally the more inventive or humorous aspects in creative personalities.

Well known but still strapped in 1918, Edna St. Vincent Millay playfully wrote to Monroe for an advance on her "so stunning verses" awaiting publication. In a postscript, Millay added: "I am *awfully* broke. Would you mind paying me a lot?" In contrast, Robert Frost, famous and prosperous thanks in part to early support from Pound and *Poetry*, assured Monroe after she presented him $200 in 1922: "I don't care what people think of my poetry so long as they award it prizes." Like other artists, poets have a strong competitive sense, and none was more competitive than Frost. In a society where cash is life's report card, he strove to be at the head of the class.

Impetuous, egotistical, and charmingly self-deflating, William Carlos Williams was prolific but uneven in his poetry production. Monroe accepted several pieces but returned or asked for revisions on many more. Over their long, contentious but cordial relationship, the good doctor's moods toward Monroe could swing wildly between exasperation and affection. Following one too many rejections, he cheekily informed the editor in 1921: "After May 1st all poems by William Carlos Williams will be

Edna St. Vincent Millay, among the most popular poets of the twenties and thirties, was first championed by Harriet Monroe in 1913.

$50. —a piece—minimum—so get a thrill by rejecting five or six hundred dollars worth while you may." (She noted on the letter, "These ac'd, if at our usual rates.") It is hard to say what her reaction might have been had she known that Dr. Williams wrote Mitchell Dawson, a Chicago lawyer, in 1919: "Harriet Monroe and her folded diaper of a periodical is without any significance except as per cash paid for work." Even so, the pediatrician-poet kept sending his bantering letters and contributions, invited Miss Monroe to stay at his home, and remained friends with her to the end.

Monroe was also one of the very few ever invited into Wallace Stevens's house. She gave the insurance executive-poet his professional debut in *Poetry* in November 1914, and presented "Sunday Morning" in 1915 and many other masterpieces thereafter. She became his greatest champion, gave him several prizes, and urged him repeatedly, in print and in private, to publish a book. When *Harmonium* was at last printed in 1923, he was forty-four. The collection sold poorly. "My royalties for the first half of 1924 amounted to $6.70," he informed Monroe. "I shall have to charter a boat and take my friends around the world."

Amy Lowell, "the demon saleswoman of poetry," in the twenties.

For poets with steady day jobs or independent incomes, payment was (and is) still appreciated, if in their cases perhaps more important for its symbolic value. Even so, money's real worth is of course what makes things happen, as every entrepreneur and philanthropist knows. Thus the wealthy and ambitious Amy Lowell was generous to the magazine, but usually there were strings attached to her gifts. "The tremendous Amazon," as Edgar Lee Masters called her, wished her poems to be printed just so, and wanted her books reviewed with enthusiasm. When they were not, Monroe could expect reproaches.

"I believe very firmly that the 'laborer is worthy of his hire,'" she informed "dear Harriet" in 1913—then she asked for an advance on some poems. She was soon to depart for England, she explained, and would appreciate payment because "every little bit helps on a journey." She concluded with a request for a letter of introduction to Ezra Pound. In detailed reports, Lowell described what seemed to be the beginning of a beautiful friendship. Pound, sensing a potential patron as well as a willing pupil, introduced Lowell to his friends and initiated her in Imagist doctrine. Within a year, Ezra was accusing Amy of diluting stringent Imagist principles into "Amygisme," poaching on his territory, and taking over his "protégés" for *Some Imagist Poets.* Tirelessly promoted by "the demon saleswoman of poetry," as Eliot dubbed her, the anthology was a great success. (Pound's own picky selection in *Des Imagistes* flopped; some buyers even demanded refunds.) Both parties apprised Monroe at length during the ongoing unpleasantness, and their she-said/he-said accounts vividly illustrate the untidy mix of aesthetics, egotism, economics, personal alliances, and politicking that made up Modernism in its formative period.

2. The Pound Complex

In *Dear Editor* we presented several sides of these and other arguments involving Pound, and reconstructed his complicated if often misrepresented association with *Poetry.* From the correspondence files we were able to correct many distortions for a fuller if less flattering portrait of the maestro than the images airbrushed by his acolytes. Throughout his dealings, we found, money brought out the light and dark (the *chiaroscuro,* as he would say) in his character. Pound's judgment as a talent scout, skills as a manuscript doctor, selfless support of artists in need, and untiring efforts as a promoter of Frost, H.D., Eliot, James Joyce, and many others are legendary. Yet his egotism, high-handedness, and hot temper were such that he managed to alienate everyone, including those he helped most.

Pound first presented himself to Monroe as rather more influential than he actually was in 1912—"I do see nearly everyone that matters," he said modestly—but his connection with Yeats inspired confidence. Along with poems by the master, Pound sent pieces by young unknowns, including Joyce

Ezra Pound, impresario and
first foreign editor, in the teens.

"H.D., *Imagiste*" (Hilda Doolittle).

and D. H. Lawrence, whom he gathered uneasily under the banner of Imagism. (He later admitted that he hastily made up the "movement" just to get H.D. into print.) His submissions were accompanied by long letters filled with exhortations, acid comments about prominent writers, and diatribes on publishers. He also sent highly opinionated essays and reviews. His articles raised hackles (as he intended), and many of the poems turned readers off and provided fodder for newspaper parodies. "For GORD'S sake don't print anything of mine that you think will kill the Magazine," he wrote Monroe a few months into their tumultuous partnership, "but so far as I personally am concerned the public can go to the devil."

As the founder said from the beginning, her own great goal was to "build up" a public for the New Poetry. Yet she kept publishing Pound and "his" authors, unpopular though they usually proved to be. Meanwhile, Monroe and her astute associate editor, Alice Corbin Henderson, found their own innovative material nearer home. They promoted Sandburg, Edgar Lee Masters, and especially Vachel Lindsay, whose Midwestern populism was far more pleasing to *Poetry* subscribers than the imported experiments. Pound loathed Lindsay, dismissed Sandburg, and simply ignored Stevens. Tensions rose, as H.M. continued to print her catholic choices next to E.P.'s more radical offerings. But their first big squabble arose over money, the $250 prize for best poem of the first year. Pound insisted that Yeats receive it. Monroe wanted to give it to Lindsay, who was always in need of cash. Monroe capitulated, then she scrambled to find $100 to award Lindsay as a prize for "General William Booth Enters Into Heaven," the most commented-upon poem of *Poetry*'s first year. Monroe helped launch his spectacular career as a poet-performer and came to the rescue often during Lindsay's steep decline, forwarding sums from "secret admirers," doubtless from her own purse.

Monroe was quite generous to Pound as well, even when he proved disloyal. Despite his pledge to offer *Poetry* exclusive rights, within the first year he started sending work by himself and "his" authors elsewhere. His letters to Monroe began to bristle with barely disguised contempt, even though *Poetry* was one of Pound's few steady sources of income after 1914, when he became persona non grata at mainline English journals because of his intemperate remarks in the short-lived *Blast.* When she was forced to cut rates that year, Monroe kept paying him full price.

Without telling her, in 1917 he joined the rival *Little Review* and declared in his first article for the competition: "*Poetry* has shown an unflagging courtesy to a lot of old fools and fogies whom I would have told to go to hell tout pleinment and bonnement." At the time, Monroe was embarked on her second five-year campaign, and Pound's slam did not make her fund-raising any easier. Instead of asking Pound to resign, she accepted his "Draft of Three Cantos" and paid him £21 in advance—and apologized she couldn't afford more. Although he stayed on the masthead until 1919, his editorial role was over in 1917. But he continued to heckle Monroe, and she said nothing.

With the passing years Pound claimed ever more credit for Monroe's enterprise while deprecating her substantial labors. When he presented a revisionist account of his years at *Poetry* in *The English Journal* in 1930, Monroe offered a rebuttal, which few saw. In a rare act of self-defense, she pointed out: "The wrecks of his wild runs strew the path of progress." If she had let Pound run *Poetry*, she added, it would have gone the way of the many other journals with which he was also involved.

Pound was a prodigious propagandist for authors he promoted, and for himself. His version of his time with *Poetry* became the standard version, passed down in the histories. Monroe herself abetted his mythologizing in *A Poet's Life*, her posthumously published autobiography (1938), by putting a positive spin on their many conflicts. She was highly selective in presenting his letters and carefully edited out the rough spots. Ever gracious, she observed only that Pound continued to prod. "And if his stings and stabs should cease," she wrote in 1935, "it would mean for me the loss of life's most deliciously acrid flavor."

3. The Great Depression

By 1930 all of *Poetry*'s first competitors had gone out of business, and its days appeared to be numbered too. As the depression deepened, the deficit tripled and Monroe lost half her supporters. Now seventy, she believed even if the magazine hung on a few more years it couldn't survive after her death. She began to make final arrangements. In May 1931 she bequeathed all of *Poetry*'s assets to the University of Chicago, including books, manuscripts, correspondence files, and journals. Before she finalized the deal, Monroe consulted Pound, who praised her for getting the Chicago "porkpackers" to pay for poetry. *Poetry* managed to hold on, but

The founding editor at
Agnes Scott College, 1921.

in an April 1932 editorial, "Volume Forty," Monroe doubted "whether there will be a *Volume XLI*." All that was needed was an annual subsidy of four or five thousand dollars—better still, $100,000 for a permanent endowment. If any readers knew of a millionaire who could provide it, would they kindly inform her?

Anxious letters poured in from poets and readers, while newspapers across the country ran articles and editorials decrying the possible loss of such a "cultural asset." Many small donations trickled in, subscriptions increased, and some poets requested "no payment" for their work. Then, in 1933, an emergency grant from the Carnegie Corporation was received. It was renewed for three years, and the magazine survived another decade.

Despite *Poetry*'s own difficulties during the depression, the editors went to great lengths to answer calls for help. The most poignant pleas and thank-you letters came from younger poets, who were frequently desperate. Monroe printed the poems of Harry Brown, a poor, precocious sixteen-year-old, gave him prizes, and helped get him into Harvard. (He eventually became a successful novelist and screenwriter.) She also saw to it that the young Louise Bogan, George Dillon, and Paul Engle received fellowships. (Engle recounts his adventure with Miss Monroe as a lad in 1933, in his letter of June 1987, printed below.) Jobless or barely getting by, many young writers were drawn to socialist politics. Monroe was unimpressed by most of their material, but she did print many leftists. Among the scores of other emerging writers *Poetry* presented in the thirties were Theodore Roethke, May Sarton, Paul Bowles, Robert Fitzgerald, Ruth Lechlitner, J. V. Cunningham, Robert Penn Warren, Lorine Niedecker, Josephine Miles, Mary Barnard, Stanley Kunitz, and Elizabeth Bishop.

Returning from a P.E.N. Congress in Buenos Aires in the fall of 1936, Monroe decided to fulfill a dream to see the Andes and visit the Inca ruins. The journey overland was hard and the high altitude an added strain. When she reached Arequipa (or "place of rest"), she was exhausted, but determined to push on to Machu Picchu. On 25 September she suffered a massive stroke and died the next day. She was buried in Peru. Newspapers nationwide ran obituaries and articles praising Monroe's many efforts on behalf of American poets. Monroe's family, the *Poetry* staff, and many poet-friends resolved to keep the magazine alive as her most fitting monument. Morton Zabel, her longtime associate editor, kept *Poetry* afloat for another year. After the twenty-fifth anniversary he turned over the duties, and mounting deficits, to George Dillon in November 1937.

4. George Dillon and Peter De Vries

Like Zabel, Dillon had served as Monroe's assistant while still in college. He had published his first book in 1927, when he was twenty-one, and won the Pulitzer Prize for his second in 1932. In 1936 he and "Vincent" Millay collaborated on a translation of Baudelaire's *Flowers of Evil*. Dillon was a reticent fund-raiser, but fortunately a young fiction writer, Peter De Vries, joined the staff in April 1938. A very clever impromptu speaker, De Vries was soon enlisted to help balance the budget by addressing literary clubs. He quickly learned that luncheon addresses rarely result in increased subscriptions or donations.

George Dillon, age twenty-one in 1927, the year of his college graduation and the publication of his first book, *Boy in the Wind.*

While *Poetry*'s finances remained shaky, issues came out on schedule. But by the spring of 1942 there was considerable doubt whether *Poetry* would survive to celebrate its thirtieth anniversary. "Beginning the sixtieth volume of POETRY," News Notes for April 1942 opened, "we have much the sensation of starting to walk a plank." There was only enough cash to go on for one more week. A special committee hastily collected donations. In Washington, D.C., Archibald MacLeish gave a reading at a benefit co-sponsored by Mrs. Roosevelt. Disaster was averted, again.

Pegasus drawing by James Thurber, presented to *Poetry* in 1943.

In July 1942, Dillon was inducted and served in the Signal Corps in Africa through most of the war. Early in 1943, De Vries also was drafted but rejected for multiple ailments, and returned to the magazine. His wife Katinka joined the staff, former associates Jessica Nelson North and Marion Strobel Mitchell came back to lend a hand, and John Frederick Nims served as a part-time reader. Soldier-poets passing through Chicago frequently stopped by the Erie Street office and were taken to dinner and entertained. However straitened its circumstances, *Poetry* maintained its tradition of hospitality.

Throughout the war years, De Vries and the staff had to devote ever more time to fund-raising. Decades later he recalled alternating editorial duties "with time-outs to beg, borrow or bludgeon our tiny salaries out of civic-minded persons. I say civic-minded because Chicago has always been proud of *Poetry*'s deficit." Squadrons of volunteers were mobilized to help with programs—readings, lectures, musicales, anything but rummage sales—to make up the deficits. One

Kenneth Koch about the time of his first appearance in *Poetry*, at age nineteen, in 1945.

program in 1943 featured the humorist James Thurber, who immediately recognized De Vries's similar talent. He introduced De Vries to Harold Ross, the legendary editor of *The New Yorker*, who quickly added the witty Chicagoan to his eccentric staff. Between July 1944 and late 1946, De Vries divided his time between the two magazines. Among his later discoveries were Gwendolyn Brooks in 1944, James Merrill in 1946 (at age nineteen), as well as Kenneth Koch and John Ashbery, also minors when both debuted in November 1945.

Sergeant George Dillon in a snapshot taken while he was stationed in Paris, 1945.

Sergeant George Dillon was with the vanguard during the liberation of Paris on 25 August 1944. In fact he announced the news from his radio post in the Eiffel Tower. He returned to the States and, very reluctantly, to the editorship in April 1946. Editorially and financially, the postwar period was difficult. As costs escalated with inflation, the magazine approached more than three dozen foundations for support. Every application was rejected. Finally the Bollingen Foundation awarded $15,000 for 1947, then renewed the grant for two years. During this uncertain period *Poetry* was enlivened by first appearances of John Berryman, David Wagoner, W. S. Merwin, William Stafford, Margaret Avison, Richard Wilbur, and Donald Justice.

Although the magazine was saved again, the constant money worries finally took their toll, and in March 1949 Dillon resigned and was succeeded by Hayden Carruth, then twenty-eight. After service in Italy, Carruth had entered graduate school at Chicago. He joined *Poetry* as associate editor in the spring of 1948. Although he had control over prose, he shared the decisions on poetry with Marion Strobel and John Nims, an arrangement that soon proved unworkable. With the Bollingen money running out, the situation became desperate. Although ill suited to the task, Carruth tried diligently to find new donations. His many solicitation letters and personal visits came to nothing. At the end of November, Carruth and the staff debated who would call and tell the printers to stop the presses. He prepared a statement that *Poetry* was closing. An hour later, a telegraph arrived. The Bollingen Foundation had decided, after all, to give the magazine an absolutely final grant.

Carruth felt he should now have full editorial authority. Unfortunately, conflicts over editorial policy and personality clashes between the young editor and older trustees had now grown to the point that differences were irreconcilable. Both sides presented position papers, but Carruth's opponents had already lined up allies and proposed Karl Shapiro as his replacement. When the board met again in early January 1950, they had their way. Shapiro was invited and accepted immediately.

5. Karl Shapiro

Then at the height of his fame, Shapiro had a long history with *Poetry*, which had "discovered" him in 1940, printed him often, and awarded him prizes. In

1945 he won the Pulitzer Prize for *V-Letter*, his book of war poems. In 1947 he was appointed Consultant in Poetry at the Library of Congress and began teaching at Johns Hopkins, but didn't like the job. "I needed to escape the academy," he recalled in 1987, "and Editor of *Poetry* seemed like a beautiful and exotic alternative." Shapiro's five-year tenure turned out to be the rockiest in the magazine's history.

Always outspoken, Shapiro seemed to court controversy. His policy at *Poetry*—or, as he boasted to reporters, his *lack* of a policy— was sometimes disconcerting. One of his first decisions was to remove from the cover Monroe's beloved Whitman motto: "To have great poets, there must be great audiences too." Then he removed Geraldine Udell, who had been Monroe's secretary and befriended many poets in her quarter-century as business manager. Shapiro's wife, Evalyn, took over her duties, without pay. Several trustees resigned in protest. Editorially, Shapiro started with a clean slate too, since there were few accepted poems in the files.

Karl Shapiro shortly after winning the Pulitzer Prize for poetry in 1945.

Among the more notable younger poets who debuted under Shapiro were May Swenson, Frank O'Hara, James Dickey, Anthony Hecht, Philip

Booth, Galway Kinnell, and Adrienne Rich. But throughout his term Shapiro tilted heavily toward his contemporaries: Delmore Schwartz, Muriel Rukeyser, Richard Wilbur, Theodore Roethke, John Ciardi, John Nims, and Randall Jarrell. All were well schooled in the Great Tradition, and in their own work they followed the norms of academic poetry: compression, allusion, irony, "intellectual" content, and exceptional technique displayed in forms crafted with high finish—in short, precisely the poetic values that would be abandoned or attacked by the rebels of the late fifties and sixties.

Born in the teens and twenties, the glory days of Modernism, and following the bold pioneers of the New Poetry, the "Middle Generation" could also boast brilliant artists. But living in the shadow of giants was not easy. The "anxiety of influence," not to mention the angst of growing up during the dismal depression years, left psychic scars. The war inflicted additional wounds. While they came to be largely sheltered from the poverty and insecurity associated with their craft, many poets who rose to prominence after the war had problems perhaps more profound and intractable than physical want. Compared with the general population, a disproportionate number suffered from alcoholism and serious mental illnesses. Many had to be institutionalized, repeatedly, and several committed suicide. Still, the future for American poets, as for the U.S. generally, looked bright during the fifties. After all the difficult years, the younger authors were the first able to earn a living primarily as poet-professors or creative-writing instructors as writing courses and M.F.A. programs spread rapidly.

While under Shapiro's hand, *Poetry* continued to represent the best in current poetry, but the prose section became contentious. Edward Dahlberg's bizarre assault on Conrad Aiken's *Ushant* in 1953 caused an uproar. Hugh Kenner's acerbic critiques made him notorious. Many other reviews provoked negative reactions. But Shapiro discovered the business side of the job was even more troublesome. In late 1950, *Poetry* had a deficit of $20,000. After much lobbying, the Bollingen Foundation pledged another $7,500 for 1951 and $5,000 for 1952. Shapiro promised not to ask again. He had problems balancing his personal budget too, and had to take teaching jobs and give readings and workshops. In 1952 he also became editor of the Newberry Library's *Journal of Acquisitions*. He persuaded the director, Stanley Pargellis, to join the board. The library would eventually rescue the magazine, twice.

Shapiro was able to save on salaries when he invited the wealthy Isabella Gardner on as first reader. She served without pay and became his closest confidante. By January 1952 the magazine was losing $500 a month. The ten-year cycle was repeating itself, and it appeared *Poetry* would not reach its fortieth anniversary. Again several foundations were approached; as usual,

Evalyn Shapiro, Isabella Gardner, and Karl Shapiro in the *Poetry* office, early 1953.

they all said no. The only hope seemed to be to make another appeal to the Bollingen trustees—rather awkward, given Shapiro's pledge. Even so, they gave a small award for 1953, and then another, *truly* final, grant in 1954.

After *Poetry* celebrated its fortieth anniversary, matters went from bad to near bankruptcy. Ellen Borden Stevenson, the heiress to a condensed milk fortune and ex-wife of the Democratic presidential candidate, became board president in January 1953. In May she offered the magazine space in the old Borden family mansion, which she was converting into an Art Center. But the red ink still spread. Even the office's extra set of bound volumes had to be sold; the post-1936 *Poetry* archives followed. Ellen Stevenson had promised to assume financial responsibility until the end of the year. Then she changed her mind. (She had believed income from her Center would cover expenses; her business manager informed her otherwise.) She had lent $2,000 to the magazine and wanted repayment. *Poetry* now had only $100 on hand. In June 1954, the board met in emergency session, where Mrs. Stevenson's letter of resignation was read. Since the magazine was no longer welcome in her house, Dr. Pargellis offered it rent-free space on the unheated top floor of the Newberry Library.

After almost five years of turmoil, Shapiro needed a break; he informed the board he wished to leave within six months to a year. He was soon offered a visiting professorship at Berkeley, to begin in January 1955. As his stand-in he recommended Henry Rago, who had been on staff only a few months. By early spring 1955, Shapiro decided not to return, though he asked that his resignation not become official until September. Rago was firmly in control months before the masthead was changed. The trustees had voted to make Rago "temporary" editor. He remained fourteen years.

6. Henry Rago: The Early Years

Although his editorial experience was limited when he took the reins, Rago had an association with *Poetry* going back to 1929 when he was in high school. His father was a businessman (Rago Brothers Funeral Homes) and took a practical attitude toward his son's poetry writing: he brought the fourteen-year-old to Harriet Monroe for a professional opinion. She encouraged the boy, commented on his verses, and called him "my protégé." He was first printed in *Poetry* in 1931.

After studying law at De Paul, Rago took degrees in theology and philosophy at Notre Dame. He served in Army Counter-Intelligence during the war (he met T. S. Eliot in London during the Blitz) and was among the first soldiers to enter Paris after the liberation. In his three years there, Rago visited Alice B. Toklas and talked poetry with Gertrude Stein. In 1947 he began teaching at the University of Chicago, where he became known as a great lecturer and formed a close friendship with Hayden Carruth. Henry liked to take Hayden to a club run by "Bottles" Capone, brother of Al, whose funeral Rago Brothers had conducted. He remained devoted to him through the often difficult years after Carruth left *Poetry*.

When the University failed to reappoint Rago in 1954, he accepted Shapiro's invitation to join the staff that fall. As editor he was a strong manager and successful money-raiser, unlike most of his predecessors. His approach to both the business and literary sides of the operation was lawyerlike: meticulous in every detail. Within a year, *Poetry* went from what Rago later described as "the leanest and meanest time" in its history to unprecedented prosperity. For, ironically, almost as soon as Shapiro left Chicago, *Poetry*'s fortunes turned.

While *Poetry* was teetering on the brink, an angel stepped from the wings. J. Patrick Lannan, a Chicago financier and art collector, proposed a big annual benefit—to be called Poetry Day—featuring a reading by a major poet, followed by a dinner and an auction. Lannan persuaded publishers, booksellers, and art dealers to donate first editions, paintings, and other items. Robert Frost was invited to be guest of honor and read to a packed house on 13 November 1955. The auction attracted 168 high-bidding guests, including presidents of large corporations and directors from major libraries and museums. When the evening was over, *Poetry* was $29,000 richer.

So the pattern was set, though the auctions were later dropped. In 1956, Carl Sandburg drew an even larger audience than Frost. T. S. Eliot agreed to come in 1959, and the crowd that lined up at Orchestra Hall could have filled it twice over. W. H. Auden and Marianne Moore were only slightly less popular in 1960 and 1961. In 1962, Frost returned to give the reading, one of his last, in celebration of *Poetry*'s Golden Anniversary.

Thom Gunn about the time of his first appearance in *Poetry*, 1955.

After two and a half years in the Newberry, *Poetry* was able to move to rented space a block away on State Street. Drastic economizing had forced Shapiro to slash printing expenses. *Poetry* was put out with ugly typography on cheap paper bound with staples. It was in this low-budget format that Philip Levine, William Dickey, Donald Finkel, Thom Gunn, Donald Hall, Mona Van Duyn, James Wright, and other new talents made their first appearances in *Poetry*. Rago made it a priority to restore the magazine to its former grace, and Greer Allen's elegant new design was introduced with the January 1957 issue.

After the first Poetry Day, Rago was freer to concentrate on editing. Probably no other editor expended more energy on every aspect of running the magazine, or spent more time communicating with poets. Toward all who sent work, first-time submitters as well as old contributors, he was remarkably kind. Rago's detailed, gentle suggestions for changes made it difficult to argue with him. He was so courteous in returning manuscripts that he got letters of appreciation from poets he rejected. Rago also worked tirelessly at promotion, and in each annual report he was able to announce steady increases in subscriptions, advertising, and national media attention. By the fall of 1962, circulation reached almost six thousand, making *Poetry* the largest of the little magazines at the time.

Recognizing the opportunity the fiftieth anniversary presented, in 1961 Rago began to work on several projects for the celebration, including three special issues. *Poetry's* special Golden Anniversary issue was the largest to date, at 160 pages, and featured work by almost 60 poets from both sides of the Atlantic. The most notable of the younger generation mingled with several of *Poetry's* famous longtime contributors—Aiken, Frost, Cummings, Graves, Jarrell, Rukeyser, Spender, Williams, Zukofsky. Rago was even able to get a piece from the almost silent Ezra Pound, to whom he also presented a special $500 prize, named in honor of Harriet Monroe. Along with a section from Canto CXIII, the issue printed facsimiles of the opening of the "Three Cantos" from 1917 and the manuscripts of "Prufrock," "Sunday Morning," and poems by Joyce, Williams, Frost, Moore, Crane, and Yeats. The number sold out quickly and was reissued as a paperback.

Two large public events capped the birthday observance. To coincide with the jubilee, Rago arranged with the Library of Congress to put on a three-day National Poetry Festival in late October, with the theme "Fifty Years of American Poetry." Eighty-five noted poets attended. All thirty-five guest speakers, except Ogden Nash, were longtime *Poetry* authors. Rago gave the welcome. Frost, whose status as Grand Old Man was confirmed by his reading at the Kennedy inauguration, gave the keynote address. He recalled Harriet Monroe as "a great little lady": "she wanted to be thought as good a poet as anyone, and she didn't get that recognition . . . she just hid her poetry by being such an editor." Despite the Cuban Missile Crisis, which erupted midway through the festival, every seat was occupied during each session, making it the most popular program held until then at the Library of Congress.

Frost repeated most of his Festival recitations at Poetry Day, on 16 November. The crowds were so large that many had to be turned away. While a high point for *Poetry,* on the larger scene the Golden Jubilee marked the end of an era. Frost died on 29 January 1963; William Carlos Williams was gone two months later. Hilda Doolittle had died in 1961, her former husband and fellow Imagist, Richard Aldington, shortly after her. Harriet Monroe's other original contributors and oldest collaborators followed as the decade progressed: Zabel in 1964, Eliot in 1965, Sandburg in 1967, and Dillon in 1968. By then, a new era in American poetry had already begun.

CHAPTER III

A Second Poetry Renaissance

1. Making It New, Again

During the second half of Rago's tenure, 1962–1968, American poetry shifted into its most active and highly visible phase since the teens. Along with the multiplicity of styles and aesthetic viewpoints, the sheer numbers of poets, poetry courses, poetry publications, and poetry readings grew to industrial size, reaching levels never before seen in this country. Poetry seemed, for a while anyway, well on its way to becoming a truly popular art form once again, something it had not been since the heyday of Longfellow. In the 1950s poetry recitations (with or without jazz accompaniment) had acquired a hip, insider allure among the beatnik set and with would-be bohemians. But in the sixties enthusiasm for poetry carried wider, if not easily definable, social cachet, even glamour—at least among large numbers of college students. Part of the fresh appeal of poetry of the "higher," self-consciously literary sort doubtless arose from a kind of halo effect or glow by association it received from the far more popular songs of the sixties. The lyrics of the new generation of sophisticated poet-singer-songwriters—John Lennon, Paul McCartney, Paul Simon, Joni Mitchell—now reached levels of originality, thoughtful intensity, and complex artistry that were a marked contrast to the mindless formulas of the pop confections manufactured in the fifties and early sixties.

Even more important was the engagement of poetry and poetry writers, both "serious" and popular, with the larger cultural issues and political movements that grew as the decade descended into some of the most troubled years for the Republic. The times, they were indeed a-changin', as the protesting Bob Dylan droned, and dissenting voices were raised across the land. But even in the "tranquilized Fifties," as Robert Lowell called them, there were of course pockets of nonconformity and expressions of opposition to the tidy postwar platitudes from poets in the venerable Romantic tradition. After all, rugged individualism, independent streaks, and defiant Self-Reliance used to be hailed as national characteristics, as traditional as the idea of American exceptionalism.

By the early sixties, unorthodox ideas and outbursts of artistic and social rebellion initiated by the Beats and other anti-Establishment types had spread to larger groups of countercultural artists, students, and social activists. What began as analyses and critiques by small groups of dissident writers and intellectuals—some intoning the mantra of Higher Consciousness—now broadened into an increasingly angry nationwide debate about American society and government policy within the academy and among the larger mainstream population. As the Vietnam War escalated, political, social, and economic divisions deepened within the country. The issues were no longer merely philosophical, artistic, or academic.

From the strictly aesthetic standpoint, as the sixties progressed Pound's command to "make it new" was obeyed once more, and with gusto. Increasing numbers of poets rejected the academic dogma they had been taught, and had come to resent, and returned to methods pioneered by the early Modernists. Thus a second poetry renaissance was set in motion. Although it is also considered a revolution, what occurred, in stylistic terms, was less original than sometimes assumed. If the literary insurgents provoked a revolution, it was in the primary sense of the term: a circling back to the original principles and radical methods of the early Modernist experimentalists *Poetry* first championed.

By the thirties that first revolution had been tamed. As David Perkins notes in *A History of Modern Poetry*, the New Criticism smoothed the jagged edges, and academic critics and poets downplayed the more extreme methods of high Modernism, such as the ellipsis, fragmentation, and discontinuity of Pound's *Cantos* and the thick symbolism and allusion in *The Waste Land*. Instead they shifted emphasis to the Modernist ideals of economy, wit, irony, and intellectual control; and they returned to form. And so the Modernist insurgency was followed by cautious moderation, its provocative techniques supplanted by precision and polish. In the fifties the influence of Eliot's conservative later poetry and criticism was still strong, particularly his notions of emotional restraint and "impersonality." Elaborating on Eliot's ideas, I. A. Richards, William Empson, and John Crowe Ransom (whose 1941 book *The New Criticism* fixed the name) had preached the virtues of ironic distancing, ambiguity, and dexterous handling of form. The poets coming of age in the fifties were trained to read and write poetry according to New Critical standards, as neatly expounded in Cleanth Brooks and Robert Penn Warren's *Understanding Poetry* (first edition, 1938), a standard textbook in undergraduate English classes well into the sixties.

But by the sixties many postwar poets who had begun publishing in the approved formal modes began to move toward less constricting, more individual styles, notably Adrienne Rich, W. S. Merwin, Anne Sexton, and

Robert Lowell. Along with free verse and techniques harkening back to early Modernism, they also expressed more personal attitudes toward content, with many so-called Confessional poets speaking openly about private matters in ways unthinkable under Eliot's philosophy and New Critical doctrine. Younger poets particularly identified with the daring originality, free-spiritedness, and iconoclasm of the old avant-garde. Large numbers were inspired by the example of that great American original, Walt Whitman, and by William Carlos Williams, who was finally out from Eliot's shadow. (In the forties and fifties, Dr. Williams had happily received house calls from admirers and acolytes, including the teenage Allen Ginsberg and the young A. R. Ammons.) Spontaneity, candor, experimentation, unconventionality, distrust of Tradition, and challenges to Authority again became major motifs.

Literary innovators of the early Modernist movement had found models in the advanced theories and methods of the visual artists of their time, particularly the Cubists, Surrealists, and Futurists, and adapted their use of collage and other disjunctive techniques to poetry. The aspiring poets of the sixties went back to those originals in painting and poetry, and updated or recycled their methods, and for the same reasons: as effective ways to approach the complexity of modern consciousness and to express the feelings of uncertainty, fragmentation, and alienation in modern American life that were, if anything, even more acute during the cold and hot wars of the Nuclear Age. Many of the postwar generation—and not only the so-called New York School—also followed the example of the artists in the contemporary avant-garde, especially the Abstract Expressionists and Action painters, with their self-referential emphasis on process: the work of art, verbal as well as visual, being a record of its own making.

Above all, the notion of orthodoxy, arbiters, and a dominant style became unacceptable, in fact irrelevant, to the Now Generation. Growing political, philosophical, and social diversity added to the new vitality and variety in American poetry, reflected in the large number of literary sectarians who separated themselves into ideological-aesthetic subgroups. Subject matter aside, for them the form of a poem (or lack thereof) came to symbolize ideas and values beyond the "merely" artistic. The *free* in free verse now carried political or moral implications, as the term was facilely identified with liberty, spiritual and social liberation, or liberality in general.

Quarrels among practitioners of the new styles and between increasingly hostile conservative and liberal factions were no less combative and often far more caustic than the theoretical and technical debates over form and *vers libre* during the first poetry revolution of 1912–1922. By the mid-sixties the disputes were seldom limited to abstractions or literary procedures, as partisan poets became voices of and sometimes leaders in social and political

struggles as well. The variety of approaches to poetry began to mirror the
larger upheavals in an American culture again in rapid flux.

Among the students of the Baby Boom generation—the largest group of
young people ever to attend college—the increased questioning of and an-
tagonism toward academic authority, big business, and "the military-indus-
trial complex" (the phrase was coined by President Eisenhower, who knew
whereof he spoke), as well as rigid social conventions in general, culminated
in the late-sixties campus uprisings. The political activism and civil disobe-
dience of students generated further opposition to the Vietnam War and
gradually helped mobilize ever larger portions of the population as the
conflict dragged on and casualties and costs mounted.

Following upon the manifold disasters of the violent, pivotal year 1968—
with its horrific assassinations, urban riots, military escalations, protest
marches, and chaotic Democratic National Convention—the country was
beginning to be transformed by the largest social upheavals since the Great
Depression. The civil rights struggles rekindled by the younger generation
of militant black leaders were followed, in turn, by the rising women's, gay,
and other liberation movements among diverse minority and ethnic groups.
The rapid succession of the social struggles, countercultural clashes, and political causes now transforming the country would inevitably change the
aesthetic landscape as well, and the concept of poetry from then on.

Effects of these changes on all levels, from pop culture to secondary
and higher education to Congress and the courts, were more profound
than even the most optimistic participants could have imagined, and
longer lasting. Conservatives in education, religion, and politics were out-
raged, and many never reconciled themselves to the reversals to the status
quo or the philosophies behind them. Thus ensued the increasingly acrimonious and intolerant culture wars. It would take decades before conservatives and "neo-cons" would be able to reverse the revolution, at least
in part, and for censorious fundamentalists and the radical right to exact
retribution.

2. *Poetry* During the Later Rago Years

It is a measure of Rago's openness and of the magazine's continuing prestige that old practitioners and young experimentalists alike were accom-
modated in *Poetry*. Rago's tact and generosity helped him negotiate the
confrontational sixties and sustained his relations with a wide range of writers who were often not on speaking terms with one another. Having won
back many people who had been offended during the Shapiro years, Rago
worked assiduously to represent the best in both traditional modes and the

latest fashions, but he was particularly welcoming to younger poets, whether formalists or free spirits.

Considering his conservative background, deep admiration for Eliot, and belief in New Critical standards, Rago was surprisingly broad-minded. He was especially receptive to the poets associated with Black Mountain College. Between 1955 and 1962 he had published nearly two dozen poems by Robert Creeley and almost as many by Robert Duncan and Denise Levertov. Charles Olson, the theorist of this Projectivist group, appeared more selectively in 1962 and after. Creeley remained a great favorite with Rago and published more than forty poems in the magazine in the sixties; Levertov contributed about two dozen during the same period.

Henry Rago in his office at the Irving Apartments, 1018 North State Street, early sixties.

Rago was extremely supportive to James Dickey early in his career and continued to be helpful as his reputation grew. Besides printing his poems and seeing that his books were carefully reviewed, Rago offered Dickey advice, prizes, and reading gigs. Rago also had cordial relations with the contentious Robert Bly and helped publicize Bly's anti-war activities in the mid-sixties. Throughout the decade *Poetry* regularly featured Bly's work (some two dozen pieces) and printed groups of poems by others sometimes labeled as the Deep Image "school," particularly Donald Hall and James Wright. Frequent contributors likewise included writers loosely if inaccurately linked as Surrealists, including Galway Kinnell, David Ignatow, and W. S. Merwin, who had no less than thirty poems in *Poetry* during this period of radical transformation to his mature style—elliptical, imagistic, unpunctuated—in the mid-sixties.

Robert Creeley, with Bobbie Hall, his second wife, before the entrance to the *Poetry* offices, late fifties.

Most of poets in the New York School were presented in *Poetry* many years before that misleading title was applied to those rather disparate individuals. (The Manhattan art dealer John Bernard Myers affixed the name to an anthology of the young poets he printed in the fifties, hoping the prestige of their better-known friends among the New York painters would rub off on them.) Kenneth Koch and John Ashbery in fact debuted in the November 1945 issue, while still in their teens, and they contributed about twenty poems each during Rago's editorship. Frank O'Hara made his first appearance under Shapiro in 1951 and continued to receive eager acceptances from Rago up to his untimely death in 1966. (O'Hara was struck by a Jeep dune buggy on Fire Island as he stood on the beach late at night and died of multiple injuries on 25 July 1966, a few months after his fortieth birthday.) In the fall, with O'Hara's brother Philip, Rago set up the Frank O'Hara Prize of $500; the first winner was Gary Snyder. *Poetry* also printed four of O'Hara's poems posthumously in 1969. James Schuyler began to appear in the mid-sixties.

Although the assertion is often repeated that *Poetry* ignored or rejected the Beats, the record indicates it was the other way around. In May 1957 Rago sent a letter of support to Lawrence Ferlinghetti for use by the defense at the *Howl* obscenity trial. (The respected editor of *Poetry* was, incidentally, also a member of the City of Chicago's censorship board.) The *Poetry* staff entertained Allen Ginsberg, Gregory Corso, and Peter Orlovsky at the office in 1959. Throughout his years Rago welcomed and printed other countercultural and Eastern-influenced poets from both the East and West coasts—Kenneth Rexroth, Lew Welch, William Everson (Brother Antoninus), as well as Snyder—and was quite eager to publish Ginsberg too. But an editor cannot present work by authors who decline to submit any.

Ginsberg's versifying father Louis suggested a father-and-son appearance, repeatedly, but Rago wasn't keen on the elder's artifices. Rago invited Allen to send poems early in 1966 and immediately accepted "Wichita Vortex Sutra (I)" when it arrived in April. Unfortunately Rago couldn't present it: Ginsberg informed him that student pacifists in Omaha had already printed it in a mimeographed magazine. A similar technicality prevented a later offering from appearing. In any case, *Poetry* published reviews of almost all the books of the Beat poets. (Ferlinghetti's *Pictures of the Gone World* received *two* notices in October 1956.)

Whatever his personal preferences, Rago showcased the wide spectrum of the shifting aesthetics of the sixties in *Poetry*, from Ammons and Ashbery to Louis Zukofsky and Paul Zweig. Ammons gave him some of his most important early work, including "Gravelly Run" and "Expressions of Sea Level." Rago presented nine long sections from Zukofsky's magnum opus "*A*," which Harriet Monroe had begun publishing in 1931. Other particular favorites of the editor's were Marvin Bell (almost three dozen pieces), Michael Benedikt (twenty-eight), Barbara Howes (eighteen), Donald Justice (twenty-eight), Lorine Niedecker (fifteen), Charles Oppen (twelve), Winfield Townley Scott (twenty-four), William Stafford (twenty-four), Charles Tomlinson (thirty-one), Mona Van Duyn (fourteen), and David Wagoner (twenty-two). Some writers Rago printed in abundance proved less favored by history, including Raymond Roseliep (1917–1983), a Jesuit priest and prolific haiku author who contributed thirty-two poems; Larry Eigner (1927–1996), thirty-eight; Aram Saroyan (b. 1943), seventeen pieces, including a one-line stunt that repeated a single word (*night*) across two pages; and forty by Hy Sobiloff (1912-1970), a New York businessman.

But during the last half of Rago's tenure almost every poet of prominence or promise appeared with at least one or two groups usually of four to six poems, including Wendell Berry, John Berryman, Turner Cassity, Donald Davie, Robert Duncan, Alan Dugan, Richard Eberhart, Clayton Eshleman, Kathleen Fraser, Donald Finkel, Jean Garrigue, Louise Glück, W. S. Graham, Thom Gunn, Donald Hall, Michael S. Harper, Jim Harrison, William Heyen, Daniel Hoffman, John Hollander, Anselm Hollo, Theodore Holmes, Barbara Howes, Ted Hughes, Richard Hugo, Elizabeth Jennings, Le Roi Jones (later Amiri Baraka), Donald Justice, Carolyn Kizer, Philip Levine, Michael McClure, Thomas McGrath, James Merrill, Thomas Merton, Josephine Miles, Herbert Morris, Samuel French Morse, Howard Moss, Lisel Mueller, Leonard Nathan, P. K. Page, Sylvia Plath (her final poems were submitted by Ted Hughes), M. L. Rosenthal, Gibbons Ruark, Ernest Sandeen, Hugh Seidman, Anne Sexton, Harvey Shapiro, Karl Shapiro, Helen Singer, Robin Skelton, Stevie Smith, Gilbert Sorrentino, Raymond Souster, Kathleen Spivack, George Starbuck, Dabney Stuart, May Swenson, James Tate, Eleanor Ross Taylor, Richard Tillinghast, Constance Urdang, Jean Valentine, Mark Van Doren, and Vernon Watkins.

Many who contributed poems to *Poetry* did reviews for the magazine as well, even though in several cases they had never written criticism before Rago approached them. Rago seemed unconcerned by their lack of experience; with very few exceptions, those he asked found it hard to say no, and the editor's instincts about their abilities in prose turned out to be sound. Despite his initial hesitations, A. R. Ammons, for example, acquiesced and eventually reviewed a dozen collections, including Ginsberg's *Reality Sandwiches* in 1964. Michael Benedikt reviewed three dozen volumes, M. L. Rosenthal and X. J. Kennedy each wrote more than two dozen notices, and Wallace Fowlie almost an equal number, many of them French titles. Frank Lentricchia provided a dozen reviews of books on poetry history and theory. But the yeoman work was performed by Hayden Carruth, who covered sixty-four books over Rago's last seven years and

William Stafford, a frequent reviewer in
Poetry, did conservation and forestry
work as a conscientious objector
during World War II.

was invariably judicious and fair-minded. William Stafford provided sixty-five generous critiques. Richard Howard was even more prolific, offering almost one hundred pointed assessments (and frequently raising ire) during the same period.

James Dickey proved a perceptive and lively critic with some three dozen reviews in the sixties and provoked a huffy response from the ever-touchy Conrad Aiken for his pan of Aiken's unfortunately titled *The Morning Poem of Lord Zero* in 1963. Aiken had had unhappy relations with *Poetry* almost from its inception, and was still smarting from the outrageously unfair review his *Ushant* had received from the vengeful Edward Dahlberg in February 1953. (Shapiro had a minor scandal on his hands and had to apologize for the many errors in Dahlberg's bizarre article; see *Dear Editor*, Chapter XVII.) Dickey's review of *Lord Zero* opened with the observation:

> The course of poetry appears to have turned away from Conrad Aiken, leaving him an industrious and unfashionable Historic Personage with space in all the textbooks and anthologies and very few readers. Beside the work of those poets who sweat for the ultimate concentration— [Dylan] Thomas, Robert Lowell, John Berryman—Aiken seems terribly low-keyed and diffuse. His long later poems, in fact, seem very like words murmuring endlessly to themselves in poetic terms without in the least resembling poetry as we have come to believe it should be.

Dickey grew even more negative from there, opining, among other things: "The sense of necessity that art alone makes possible is almost totally absent, and one surrenders to the serious, musical murmur as to a long after-dinner nap in which one dreams of poetry dreaming that it is poetry." While affirming the traditional hands-off policy toward reviewers, Rago acceded to the offended author's request and printed Aiken's ill-conceived letter of protest in the March 1964 issue. Aiken never contributed to *Poetry* again. Dickey went on to present another dozen sharp reviews in the magazine before the decade was out.

Besides keeping up with the evolving American scene, Rago continued to offer periodic surveys of poetry abroad. In his first years he assembled foreign issues devoted to poetry of Japan (May 1956), Israel (July 1958), and India (January 1959). In May 1962 he published another British issue, and the July 1962 bilingual issue was devoted to Yves Bonnefoy, translated by Galway Kinnell. In October 1964, Rago presented a special Greek number with work by Odysseus Elytis, Nikos Gatsos, George Savidis, George Seferis, and others, translated by Edmund Keeley, Philip Sherrard, and Ruth Whitman. Throughout the rest of his tenure Rago printed many translations from contemporary French, Italian, and other European poets as well.

He also published two special editions devoted to longer poems, sequences, and works-in-progress. The first double issue, October–November 1963, carried new pieces by Berryman, Bishop, Jarrell, Kizer, Levertov, Lowell, Olson, Roethke, Karl Shapiro, Snyder, Tomlinson, Zukofsky, and others. A second double issue, with 190 pages of longer poems, was published in April 1965, consisting of contributions from Wendell Berry, Bishop (translations of work by Carlos Drummond de Andrade), Carruth, Creeley, Duncan, Kinnell, Koch, Levertov, Charles Olson, Rich, Sandeen, Sexton, Snyder, Tomlinson, Theodore Weiss, and Philip Whalen. In his Foreword to the anthology, Rago wrote: "We have made the point here more than once that poems are made by poets, not by groups or power blocs or enterprising journalists."

T. S. Eliot died on 4 January 1965, and Rago offered tributes to his hero in the March 1965 issue. He recalled being introduced to Eliot in London in 1943 through Robert Speaight, who played Thomas in the original production of *Murder in the Cathedral*, and told of their meetings during the second Blitz when Rago was serving as a lieutenant in Army Counter-Intelligence. On one occasion Eliot took him to lunch at the Garrick Club and offered to hold Rago's manuscripts until he found permanent quarters on the Continent. The editor recounted their later meetings in Paris, where Eliot introduced him to Paul Valéry, whom T.S.E. addressed as *"maître,"* and took him to dinner at the fashionable Bristol Hotel. (At their last get-together in London, in August 1961, Rago noted, over lunch Eliot had a large draught of beer, on doctor's orders.) He concluded that Eliot "more than any other writer of the twentieth century, has given our age its complete expression," and declared: "Of all the poets I have ever known, old or young, he was the kindest."

T. S. Eliot in the early sixties; he made
his professional debut in *Poetry* in 1915.

News Notes for June 1965 reported on Eliot's memorial service in Westminster Abbey on February 4, where Sir Alec Guinness read from the poet's works and the choir sang Stravinsky's setting of lines from *Four Quartets*. Lionel Trilling and Cleanth Brooks, then cultural attaché to the American embassy in London, attended as representatives of President Johnson, who "sent a message in tribute from the White House." Others present included Ezra Pound ("who made the journey from Italy expressly for this occasion"), Stephen Spender, Christopher Fry, Henry Moore, and Dame Peggy Ashcroft. Rago's remarks in *Poetry* were reprinted as *T. S. Eliot: A Memoir and a Tribute* in a pamphlet designed by Greer Allen. In further remembrance, Poetry Day for 1965 on 21 October featured a preview of the Goodman Theatre production of *The Cocktail Party*. At the dinner, Rago read a message from Valerie Eliot, after which a recording was played of Eliot's 1959 Poetry Day reading before "the largest crowd ever gathered in Chicago to hear a poet."

Besides his admiration for the artist and his personal gratitude for the master's friendship, Rago appreciated Eliot's long association with *Poetry* and his assistance over the years. Like several other earliest contributors, Eliot did not forget the magazine's importance at the start of his career, and his Poetry Day appearance helped sustain it, as did Frost's SRO performances in 1955 and 1962. Eliot's reading and the dinner and auction garnered some $30,000. Frost's 1962 appearance brought in almost $19,000; he declined the honorarium and even paid his own travel expenses.

Poetry had stayed safely in the black for several years thanks in large part to these benefits, but by 1962 Rago had to warn of declining reserves and the need for additional support. One board member proposed setting up a "fiftieth anniversary fund," but nothing came of the idea. Instead Rago redoubled his fund-raising efforts and was able to balance budgets by piecing together foundation grants and other aid from several sources. He made arrangements with A.M.S. Press in New York for sale of reprints of the magazine, with half the proceeds on full sets to go to *Poetry*. He convinced the Bollingen Foundation to underwrite the several fiftieth-anniversary special issues through a $5,000 grant, and he procured $2,000 awards from both the Robert McCormick Foundation and Hy Sobiloff's Ambrook Foundation, which were renewed three and four times. (Sobiloff drove a hard bargain: Rago tutored Sobiloff on his poetry for several years in exchange for his largess, but the gifts pledged were sometimes slow in arriving.) Beginning in 1962, the Ingram Merrill Foundation offered $2,500 annually to underwrite payments to authors, and thanks to James Merrill this support was regularly increased as the annual grants extended well into the nineties. For many years as board chairman, J. Patrick Lannan gave annual gifts of $4,000.

In 1965 Rago approached David Rockefeller for a $45,000 donation. They had served together in the Counter-Intelligence Corps in Paris from 1944 to 1947 and remained friends after the war. In his gracious reply of 1 June 1965, Rockefeller declined to contribute the full amount because of numerous other obligations, but agreed to pledge $22,500 in securities over three years, provided the sum was matched. (Rockefeller made it clear that the challenge grant was a onetime offer.) While net income from Poetry Day dropped from $20,000 in 1964 to $4,750 in 1969, these and other grants, along with the extra revenue earned when the annual subscription rate was finally raised to $10 in 1965 and then to $12 in 1968, kept the balance sheets safely in the black through most of the decade. Rago promoted the magazine through exchange ads with other literary journals and through direct-mail campaigns to high schools and libraries, and attracted good (and free) publicity for the Poetry Day readings and special issues. Thus circulation slowly but steadily increased during his tenure, rising from about 5,900 in 1964 to almost 7,600 paid subscriptions and newsstand sales in 1968, making *Poetry* the largest of the little magazines, even though it lacked the institutional sponsorship typical of such journals.

3. Correspondence 1962–1966

In the voluminous files from the last years of Rago's tenure, a large number of letters are provoked by reviews, and many responses come both from the authors critiqued and from contributing writers and regular readers who add their particular opinions about books and poets in the news. James Dickey is a topic of discussion in letters from several fellow poets, and he himself keeps in regular contact. Ezra Pound in his increasingly silent old age is the subject of messages from his longtime disciple and publisher, James Laughlin of New Directions, and his best critic (and formerly a frequent *Poetry* reviewer), Hugh Kenner.

Mrs. William Carlos Williams writes of her late husband's generosity to literary magazines, and of his beloved dog. John Berryman sends apologies for taking so long in sending new work, and Delmore Schwartz gives evidence of his sharp decline. Berryman and David Wagoner share their feelings on the loss of a friend and mentor, Theodore Roethke. Other missives recall odd and amusing contretemps, such as the award of a gold (or was it merely gold-plated?) medal to Robert Graves. An elderly gentleman writes from Florida to reveal that he was the model for Frost's Hired Man.

Reports from Lew Welch and Robert Duncan bring news of the growing excitement of the burgeoning San Francisco poetry scene, while from the East Coast the young Gerard Malanga keeps Rago abreast of latest adventures at Andy Warhol's Factory. (On one of his regular trips to New York, Rago checked out the scene for himself.) Throughout these years, several other emerging poets with offerings for *Poetry* or newly appearing in its pages share their ideas in frank and often funny cover letters, including Jim Harrison, Charles Simic, Lisel Mueller, Larry Woiwode, and Alan Dugan. Basil Bunting, an old contributor and former Pound protégé, offers a new poem, "Briggflatts," following encomiums from Robert Creeley. Every year during this period Rago presents about thirty poets who are making their *Poetry* debuts.

T. S. Eliot to Henry Rago   *Faber and Faber, Ltd,*
                                               London, 15 June 1962

Dear Mr. Rago,

Thank you for your letter of June 5th. I am most interested to hear of the golden anniversary number, and would wish to congratulate *Poetry* on its survival for these fifty years, and express the hope and confidence in the perpetuity of the magazine. I only regret that I have no poem in a condition in which I should care to offer it to your, or any, public, and therefore cannot pay you the only kind of tribute that would be really appropriate to the occasion. If I had something that was previously unpublished anywhere, which I was willing to print, I would certainly give you the opportunity of publishing it.

What you say at the end of your letter gives me much pleasure, and I was very happy to have been of some service to *Poetry* on that visit to Chicago [in 1959, as guest of honor at Poetry Day].

With all good wishes from my wife and myself.

Yours sincerely, / T. S. Eliot

The beginning of "The Love Song of J. Alfred Prufrock," as marked up for the printers, was reproduced in the special Golden Anniversary Issue (October 1962) along with the opening pages of Yeats's "The Scholars," Pound's "Three Cantos," Stevens's "Sunday Morning,"

Williams's "The Botticellian Trees," Marianne Moore's "The Steeple-Jack," and other famous pieces first published in *Poetry*.

Hugh Kenner to Henry Rago   *Santa Barbara, Calif.,*
                                                    23 November 1962

Dear Henry:

That [special prize to Pound] is by all odds the finest gesture at which you have ever connived; and the marmoreal ring of the citation is worthy of the occasion: ". . . with the effect of so precise a testimony." Precisely.

I am pleased that he wrote you. Is it proper for the historian of the Pound Era to enquire as to the wording of his response?

If I can bring this book off it will go like the Nautilus [U.S. nuclear submarine] under the ice-pack, great gyroscopes turning, plotting the invisible currents, and surfacing from time to time at assigned points for a look at the terrain. The stylistic problems alone are perplexing. . . . I shall try to make the Marianne piece for you another trial run. This job will have as many interwoven strands and variant manners as *Ulysses*.

I wish I could have gotten to Washington. Guy Davenport represented NR [*New Republic*] there, but I think was unable to get near you. Louis Zukofsky reports that you and he exchanged words at last.

Best to you all from us both, / Hugh

The Harriet Monroe Memorial Prize, ordinarily $100, was raised to $500 for Pound. The citation read in part: "That the prize bears the name of the founder of *Poetry* makes this choice all the more pleasing. No other person in the history of this magazine helped her as much to do the proudest things that *Poetry* has done." For E.P.'s response, see *Dear Editor*, p. 452.

Delmore Schwartz to Henry Rago   *Syracuse, N.Y., 6 December 1962*

Dear Henry:

During the Poetry Festival [at the Library of Congress in October] I misplaced my copy of *Poetry*'s Golden Anniversary issue, which I thought was very good, and I wonder if you could send me another one at my new address.

I'm sorry we weren't able to see more of each other in Washington, but those three days of the festival were rather hectic. I do hope that if you are ever in this area you will call me.

Best, / Delmore

Like John Berryman, Schwartz had in fact been drunk during most of the proceedings; he was arrested for smashing the furniture in his hotel room; see *Dear Editor*, Chapter XVIII, p. 442.

James Laughlin to Henry Rago   *Norfolk, Conn., 18 December 1962*

Dear Henry,

I do want to thank you so much for sending me the marked copy of the program of the auction. It is always most interesting to compare the various prices, and I am happy indeed that the D. H. Lawrence manuscript brought in $130. . . .

This morning Hayden [Carruth, then working at New Directions] brought up to show me your latest issue with the wonderful news of the fine prize for Ezra. I am delighted. And I think the editorial comment that went with the prize was very graciously and deftly handled, by you, I assume.

Are these prizes taxable as income? If so, I ought to let Mr. Gleason in Boston know about it. I have no doubt you have had test cases, or legal rulings, on this point before, and can readily let me know how it stands.

The latest reports on Ezra are fairly encouraging. He is staying in a little house in Venice, and apparently plans to remain there for the winter, since it is so much easier to heat than the [Brunnenburg] Castle [near Merano in the Alto Adige (Tyrol) in Northern Italy]. I don't believe he is writing much of anything, but at least he is feeling better. His daughter Mary [de Rachewiltz] may perhaps be coming to this country for a short visit early in the new year. Omar, his son, as you may have heard, is now Headmaster of the American School in Tangiers.

With Christmas wishes and for 1963,

James Laughlin

William Dickey to Henry Rago   *[San Francisco, Calif.],*
14 January 1963

Dear Mr. Rago,

. . . I've been very pleased by the news stories that have reached me about the Union League Prize. The only problem I have at the moment is to try to get the Internal Revenue to decide whether it's tax deductible. That's the kind of question I can't feel Shelley ever had to answer.

Thanks for reading these poems,

Yours, / William Dickey

James Dickey to Henry Rago   *Portland, Ore., 3 March 1963*

Dear Henry,

Thanks so much for your note. Sure, I'll take on the Aiken for you, plus the chronicle you see shaping up in future. I have plenty of time here. . . .

Could you help me with a problem? I want to write some poems under another name—a couple of other names, in fact—to see if I can take on different "writing personalities" in case I get tired of the one I have. I'd like to send some of these to you and see what you think of them, but, in case of publication, I wouldn't want my real identity known. Is this a legitimate pursuit, in letters? A Portuguese poet named [Fernando] Pessoa did this some time ago—he had *four* alter egos! —and I wanted to try it, just to see what would happen. On the other hand, I don't want to submit poems to my editors—such as yourself—without letting them in on what I am doing; that would somehow seem wrong to me. Could you advise me on this? If you don't think it's a good idea, I'll publish the poems under my own name, though they're quite unlike anything I've ever done before. . . .

Rago replied 19 March that he thought it was a good idea, but suggested Dickey let editors know what he was up to, and to indicate in biographical notes for published pieces that the author's name was a pseudonym.

Henry Rago to Mona Van Duyn   *Chicago, 15 March 1963*

Dear Mona,

Thanks for the review, for which I enclose our acceptance notice.

I feel just a little hesitation over your treatment of Howard Moss; I don't mean your opinion, which I would never have any business commenting on unless it involved some outrage against either fact or reason, but the expression of it. I think the whole tone could be a little more humane, and every point still made. I feel this all the more because we have gone out of our way to review the book after so long a wait; it would seem that we were making some quite special point of all this: the emphasis in all you say would be doubled in this context.

Can you feel at all what I'm saying? (I don't know Howard Moss at all except by correspondence, as I know almost everyone else. I feel only the same obligation to him that I feel to all the poets whose best work we have published.) . . .

These are his selected poems, pretty much the work of his lifetime thus far; so I risk being a nuisance with these suggestions. . . .

Mona Van Duyn to Henry Rago   *St. Louis, Mo., [17 March 1963]*

Dear Henry,

Your letter came today, and I hasten to answer—Moss and [Josephine] Miles have certainly waited long enough already. . . .

Let me say right off that I am not at all offended by your request that I revise the review and will do so as fast as I can. But in explanation: I don't feel that the review of Moss was unfair, even in tone, to *my* sense of his book. I was disappointed in it when I first read it, and so left it to last, hoping I could see it more brightly; that is, I really gave it an extra effort in this reading. But it seemed even worse to me, possibly, as I suggested in the review, in its defense, by being juxtaposed against the other two. I felt freer to hold these books up against my own highest standards *because* they were the works of established poets—I never do this with young poets, trying rather to read them on their own terms.

However, I am totally convinced by one of your points—that it might seem after so long a wait that a special point was being made of criticizing Moss. *Poetry* has very high standards of courtesy toward its poets, which I approve of, and would wish to conform to. Besides, there would be still *more* delay getting a more sympathetic reviewer to do Moss. Thanks for pointing out ways of revising—they will help. . . .

I'll get a new Moss review to you as soon as possible.

All good wishes, / Mona

In a later note (undated) with the revised review, Van Duyn wrote: "This is about as far as I can go without disliking myself. I hope you'll feel free to get another review, if you want to take the time. I'll send the book to anyone you say." Her review of Moss's *A Winter Come, a Summer Gone*, Ashbery's *The Tennis Court Oath*, and Merrill's *Water Street* (among others), appeared in July 1963.

James Dickey to Henry Rago   *Portland, Ore., 23 March 1963*

Dear Henry,

Thanks so much for your letter. I have the Aiken book also, and am—as is my wont—starting slowly through it. I will have it done in plenty of time for your April 15th deadline, and can also begin working on the chronicle as soon as we have chosen the right books, and enough of them. The four books you mention—the Wright, Jeffers, Hodgson and Swenson—will be fine to look at as a starter. There are, though, about a couple of things that you and I ought to go over preliminary to my reviewing them. First, I have just written a piece for Bob Bly's magazine, *The Sixties*, on Jim Wright's work; this will appear under the name of the inescapable Crunk, and not my name, so perhaps that would not constitute a hindrance to my treating his book. But, since Wright gave my first book such a glowing treatment a year or so ago, I am a little afraid that my review of his book, which would be largely favorable, as it was in the *Sixties* article, would seem a little the case of quid pro quo, noblesse oblige, or something. If you think these don't constitute serious objections, then I'll be glad to do Wright's book. May Swenson, for some reason, keeps sending me all her books as they come out, as well as publications of the house— New Directions, evidently—where she works. I have never met Miss Swenson, but I have a feeling that maybe all these books reach me from her because she knows I am a reviewer—I may be mistaken about this of course; it's just that I can't really think of any reason why she might send me books—somehow expects a favorableness from me that

James Dickey, a frequent contributor of poetry and prose, in the mid-sixties.

I am not really prepared to give. Again, if you don't think these are valid reasons for *not* reviewing I'll be glad to review.

By the way, has my own *Drowning With Others* been reviewed in *Poetry* as yet? . . .

Thanks so much, Henry, for your advice on using a pseudonym; largely on that advice I've decided to go ahead with project X, as I outlined it to you. As soon as I get some poems that satisfy me from either Jesse Shields or Boyd Thornton—the names I'll (tentatively) be using—I'll send them on to you; on first acquaintance they seem (intermittently) exciting guys. . . .

Yours, / Jim

Drowning With Others was reviewed by Richard Howard in the current (March 1963) issue.

Philip Levine to Henry Rago   *Fresno, Calif., 6 April 1963*

Dear Mr. Rago,

Thanks so much for helping with the two poems; they are two that I wanted read by as large an audience as I could reach, and I'm afraid my book [*On the Edge,* his first volume] won't reach much of an audience. . . .

Before I sign off I really feel obliged to mention one poem you printed last year; it was by James Dickey, a man I know in no way and whose reviews I've read and disliked. But the poem you printed on his father, a poem situated in front of one of those enormous hospitals, overwhelmed me. I went back and reread a lot of his poems I had sitting around in various copies of *Poetry.* How did I miss him? He's a terrific poet.

Thanks again.

Sincerely, / Philip Levine

Dickey's "The Hospital Window" (January 1962) became one his most often reprinted poems.

Denise Levertov to Henry Rago   *New York City, 26 April 1963*

Dear Henry,

Yes, I did see Richard Howard's review [of *The Jacob's Ladder*, March 1963] & didn't think it was destructive at all. When he said those lines about the dog drinking were "dreadful" I think he just didn't understand what I was trying to do (i.e. he may not have caught the reference to Basket, Gertrude Stein's dog from whom she said she learned what a sentence was, listening to him drink). But for the rest, what he is doing is challenging me to attempt more, & I would sooner such a tonic kind of review than a flabby eulogy, any day. I read it at Archie Ammons's & still don't have a copy but will get one tomorrow for I want to reread it. . . .

Love— / Denise

Randall Jarrell to Henry Rago   *Greensboro, N.C., 5 May 1963*

Dear Mr. Rago:

Your double number in the fall sounds nice, and I do have something long I'd like to give you for it—a poem named *The Lost World*. I'm hopeful

that a lot of the people I'd like to have read it would see it in *Poetry*. I'll send it along with this letter— do tell me how you like it.

We enjoyed getting to see you in Washington [at the Library of Congress Poetry Festival]—your double number of *Poetry* was awfully good and attractive-looking, I thought.

With all best wishes.

Yours, / Randall Jarrell

Randall Jarrell, a favorite of Karl Shapiro and Henry Rago, died after being struck by a car in 1965.

"The Lost World" was printed in the October 1963 issue and became the title poem of Jarrell's last volume. He gave a speech at the festival surveying the past "Fifty Years of American Poetry"; it was later printed in *The Third Book of Criticism* (1970).

Delmore Schwartz to Henry Rago   *Syracuse, N.Y., 5 May 1963*

Dear Henry,

Please excuse me for not answering your letter sooner, but I was waiting to see if the depressed frame of mind I've been in lately would lift and I would be able to go over manuscripts in first or second draft and find something for your new project [the long poem issue]. When I'm in this state of mind nothing seems very good or even good enough and I certainly don't feel able to do the rewriting that is always necessary. So you better not count on anything from me. I will send you new poems when I can. Meanwhile, best wishes for your double number which is a wonderful idea and which I should think would be possible on a yearly basis too.

Best, / Delmore

Schwartz did not contribute to the special issue. He died of a heart attack in 1966, at age fifty-two, in the lobby of his Manhattan hotel. His body lay unclaimed for three days at Bellevue Hospital, where earlier he had been committed for psychiatric treatment.

James Dickey to Henry Rago   *Portland, Ore., 11 May 1963*

Dear Henry,

Glad you like the Aiken review. Sure, we can change the things you point out. . . . As to the next review: all the books you mention are fine, though I really think I should steer clear of Wagoner, having just been his house guest for a very expensive (for him) weekend in the country. . . .

Thanks for your good news about the tour this coming winter. On the strength of your first letter, and following your suggestion, I have made my plans known to Reed [College] and The Authorities, and have also alerted a good many people throughout the Midwest. I hope very much that during the swing through I will be able to get together with you and Juliet again. Tell Juliet, by the way, that I have a whole lot of new stuff to show her on the guitar; I'm taking lessons from a student of mine who is really a whiz. . . .

Helmets, the new book of poems, will be out in about eight months. I have started two new books, *Reincarnations* and *Unknowing*, and a tentative third one, *The Stepson*. Jesse Shields and Boyd Thornton [his alter egos] are toiling away slowly under my merciless tutelage, and hope to have something to submit before too much longer.

My best to you, Henry, as always.

All yours, / Jim

Rago helped set up readings for Dickey in the Midwest "circuit"; the series was funded by the Rockefeller Foundation and administered by Robert Mueller at *Poetry*.

Arthur Freeman to The Editors   *Society of Fellows, Harvard University,*
15 May 1963

Dear Editors:

I'm afraid it's a little late to register a complaint about a review (June, 1962, issue of *Poetry*) but I only now saw it, and print lives. The notice by Marya Zaturenska of my book [*Apollonian Poems*] (pp. 193–194) I find a little annoying, chiefly because it is stupid and illiterate, not to say pompous. Misleading, too. Miss Z. quotes seven lines of my poetry to prove a point of some sort, and in the course of seven quoted lines makes a total of *nine* errors. I ask you! Not only is the passage unkindly ripped out of context, wherein it is clearly satiric but out of which it only looks gawky, but: (1) a line is dropped out altogether, (2) there are three punctuation errors, and two words capitalized which I didn't, (3) the line arrangement isn't observed, (4) an italicized word is left in roman, (5) a word is idiotically pluralized whereby a rime is destroyed, and (6) the town I'm writing about, which Miss Z. accuses me of maligning ("a once-famous city," she mourns) is misspelled by her. And if there were any question of it being the printer's fault, he is absolved a line later, where Miss Z. repeats her spelling error. Such reverence she has. (For good measure, she also misspells "Istamboul," which must prove something or other.)

Now I think this is pretty inexcusable. If I'm going to be panned, I think I have at least a right to be panned for what I wrote, not for what Miss Z. rewrote. More people, after all, read *Poetry* than read me. What is especially galling is the last sticky sentence of paragraph one of p. 194, where Miss Z. urges me to stay home and "do a little reading in history." She questions my scholarship—she, who demonstrably lacks a ~~gazeteer~~ gazetteer (I misspelled that but I went and looked it up), at the very least.

Please pass this along to Miss Z., if you will, along with my assurances (1) that I never wrote a word about Switzerland, (2) she's wrong, my hotels were always two-dollar flea-bags, and (3) that I can't sell a thing to the *New Yorker*. Even by quoting her.

Best, / Arthur Freeman

In April 1966, H.R. asked Freeman to review books by Donald Davidson, May Sarton— and Marya Zaturenska. Freeman begged off, reminding him of his previous dealings with her: "I don't much care for her poetry, regardless of this skirmish, but I fear any reaction of mine, particularly in *Poetry*, even if not deliberately prejudiced would seem so. . . . My new book, incidentally, is coming out May 4, if you don't already have a copy. God save me from Miss Z."

Louis Ginsberg to Henry Rago   *Paterson, N.J., 12 June 1963*

Dear Mr. Henry Rago:

Enclosed please find a new poem of mine, called "News Every Hour on the Hour". I have tried in some of my more recent poems to smuggle, to the best of my disability, some felicity into my lines in hopes that you might slip a few of my poems into the pages of your magazine.

Under separate cover, I am sending you a few poems of my older son, Eugene Brooks, who also writes poetry. He is a lawyer in N.Y. and has appeared in a number of places. . . .

Has Allen sent in any poems to you? (It might be interesting to have a group of poems by father and two sons.)

Be that as it may, there is that bent of poetry in the family: if we keep up our bent we'll be broke. I myself have been around quite a while, baiting the Muse. I have retired some [sic] high school teaching but teach two nights a week at the Rutgers local center. Mornings, I go from bed to verse. In fact, if you want to make a living, you can't do verse. Then I take milk of amnesia for relief.

So keep an o-pun mind. Best wishes from

                                                        Louis Ginsberg

Ginsberg repeated the suggestion, twice, but H.R. did not care for the father's work. He was first printed in *Poetry* in 1927 and for the last time in 1947.

John Berryman to Henry Rago   *[Providence, R.I.], 22 July 1963*

Dear Henry—

Henry [in the "Dream Songs"] seems to be inter'd in heroes lately—wh. makes it hard on me. I'll send you with this a *seven*. I can't go into the archives, exc. to find the 'anthrax-ray' one, wh. I actually like; or— seem to remember to like.

Good luck w. yr number, & vacation. Cheers to yr lady & offspring. . . .

Have you seen, can you get rights to Sylvia Plath's final poems (*Observer*, 17 Febr.) and for a biog'l piece on her? They are rare.

Of course you can have more of my songs to tuck in if you want. I just get mortally tired.

Best— / John

John Berryman in an undated snapshot from the early sixties.

Berryman had written 17 July: "Will ob[lige], swiftly as poss. Trouble is, I hate the damn Songs at present."

Gustav Davidson to Henry Rago   *Poetry Society of America,*
                                          New York City, 19 August 1963

Dear Mr. Rago:

Mr. [Charles] Tomlinson (*Poetry*, Aug. '63) evidently does not know all the facts re the awarding of our gold medal to Robert Graves, and so characterizes the Graves article (in his *Oxford Addresses on Poetry*) as "charming" rather than as bad taste. Furthermore, Mr. Tomlinson takes at face value Graves' statement that the medal was not gold, only "gold-plated," thereby further perpetuating a falsehood and a calumny.

Mr. Graves has held up The Poetry Society of America to ridicule and scorn by stating that we deliberately deceived him in awarding him a medal purporting to be gold when we knew all along that it was not. This, too, is false.

When Mr. Graves' book appeared (*The Oxford Addresses*), it was brought at once to the attention of The Medallic Art Company, which struck off the 10 medals. The Medallic Art Company is a 100-year-old firm of whose integrity there can be no question. The invoice of the firm, when it billed the Society, read: "10 14kt. Droutzkoy gold medals." We paid the then current price of 14 carat gold and its use in making up the medals ($571.83). . . .

It should be pointed out that Mr. Graves was very proud and honored to be the recipient of our medal (his own country had not, up to then, honored him in this fashion). He was also honored, he said, to share the dais with Robert Frost, Marianne Moore, and others. However, he came to our 50th Anniversary Dinner fortified with a touchstone which he produced from his pocket. He brought it, he declared, for the purpose of testing the gold content of his trophy. This was done in no spirit of levity but in all earnestness, as later events proved. Mr. Graves was the 10th recipient—and final recipient—of the medal, and none of the preceding recipients ever dreamed of putting the medal to a test, in public or in private, as far as anybody knows. On his return to Europe, Mr. Graves sought out a jeweler who would confirm him (and, as Mr. Graves asserts triumphantly, did confirm him) in his presupposition that the medal was not gold, and then made capital of the matter at the expense of the Society that honored him. . . .

I believe that, in fairness to The Poetry Society of America, the foregoing facts should be made known. I believe that your magazine, knowing the facts, would not wish to lend itself to further perpetuating a falsehood and a calumny.

Sincerely yours, / Gustav Davidson,
Executive Secretary

In his essay, "Poetic Gold," printed in *Oxford Addresses on Poetry* (London: Cassell, 1961, pp. 85–96), Graves recounts his reaction to the awards program (attended by six hundred people at the Waldorf-Astoria) in a joking manner. Throughout the dinner, Frost, who traveled from Florida especially to see Graves, made sly comments; in his acceptance speech Graves drew an extended analogy between the rarity of real gold in medals and of genuine poetic talent. In his letter of 20 January 1964 (below), Graves justifies his reactions to the prize and essentially repeats his version of the affair as presented in the *Oxford Addresses*. Davidson's letter was printed in the December 1963 issue, pp. 200–201. In his review of the *Oxford Addresses*, Tomlinson wrote only: "The book contains a charming account of the gold medal awarded to Graves by the Poetry Society of America that turned out not to be gold."

Robert Graves to Henry Rago   *Deya, Mallorca, Spain,*
                                                  20 January 1964

Dear Henry:
    Would you like to print this? Excuse the mess!

                                                  Yours ever, / Robert
Dear sir:
    Gustav Davidson knows perfectly well that I am neither a liar nor a snob; and so should everyone else who has met me. (But I admit that at least three Germans in my life have accused me of being no gentleman.) He also knows that I never insulted the Poetry Society of America, but that Robert Frost (the Honorary President) and I shared a joke about touchstones & the acid test for poetry in which Dr. Clarence B. Decker the President was poet enough to join.

    —In American Law a gold medal is legally marked "14 kt" if it has at least seven one-millionths of gold in its plating. If manufacturers apply to the Director of the Mint for gold used in a particular order, it is perfectly ethical for them to spread its use to other products. The medal I got was *not* gold, although a gold medal—perhaps it was only the original design sample?—and even so the 57 dollars paid for its manufacture was not excessive. The honour was all that mattered, as I told

Robert Graves in later life; he first appeared in the magazine in 1919.

Dr. Decker; but in my speech at the Celebration I had dwelt on the intrinsic and extrinsic riches of gold and poems—also on jasper touchstones and on the etymology & metaphorical use of *Karats*. So the chance discovery—forced on me later by an old Palma goldsmith of my acquaintance, who asked to see it because he had never in his life seem a real *golden* medal, that my particular Alexander Drouzkoy Award would not stand up to the acid-and-touchstone test—amused Robert Frost & myself as ironical.

No more than one gold medal in a thousand is golden (and this figure does not even include the Olympic Games awards) just as there is no more than one prize poem in a thousand has any gold value at all higher than the seven one-millionth plating requirement. No Spanish gold medals are made of gold, nor are any British ones except one or two struck by special Royal Warrant. Of all this I had been innocent at the time of my speech. The touchstone that I produced as a gimmick had been brought to America as a present for the son of a poet, named Jasper, not to test the medal.

I hope this puts me straight with readers of *Poetry*. They can find the whole story in my *Oxford Addresses on Poetry* (Doubleday).

Ironically yours, / Robert Graves

In his *Oxford Addresses*, Graves states he wrote Dr. Decker, thanking him for the honor and said he would spend the $100 check that accompanied the medal "on a real-gold replica, taking care to use the original red ribbon and pin." He adds that he told Dr. Decker he should have "revealed the truth before the banquet ended." Graves gave the letter to Frost, to forward or not, as he saw fit; Frost passed it on "('gleefully,' I hear)". This letter was printed in the April 1964 issue, under the title "Gold, in Medals and in Poems."

Mrs. William Carlos Williams to Henry Rago   *Rutherford, N.J.,*
                                                              3 September 1963

Dear Henry Rago—

I'm pleased that Bill's poems will appear in "Poetry." I've gone thru a mass of manuscripts but find no more.—

Bill was so generous to the little mags—he would write a "pome" and send it off—all in one breath. —Sometimes I'm sure it might have been better if he hadn't been so prompt! But that was Bill!

It's just *too* bad that a color photo of "*Stormy*" couldn't have been published with the poem! —What a dog! Jim Laughlin and his wife fell in love with him when they came home with me after the services for Bill—and promptly bought one from some fancy kennel—but they report 100% love for him.

If there are any books of Bill's that *Poetry* does not have—books of Paterson—etc., let me know. —I'd be delighted to give them to the collection. So, speak up—

If ever you are about here, please do at least *call* me. I am just as much as ever interested & involved with the modern poets. I love them.

With my best wishes,

Sincerely— / Florence Williams

Williams's short, humorous poem to his dog was printed in the Golden Anniversary issue.

John Berryman to Henry Rago   *[n.p.], 9 September 1963*

Dear Henry,

I expect I am getting soft in the head—ruined by the deaths of Roethke [1 August] & MacNeice [3 September]—but I like some of these songs. I am out of money or nearly, since people owe me money, for a week or so: would it damage your budget if you paid me immediately, or as soon as possible, for these? *minus* $6 for the ten-to-be-sent, a list of which I enclose.

Ted's [Roethke] death hit me, and over several days I made up two songs, one of which I killed, the other of which was taken so fast by [Arthur] Crook [editor] of TLS that he apologized for not sending me a proof. . . . I printed it abroad because I can never think of where the hell to send anything here that won't take months to see, and I generally hold my stuff for years, much less months, but sometimes one gets bored with this procedure. I just had an interesting letter from [Vernon] Watkins about it.

Notes on Contributors: Farrar Straus prob'y do 75 *Dream Songs* next spring, Faber perhaps later. *Ramparts* gave 15 their first prize, $700, in May. Visiting at Brown last year; sabbatical this, again on leave fr the Univ of Minnesota, Humanities Programme (*not* Engl Dept). . . .

Despite his problems with alcohol, Berryman was able to maintain his academic career and held several visiting positions; Allen Tate was instrumental in getting him the regular post at Minnesota.

David Wagoner to Henry Rago   *University of Washington,*
                                  Seattle, Wash., 20 September 1963

Dear Henry:

Thanks for the kind words, and congratulations on a couple of recent issue of POETRY. How the hell you manage to keep up the standards you do month after month, I can't imagine.

And thanks also for the memory of Ted Roethke's praise for me. As you probably know, I value his opinion a great deal. He was my teacher at Penn State in 1947, and the first poem I wrote for his class (and for his voice, because he could fill a room with the boom and the gestures) came out in POETRY the next year—called "Marsh Leaf," a dismal dripping of a poem, but mostly mine own. They've asked me to teach his classes in the fall; though I've done it before when he was on leave, dipping himself off the shores of Ischia or Ireland, this time it will be tough. I can't even begin to match the intensity he could achieve in a classroom in his prime. The son of a bitch was a magician as a teacher, and the new book will show what he was becoming as a poet. And that isn't all: he left behind a tremendous collection of notebooks, full of the maddest and most wonderful work of all, which only a few close friends ever had much of a look at: not whole poems but fragments, aphorisms, scurrilous diatribes, libelous literary observations. It will all come out in time, I guess. Beatrice [his widow] is rightly guarding the material like a centurion, but when I broached the possibility of making a few essay-like aggregations of some of the stuff (that is, organizing some of it by theme and/or mood and/or style) for magazines, she said she'd like me to try it this fall. There are *trunks* full. She needs money. He left her the house, two cars, his books, his royalties, and damn-all else.

Would POETRY be interested in seeing parts of this strange stuff? I know that's a silly question; of course you would, just as a matter of interest. But when I get a better idea of what I can do with it (the stuff will be published in its entirety someday, I'm sure, as with Coleridge and Blake) I'll know whether some of it can stand in short pieces or whether it requires bulk. At any rate, more news later. First comes the problem of transcribing some of the tougher handwriting. . . .

Best, / Dave

"Straw for the Fire: From His Notebooks," arranged by Wagoner, appeared in November 1964; "The Stony Garden," also in a version by Wagoner, was printed in November 1968. Roethke received the National Book Award posthumously for *The Far Field* (1964).

Allen Ginsberg to Henry Rago   *San Francisco, Calif.,*
                                                    14 October 1963

Dear Mr Rago:

Enclosed find a note by me on poetry by Philip Lamantia & Poetry's review of it by Richard Howard—both of them old friends of mine so my note aimed at pacifying not hasseling [sic].

Talking it over with Philip Whalen, I asked him why he'd never been printed in Poetry, he said he's never submitted never been asked—I offered to send in a mss. for him as he seemed hesitant. Enclosed a fine poem by him, characteristic of his work.

Allen Ginsberg, with William Burroughs and Philip Whalen,
in an undated photograph sent to *Poetry* probably in the late sixties.

When I have been home sufficiently long to type up writing I've done during several years absence I will submit a poem to you also. Been away 4 years.

As ever / Allen Ginsberg

Henry Rago to Allen Ginsberg   *Chicago, 22 November 1963*

Dear Allen Ginsberg,

We've been in our busiest time here, so I've been slow to thank you for your letter and for all else that came with it. The letter on Richard Howard's review of Lamantia we'll be glad to print in the first available issue. . . .

I look forward too to seeing the poems, your new ones I mean, as soon as you have them typed and ready to send.

I don't feel quite strongly for the Philip Whalen poem to keep it for PO-ETRY, though I've seen others of his elsewhere that I would have been glad to have in the magazine. I hope he won't take this as an indifference to his work, or to your own good offices. Do tell him to try us again, and to expect that there'll always be picking and choosing. I just don't make the kind of commitment to this poem that its full length demands of me.

I remember the afternoon we had together at POETRY, and I often hope that all things go well with you.

Yours sincerely, / Henry Rago

Ginsberg's letter on "Lamantia as Forerunner" was printed under Correspondence, January 1964. Howard said of Lamantia's work that Ginsberg had already written "the poems these spasms so relentlessly parrot." Ginsberg asserted they shared "similarity of sources" and that Lamantia's interest in "surreal composition notoriously antedates mine and surpasses my practice"; in a footnote he added that Howard was "an excellent fellow otherwise." Whalen's first (and only) appearance in *Poetry* was "Invocation and Theophany" in April 1965.

David Ignatow to Henry Rago   *New York City, 1 January 1964*

Dear Henry Rago:

A happy new year to you and all the staff of *Poetry*. I thought a happy omen, at my house last night, was the playing of Bach on our piano as 1964 ticked in. The playing seemed to say for me that there will be more composure, restraint of violence in the days to come than we were witness to last year, that sad, terrible year which nearly crucified us with our President's death. None of us present at my house could cease from thinking about or being influenced in our conversation by his death. It was a quiet, calm gathering, such as I hope with all my being will develop everywhere in the world in days to come, and compassion on us all. Amen. . . .

Cordially, / David Ignatow

Conrad Aiken to Henry Rago   *Savannah, Ga., 18 January 1964*

Editor, POETRY
Dear Sir:

It may seem a little odd for an "unfashionable Historic Personage" to reply to your reviewer, but I do think I owe it to my publishers, and perhaps to Mr. Dickey himself, to put him right about a few things. It is that Mr. Dickey is very, very sorry for me, and that my poems, if for the moment I may call them so, cause him such extreme distress, and he goes on about it at such length, and in such a fever, that I feel it is only merciful to put an end to his suffering. The *soi-disant* poems I will continue to allow to speak for themselves, as they should. But when Mr. Dickey (whom I assume to be considerably younger than myself, and ought, therefore, to be wiser) says that this industrious and Historic Personage has "very few readers," I am afraid the facts do not support him. In the same mail that brought Mr.

Dickey's *cri de coeur*, his lament for one who so clearly ought to have been long since dead, came the latest royalty report from the Oxford University Press. It showed earnings—for the six months just past—of between seven and eight hundred dollars on the four books: A LETTER FROM LI PO (not A LETTER TO LI PO, Mr. Dickey), COLLECTED POEMS, SELECTED POEMS, and THE MORNING SONG OF LORD ZERO. It showed also, as these reports have continually shown for the past ten years, a steady and marked rise in sales, even for the prohibitively priced COLLECTED. For one who is not a teacher-poet, nor a traveling-salesman poet—those who lecture or read at the drop of a thin dime—I don't think this is too bad; and it ought to help to relieve Mr. Dickey's mind to know that SELECTED POEMS, published in May 1962, is sold out, and that MERIDIAN BOOKS will bring it out as a paperback this spring. The PRELUDES, too, which came out so long ago that I daresay Mr. Dickey doesn't recall them, may also come out as a paperback. And finally, of the three books *about* this unfashionable Historic Personage which came out last year, Jay Martin's CONRAD AIKEN: A LIFE OF HIS ART is to have a second printing.

May I hope, therefore, that Mr. Dickey now feels a little better about it all? *I* certainly do.

yrs , / Conrad Aiken

In his reply to Aiken 24 January 1964, H.R. agreed to print his protest but tried to dissuade him, adding: "I could hope that on some reflection you might decide that many of us would assume in any case not only what your letter says but vastly more than that."

Conrad Aiken to Henry Rago   *Savannah, Ga., 28 January 1964*

Dear Mr Rago:

Thanks for your letter. Heaven knows I don't want to seem pernickety about this, but it seems to me that you seriously underestimate the damage done to me and my publisher by that review of Dickey's. In stating that I have few readers he comes precious close to libel. No, this sort of irresponsible assassination (cf. the outrageous review of USHANT which Shapiro published) should not be allowed to go unnoticed, and I think Dickey deserves to be rebuked and corrected, and the facts put right, in POETRY, many of whose readers might otherwise have acquired—and passed on to others—a false impression. Not only that, either; for the sheer bad manners of Dickey's piece are inexcusable. I'm surprised, frankly, that you don't yourself see all this!— Anyway, I'll be grateful if you WILL publish my letter. I could, as you suggest, have said much more, but it was no part of my intention to defend the work itself. But I do object to being called dead! I suspect TIME was echoing Dickey when it described me as a kind of Smith-sonian Institution. But that at least has the virtue of being funny!

Your sincerely, / Conrad Aiken

Aiken's letter appeared in March 1964. For details of the controversy surrounding Edward Dahlberg's review of *Ushant*, see *Dear Editor*, introduction to Chapter XVII and pp. 403-407. See also Roger Hecht's letter below.

James Laughlin to Henry Rago   *New York City, 25 February 1964*

Dear Henry,

Many thanks for your note of February 21st. . . .

Ezra is considerably better in health these days. There is a picture story on his life in Venice coming out in *Life* on March 27th, if they keep to schedule. They play up the pathos of his present situation, but actually, he is more cheerful than they make him sound. He still talks vaguely of a visit here, but I have my doubts. I think he realizes that Italy is his real spiritual home, and that he would be a fish out of water over here. . . .

As ever, / James Laughlin

Roger Hecht to Henry Rago   *[New York City], 20 March 1964*

Dear Mr. Rago:

. . . with reference to the Aiken letter in the March issue, I confess my-self shocked at and by the spectacle of such bad manners. The central con-tention that James Dickey made, that Aiken's work is not widely read, is hardly disproved by a battery of the Aiken sales figures. That new editions of several Aiken books are scheduled is also irrelevant, and bespeaks an at-titude of plain and disgusting salesmanship, which combined with the in-ordinate heaps of pity that Aiken bestows on Aiken makes the entire letter seem false and unworthy of so eminent and battle-tried a man as Aiken must be. I say this with extreme reluctance, for I know Dickey's poems and opinions—if there's any difference—all too well. And I realize that Dickey always has been and remains an advertising man—a person interested in persuasion more than in anything else. Nevertheless, I believe Dickey's re-view should have stood as it was without the petulant answer Aiken wrote being printed. . . .

Many people buy books of poems, Mr. Rago, and place these in their homes as women place trinkets at the waist, the breast, the neck. The trin-kets, the volumes, may be valuable and beautiful in themselves; but they are not purchased or displayed for anything other than the hope that a man, a guest, will note their presence and offer compliments to the woman, the hosts, as the case may be. Also, many volumes of poetry are purchased for English classes and are carefully misplaced or given away after term's end. . . .

I say all this with reluctance, but Aiken obviously cannot tolerate a harsh review of his work, and the pages of POETRY, if opened once to the whining of poets who feel their works to have been mistreated, cannot logically or fairly be denied to any poet who has had work reviewed in POETRY. I fear in fact that you may have set an unfortunate precedent by printing the Aiken letter. It should not have appeared. It does not merit the currency it received. . . .

Let me in humorous conclusion note that in recent years more and more of the poets and poems in POETRY appear to be housebroken and apron-stringed and less and less of what in the last century was called "manly" appears. Poems about ideas, poems about events, poems about persons other than lovers, children and mistresses, I gather arrive at your office with greater and greater infrequency. I should not be altogether surprised were more of the women poets to become in their poems and perhaps in their lives as shrill and strident with frustrated femininity as Miss Kizer and Mrs. Sexton already are. By which I return to James' note for the subject of the novel that, when written, became THE BOSTONIANS: he wanted to deal with something idiosyncratically American, and he found "the decline in the sentiment of sex."

I am sorry. This is much too long.

Blessings and stay well— / Roger

Robert Duncan to Henry Rago   *[San Francisco, Calif.], 26 May 1964*

Dear Henry/

Yes, I certainly wld like to get to writing that piece on Dickey's *Two Poems*, and I am writing to him in this same mail to enquire about a copy of the book. Wld you send the review copy from POETRY to be sure to cover? While at Denise Levertov's in New York I read *Helmets*, finding there even more to excite my major sympathies. He dwells in a spiritualized world, close upon the presence of Nature's magic and upon the visitations of what theosophists call the astral—shades of our own living; but without faith, I judge from what I have read, there being neither God nor angels nor gods in the structure of his imagination. Yet God must be there, for his work has grace—poetic grace that I am sure stirs in us from the Grace of the created world from its creator.

The visit with you on my way East was a great pleasure. If the possibility you mentioned of my reading on the mid-West circuit this coming Fall or next Spring matures, it may not be too long before we might have time together again.

Yrs, / Robert Duncan

Lew Welch to Henry Rago   *Mill Valley, Calif., 31 May 1964*

Dear Mr. Rago,

I finally have a fairly permanent address—will be here for at least 6 months. . . .

Gary Snyder is back from Japan for a while & we have organized a giant reading as per the attached. . . .

S.F. and the Bay Area grow more responsive to poetry every day. Gary, Phil, and I have been on the radio (FM), the Chronicle loves us, (maybe a whole column by Ralph Gleason, local jazz column writer & very good man), everyone very excited. I just predict 1,000 souls. . . .

General problem: big fear/hate thing called war between hip & square. Poet seen as frightening hippydip. Incommunicable (poets!) folks who mumble, snarl, etc. etc.

Cause for Real Hope: All folks delighted by actual article. Express huge need for Poetry. Prove this by quick pickup of the poems (in this town you can hardly get a 50 line structure out, out loud, for interference of shrieks of laughter, cheers, etc.).

For all the reasons we all know (and which, I say, we must forget—no blame, as I Ching says) the whole thing got hopelessly fucked up. Ginsberg in NY beautifully correcting things. We 3 (and dozens of others) here in SF also putting it right. Or trying to.

And, weirdly, all this is happening without any real change in approach. The poems are actually tougher. I wear long hair and black boots. Why not? I'm handsome and vain. Synder has a beard, patched jeans, a wild little over-the-shoulder black Jap bag thing. Of course! Poets have to carry books, mss., all manner of clumsy articles. Whalen wears funky old over-all-type jeans, immaculately clean, simply because he's portly & can't make it in Levi's & he's poor, terribly poor. . . . [sic]

How to say anything without causing a new confusion. That's what actually went wrong. One answer. Write more. Write more accurately. Write tough.

Every time we cheat, even unknowingly, thousands "die of our cowardice."

How great to have our job at a time like this—eh Henry?

Lew Welch

Can't you figure a way to make this reading? Worth it. Also, June in SF unbelievable. Try. W.

Charles Simic to the Editor   *New York City, 2 November 1964*

Dear Sir,

I'm submitting eight poems for your consideration. I have published a little previously (Chicago Review) and will have some poems in the next issue of "The Beloit Poetry Journal."

I have left my studies at NYU to become a house-painter, this being more profitable and in every respect more educational. I have majored in Slavic studies and I'm using whatever knowledge I have to translate some Yugoslav and Bulgarian poets.

Cordially yours, / Charles Simic

Simic first appeared in *Poetry* in 1970, with two poems.

Robert Creeley to Henry Rago   *Placitas, N.M., 26 November 1964*

Dear Mr. Rago,

This comes late indeed, but it occurs a pretty faint group—at least in my own mind. . . .

I don't know if I mentioned, in the last note, having seen Basil Bunting in Newcastle. I was very impressed by him—he is extraordinarily intelligent, and very usefully perceptive, I felt, about poetry and all that relates to it. Too, he was at work on a long poem—some 70 lines of which he read to us—and I think it will be a very fine one indeed.

My best to you, / Robert Creeley

P.S. (November 27th) I've just had your very helpful letter concerning the poetry [reading] circuit and [associate editor] Bob Mueller's having had to go into the Navy (which sounds difficult). I'm, sorry the circuit is not now possible. . . .

I did have a very happy visit with Charles and Brenda [Tomlinson], and their very pleasant daughters. I read at Bristol, and then with them at their home—such a lovely lovely place it is! Charles is, for me, the most actively intelligent man there. . . . The only other, really, who centers as he does— and has had of course a long record of having done so—is Basil Bunting, and I do wish contemporary British poetry would make use of their ability, in a substantial sense. . . . But the younger men seem not even to have heard of him, which is a shame. Anyhow I'm hopeful of something now happening to put him back in the record. I think that both he and Louis Zukofsky are invaluable, in very much the same way—elsewise the whole "record" of that generation reads incorrectly.

Mueller formally resigned his position a year later; he had directed the Midwest section of the poetry circuit, a series of readings around the country funded by the Rockefeller Foundation.

Jim Harrison to Henry Rago   *[n.p.], 6 December 1964*

Dear Mr. Rago,

I believe Denise Levertov mentioned my work to you during the recent Chicago trip. In any event, here are ten short poems I hope you'll take a look at.

I've not been published before, not even in the smallest periodicals, though I haven't tried in the past few years. I've only been doing good work for a year now.

I have a job as a delivery man for a book wholesaler. I'm 26, married, and have a daughter. I have a B.S. in Comparative Lit. from Mich. State U. and part of an M.A. but I turned out to be a bit too loony for teaching and scholarship. I was born in Grayling, Michigan but have lived most of my life in Reed City (north) and Haslett. My father was a conservationist.

The people at W.W. Norton have been "looking" at a ms. of mine for two months now but haven't decided. I still sleep well.

Sincerely, / Jim Harrison

P.S. —I send this "special delivery" because there's a mail machine where I work. Creeley has a nice poem about postal people burning ms.

Harrison's first contribution, "Dead Doe," was printed in August 1965.

Basil Bunting to Henry Rago   *Wylam, Northumberland, England,*
                                              13 December 1964

Dear Mr Rago,

Thank you for your letter. . . .

I am, as Creeley told you, engaged on a 'long' poem; but it is not a long poem in the sense that the Cantos, or Zukofsky's A or the other, general commentaries on the times are. It may be slightly longer than The Spoils, which *Poetry* published whole; but it is too soon to say how much of its intended contents will have to be cut out when I get down to the more arduous part of the work after the first draft is finished. Anyway, it was from the first my intention to offer the whole thing to you when the time comes. I think it will be sufficiently different from the current fashion to make some impression, and it will have a shape which is the necessary setting of the parts although two or three, short lyrics imbedded in it could, I suppose, be taken separately without losing too much of their effect. . . .

Since I drudge to live, it is taking a long time to write. Perhaps it may be ready next summer. (Its name is BRIGGFLATTS).

Yours faithfully / Basil Bunting

James Laughlin to Henry Rago   *New Directions, New York City,*
                                                                      8 February 1965

Dear Henry,

I don't think I have yet thanked you, as I want very much to do, for the most heartwarming letter that you sent me not long ago. . . .

I was really quite astonished to read in the paper the other morning that Ezra had attended the service for Eliot in the [Westminster] Abbey. I had spent several days with Ezra in Venice in January, and knew that he wanted to go, but I never thought he would be able to get himself organized to do it. I found him in pretty good shape physically for a man of his age, but still plunged in that terrible melancholy, and so withdrawn into silence that he hardly speaks at all. He told me also that he had not been able to write anything for months.

                                            With best wishes, as ever, / J.

Robert Duncan to Henry Rago   *[San Francisco, Calif.],*
                                                                       1 March 1965

Dear Henry/

Enclosed the proofs for "The Fire." I hope my notations are clear: The parenthesis "(This is Piero di Cosimo's great painting . . ." etc.) is part of the text; not, as it seems to have been taken, a footnote to the title. In the original typescript I had spaced the lines out, space-and-a-half, so that single-spaced sections were distinguished; to keep this break where I wanted it, I have introduced some stanza breaks. I felt the phrasings of the typescript absolutely necessary to the movement.

Is it some solace for our times—I'm thinking of this terrible satanic bombing of Vietnam South and North and the daring of, even stirring up of, whatever nest China is—that we are not the first ones or the only ones who must make our lives in a time of the shaking of the Tree of Good and Evil? Is Satan indeed, as the Church teaches, absolute in his enmity to Creation? Seeing the travesty of Lincoln that LBJ puts on or the jolly grimacing mask of [Hubert] Humphries [sic] (having won over the evident evil of [Barry] Goldwater's presentation), I am shaken in that heresy I would hold that Satan will be redeemed in the end of time, even as Christ has redeemed Adam. For these men, if they know what they do, are terrible men.

I hope soon to have some new work to send you for future issues. And when I see my way I mean also to rework the passages you were interested in in the polemical essay I sent you.

                                            Sincerely, / Robert Duncan

Andy Warhol with Gerard Malanga at The Factory, June 1963.

Gerard Malanga to Henry Rago   *Bronx, N.Y., 22 March 1965*

Dear Mr. Rago:

It is good to hear from you. What I thought when I received your letter was that you were sending me proofs of my poems. Your letter was a complete surprise.

I have always found book reviewing a challenge; but [Louis Zukofsky's] *Bottom* is certainly a challenge. Yes, I will take the responsibility of meeting a deadline. . . .

When you come to New York I do hope you will have time to see me. I can be reached any day after 2:00 P.M. at EL 5-9941 / the address: Andy Warhol, 231 East 47th Street. We would like to include you in Andy's new personalities movie. I was also wondering if you would consent to give me some of the your unpublished poems for inclusion in the third issue of *Nadada?* . . .

Write soon.

Best wishes, / Gerard Malanga

Maurice English to Henry Rago   *University of Chicago Press,*
1 April 1965

Dear Henry:

As you know, the Harper Memorial Library of the University of Chicago is the repository of the papers of Miss Harriet Monroe. These papers constitute, of course, an invaluable record in connection with the history of *Poetry* Magazine, but also shed light on the development of poetry generally in the United States and in the English-speaking world during the first half of the century, and on the thoughts and activities of many distinguished American writers.

The desirability of publishing a selection from these papers is of course quite obvious, and the approach of the seventy-fifth anniversary of the University of Chicago seems like a propitious time to proceed. The press and the members of the faculty with whom we have talked thought it would be very helpful if we could have the opinion of your and the past editors-in-chief of the magazine as to who might most appropriately be asked to do the editorial work connected with this proposal to publish a selection of the Monroe correspondence with the necessary annotations and, of course, an introduction.

We would be very grateful for any nominations that you would care to make to us (which will be held in confidence), and would appreciate also any comments or suggestions that might be helpful in developing this proposal. May we look forward to hearing from you?

Cordially, / Maurice English, Senior Editor

H.R. recommended George Dillon as "the natural choice . . . he worked closely with Harriet Monroe . . . is intelligent, learned, and scrupulous." Dillon declined the offer. Karl Shapiro was asked and agreed to take on the project, but nothing came of it. See Shapiro letter of 5 November 1966 below.

Gerard Malanga to Henry Rago   *Bronx, N.Y., 9 April 1965*

Dear Mr. Rago:

I was very happy you had the opportunity to visit Andy's "factory." I hope when you are in New York again you will drop by.

Yesterday I picked up Zukofsky's *Bottom* from LeRoi's [Jones] wife. Some Book! From the looks of the publisher I'd question the fact that Zukofsky put any money into it.

Andy and I will be going to Paris on April 29th and will be away for a month and a half. I will be able to get the reviews to you sometime in June or July. I cannot promise an earlier completion.

Last night I went to Diane DiPrima's East End Theatre to see Piero [Heliczer] and Angus MacLise read poems and play instruments. Another poet, Paolo Lionni was on hand in the orchestra as well as many other underground celebrities. It was very exciting and the concert lasted almost three hrs.

In a couple of wks you shd have copies of "stillies" from your portrait movie.

Best wishes, / Gerard

P.S. Do you think Wag Lit Mag could get a mention in the News Notes column. GM.

Ron Padgett to Poetry   *New York City, 27 April 1965*

May Sarton to Henry Rago   *Munsonville, N.H., 11 May 1965*

Dear Henry Rago,

I enclose a sort of Greek Sampler, part of a book to be called *A Private Mythology* which Norton will publish early next year. I hope very much that you will wish to publish these as a unit. Maybe it is a lot to expect. It is 27 years since my first book of poems was published and it is quite clear that I have never made it, and risk becoming a sort of *dodo*. But it has always been my belief that I am, although a fast beginner, a slow maturer—perhaps at least I am beginning to say some of the things [sic].

In August Norton brings out a terribly risky novel I have written about being a woman and a poet. I expect the worst, but sooner or later I had to try to say it. It is called *Mrs. Stevens Hears the Mermaids Singing*. I expect only sneers and clots of mud, but between me and God, I know it is good.

Well, enough of me—take a look.

Yours, respectfully submitted (as they say on college committees!)

May Sarton

Rago did not accept the poems.

Robert Duncan to Henry Rago   [*San Francisco, Calif.*], *19 May 1965*

Dear Henry,

It is a proud issue [April 1965]. For me, Denise's "Olga Poems" and [Gael] Turnbull's "Twenty Words: Twenty Days" present a major challenge for what poetry can be. That immediate to life! I had seen parts of the "Olga Poems" last spring in New York, and in some way seen them without recognition. I mistrusted I know the personal occasion. But now the greater joy and excitement in the work to follow how fully the whole thing has been communicated. Those long lines, where the numbers can be felt but cannot have been calculated—perhaps the "everything flows" lead that way—

As Turnbull's intelligence, his attention and charge appropriate everywhere in each area Creeley, Charles and I all seem to have furnisht with of our best—"Cole's Island" is a lovely directly accessible poem. And it is thinking of these, that I see the "Olga Poems" and "Twenty Words" as more than their best, as lifted up into something that becomes ours beyond theirs. Humanity is more vitally us than personality.

Wendell Berry, whose work I have followed since I knew him and saw him again in New York, in this sequence [from "The Handing Down"] comes into his own for me—an appropriate every sense of it since he has to be so much with the man's growing into his life "His days / come to him as if they knew him." The idealization of man, house, love has taken over and overrides, I realize, rifts the real world show. But the loving idealization is rarer in its success today than the hating idealization—the world of Beckett or Burroughs that overrides unions reality reveals.

Both Snyder's and Whalen's work ["Through the Smoke Hole" and "Invocation and Theophany," respectively] were fine. The inferno of Galway Kinnell ["The Mystic River"] with its spirit at times of Dante and of Blake, perhaps because it rode sentiments of outrage and not confrontions with the particulars of evil, lost energy; phantasies of a social anger.

These are terrible times—with a man who to fight the idea *communism* has armed tyranny in Viet Nam and in the Dominican Republic, and for humanitarian reasons, to save lives, has sent troops to kill the people of Santo Domingo. "We're to kill the civilians before they shoot us," one common soldier (a boy) interviewed on T.V. That Johnson may be insane, a dull-minded man consumed with the megalomania of absolute power— the mandate!—is part of the terrible possibility. I think he is a figure, as Hitler was, of the Wrath of God, that terrible wrath that consumed Christendom as Catholic and Protestant piled the corpses high to eradicate ideas. And I have in my obedience to the poet in me felt the thunder of that God-voice shake my body, my lines. I want now I realize to hold to what humanity I can (so I am moved most by Denise and Gael who write, as they do, from the depth of their humanity)— As often I turn to the thot [thought] of Zukofsky for his intellectual caution because I so used it.

Dante made his descent into Hell attended by the caution of Virgil. Kinnell needs a more firm guide than Henry David [Thoreau]. I think I had given myself a false mandate in the name of the poet.

Henry, this was meant as a letter of thanks from me as a reader as well as writer, and if I've got off into my troubled thought it's because I am also a friend and you, then, not an editor for me—and more because to write at all I had to write some of these things too.

I hope soon to find the time to get my notes on derivation and on the articulation and juncture of lines done—as you rightly wanted of me— without the polemical wrath that would leave wounded or dead those who do not see things as I do.

Robert

Wade Van Dore to Henry Rago   *Clearwater Beach, Fla.,*
                                                 14 June 1965

Dear Mr Rago:

Noting the letter to you in Selected Letters of Robert Frost, I'm moved to write.

Having known Frost probably as well as anyone outside of his family and [Louis] Untermeyer, I'm writing a book largely about him which Holts have suggested I call "The Life of the Hired Man". I'm including most or all the thirty-two letters Frost wrote me, the first of which, in the Selected Letters, is number 221. If you take the time to read the write-up about me there you'll see that I was Frost's "hired man" on three of his farms. As a matter of fact he wanted me more as housekeeper and companion than as a hired man.

Here is my story about Harriet Monroe. Coming down from the north woods of Canada in 1928 or early 1929 where I had been guiding moose hunters and living like a hermit, I stopped in to see her. Carrying a few newly written poems with me, on letting her read them she exclaimed, "I'd like to lead an issue with six of these". This of course pleased me, but the poems were very young and I felt they needed seasoning. So I suggested I retain them for a time but I promised to return them in a few months.

But when I sent her the same six poems giving my address as of South Shaftsbury Vermont, in care of Robert Frost, she rejected the poems emphatically. And Frost who'd brought her note home from the post office and handed it to me was much hurt. He paced the floor for a full half hour. He thought she had made the rejection just to wound him, and maybe she had—though it could have also been jealousy—her wanting to be my total "discoverer".

So I never got into *Poetry*. I made the *New Republic*, the *Atlantic* and the *New Yorker* and others but I felt that so far as *Poetry* was concerned I was forever black-listed.

Becoming a recognized poet does indeed require a lot of luck. Frost told me he never expected to have wide recognition after twenty years of writing. It was a case of long-delayed luck with him finally—or his knowing how in person to deal with Britishers. He said he never asked for anything and that is why they gave him so much. . . .

One of the last poems I showed him was about a farmer who lived near him at Breadloaf. I got to know this man through spending the summer of 1943 with Frost there. Frost was tickled with this poem and asked for a copy so he could, as he said, "carry it around and read it to people". This was the era when the government started to pay farmers for *not* farming, remember? This practice was of great interest to Frost, and my calling it a "sop" in the poem made what he called one of those "lucky" rhymes. It's just a short character study which I imagined was unsuited to name magazines, so I've never submitted it. I wish you would take a hard look at it to see if it isn't too far off to use in *Poetry*. After all these years I think the magazine owes me a little poetic justice. I don't ask to "lead an issue". One poem to lead me off in my re-emergence as a poet would be fine!

Sincerely yours, / Wade Van Dore

Henry Rago to Wade Van Dore   *Chicago, 6 July 1965*

Dear Mr. Van Dore,

I am sorry to return your poem "Mountain Notes on a Vermont Farmer." I have been interested to see it, though I did not feel persuaded to put it among the comparatively few choices for the magazine. . . .

I think I should say—for there is no choosing, finally, between friends—that I knew Harriet Monroe too and valued what she gave me. I am pleased to add to your story, that I heard Mr. Frost pay high tribute to her on the stage of the Coolidge Auditorium at the Library of Congress, on the Fiftieth Anniversary of POETRY. A few months before he died, he gave a reading in Chicago for the benefit of this magazine, which she founded, and declined both his honorarium and his travel expenses. We had hours of private talk that weekend; I don't think I'd put his whole attitude toward Harriet Monroe or her magazine on one episode. Finally, I would say of that episode that whatever the basis of Miss Monroe's judgment in rejecting your poems, I should be greatly shocked if that judgment could be traced to malice or vindictiveness. I never saw any manifestation of either quality in her. Ezra Pound's testimony in the Memorial Issue of POETRY shortly after her death makes the same point with emphasis; and he saw her straightness of motive put sometimes to hard tests.

Yours sincerely, / Henry Rago

Donald Justice to Henry Rago   *Program in Creative Writing,*
                                  University of Iowa, Iowa City, Ia.,
                                              17 June 1965

Dear Henry,

Here are some poems for you to consider. . . .

I've had a strange year. The Actors' Workshop at San Francisco State was really very good and quite interesting to be around, but we didn't like San Francisco. So it came as almost a relief to me when the company decided to take the offer at Lincoln Center and disband, leaving me and the other writer Ford [Foundation] had assigned there (Jack Hawkes) free to go where we wanted. We both headed for Florida. . . .

Perhaps this isn't the proper time or place to mention it, but since I've gone this far, let me go on to say something else fairly personal. I'm not very happy with the situation here at Iowa—though many of the academic securities, such as tenure & a decent salary, etc., have drifted my way—and if you should know or learn of an available opening elsewhere, I'd appreciate your letting me know about it.

Also to continue the theme, briefly: another way out occurs to me—applications for grants like the Guggenheim—and I wonder if you would be willing to recommend me, when the time comes next fall, for a Guggenheim.

With best regards, / Don

Gerard Malanga to Henry Rago   *New York City, 21 July 1965*

Dear Mr. Rago:

Thank you for your letter of July 16th. Everything is calm at "the factory" at the moment. Dan Cassidy is floating around the place on LSD and we, along with my friend, novelist Chuck Wein, are awaiting an interviewer to come and interview us on an article they are doing for a magazine called *Moderator*, which is distributed to most colleges and universities across the country . . . we were all photographed yesterday in leather jackets and T-shirts in the subway and in front of auto wrecks in front of a police station and on parked motorcycles. Great fun!!!

I hope you don't mind me phrasing the contributors' notes the way I have. . . . I want the contributors' notes to read as it is because the Zukofsky piece is so overwhelming that anything about me wouldn't be fantastic. OK? Anyway, it's different.

The stillies are in the process of being paid for by the photo editor of the Warhol book. Dan Cassidy will be sending you some poems very soon. He's never been published in *Poetry*.

All my best, / Gerard

The contributor's note read: "GERARD MALANGA is Gerard Malanga."

Basil Bunting to Henry Rago   *Wylam, Northumberland, England,*
                                                    10 August 1965

Dear Rago,

(May we drop the formality of Mr?) Thanks. . . .

I know the difficulties of finding even a modest amount of space in a well-run magazine let alone about 750 lines; and you, no doubt, know the impatience of authors. There is a momentary spate of publicity about me in England at present and I would like to have taken advantage of it to get a good circulation for whoever presently makes a pamphlet of Briggflatts, particularly as several publishers seem determined to bring out my collected poems sometime next year, which will limit the time available for selling a pamphlet; but it is more important to me to appear in Poetry, which published my Villon 35 years ago and nearly everything considerable I have written since. . . .

I had also better say that I know there are inaccurate and incomplete mss copies floating around. It has been more copied by industrious penmen than any poem I ever heard of, Lord knows why, one copying down another's errors and so on. Over that I have no control. I suppose it is theoretically possible that some pirate might print one of these garbled copies without consulting me, but I don't believe it. I'd make one hell of a fuss if it happened. But the existence of this curious mss circulation is another reason for hastening the printing as much as possible. . . .

Yours faithfully, / Basil Bunting

"Briggflatts" was published in the January 1966 issue and was awarded the Levinson Prize ($500) in October. Rago asked Bunting to be the reader for the 1967 Poetry Day, but he declined the invitation, saying he did not wish to appear on a program with other poets.

Jim Harrison to Henry Rago   *Kingsley, Mich., October 1965*

Dear Mr. Rago,

Please send along the books you mentioned. . . . Am reasonably familiar with what they're up to—I can't promise you a spleenless notice.

I'm still doing construction work though it will soon end with cold weather. When there's no work I hunt partridge & rabbit.

My "suites," though, go well. I hope to finish the first by the end of the month. A revisionist.

I won't reach Chicago or your office this Fall—couldn't raise bus fare to Kalamazoo!

Yrs., / Jim Harrison

Harrison's review of Ammons's *Tape for the Turn of the Year* appeared in February 1966; he reviewed five other volumes in the June 1966 issue.

Robert Watson to Henry Rago   *Greensboro, N.C.,*
15 November 1965

Dear Henry,

Here are three poems for the consideration of *Poetry*. . . .

In Greensboro we are all still stunned with Randall Jarrell's death. I had driven him to the hand clinic at the hospital in Chapel Hill only four days before. Though his death was first reported in the news as suicide, later evidence suggests it was an accident: he was hit by a car on a narrow, dark road.

Sincerely, / Bob

While walking along the lonely road, Jarrell was struck by a car and died 14 October 1965; some suspected he had deliberately jumped into its path. His death was ruled accidental, and the driver was not charged. Jarrell suffered bouts of depression, and had recently attempted suicide by cutting his wrists and was hospitalized; after treatment he seemed to be well again.

Richard Hugo to Henry Rago   *Missoula, Mont., 29 December 1965*

Dear Mr. Rago:

Sorry I keep missing you in Chicago. . . .

Can I beg off this review? I expected to be asked to review individual volumes of modern verse. I'm afraid I'm really unqualified to review the Clancy or the Reeves book, tho the others might be fun. I should explain that I was out of school for almost fifteen years before I came back as a teacher and really don't have the background built up yet to handle the Cassell book [*The Cassell Book of English Poetry*, edited by James Reeves]. But could you keep me in mind for new individual books of verse? Sorry I'm such an uneducated slob, but if you worked 13 years for Boeing, those rivet guns, industrial procedures and cost savings reports wouldn't have done you much good I can assure you. . . .

Thank you also for your kind hopes that things go well. I fear not tho. After 14 months of separation my wife and I have settled on divorce. I suppose that will at least put an end to this limbo, but I'm afraid things haven't gone well for me at all for quite some time. My only advantage is my incredible ability to feel sorry for myself. I find that I am a consistent and dependable source of sympathy for me, so you need waste none on my behalf.

All best wishes, and I return your hope, only this time that things go well for you.

As always, / Dick Hugo

Gerard Malanga to Henry Rago   *New York City, 30 December 1965*

Dear Henry:

I have enclosed fifteen new and very recent poems. Maybe we can aim for a larger selection if the other long ones that you still have don't work out for you.

I've been rehearsing "au go go" dancing with Edie [Sedgwick] for a new Rock 'n Roll group called The Velvet Underground. You'll be hearing a great deal about them in the very near future. They're better than The Beatles and the Rolling Stones combined.

All my best to you for the new year,

Gerard

Hayden Carruth to Henry Rago   *Johnson, Vt., 28 January 1966*

Dear Henry,

Thanks for your note, and I'm glad the new Auden piece seems more suitable. . . . We visited Adrienne Rich and her husband in Cambridge two weeks ago, first time I have strayed into literary society for years and years. Met Lowell and liked him very much. (The only other time I saw him was that fearful night at the Tates' on Harper (?) Avenue years ago.) But I fell sick down there too, and so didn't see much of the city of Longfellow and the elder Lowell. Just as well, perhaps. Did I say to you how much I liked Adrienne's piece on Lawrence [*The Complete Poems*, edited by Vivian De Sola Pinto and F. Warren Roberts] some months back [June]? I think she has a great talent for prose criticism that no one has ever brought out, and that she herself is unsure of. You ought to put her to work more often, though she is slow and probably isn't good for more than a couple of pieces a year anyway. I'll tell you one thing she could do perfectly: that's a retrospective piece on Sylvia Plath. She has studied Plath poems with care and enthusiasm, and could write well about them, I'm almost certain. . . .

Best to all, as ever.

Hayden

Rich reviewed six anthologies in August 1966 but did not write on Plath.

Larry Woiwode to Henry Rago   *Brooklyn, N.Y., 21 February 1966*

Dear Mr. Rago:

Since I last sent you something, in 1964 (you've replied each time with a kind note), I've been busy changing courses. In '64 I turned from poetry altogether, to fiction, and since have sold seven stories to the New Yorker, and now have a first reading contract—for fiction, only—with them. In the past few months I've been gradually going back to my poetry (the New Yorker recently bought one poem), and I wanted you to see some of it.

Most of my old records were lost or destroyed in a series of moves, so perhaps you've seen one or two of these once before, but I hope not, and if you have, I'm hoping you won't even notice, they're in such different shape. And I hope, too, that there are some here you like.

Sincerely, / L. Woiwode

The poems were not accepted.

CHAPTER IV

The Late Sixties:
Protests and Poets

1. Growing Opposition to the War

Following the assassination of John F. Kennedy on 22 November 1963, Lyndon Johnson inherited several unsettled domestic and foreign policy issues. The new president was highly successful in enacting civil rights and other social legislation. He even got Congress to provide major funding ($268 million) in 1965 to establish what became known as the National Endowment, which through the leadership of Carolyn Kizer, the first head of the literature section, gave substantial awards to poets, Hayden Carruth, Mona Van Duyn, and Maxine Kumin first among them. (A News Note for October 1966 added that the Endowment was also offering sabbatical grants "to writers who teach for a living.") But Johnson's ambitious domestic plans and hopes for what he called the Great Society were overshadowed by increasing dissent over his administration's policies in Southeast Asia.

By 1965 U.S. involvement in Vietnam had grown exponentially, and with each escalation, resistance grew across the country. From President Kennedy's initial commitment of 3,200 troops (and $65 million in military equipment) in 1961, the force was expanded to 16,000 in July 1964. Then, on 4 August, North Vietnamese torpedo boats shelled and slightly damaged a U.S. destroyer doing intelligence work in the Gulf of Tonkin; later that day there was allegedly another assault on the ship. It is still not clear whether the so-called Second Attack actually occurred, but the "incident" served as sufficient pretext for Johnson to order immediate air strikes in retaliation. Meanwhile his advisers drafted the Gulf of Tonkin Resolution, which Congress passed on 7 August. It authorized "all necessary measures" to defend U.S. troops and allies in Southeast Asia, and was used to justify later military activities, including those initiated during the Nixon years.

With help from Russia, and much more later from China, North Vietnam stepped up its attacks, often using the Ho Chi Minh Trail through Laos to infiltrate guerrillas into the South. Saigon's own army was inadequate, but the U.S. commander-in-chief, General William Westmoreland, optimistically predicted that with increased U.S. forces the Communist advance could be contained. By late 1965 there were 180,000 American combat troops in South Vietnam. Hanoi responded by increasing the regular and guerrilla forces of its People's Liberation Army to perhaps 220,000. By mid-1966 U.S. forces reached 350,000. A year later that figure grew to 486,000.

Anti-war activities began to mount a month after Johnson authorized sending in the first combat units in the spring of 1965. On 17 April the Students for a Democratic Society (SDS) organized the first large anti-war rally in Washington. Some sixteen thousand people peacefully picketed the White House, then marched to the Capitol singing and carrying signs declaring "No More War." By the fall of 1965 opposition had grown considerably, and demonstrations were held in forty cities across the country in October. A favorite chant was "Hey, hey, LBJ, how many kids did you kill today?" Certain demoralized soldiers in Vietnam wrote as their motto: "We are the unwilling, led by the unqualified, doing the unnecessary for the ungrateful."

Between 1961 and 1963, 392 U.S. forces were killed in Vietnam. By the end of 1965, 1,863 more had died there. Despite sharp debate and strong misgivings, Congress authorized $12.8 billion in January 1966 to continue the war. In the summer large race riots broke out in Chicago, Cleveland, Brooklyn, Dayton, San Francisco, Atlanta, and other cities; there were scores more the following year. Meanwhile U.S. bombing increased in Vietnam, and Agent Orange and other chemicals began to be used to defoliate the jungle in order to expose enemy guerrillas. Financial costs of the war were now running to $1.2 billion a month, according to the Treasury Department. Casualties were 970 in September 1966 alone, with 145 killed in one week; the total combat deaths for the year were 6,143. By the end of 1967 another 11,153 U.S. troops had died. In 1968, the highest point for casualties, 16,592 more deaths were added to the toll.

Statistics indicate only part of the larger costs of the war, of course, to the soldiers, their families, and the character of the nation, as well as its international reputation. By war's end, 58,193 soldiers were dead, more than 150,000 wounded, and at least 21,000 permanently disabled. Over the duration, more than 3 million served in the undeclared war; their average age was 19. The Veterans Administration estimates that 830,000 Vietnam vets suffered from post-traumatic stress disorder; 480,000 exhibited symptoms so severe as to classify them as disabled. Several hundred thousand American troops were also exposed to Agent Orange, with untold health consequences years later. Total cost of the war over three administrations was at least $176 billion. Estimates of the number of Vietnamese who died during the conflict vary greatly and may never be known for certain, but figures released by the Vietnamese government in 1995 put the number of combatant deaths at 1 million and civilians at 4 million.

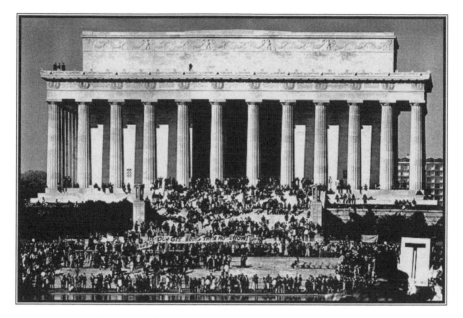

Anti-war demonstration at the Lincoln Memorial,
Washington, D.C., the morning of 21 October 1967.

In May 1966, Galway Kinnell wrote to Rago about the series of poetry
"read-ins" he and Robert Bly had organized at colleges and community
centers across the country. These and many other such programs involved
scores of poets of all ages who wrote in widely different styles. They attracted thousands of participants, and, like the "teach-ins" and "be-ins,"
these protests were almost always peaceful, in keeping with their pacific intentions. As the war dragged on and the mood grew angrier, rallies became
far less tranquil.

Of the many anti-war demonstrations during these years, the most dramatic was the March on the Pentagon, 21 October 1967. It was the climax
of five days of protests across the country against the draft and U.S. policy
organized by the National Mobilization Committee to End the War in
Vietnam (a k a "the Mobe"). As many as 100,000 people gathered calmly
at the Lincoln Memorial to hear anti-war speeches and to witness the
burning of draft cards. Led by the chairman of the committee, David
Dellinger, who declared that the days of peaceful protest were over, a crowd
of more than 50,000, many of them hippies in colorful attire, marched to
the Pentagon. Along with the thousands of students and ordinary citizens,
many clergy participated, as well as the noted baby doctor Dr. Benjamin
Spock and several prominent poets and writers. Besides Spock, the most

Protestors met armed forces at the Pentagon, late afternoon of the same day;
the sign may have been carried by a government provocateur.

visible among the speakers were Robert Lowell, who later wrote two sonnets about the March, and Norman Mailer, who reported on events in his
"novel as history," *Armies of the Night*, which won the Pulitzer Prize for
1968.

But the theatrical flare and appropriately absurdist Dada gestures were
provided by Abbie Hoffman and Jerry Rubin, the leaders of the new Yip-
pie (Youth International Party) "movement." (In August, Hoffman—who
denied the Yippies had leaders or could be "organized"—had disrupted activity at the New York Stock Exchange when he dropped wads of dollar
bills onto the trading floor from the visitors' gallery.) Allen Ginsberg composed a mantra that was chanted to "levitate" the Pentagon while Rubin
and Hoffman, in an Uncle Sam hat, attempted to "exorcise" the evil spirits
from the premises.

Six thousand U.S. marshals and troops were called up to protect the
building. Hippies, in an expression of Flower Power, placed blossoms into
the bayoneted rifle barrels; but when a large splinter group (some said the
SDS) stormed the line and tried to enter the Pentagon, the federal forces
began clubbing demonstrators and tear gas was released. Chaos ensued and
rioting continued into the night, during which time 681 people were arrested, including Mailer and Hoffman. Although the rally ended in a rout,
many historians consider the massive demonstration a major factor in John-

son's decision not to run for re-election. By the end of 1967, public approval of the war dropped to 35 percent.

Even more depressing news on several fronts followed in 1968, one of the most tumultuous years globally since World War II. The North Vietnamese observed their New Year by launching the Tet Offensive on 31 January. Some 84,000 Viet Cong guerrillas and regular troops attacked hundreds of South Vietnamese cities and villages, and twelve American bases, then entered Saigon where they took over the U.S. embassy for six hours—the siege was filmed by American television and broadcast on the nightly news—before a major allied push forced them into retreat. During Tet the United States lost over a thousand soldiers, the South Vietnamese suffered 4,000 casualties, and perhaps 400,000 people were left homeless. The wide and rapid thrust of the assault belied the rosy prognoses for "success" the Pentagon had been putting out, revealing how military advisers had misled their commander-in-chief as well as the country. Tet marked the decisive turning point in public opinion about U.S. involvement in Vietnam. Polls taken shortly afterward indicated President Johnson's approval rating on his conduct of the war had now slipped to 26 percent.

2. *Annus Horribilis*: 1968

Newspaper headlines and capsule comments may serve to highlight the continually surprising and often tragic events during the following months:

In February, Illinois Governor Otto Kerner issues his report on the 1967 race riots, rejecting conspiracy theories and naming racism and police brutality as the causes. Kerner warns that the country is moving toward two "separate and unequal societies."

On March 12, Senator Eugene McCarthy, Democrat of Minnesota, makes a surprisingly strong showing in the New Hampshire primary on an anti-war platform; expected to get only 20 percent, he wins 41.9 percent of the vote. That day the *New York Times* reveals that General Westmoreland has requested an additional 206,000 troops. Encouraged by McCarthy's success, Robert Kennedy announces his own candidacy for president on March 16th. (On the same day the My Lai massacre occurs; the killing of 500 Vietnamese civilians by American troops is concealed for a year.) On March 31, President Johnson makes a dramatic announcement on television that he will not run again, and says he intends to stop the bombing in North Vietnam. North Vietnam says it will meet with U.S. representatives.

On April 4, Martin Luther King, Jr., is assassinated in Memphis. Riots break out in Washington, D.C., New York, Chicago, Detroit, and a hundred other cities; the National Guard is called out. On April 10, Congress

approves the Civil Rights Bill of 1968, which prohibits racial discrimina-
tion in housing, schools, and voting. On April 28 a thousand students bar-
ricade themselves for three days in five buildings at Columbia University,
protesting university involvement in studies for the Pentagon. Police eject
them and arrest seven hundred. (Meanwhile, on April 29, the musical *Hair*
opens on Broadway, breaking long-standing taboos on nudity and vulgar
language in the theater.) On May 10, university students riot in Paris. A
shantytown is set up by blacks, Mexicans, and Native Americans on the
Washington Mall on May 11.

On May 13 the United States and North Vietnam begin peace talks in
Paris; negotiations will stop and restart repeatedly over the next five years.
On May 17 nine anti-war demonstrators seize Selective Service draft
records in Catonsville, Maryland. The poet, activist, and Jesuit priest Daniel
Berrigan and his brother Philip are arrested. (Daniel disappears, continues
to aid the anti-war movement, and is not apprehended until 1970; he serves
time in Danbury Federal Penitentiary.)

On June 5, Robert Kennedy wins the California primary; immediately
after his acceptance speech he is assassinated by Sirhan Sirhan and dies the
following day, at age forty-two. On June 19 the Poor People's March is held
in Washington. On July 1 the nuclear nonproliferation treaty is signed;
France and China are not parties to it. On July 23, Palestinian terrorists hi-
jack an Israeli airliner and fly it to Algeria—the first such act for political
purposes.

On August 8, Richard Nixon wins the Republican nomination for president on the first ballot in Miami Beach, defeating New York governor
Nelson Rockefeller and California governor Ronald Reagan. Nixon
promises "an honorable end to the war in Vietnam." August 20–31, Czecho-
slovakia, which only six months earlier had celebrated a "Prague Spring" of
liberation, is invaded by the Soviet Union and 200,000 troops from Warsaw
Pact nations; reformist Communist leader Alexander Dubcek protests and
is demoted.

On August 28 the Democrats meet in Chicago for their national convention amid oppressive heat and bus, taxi, and telephone strikes. About
twenty thousand anti-war demonstrators hold a "festival of life" with dancing and poetry readings in Grant and Lincoln parks, though Mayor Richard
J. Daley refuses to grant permission to parade or to sleep in the parks. He
also requests five thousand National Guardsmen and seven thousand federal troops to buttress the city police force. At the boisterous convention,
Vice President Hubert H. Humphrey wins the nomination. Followers of
Senator Eugene McCarthy and Senator George McGovern (who tries to
rally Robert Kennedy's supporters) attempt but are unable to modify the
pro–war party platform.

Militants, including Abbie Hoffman and Jerry Rubin, Black Panther leader Bobby Seale, and Tom Hayden of SDS, gather their followers in the park in front of the Hilton Hotel, Democratic party headquarters. With several TV stations broadcasting live, some 5,000 angry protesters shout "The whole world is watching"—then tear gas is released and police and troops charge using nightsticks, clubbing all in sight, including 63 newsmen, and drag people off and pack them into paddy wagons. About 1,000 demonstrators are injured, 101 hospitalized; 192 police are hurt, 49 hospitalized. Eventually, in March 1969, Hoffman, Rubin, Hayden, Seale, Dellinger, and three others are indicted for conspiracy and inciting a riot, and become known as the Chicago Eight—then Seven, after Seale creates an uproar at trial by calling Judge Julius Hoffman a "fascist pig," among other things, is gagged and tied to his chair, and finally severed from the case.

In other news during the summer and early fall of 1968, in September Arthur Ashe becomes the first black to win the U.S. Open tennis championship. Nixon appears on the most popular TV program, *Laugh-In*, to ask: "Sock it to *me*?" Jacqueline Kennedy marries Aristotle Onassis on the isle of Skorpios. And at the Olympic Games in Mexico City in October, black sprinters bow their heads during the U.S. anthem and raise clenched fists in a black-power salute, are suspended, and then thrown out of the Olympic Village.

On November 5, Nixon wins the presidential election by just 500,000 votes, or 2.3 million fewer than he drew in his loss to Kennedy in 1960. Republicans and Democrats narrowly split the popular vote, but third-party candidate Governor George Wallace of Alabama takes 13.5 percent, and 45 electoral votes, enough to hurt Humphrey in industrial states.

By December 12 U.S. combat casualties in Vietnam have reached 30,057—with 9,557 deaths in the first six months of the year alone, more than in all of 1967. Troop levels finally plateau at 540,000 for the war, which has become the longest in American history.

3. *Annus Mirabilis*: 1968

Despite political and social upheaval, or perhaps because of it, the intellectual and cultural ferment in the country during this period remains extraordinarily impressive forty years on. Amid so much depressing news in unhappily eventful 1968, one still marvels at the unusually large number of memorable achievements, along with needful diversions, produced by artists and entertainers that year. Besides *Hair*, other hits on Broadway are *Boys in the Band*, *The Great White Hope*, and *Promises, Promises*. (And Luciano Pavarotti makes his debut at the Metropolitan Opera in *La Bohème*.) Hit movies of 1968 include *The Graduate, Funny Girl, Rosemary's Baby, Planet of the Apes, 2001: A Space Odyssey,* The Beatles' *The Yellow Submarine, The Lion in Winter, The Odd Couple, The Producers,* and *The Good, the Bad, and the Ugly.* Academy Awards in various categories go to *In the Heat of the Night, Guess Who's Coming to Dinner, Cool Hand Luke,* and *Bonnie and Clyde.*

Among the top hit singles of 1968 are "Hey Jude" (The Beatles), "I Heard It Through the Grapevine" (Marvin Gaye), "People Got to be Free" (The Rascals), "Mrs. Robinson" (Simon and Garfunkel's theme song for *The Graduate*), "Hello, Goodbye" (The Beatles), "Hello, I Love You" (The Doors), and "Born to be Wild" (Steppenwolf). In November The Beatles also release their groundbreaking *White Album.*

Best-sellers and critically acclaimed books of 1968 include Carlos Castaneda's *Teachings of Don Juan,* Eldridge Cleaver's *Soul on Ice,* Arthur Hailey's *Airport,* Peter Maas's *The Valachi Papers,* Desmond Morris's *The Naked Ape,* Alexander Solzhenitsyn's *The Cancer Ward,* Gore Vidal's *Myra Breckenridge,* and Tom Wolfe's *The Electric Kool-Aid Acid Test.*

In 1968 the first *Whole Earth Catalogue* is published and indicates the hippie movement is attracting many people beyond the counterculture. In fashion news, Calvin Klein and Ralph Lauren begin clothing lines. At the same time antique clothes and secondhand "granny" dresses become the rage with hippies. As the drug culture spreads, so does Eastern philosophy, and along with it the wearing of sandals, embroidered caftans, Afghan coats. "In" styles for both men and women feature bell bottom pants, long hair and Afros, headbands, jangling bracelets. Meanwhile members of the women's liberation movement protest the Miss America pageant and throw girdles, curlers, and *Cosmo* into "Freedom Trash Cans" in several cities. Early in 1968 Christiaan Barnard of South Africa performs the first heart transplant. On Christmas Eve the Apollo 8 astronauts circle the moon for the first time.

4. Correspondence 1966–1968

Hardly surprising, the war in Vietnam and the growing opposition to it are frequent topics in correspondence to *Poetry* in 1966 and 1967, and several poets reflect on the conflict at home as well as abroad. Galway Kinnell appends to his letters long lists of participating poets and colleges for the "read-ins" he and Robert Bly have organized from Oregon to Illinois and Ohio to the Eastern seaboard; Rago publishes the names in the June and July issues. Allen Ginsberg, another prominent peace activist, writes from San Francisco and Omaha during his many cross-country trips. Kenneth Burke encloses satiric verses about the policies of the Johnson administration. Denise Levertov sends greetings on the eve of her husband's trial in Boston, where he, Dr. Benjamin Spock, Yale chaplain William Sloane Coffin, and others are charged with conspiracy for burning draft cards and helping eligible men avoid induction.

Other correspondents write about the usual literary matters and authorial concerns: to introduce themselves and submit work; to update the editors on their latest news and awards; to report on their travels or pass on word about friends; to ask for recommendations or to say thank you for favors received; to comment on or complain about poems or reviews in recent issues; to ask for advice. Leonard Nathan remarks on Allen Ginsberg's trip to

Galway Kinnell, organizer of many readings by poets against the Vietnam war, in the late sixties.

India and describes the burgeoning poetry scene in Calcutta. Louis Ginsberg sends a pun-filled missive suggesting, yet again, a father-son appearance. Malcolm Cowley recalls his first publication under Harriet Monroe. And John Ashbery writes during a nostalgic visit to Paris.

For his contributor's note in the December 1968 issue, Robert Chatain, a young soldier whose work was accepted for *Poetry* while he was on active duty, writes from Vietnam: "In fourteen days I get out of here, and out of the Army at the same exquisite time. If I had the resources I would print this information on formal announcements and mail it, at government expense, to everyone I know. . . . My wife and I don't have the faintest idea where we're bound for. The series of poems, sixty-seven of them, is almost finished; I am calling them 'united / states'. . . ."

Robert Bly to Henry Rago   *[Madison, Minn.], 24 March 1966*

Dear Henry,

I'm enclosing a copy of a *Times* clipping. You may be able to use it for a news note. The "read-in" is a sort of unhappy name donated by the newspapers, but the idea is just to have not a group of political people on stage but a group of poets who testify by the presence of their bodies on stage that they are opposed to the course of the war in Vietnam.

I have wanted for a long time to thank you very much for sending the Sixties [Press] books out for review consistently! That is encouraging. I think all the reviews have been very fair as well—I was pleased with all of them. . . . Reviewers often refuse to give an opinion! . . .

                                        With all good wishes! / Robert

Allen Ginsberg to Henry Rago   *New York City, 19 April 1966*

Dear Mr Rago:

Enclosed find the first part of a long poem I wrote on recent Midwest trip. A longer larger section being mantric Unilateral Declaration of End of Vietnam War will be in Village Voice in a few weeks.

I've regarded your invitation to submit poetry to Poetry highly enough to withhold from doing so till I had a poem I feel would be equal to the occasion as a debut piece for historic Poetry—in my judgement [sic] the enclosed would be appropriate so I commend it to your attention.

It was written on UHER Tapemachine as part of a series of experiments in composition aloud. Bob Dylan the young minnesinger had given me the gift of enough money for a precision instrument which was portable. So the poem's written, in a car.

                                        Best wishes— / Allen Ginsberg

[*In left margin:*] I would appreciate an early reply as I have promised mss. to many places and wish to keep my promises.

Rago accepted the poem on 9 May, with a query: "on page 1 the typescript has Melleville. Do you mean it this way—it could be a triple pun—or would you like to make it simply Melville?"

Allen Ginsberg to Henry Rago   *New York City, 18 May 1966*

Dear Mr Rago:

I am really very happy that you accepted the Wichita poem for Poetry. I like it as a poem and statement. Thank you for your kindness. Melleville should be spelt properly Melville, it's my sloppiness here. I know you are crowded up with earlier mss. but I hope there won't be too long a delay in printing the poem: I've waited so long to publish a text in Poetry that now I am eager to see one in place. But I know you have a large backlog so I'll tarry in patience. . . .

Thank you again for your courtesy to the poem of my own that I sent you.

                                        As ever, / Allen Ginsberg

Galway Kinnell to Henry Rago   *New York City, 12 May 1966*

Dear Henry,

As you know there have been a number of "Read-ins" protesting the war in Vietnam. It is astonishing how the poets have risen to the occasion, far more than the novelists or other writers. I'm sending you a list of all those poets who participated, hoping you can print the list in your "News Notes," for I think it's extraordinarily impressive. I know you aren't able to be at Minneapolis, but may we add your name as having sent a message? I have put it in on the enclosed list feeling sure you will agree.

With warm regards, / Galway

Kinnell enclosed lists with the names of sixty-nine poets who participated in readings protesting the war and eight others who could not attend but sent poems to be read. The list of locations included twenty-two campuses from Portland, Oregon, to St. Cloud, Minnesota, to New York City. Kinnell sent a list of eighteen additional readers in May. Rago ran the lists in the June issue and printed an additional one in August. In September 1966 *Poetry* printed Bly's "March in Washington Against the Vietnam War." The first anti-war march on Washington had taken place 17 March 1965; the most famous one occurred there 21 October 1967.

Marvin Bell to Henry Rago   *Iowa City, Ia., 28 May 1966*

Dear Henry:

I'm sick at heart over my lengthy delay in reviewing for you the four anthologies. . . . I seem to receive "fan" letters whenever you print something by me in *Poetry*, and the last review you published drew admiration I respected and welcomed. . . .

When we discovered our need for another poet-teacher for the second semester of this school year, I suggested you, and hoped you would be available. Of course, George's [Starbuck] call to you determined quickly that you were not. But I hope, still, to have the opportunity to hear you instruct. I have always heard, not surprisingly, that you are a superb teacher. . . .

Although May is nearly over, I am enclosing twenty poems for your consideration. I have been accumulating these for you during the past thirteen months. . . .

The reference to "Henry" in "The Membership" is an allusion to the "selves" in Berryman's Dream Songs. Do you think it requires a footnote? (One of the pleasures related to participating in a number of the recent read-ins was a visit to Berryman, while in Minneapolis at Bly's invitation for a set of them, and listening to Berryman separate "Henry" from himself.)

Sincerely, / Marvin Bell

Robert Duncan to Henry Rago   *[San Francisco, Calif.],*
                                                        1 June 1966

Dear Henry/

Just as POETRY is announcing again that it will be reading only new poets for the summer months, I am sending you a group of poems by another new poet here, David Bromige. I am particularly struck by "Weight
Less Than a Shadow", where the dream experience, the dream-use of
words and images as puns and assonances, and the highly individual feeling of the free-verse line, most cohere. So, as I have always in hopes and
mind to do, I askt Bromige if I might "introduce" his work in writing to
you and submitting a group of recent poems for him. Again, it is something of a pride (prize) of the recognizer I take great pleasure in; and it
will be gratifying if you too agree. In all events, I know you will be interested in following Bromige's work.

POETRY is beginning to reflect quite a bit of the poetic activity of San
Francisco—it was always San Francisco's neglect of POETRY that made it
otherwise, and I am glad that the ice is beginning to break.

Perhaps having taken on too many commitments to do Prefaces (two to
new books forthcoming of mine; and then one for the Alchemical Papers
of Thomas Vaughan), I am in an almost stagnant period. You will have first
serve, when I have some poems again.

                                          Yours, / Robert Duncan

H.R. published the poem mentioned in April 1967. Bromige also had a group of five poems in the March 1968 issue.

Allen Ginsberg to Henry Rago   *[n.p.], 3 June 1966*

Dear Mr. Rago:

Alas the poem I sent you ["Wichita Vortex Sutra (I)"], I had left a copy
with students at Nebraska University & I hear rumor that they mimeographed it for sale cheap to benefit local student poesy/pacifist magazine.
I'm not sure & have written to check up. I think that must constitute "publication" maybe & thus make poem ineligible for Poetry Magazine publication, which I regret. I'll let you know for sure when I hear, in a week or
so. I don't mind but I am disappointed not to have that poem in Poetry especially after you'd been generous enough to accept it.

I'll write you when I'm surer as to status of the poem. But I thought best
send you this note in time.

                                          As ever / Allen Ginsberg

Allen Ginsberg to Henry Rago   City Lights Books,
                                              San Francisco, Calif.,
                                                   14 June 1966

Dear Mr Rago:

I've found that students at Lincoln, Neb. mimeographed the poem, and that was picked up by a mimeographed 500 copy magazine *DO IT* in Omaha. So I guess that excludes the text from Poetry. Please let me know. I'm sorry to have confused matters so by my looseness with mss. But it hadn't occurred to me in practical terms what wd happen, as I gave them a copy of the poem the day after it was written. Send me a card here please—

As ever, / Allen Ginsberg

H.R. replied 20 June that the poem's appearance even in a mimeographed magazine constituted prior publication, according to *Poetry*'s long-standing policy. He thanked Ginsberg for his thoughtfulness in informing him as soon as possible, adding: "I couldn't be more sorry. Let us hope that you will have POETRY in mind for the next thing you do that would make for an auspicious 'presentation' in our pages."

Hayden Carruth to Henry Rago   *Johnson, Vt., 28 August 1966*

Dear Henry,

I'd been typing these things up—a big job!—for several days when the news of the government grant [from the NEA] came yesterday; somewhat prematurely, but you know how these things are. It threw me into a loop, frankly. I had been feeling unsure of myself anyhow, and now this added pressure: can the poems support it? Won't they just seem insignificant and terribly inadequate to the people who have been so kind to me? Etc., etc.

However, first things first, and in this case first is thanks. So much. The Harriet Monroe Award, the Brandeis Award, all those *Poetry* prizes, the recommendations for fellowships, and now this—you have done a tremendous amount for me. I don't know really how to say what I feel. I am sensible of all of it, deeply sensible. And I think you know that in my case all these helps have served much more than their ostensible literary purpose, because they have enabled me to remake my life in the way it seriously needed remaking. Without them I simply could not have done it. I just hope my writing has been intelligent enough, useful enough to have earned at least a little of all this munificence.

As for the poems, it would be inexcusable to send any editor such a large batch, and all I can do is plead the non-professional and supra-professional nature of our relationship. . . . For long periods I haven't written anything at all, and have just slumped, feeling extremely unpoetic. Most of these poems have been done for or after particular occasions, usually very rapidly—some are fragmentary. I honestly can't judge them or tell much about them. . . .

If you haven't time or strength to read all this stuff, I'll understand.

Meanwhile many, many thanks again. From all of us. And do let us know how your summer went, and your other news.

Love to all, / Hayden

Malcolm Cowley to Henry Rago   *Sherman, Conn., 6 September 1966*

Dear Henry,

I'd like to query you about the idea of sending some verse to *Poetry*. The query requires some explanation. At present I'm working on old and new poems for a volume to be called (if I don't change my mind) *Blue Juniata: Collected Poems.* . . .

I used to have a pretty close connection with *Poetry*. Harriet Monroe was the first editor to publish a group of my poems, in I think it was, my God, 1920 or 1921. There was another group in 1923, and still another in 1926 that won the Levinson Prize of $100 (which I used to make the down payment on a farm in this neighborhood). When *Blue Juniata* came out in 1929, it was the first choice of a poetry book club that Miss Monroe had organized (the club didn't long survive the Wall Street crash). Later there were other groups, but alas, not frequently, and my last poem in *Poetry* must have been around 1950. There were ten years when I didn't write any new ones.

My idea is this. I'd like to put together a group of Pennsylvania country poems, like the first three groups I published in *Poetry*. The first poem (now in process) and the last (just finished) would be new ones. The three or four intervening poems would be old ones, first published in *Poetry* and now pretty drastically reworked.

Of course you can't pass judgment from this prospectus. You'd have to see the group, and it won't be ready until that first poem is finished, which might be two or three months from now. But my query is only about your degree of hospitality to the idea. I think it might have a certain value for the magazine, as an affirmation of continuity over the years. What do you think?

Cordially, / Malcolm

Rago asked to see the poems, but said he would be mostly interested in new work; printing older poems, even if reworked, might be a problem, given long-standing *Poetry* policy to print only previously unpublished work. Cowley's "A Countryside, 1918–1968," was printed in June 1968.

John Ashbery to Henry Rago   Art News, *New York City,*
                                        21 October 1966

Dear Mr. Rago,

I can't tell you how pleased and
honored I feel at receiving the
Union League Civic and Arts Foundation Prize from *Poetry*. This was a
wonderful piece of news. I am writing to Mr. Martin to express my appreciation. And thank you.

Although I hate to ask you for a favor in the same breath as thanking
you for one, I had been meaning to
write you to ask if you would be kind
enough to recommend me again for a
Guggenheim. You did once several
years ago, but last year I neglected to
re-apply in time and must go through
the whole process again. If you could
find time to do this I would certainly
appreciate it.

John Ashbery in 1960.

I am very glad you like my two
pieces on Frank O'Hara. I would
have been very happy to write one for *Poetry*, but did not think of suggesting it since I could not remember reading any articles of that kind
there. I don't think I could do another one, and in fact declined doing one
for *Art and Literature* since not only is it painful but it is very difficult to express one's sense of loss in different words several times. Perhaps Kenneth
Koch would like to write one, however. . . .

Sincerely, / John Ashbery

Karl Shapiro to Henry Rago   Omaha, Nebr., *5 November 1966*

Dear Henry:

I am in Omaha, as I told Julie [McLachlin, the secretary], helping to
move my new family. We should be there by next week.

Teri Baldwin (my wife-to-be) and I want to talk to you about a contract
we have signed with the U of Chicago Press. We are co-editing the *Poetry*
correspondence for publication. It is a massive correspondence, I imagine,
and we are happy that we were picked to do the job. We haven't looked at
the collection yet but want two copies of the [magazine] Index as soon as

possible. Are they available at *Poetry*? And of course we want to get your ideas about this book and as much help from you as you can give.

I don't know whether any of this information, personal and editorial, is still sub rosa. . . .

We hope to come to dinner soon, if the invitation still holds.

All the best to you and Julie

Karl

Rago had recommended George Dillon for the job; see Maurice English letter of 1 April 1965.

Leonard Nathan to Henry Rago   *New Delhi, India,*
                                                  24 December 1966

Dear Henry Rago:

Some more from India, though not, I guess, Indian. This place is incredible, not the least for its literary life. Ginsberg left quite a trail, but there is an Indian twist to it. For Beats, they have their "anti-poets" writing, obviously "anti-poetry." I am to address these people soon, mostly young. In Calcutta a group of free-wheelers—I guess of the Beat variety—began a monthly magazine for verse. It soon became a weekly, then a daily, then— so help me God—an hourly; they printed, so I hear, seven in one day. I guess the poets lined up in front of their door, with poems hot off the pan, or finishing them up right there.

Though many Indian poets seem a bit bewildered by their own relation to their tradition and to what's going on in the west now, things seem lively enough. Like the local politics, Indian poetry seems going every which way, but, unlike the politics, some of the poets seem to be getting somewhere. What chiefly they lack—so far as I can tell—is a good practical criticism, a thing we may have too much of. And then politics gets in the way, not just poetic politics. The tendency is for the manifesto to substitute for thinking hard about individual poems and poems in general. But nobody is curling up in silence and that means, if nothing else, there is plenty of life. And out of the collision of east and west—it is no less than that—something may come that is larger than either. If it doesn't, there will have been a lot of joy on the way.

Best wishes for the new year.

Cordially, / Leonard

Ted Berrigan to Henry Rago   *[n.p.], 27 January 1967*

Dear Mr. Rago:

Earlier this evening I was telling Ron Padgett how, when you returned my last batch of poems, you included a note on the poems, saying they were rather "mild." Ron said that your note was wildly hilarious, or rather we both said it at once—it was so inspiring that we decided to send you some more poems which, I hope, are not so mild as the previous ones.

Now, don't you go Aram Saroyanesque on us by inverting the "m" in your next reply.

Yours in good humor,

Ted Berrigan

David McReynolds to Robert Mueller   *New York City,*
31 January 1967

Dear Robert Mueller,

I think you might be interested in the two items that I have enclosed. The first is a sheet of ads ready to run by publications using a photo offset process. It may be that you would want to help us reach men of draft age with information on their legal rights to apply for the classification of conscientious objector and might be willing to run one of these three ads in your magazine. We have a small budget that we are using to place these ads in those publications that insist on money and I am turning to you in the hope of charity, as our ad budget is now exhausted.

Second, a copy of "Up Tight With the Draft?" is enclosed—you might want to give it a plug.

Certainly we would be grateful for whatever you can do and send you our best wishes for the success of *Poetry*.

David McReynolds

The pamphlet did not receive a plug, though Rago did mention various anti-war activities in News Notes. Robert Mueller, the managing editor, had been called up for active duty in the navy in 1965; after more than a dozen years on the *Poetry* staff, beginning as assistant editor, he resigned his position in 1966.

Robert Bly to Henry Rago   *Madison, Minn., 21 February 1967*

Dear Henry,

We are doing a reprint of the booklet called A POETRY READING AGAINST THE VIETNAM WAR, and I'm currently choosing a few substitutes for the empty spaces representing the absence of Cummings! I thought I would put in [Robert] Duncan's *Uprising*, and that wonderful poem of Denise's [Levertov] you published, called *Life at War* [June 1966]. I have Denise's permission, and I would be pleased then to have the permission of *Poetry*. We will acknowledge your prior publication in our acknowledgements page. . . .

I don't know what to think of this new development involving the creation of a *third* organization of literary magazines, CCLM [Coordinating Council of Literary Magazines]! I would have preferred that subsidies come from foundations, rather than from the government. However, I suppose ALMA [Association of Literary Magazines of America] should be grateful that it wasn't subsidized by the CIA. . . . [sic]

Warm wishes, / Robert

A January 1967 News Note announced the publication of the anthology, which was gathered by Bly and David Ray and put out by American Writers Against the Vietnam War; the collection was distributed by Bly's The Sixties Press (Madison, Minnesota) and priced at $1.00. In 1990 CCLM was renamed the Council of Literary Magazines and Presses (CLMP).

Louis Ginsberg to Henry Rago   *Paterson, N.J., 23 February 1967*

Dear Mr. Henry Rago:

Greetings! As the Southern delta gentleman said, "How's bayou?"

Am enclosing five poems in hopes you might like some enough to smuggle them into your magazine.

As you might know, I have two sons also writing and publishing poetry: one Eugene Brooks, a lawyer; and the redoubtable Allen.

No doubt, poets are born, not paid; they may not get cash though sometimes they get cachet.

Almost a year ago, Allen and I gave a joint reading at the Poetry Society of America in N.Y. Since then, we have received many offers from colleges. We have been booked for joint readings . . . I am enclosing a clipping about the Poetry Society reading from the N.Y. TIMES.

Lately, in my mementopause, I have been invaded by a affliction of puns. So, when Spring comes, a young man's fancy, but a young woman's much fancier. Then the boys are gallant and the gays are buoyant.

Be that as it may, I hope that some of my poems may please you.

Yours for an o-pun mind,

Louis Ginsberg

Besides the clipping from the *Times* of 1 April 1966, Ginsberg enclosed a complete bibliography.

James Schuyler to Henry Rago   *Southampton, N.Y., 7 April 1967*

Dear Mr Rago,

I enclose a poem, *Seeking*, for your consideration. Also a book, which I had thought John Myers had sent you, though I gather I was wrong.

The way in which you memorialized Frank O'Hara was most beautiful and moving, I thought. More would have said less.

Yours sincerely, / James Schuyler

In October, as an obituary notice Rago ran the lines: "Wind, you'll have a terrible time / smothering my clarity. . . ." Schuyler's *May 24th or so* was printed in a limited edition by John Bernard Myers in 1966; a director of the Tibor de Nagy Gallery, Myers first affixed the name "New York School" to Schuyler, Ashbery, O'Hara, and Koch, to associate them with the New York painters. Myers also printed poems and articles by them in his mimeographed magazine *Semi-Colon*, and later edited the anthology *Poets of the New York School* (1972). A News Note for April 1968 reported that MoMA had published a memorial volume of poems by O'Hara, *In Memory of My Feelings*, edited by Bill Berkson, with sixty drawings by thirty artists, including de Kooning, Motherwell, Rivers, Frankenthaler, Johns, Oldenburg, Marisol, Lichtenstein, Freilicher, and Rauschenberg: "Each artist was given a poem or, in some cases, more than one poem to realize in his own medium as he saw fit."

James Dickey to Henry Rago　　　*Leesburg, Va., 2 June 1967*

Dear Henry:

I have been meaning to write you for some time, simply to let you know I haven't forgotten about *Poetry*, and that I regret very much the fact that I haven't published anything with you since "The Firebombing," three or four years ago. Now that I have the big *Poems 1957-1967* finished, finally, I can turn to some new things, and I'll be able to let you look 'em over in maybe two or three months, if all goes well. But do know that I have *Poetry* in mind, and will give you whatever I think is good enough.

May I make one small request about the new book's reviewing situation in *Poetry*? I ask only that you not turn it over to anyone of the Bly faction (though Jim Wright would be OK, though he's already reviewed one book of mine for you). Bly insists that there is bad blood between us, principally because I told him I would have nothing whatever to do with his clique, claque, movement, or whatever it is, and he now tells me he is "after me." I thought you would

Robert Bly, noted anti-war protester and literary polemicist, in the mid-sixties.

probably want to know about this, for you can't get impartial reviewing done under such circumstances. The last fellow that reviewed me in *Poetry*— at least insofar as I know—was Wendell Berry, who had just prior to that published an open letter in the *Sewanee [Review]* denouncing me for my views in an article I did that included some harsh words on his friend Robert Hazel. Yet, though he had some reservations (this was *Helmets*, as I remember), he still was very fair indeed, and as a consequence he and I have become good friends. But Bly and those that follow him (John Haines, Louis Simpson, et al.) are not that large-souled. They are vindictive and re-venge-minded, and these things have nothing to do with evaluation of po-ems, being personal reasons for finding fault with literary works. Well, I won't go on and on; all this shall be as you wish.

   . . . Also, do you have Lisel Mueller's address? I'd like to get in touch with her about a personal matter. Also, I admire what of hers I've read.

   Let me hear from you on these matters whenever you can. I'd appreci-ate it.

All yours, / Jim Dickey

Later in June, Rago asked Dickey to read at Poetry Day, along with William Alfred, whose play *Hogan's Goat* was the surprise hit of the 1965–1966 season in New York. He also invited Basil Bunting, who declined; he was replaced by James Merrill.

Lisel Mueller to Henry Rago   *[Lake Forest, Ill.], 27 June 1967*

Dear Henry,

   Recently I saw some mention of an "Artists Against the War in Vietnam" festival being planned in Chicago, and I got the impression that poetry was to be included among the arts. I don't know the planners of the demon-stration, and I thought that perhaps you might, and that you might be kind enough to put me in touch with the proper person. I'd like to offer my help in some capacity or other. My outrage against this war is matched only by my frustration over not being able to take any action against it—a frustra-tion which I know I share with a great many people, but which I aug-mented by the totally uninvolved nature of the area in which we live, as well as by the fact that, being neither an academic person nor a church member, I have no "group" through which to work. So if you know whom I might contact, I'd be grateful if you'd let me know.

   My best wishes for a beautiful summer,

Lisel

H.R. note, bottom of page: "I think she should also write a note to Mr. Harry Bouras, saying she does so at my suggestion . . . she can reach him c/o WFMT [the FM radio station where he was the art critic for many years]. Mr. Bouras is helping to organize a protest of artists from the Chicago area (painters, writers, etc.) to take place sometime in the fall." Paul Sills, the theater director, was also one of the main organizers.

Samuel French Morse to Henry Rago   *Hancock Point, Me.,*
                                                       22 July 1967

Dear Henry:

I enclose the review. A second reading of MacDiarmid's *Collected Poems* left me as much unsatisfied as the original acquaintance had done—and somewhat irritated. His "Verses Written During the Second World War" remind me of Joyce's comment that the trouble with the war was that it prevented people from doing what was really important, i.e., reading *Finnegans Wake*. Violent nationalism cum communism seems to have produced in H.M. a contempt for anything but his own ego. Perhaps there ought to be another notice, on the other side. . . .

All best wishes, / Sam

His review of *Collected Poems of Hugh MacDiarmid*, edited by John C. Weston, was printed in May 1968.

James Merrill to Helen Lothrop   *Stonington, Conn., 31 July 1967*

Dear Miss Lothrop,

Thank you for your letter. I'm awfully glad I decided to say yes [to Rago's invitation to read at Poetry Day]. I will be at the above address surely through Labor Day. . . . After that I expect I shall go to Athens for anywhere from 3 to 8 weeks. . . .

Don't worry, I'll be there on the 16th [of November] by early afternoon. I may be staying with Daryl Hine if he still has room. He is one of your contributors. He has no evening clothes, but might he be invited to the Thursday reception? . . .

All best, / James Merrill

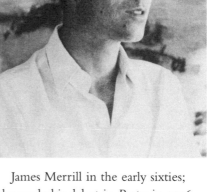

H.R. wrote 14 August, on his return to Chicago, assuring J.M. that Hine would be invited to the reception. Merrill did not mind sharing the stage with William Alfred and James Dickey.

James Merrill in the early sixties; he made his debut in *Poetry* in 1946, at age nineteen.

Alan Dugan to Henry Rago   *New York City, 16 January 1968*

Dear Henry Rago:

This is a pissed-off letter. I have two complaints. 1. I saw that I got the Levinson Award but I haven't received the money. 2. I hear from a friend that the U. of Chicago published a version of the commemorative number of *Poetry* with some of my poems in it. Couldn't you tell me, let alone pay me? Everybody makes money out of these things, from the paper salesman to the typesetter, and only the primary producer goes unpaid and un-notified. What gives?

Yours angrily & I'm not kidding,

Alan Dugan

Henry Rago to Alan Dugan   *Chicago, 19 January 1968*

Dear Alan Dugan,

I enclose a copy of the letter sent to you at your address in Mexico on 30 October 1967, telling you that we had awarded you the Levinson Prize. The decision was mine, in consultation with my colleagues, Wallace Fowlie and Joseph Wiley.

As I say in my letter the Levinson is our oldest prize. It is also our most distinguished and it carries with it the largest amount of money: $500, the check for which I enclosed with that letter. I meant to do you the highest honor I bestow in POETRY's name in any one year; I also meant to do you some good with the money.

If all this didn't reach you I'm sorry of course; but I am even more sorry to receive the kind of letter you write instead of the reasonable and civil inquiry that was possible and that should have occurred to a poet who has had more care for his work from POETRY than from any other magazine.

The University of Chicago Press has not published "a version" of our Golden Anniversary Issue. It has done a reprinting of that issue for us, the text exactly as it was in our first printing. POETRY has the right to print any number of copies of a single issue and any number of printings. We used the University of Chicago Press rather than simply the University of Chicago Printing Department, which does print every issue of POETRY, because this was the best way to arrange the financial burden that reprinting and distribution would mean; it also insured a much wider audience than we could get by our usual means of distribution.

Yours ever sincerely, / Henry Rago

Another check was sent within the week.

Nan M. Eaton to The Editor   *Greenfield, Mass., 1 March 1968*

Dear Sir:

I'm a young poet, not an old fogie, and enjoy new and creative writing. However, in thoroughly reading your publication on its arrival today, it's obvious somebody's putting you on. And you as editor are being sucker enough to print it. Probably if I put this letter in lines one inch long you'd print it.

My criticism is not the result of sour grapes, as I've never submitted any of my work to your magazine, and never will as I wouldn't want my work associated with the type thing you publish, with one or two passable exceptions. From any standard, modern or traditional, the work you print is largely bad.

Some people assume that any trend that is new is necessarily good simply because it's different, though it may have no other merit. This is not a rejection of modern poetry, as I do enjoy good modern poetry, but a criticism of the type thing you choose to represent modern poetry.

I consider my purchase of your book a waste of one hard-earned dollar. I wish I had a subscription so I could cancel it.

Very sincerely, / Nan M. Eaton

Kenneth Burke to Henry Rago   *Andover, N.J., 3 March 1968*

Dear Henry,

Finally digging out after our return to NJ, I find thy welcome note of Jan. 23rd.

. . .

Incidentally, in some of my more morbid moments, I have been doing little jingles of hate anent The Administration's stupidities. (Brutal as the outfit is, I believe it is less brutal than stupid. Imagine squandering 27 billions a year to tear apart little Vietnam, and all in the name of "cost effectiveness"!) I thought that, gossipwise, you might be interested in this one, which I quixotically sent to [anti-war presidential candidate Senator Eugene] McCarthy, hoping that it might prove usable by his speech-writers (it's a reference to Johnson):

> He got us tangled in a situation
> that would defy the best of us,
> through having access to misinformation
> that was denied the rest of us.

. . .

Here's one among several I peddled (though they have not yet been published): "the while the war drags on / reports of experts vary / how much we pay Saigon / to be its mercenary."

Wadda woild!

Polygraphically thine, / K.B.

McCarthy was himself a published poet, but not noted for his public-speaking ability.

Allen Ginsberg to Henry Rago   *New York City, 12 March 1968*

Dear Mr Rago:

Enclosed find an unpublished recent poem. An early draft w/holograph (early draft i.e. original composition half this length will be privately published in a month or 2 in England Cape-Golliard): & this version is the last poem in a book Planet News Poems 1961–67 I sent last week to Ferlinghetti; he says the book won't be ready from City Lights till June–July.

I dont know if under these circumstance the poem can find place in Poetry, i.e. whether publication of first draft holograph earlier forbids & summer publication w/City Lights gives you too short a time.

I have been doing the best I can to keep things straight, have wanted to send you a ms long time, but waited till I had something worthy.

If circumstances and time (or quality of poem) preclude swift printing in Poetry I'll try again later with something else.

OK—

as ever / Allen Ginsberg

There was not enough time to get the poem into print in *Poetry* before the book came out. The collection included Ginsberg's poem "The Pentagon Exorcism."

Robert Chatain to Henry Rago   *Long Binh, Vietnam, 19 April 1968*

Dear Mr. Rago,

Thanks for your letter, and for your estimation of the poems. I am honored.

Here are the corrected copies of the fourteen poems you chose, revised (I hope) not too extensively. I'm also enclosing the original copies which you picked out, so you can examine any changes I have made. . . .

You might be wondering how I, warrior, can get my hands on an electric typewriter. We Americans go to war with all our toys. Somehow I enjoy the thought that, in the heart of the jungle we are defoliating, in the land we have turned into a new moonscape, there is a peasant dressed in black who lives for the minute he may bury his machete in the bowels of my sleek Remington.

My best to you, and thank you for taking such good care of the poems which Doug [Mitchell] gave you.

Bob Chatain

Chatain's poems appeared in the December 1968 issue; he was discharged from the army shortly afterward.

Denise Levertov to Henry Rago   *Cambridge, Mass., 17 May 1968*

Dear Henry,

Some Resistance Kids at U of Chicago want to include "An Interim" (that poem of mine you have accepted) in a sort of collection of documents they are mimeographing (or photo-copying from typescripts) to distribute at the "Workshops on Alternatives" being held for U.C. students and their parents at the "Vietnam Commencement" June 6th. If this is not a regular printed publication, would it be OK with you? Or would it preclude the subsequent publication of the poem in *Poetry*? I would like *very much* to be included in what they are doing—but of course I don't want to get in the way of *Poetry*. If there is some urgency about it, I am enclosing 2 *yes or not* p.c.'s, one to me, one to David Worstell, the boy who is gathering this material, the rest of which will consist of statements by draft-refusers & C.O.'s [conscientious objectors] mainly.

Denise Levertov was active with her husband Mitchell Goodman in opposing the Vietnam war.

Lovely to see you & Juliet—I think I already wrote that . . . We're here for the trial, which begins Monday. . . .

Love / Denise

Levertov's husband, Mitchell Goodman, was tried with Dr. Benjamin Spock, the Reverend William Sloane Coffin, Jr., chaplain at Yale, and Professor Michael Ferber in federal court in Boston; the four peace activists in the "Spock case" were convicted in July of conspiracy to aid and abet young men in avoiding conscription. (A fifth defendant, Marcus Raskin, was acquitted.) Rago made an exception and agreed to the request.

Henry Miller to Henry Rago   *Pacific Palisades, Calif., 20 June 1968*

Dear Mr. Rago—

Thank you so much—and of course Mr. [J. Patrick] Lannan whom I met here recently—for this handsome gift you are making me. In the early days of the magazine I read a great deal of poetry. Today, I find it more difficult— so I'll be curious to see what "Poetry" is publishing nowadays.

I do remember hearing that you were one of those who signed the petition to the Supreme Court—and again belated thanks.

Please give warm regards to Mr. Lannan—I don't have his home address.

Sincerely, / Henry Miller

H.R. gave him a subscription to the magazine. In 1962 Rago had signed a petition in support of *Tropic of Cancer* and protesting its censorship, at the request of Barney Rosset, the publisher (Grove). See *Dear Editor*, p. 447.

William Weldon to the Editors   *Oshkosh, Wisc., 15 July 1968*

Dear Editors:

This letter is late—one issue having been published since the one of which I speak. . . . What I want to say regards the poem by Aram Saroyan on pages 162-163 in the June issue:

NADA NADA NADA NADA NADA NADA NADA NADA NADA NADA NADA

I know nights are important—even a hell of a lot of them. But ladies and gentleman I ask you . . .

Don't you think those two pages might have been used at the least to give some talented, but frustrated young wretch a wee moment in the big time—a chance to be seen in the most important literary periodical of this century. You know, as well as I, that publication in Poetry is a tremendous asset to any young poet's career. Someone or some two artists needed those pages. Many could have offered more than what Mr. Saroyan gave us.

This is not to disparage Mr. Saroyan's poems. I think he is a very capable artist. But let the rich get richer only from the goods they offer.

Audaciously yours, / William Weldon

Saroyan's piece ran as a single line repeating the word "night" across the two facing pages.

Hugh Kenner to Henry Rago   *Santa Barbara, Calif.,*
8 September 1968

Dear Henry:

Just back from Europe, where EP was observed looking more ghostlike than ever, though capable of muttering "I've seen worse" to the lady at the

Venice Biennale who wanted to know what he thought of the pop sculptures. This encounter seen and heard by me. His mind would have been occupied with the ghost of Gaudier. . . .

Ever, / Hugh

Pound's friend the sculptor Henri Gaudier-Brzeska was killed in World War I at age twenty-two.

John Ashbery to Henry Rago   *Paris, France, 24 October 1968*

Dear Henry,

Thank you for your letter about "Fragment" [first printed in *Poetry* in February 1966] and for warning me that it may now be in the public domain thanks to *Harper's Bazaar*. I am having this looked into. And again, let me apologize for their carelessness, to put the best possible construction on it, in omitting the credit line. I scolded them seriously about it and I do hope they wrote you a letter of apology as they claimed to have done, and above all that they wrote to you before publication to request permission, which they also assured me they did.

I too enjoyed our talk at the Kunitzes last spring and hope to see you again when we are both in New York. My plans are to return at the end of December and resume my work at *Art News*. Paris is a little sad—the rain it raineth every day—but not in a way that depresses one, on the contrary it is rather stimulating. I am keeping busy looking at all the things I missed while living here and re-seeing others that I've been nostalgic for, such as, yesterday, the Hotel de Lauzun on the Ile St. Louis which has a marvelous series of tiny rooms covered in gold leaf and incredibly complicated painted decoration. As an antidote I'm going in a couple of days to Amsterdam to see the de Kooning show among other things.

Best wishes, / John Ashbery

CHAPTER V

Transition and Contention

1. The Departure and Death of Henry Rago

Rago took charge of a magazine that was in general disarray and virtually bankrupt in 1955, and within a few years he not only brought it to a state of financial security previously unknown but enhanced *Poetry*'s reputation and greatly increased its stylistic purview. At the same time he expanded its global presence: by the end of Rago's tenure the magazine was distributed in every state in the Union, four U.S. territories, and eighty-two foreign countries, seven of them behind the Iron Curtain. But even with his seemingly boundless energy, by the mid-sixties Rago was beginning to feel the strain of keeping everything going. Besides being editor-in-chief, he was in fact, if not in title, the executive director of the Modern Poetry Association, primary fund-raiser and development officer, publicist, and producer of educational programs; he was secretary of the board as well. He was also a husband and father of four minor children whose support was less than easy on the editor's modest salary.

Like Shapiro, Rago had to supplement his income by teaching at various local colleges and universities and in summer writers' conferences. (He was approached about a position at the University of Iowa's Writers' Workshop but declined the opportunity since he could not leave Chicago.) Rago's brilliant skills in the classroom were well known, and former colleagues and ex-students who later joined the faculty at the University of Chicago still remembered him from his years teaching there from 1947 to 1954. These friends arranged to have him return to Hyde Park in the 1965–1966 academic year to give a series of lectures on "Religion in Intellectual Life" at the Divinity School. His performances were so well received that he was asked to repeat them the following year, during which he taught undergraduate courses and helped launch a new program in philosophy and the history of religion in the New Collegiate Division as well. In the spring of 1967 he was given a permanent chair as professor of theology and literature, with a joint appointment in the College and the Divinity School.

At the end of the 1967–1968 school term, Rago asked for a year's leave of absence from *Poetry*, beginning in the fall. He said he wanted time for "a more leisurely enjoyment of my teaching and reflection at the University of Chicago, more time to work at a new book of poetry, and in a long summer on the Continent with my family." He had received a grant from the Ford Foundation that would make the 1969 trip to Europe possible. As his stand-in Rago recommended Daryl Hine, a young Canadian poet who had recently received his Ph.D. in comparative literature from the University of Chicago. Rago had met Hine there, and though he did not know him well, he had enough confidence in Hine's judgment to ask him to be a Critic of the Month. Hine's résumé was quite impressive, and in August the board agreed to Rago's leave and to the appointment of Hine as visiting editor.

Although well published, Hine did not have much practical editorial experience when he came on board in October 1968; but he had time to acquire it since Rago thoughtfully left plenty of accepted manuscripts. Unlike with John Frederick Nims, the visiting editor during his earlier travels in 1960–1961, who had printed material of his own choosing instead of the work Rago had left behind, the editor made it clear he wanted the poems on file published. As he carefully explained in announcing his sabbatical and introducing Hine in the October 1968 issue:

> Because of the interval between the final shaping of any one issue of *Poetry* and its appearance even in an advance-copy is two months and a half . . . the November and December issues are already at the printer's. . . . I have edited the complete volume that begins with this issue, October through March 1969, and must say so to spare Mr. Hine the responsibility for my choices and sense of design. The April 1969 issue will be the first to give him all the room and freedom of motion a guest-editor should have. Meanwhile, and precisely for that purpose, he will act on all manuscripts that come to *Poetry* this month and thereafter, and on all other editorial matters; and he will see my issues through the press.

During his "leave," Rago was in Chicago teaching and would phone the office regularly and drop by on occasion, to indicate typographical errors in a newly printed issue or discuss other fine points of editing. After fourteen years it was not easy for Rago to let go. Hine soon established good rapport with many of *Poetry*'s oldest contributors, Rago's favorites, and several young aspirants. Among Hine's earliest acceptances were poems by Charles Wright, Sandra McPherson, and Robert Pinsky, all of whom made their first appearances in the September 1969 issue.

Early in 1969 Rago and the board reached the decision that his leave would be permanent. At a special meeting on 28 March 1969, Rago submitted a letter of resignation, and the board voted to appoint Daryl Hine editor, though he was not to assume the position officially until 1 October. Thus Rago arranged for the succession, with a long interval for Hine to get settled in the job. In a warm article in the *Chicago Daily News*, Van Allen Bradley praised Rago for his success on both the business and artistic sides of the magazine, and reflected on his departure:

> I think there is a higher percentage of prima donnas, egocentrics, neurotics, schizophrenics, back biters, back scratchers and plain nervous wrecks in the field of poetry than in any other profession, and I don't know how in hell Henry Rago has stood it this long as editor of the world's most influential magazine of poetry.

Bradley added: "His innumerable friendships have embraced most of the distinguished poets of the mid-century years." He concluded with the hope the association would "wind up with an editor half as talented, as conscientious and as unruffled as he has been in watching over their literary magazine, which is still the only true meeting place for genius in the magpie world of the poets."

In the March issue Hine published Rago's essay on "The Poet in His Poem." The contributor's note stated it was from his book-in-progress, *The Vocation of Poetry*, "growing out of his seminars and research on the faculty of the University of Chicago." The critical volume and the new collection of poems he planned for the summer were never completed. Henry and his wife Juliet were preparing for ten weeks abroad with their children when they attended an end-of-term party with several poet and professor friends in late May. The following day, a Saturday, Rago was not feeling well. On Sunday he was taken to the emergency room of Wesley Memorial Hospital, where he was examined by interns and released. The next day, 26 May, he was again unwell but did not wish to go back to the hospital. Later that day he was stricken with a fatal heart attack and was pronounced dead on arrival at Wesley. He was fifty-three.

News of his untimely death came as a shock, and as word spread many poets wrote to convey their memories of his help and kindness. Obituary notices praised Rago for his distinguished record and mentioned that he had brought to Chicago many established poets, most of whose careers were launched by *Poetry*. After a funeral mass at St. Thomas Apostle Church near the University of Chicago campus, he was buried in Calvary Cemetery in Evanston. *Poetry* had neither medical insurance nor a pension plan for staff at that time. With help from friends, Juliet Rago, an artist with an M.F.A. from the Art Institute of Chicago, found teaching jobs to support their four children, aged twelve through seventeen.

Two weeks after the funeral she received a large envelope from the University. Enclosed was a certificate: the prestigious Quantrell Award for Excellence in Undergraduate Teaching, presented on 14 June to Henry Rago, who "inspired in students and colleagues new visions of the possibilities of literature." Also in tribute, the University of Chicago radio station broadcast a conversation by Rago's friends and colleagues, the poet Elder Olson, the historian James Redfield, the theologian Giles Gunn, and English professor Edward Rosenheim, Jr. They spoke at length about Rago's deep interest in theology and wide knowledge of literature, his devotion to his students, and his riveting lecture style. Redfield, a former student, recalled: "He stood up very straight; he always spoke in paragraphs, in trim sentences. . . . It was this very formality that enabled him to be the kind of very personal, and, in a certain sense, very passionate teacher that he was." A transcript was published in the *University of Chicago Magazine* for July–August 1969.

Poetry Day 1969 became a memorial program, and on 14 November, Gwendolyn Brooks, Denise Levertov, Galway Kinnell, and Stanley Kunitz read in Rago's honor. The November issue of *Poetry* "In Memory of Henry Rago" printed fragments of poems by the late editor and elegies to him by the memorial speakers and Hine, Marvin Bell, Hayden Carruth, Daniel Hoffman, Richard Howard, Robert Creeley, Karl Shapiro, Gary Snyder, May Swenson, and others. In a memoir of his old friend, "Islands Waited, Wait Still . . . ," Carruth recounted how they broke into the *Poetry* offices in 1947 by jimmying a window, in order to retrieve copies of a new issue that contained poems by Rago: "Two young men burglarizing the magazine they were later to edit, though neither had the least suspicion of what was coming." Carruth added:

> I remember that later, when bad luck overtook me and I was forced into seclusion, Henry was the only person in seven years who came to see me. . . .
>
> Henry's life as an artist was more intense than any other I have known, but cruelly eroded by conflicts of responsibility, both the obvious and the concealed; yet he bore it without bitterness, as he bore all his burdens of time, and he worked with awesome care.
>
> He helped many poets, probably more than will ever be known; scores of my own poems over the years were improved by him, and this was the least of his help to me.

David Ignatow to Daryl Hine   *East Hampton, N.Y., 4 June 1969*

Dear Daryl Hine:

I thought I should convey to you and to the staff of *Poetry* my shock and dismay at the news of the death of Henry Rago. It is inconceivable as I recall the lively talk we had together last summer at Stony Brook during its Festival. This happened to be the first meeting of a relationship that started about ten years ago, with his acceptance of five poems, my first contributions to *Poetry*, and so my first meeting with him was filled with a sense of discovery for me and my impression was of a very gentle man, deeply rooted in a tradition of spirituality. When finally we parted, at the conclusion of the festival, I felt we had secured a mutual respect for each other and I was comforted in the thought that a man of empathy and intellect was at the head of *Poetry*.

The eclectic approach to poetry that he fostered was extraordinarily successful amidst its obvious perils, precisely because of this empathy. He was able to see through the sharp divisions of schools to the basic demands of language and form within each school. He encouraged a wide range of style and subject in an apparent recognition and belief in the diversity of which this nation is formed. In particular, he was steadily perceptive towards my own innate manner and almost never missed accepting among the best I had to show. I can never forget this debt to him and he will always be honored in my memory and I hope someday, as I think about him, in a poem to his person.

Sincerely, / David Ignatow

Samuel Moon to Joseph Wiley   *Knox College, Galesburg, Ill.,*
                                                      11 June 1969

Dear Mr. Wiley,

I have just learned of Henry Rago's untimely death, and I must express my shock and my sense of loss—personal loss, and loss to the estate of poetry in this country. Mr. Rago was without question the best poetry editor we had, under his guidance *Poetry* has been the one absolutely trusted forum for new work, open to its entire range, from known and unknown writers, and sensitive to their own best efforts. By his selection and grouping of my work, he has taught me my own poetry. In his two visits to Knox College he made himself a presence here, living clearly and fully the values he believed in. He was intelligent and kind, and we do not forget him.

Sincerely yours, / Samuel Moon

Gary Snyder to Daryl Hine   *San Francisco, Calif., 16 June 1969*

Dear Mr. Hine,

Although I never met Mr. Rago I came to feel very much a friend simply by mail—so it's an unpleasant surprise to hear of his sudden death. His editorship of *Poetry* made it truly catholic and representative of the best of all streams of American poetry—so that everyone trusted him and the magazine.

The poem ["The Hudsonian Curlew"]—if you want to use it—is elegiac in tone more than I'd planned (the pelican even in Baja are in danger of extinction via DDT now) and I feel fitting to a memorial issue—I think he'd like it—but use your judgment.

Sincerely / Gary Snyder

Karl Shapiro to Daryl Hine   *Davis, Calif., 14 July 1969*

Dear Daryl Hine,

I would be most happy to have you use my "Moving In" for the commemorative issue for Henry Rago. I am still shocked by Henry's death and have been unable to respond with the common courtesies. I am still writing a letter to Julie in my head.

Good luck to you and the indestructible magazine.

With best wishes, / Karl Shapiro

Carolyn Kizer to Daryl Hine   *Washington, D.C., 5 September 1969*

Dear Daryl Hine:

Forgive me for taking so long to reply to your kind letter of 11 June. I have been in Greece, and my mail was not forwarded. Of course we were all shocked to hear of Henry's death; however, it is good that the continuity was already established, and that the magazine is in such good hands.

I wish I could participate in the annual Poetry Day in memorial to Henry; alas, I shall be overseas again at that time. I've never yet succeeded in writing a poem for a memorial issue; not for want of trying. In fact, the only memorial poem I ever wrote was for a friend of mine who committed suicide because of the first Senator McCarthy—and that was written as much from rage (the fueling power, I guess) as from pain. However, I will try to write a little something about Henry, and send it along. I am not hopeful, though.

I am just getting back to writing after a three-year hiatus, working for the federal arts program; I am always rusty, but now I bear a striking resemblance to the little toy dog.

With all good wishes for your happy continuance at *Poetry*.

Yours faithfully, / Carolyn Kizer

Lisel Mueller to Daryl Hine   *[Lake Forest, Ill.], 25 September 1969*

Dear Daryl,

I wish I could contribute something to the memorial issue for Henry Rago, and I thank you for asking me; it seems the least I could do for a man who was so good to, and for, me. But I am constitutionally unable to write for specific occasions, and besides, my feelings for Henry—aspects of gratitude—don't seem to lend themselves to a public expression.

I never knew Henry well, in the sense that this implies meetings and conversations. Habitual reticence, plus the fact that for years I was tied down at home with young children and no daytime sitter, kept me from going into the city and visiting him at the office. So our contacts were by way of correspondence and seeing one another at social occasions now and then. He must have sensed that my failure to seek him out had nothing to do with unfriendliness, for he continually acted as a sort of patron, seeing to it that good things came my way. When the *Daily News* needed a poetry reviewer, when a theatre needed a poet-translator, when someone wanted a lecture about modern poetry, he suggested me. Most of the recognition I've had has come through Henry. Like a benevolent spirit, he was always somewhere in the background.

I knew this kind and gracious side of him; I also knew him as an editor who—as I can see now, in retrospect—knew how to encourage and stabilize one's development as a poet. From any batch of poems one sent him, he chose those which pointed toward a new direction. He preferred the flawed poem that struggled toward something to the easy, glossy, finished one, and by accepting such work for *Poetry*, encouraged the struggle he hoped would lead to "the knowledge of light."

This is the only way I know how to put my feelings for Henry just now; I'm sorry they don't make a poem.

Best regards, / Lisel Mueller

2. Daryl Hine: The Early Years

Daryl Hine was thirty-two when he became visiting editor. He was born in British Columbia and did his undergraduate work in classics and philosophy at McGill University in Montreal. He then went abroad on a Rockefeller Award and a Canada Council Grant. After living four years in France and briefly in New York, he entered the University of Chicago in 1963, where he took his master's and doctorate, in 1966, in comparative literature; his dissertation subject was the Latin poetry of George Buchanan, the sixteenth-century Scottish humanist. He was teaching writing and comparative literature at Chicago when Rago invited him to the magazine.

Hine began to appear in print when he was fifteen, and by his early twenties he had contributed to many of the leading journals in Canada and the United States. His early work was highly praised by Northrop Frye, at the time Canada's best-known literary critic, who predicted a bright future for the precocious author. By 1968 Hine was widely anthologized and had already published five poetry collections, a travel book, and a novel, while several of his plays and his translation of Euripides' *Alcestis* had been broadcast by both the Canadian Broadcasting Corpora-

Editor designate Daryl Hine, 1969.

tion and the BBC. Like his good friend James Merrill, Hine was (and has remained) a formalist; and like Merrill, he persisted in writing finely crafted work infused with wit and wide cultural references during a period when those artistic values were widely rejected. But throughout his nine-year tenure at *Poetry*, Hine maintained its traditions and was receptive to the new varieties of poetry, from the countercultural to the confessional. He himself wrote much poetry that was autobiographically inspired, including an epic in verse.

Nonetheless, because his own style was formal, Hine was accused of favoring similar work in his editorial choices. Such allegations of bias were nothing new. Indeed, since Harriet Monroe's very first issues—and no matter how active *Poetry*'s promotion of free-verse experiments as well as successive waves of innovative techniques in later decades—the magazine's editors were reproached for presenting traditional types of verse. Longevity can be a liability. Since *Poetry* was so long established, many assumed it was part of the Establishment, even though it was always an independent journal unaffiliated with any literary school or educational institution and— more important—virtually all of its monthly issues featured new work by aspiring authors of all persuasions.

Throughout its history, claims about *Poetry*'s supposed conservatism were retailed by literary operators, especially those rejected for publication or disinclined to pick up the magazine and actually read the contents. But during the increasingly acrimonious late sixties and early seventies, aesthetic disputes became inextricably mixed with the divisive social and political issues of the day. Opposing sides, political and artistic, were increasingly unwilling to give each other quarter. The form (or formlessness) of artistic works was taken as symptomatic of deeper philosophical issues or moral dispositions. The term *free* when joined to *verse* was often misconstrued and too easily used to impose a spurious political sense on what is, after all, simply a poetic mode or technique, equating it with democracy, liberality, and spiritual, social, or aesthetic liberation.

Because he chose to write in forms, some assumed that Hine was conservative, when his sympathies were, in fact, quite liberal. He was a strong supporter of women's rights and of the black and gay liberation movements, as reflected in many pieces he ran. He also broke with *Poetry*'s generally nonpolitical stance by publishing in September 1972 an entire issue "Against the War." In terms of poetic styles, despite claims that Hine was not as progressive as the times, detailed perusals of the almost one hundred issues he edited prove otherwise.

Although he was not enthusiastic about all the poets Rago favored, Hine adhered to the Open Door policy, and like all his predecessors he admitted accomplished work, "regardless of where, by whom, or under what theory of art it [was] written." He continued to publish many poets who had first appeared during Rago's tenure, including Adrienne Rich, May Swenson, and Wendell Berry. Besides giving Mark Strand, Sandra McPherson, and Charles Wright their first appearances in *Poetry*, Hine also accepted early work by authors as diverse as William Matthews, C. K. Williams, Stephen Dobyns, Louise Glück, Erica Jong, Marvin Bell, Alfred Corn, James Cole, Michael Heffernan, Wong May, Greg Kuzma, Tom Disch, and J. D. McClatchy.

Others well represented were Charles Simic, Stephen Berg, Timothy Steele, Marilyn Hacker, Robert B. Shaw, H. B. Mallalieu, Mark Jarman, Michael Hamburger, Sandra M. Gilbert, John N. Morris, Margaret Atwood, Dave Smith, Stephen Sandy, Jayanta Mahapatra, and David Bottoms. Among the more established figures making regular appearances during the Hine years were A. R. Ammons, John Hollander, Geoffrey Grigson, Turner Cassity, Richard Hugo, Kenneth Koch, Philip Levine, James Merrill, W. S. Merwin, James Schuyler, David Wagoner, and William Stafford. The editor's all-around favorite was probably Howard Nemerov, whose mastery of form compared with Merrill's, Wilbur's, and Hollander's (and Hine's own), and whose dry wit and sophisticated satire were inimitable. Hine gave Nemerov a rare honor by devoting an entire issue, August 1975, to his work.

Poets and general readers alike seemed to approve of Hine's selections, for after his first two years as editor, circulation of the magazine (both subscriptions and single-copy sales) rose from about 7,600 in 1968 to almost

8,200 by the end of 1970. Distribution stayed at about that level until the mid-seventies. Among Hine's innovations was to put artwork on the covers, which doubtless increased newsstand appeal. Given the first-rate contributors, the contents of the magazine were generally lively too, with extra interest generated when many new names appeared, particularly in his first years. But Hine also was successful in winning back a number of older contributors who for whatever reasons had stopped sending during the last regime, including Nemerov.

Hine often commented on the problems in filling the back of the book and lamented his difficulties finding reviewers, particularly poets, who could write decent prose. Even so, the critical section was frequently filled with surprises, such as a 1969 review by F. D. Reeve written completely in witty (and sometimes risqué) couplets. Rago had tended toward the serious and somber, but the new editor had a healthy appreciation for comedy. The waspish wit and satiric tone of several of the reviewers were not well received by the "sensitive" (and usually humorless) authors who felt their stings.

Early on Hine solicited work from W. H. Auden and received his clever, self-deprecating "Doggerel of a Senior Citizen." (In the bargain, he also took work by Auden's longtime companion Chester Kallman; they appeared together in the December 1969 issue.) Hine also convinced Auden to come to Chicago for Poetry Day in November 1971, and this second appearance (he also read in 1960) was one of the more successful benefits, netting *Poetry* $12,000.

Good cheer about finances became the norm, since the magazine's bottom line was fairly healthy throughout Hine's first years, with some balance sheets even registering profits. In May 1970 the magazine's offices moved to 1228 North

W. H. Auden in the late sixties; he first contributed to *Poetry* in 1931 and read for Poetry Day in 1960 and 1971.

Dearborn Street, a converted brownstone apartment whose walls were soon faced floor to ceiling with tightly packed bookcases. Even with the higher rent and increased costs of printing, the magazine's net losses ranged from a mere $1,628 to a manageable $5,603 in five years between 1969 and 1974.

Subscription rates finally had to be raised, modestly, from $12 to $15 per year, in October 1973. In 1971 the board, under the guidance of Ruth Horwich as president, found its way to securing health insurance for the staff, and in 1975 a pension fund was established.

As the countercultural revolution of the sixties began to turn into the new orthodoxy of the seventies, Hine took an increasingly dim view of the posturing, arrogance, and hyperbolic pronouncements of the erstwhile insurgents of American poetry. Nemerov shared Hine's opinion and took to task a fairly representative anthology of the fashionable new formlessness called *Naked Poetry* in a review printed in April 1970 under the title "The Theory and Practice of What." In their introduction, the editors, Stephen Berg and Robert Mezey, seem to invite suspicion, if not derision, by declaring: "We will put aside all the traditional modesties and say plainly what we think, that most of the best poetry written in America during the last two decades is collected in this book." Noting that about one-tenth of "the best poetry" in the volume was by the editors themselves, Nemerov dryly observes: "every poet's middle name is Mimi and which of us, given command of an anthology, would not have done likewise. Though I like to imagine that there may be poets somewhere who would not make themselves judges in their own cause." He concludes: "The impression produced on me by prolonged and repeated exposure to the selections in this book is one of deepest boredom. Dullness and self-indulgence, pretentiousness and triviality, are here in the greatest plenty."

Howard Nemerov was honored with a special issue of *Poetry*, August 1975.

Besides the pieces by the editors, the collection includes work by Rexroth, Roethke, Patchen, Stafford, Kees, Berryman, Lowell, Levertov, Bly, Creeley, Ginsberg, Kinnell, Merwin, James Wright, Levine, Plath, and Snyder, though usually weak specimens that Nemerov found uncharacteristic of their best work. With the exception of Ginsberg, *Poetry* had published all these poets, most of them many times, but Nemerov hit a nerve by saying of the editors' favorites: "Most of them do not write iambic pentameter themselves, and would gladly see it suppressed in others: 'the rhymed iambic', says one, 'which no fashionable poet would be caught dead writing these days.'"

Nemerov and Hine were not particularly concerned about fashion, and *Poetry's* tradition was, of course, to be *inclusive*, not exclusive, in its editorial policy. In the end, Nemerov dismisses the anthology tartly:

> The slogan of the poets who write long seems to be, If you can't be immortal be interminable; and some of the poets who write short can be interminable in ten lines.
>
> With that, so much of it is so humorlessly earnest, and so much of it, new as it is, so earnestly derivative. The Blake-fakery! the Whitmania! the riggish ved-antic! the sutras that have come unstitched! Naked poetry forsooth. If there is more enterprise in walking naked (as we are told there is by a poet who habitually wrote in rhymed stanzas), the representations of this book make it out to be private enterprise. And why go naked if you aren't beautiful?
>
> I think I'll go read some clothed couplets, especially if they have a sweet disorder in the dress.

This one review may well have turned whole cohorts of supposedly freethinking free-versifiers and others of the ever more conformist "avantgarde" against the editor.

But Hine's reviewers could be no less direct, and sometimes even harsher, toward writers in conventional styles who descended into mediocrity. One such drubbing, which happened to appear in the same issue as Nemerov's put-down, was Steven M. L. Aronson's review of L. E. Sissman's *Scattered Returns*, entitled "Urbane Trash." "Sissman's is the true gift of the adman sensibility moving along in time," Aronson begins. "He loves to give us trademarks, brand-names: not a steak but a 'New York steak,' not just an apple pie but a 'Hostess Apple Pie,' not just any typewriter but a 'Smith-Corona' . . . ." (Sissman was in fact an advertising man in Boston and had made his reputation mainly through his reviews in the *New Yorker* and a column in the *Atlantic*.) Warming to his task, the critic continues: "The elephantine egoism of the poems is astonishing. . . . The meeminess [sic] of it all makes one catch one's breath." But Aronson's brutal dismissal itself gives pause:

> What a flabby bore the collective hero of these poems is! Both charm and hairline attenuated, he is life's garbageman-philosopher, a smoothly-modulated nincompoop, crunchless and without instinct. One is appalled by the sheer banality of his life ("stuffing" would be a better word), and the sheer ease. He is indolent and quite simply dishonest.

Hine regretted printing the review. Not surprising, the tone of the piece provoked numerous objections. Sissman went on to produce three more books; his posthumously published collected poems, *Hello, Darkness*, won the National Book Critics Circle Award in 1978, four years after his death, from Hodgkin's disease, at age forty-eight.

Such acerbic critiques were exceptional, however, and most of the objections about the back of the book were as well reasoned as the reviews themselves. Hine received the usual kinds of complaints about his choices and perceived editorial policies, many of which were amusing, if sometimes unintentionally so. One of *Poetry*'s longtime procedural quirks, later rescinded, was the requirement that all manuscripts submitted be originals, not copies, and it provoked a series of ironic and increasingly acid epistles in protest from Susan Fromberg Schaeffer. Returned poems elicited other irritated and poignant reactions, as in the case of Diane Wakoski.

But, as usual, the most engaging communications included the cover letters introducing "new" poets and their work, the excited responses to first acceptances, and the editor-author exchanges over specific poems. Some of the more interesting missives received during this period are those from Charles Wright, especially when he goes into detail about his motives and methods, as well as the amusing messages from Nemerov, Dickey, Turner Cassity, Erica Jong, and the responses of the editor himself.

3. Correspondence 1968–1972

James Dickey to Daryl Hine   *Columbia, S.C., 5 November 1968*

Dear Daryl:

Thanks so much for your letter. I am delighted that you will print the poems, and that you want to lead off the issue in which they appear with them. When people open *Poetry* and get hit right off with that "Blood" poem [printed June 1969] they are going to be shook, I'll wager. . . .

Reviewing: yes, I will be happy to do something for you at some time around the first of the year. But I am so busy with these Franklin Foundation Lectures at Georgia Tech (culture for the engineers, forsooth!) that I can't take on anything right now.

And I would prefer not to do Berryman, in any case. I was a solid champion for him all the time he was trying this new stuff, and as far as I know I gave him better notices than anyone else did. But now the work is beginning to pall on me awfully; I am sick to death of his awful colloquial cuteness and those doctored-up lines of his, and some of this would surely get into the review, and he—being he—would think I had turned on him and "betrayed" him. And, since he has [been] or is being given the Robert Bly "attack" treatment at this time also, I am genuinely afraid that any further ill treatment would drive him over the edge, where he is always threatening to go. So I had rather let this cup pass, if I may. Might I do Rexroth for you in a couple of months, or would it then be too late?

Meanwhile, my best to you, and thank you so much for what you say about the new poems. And could you tell me whether my critical book has been reviewed in *Poetry*?

Good luck on your own new work.

Jim Dickey

Dickey published two prose books in 1968, *Metaphor as Pure Adventure* and *Babel to Byzantium: Poets and Poetry Now*, reviewed in February 1970.

Harry Brown to Daryl Hine   *[Los Angeles, Calif.],*
                                     14 December 1968

Dear Mr. Hine:

I can't help but be very pleased indeed that you took the three odes, can I? No, I can't. . . .

As for a publication date for my new book of poems, which in a weak moment I seem to have titled A LITTLE TOUCH OF HARRY IN THE NIGHT, I can't give you one at the moment. All I can tell you is that when I sent it to my New York agent I said: "Baby, get this published by next September, *or else!*" I've broken with Knopf, my publisher for 25 years, so that firm's out of the picture; besides, Knopf thinks all poets should write like Walter Benton (or maybe Rod McKuen, now that Knopf is a subsidiary of Random House). I've enlarged my agent's horizons to a certain extent by informing him that the woods are full of universities whose presses have been known to run off thin, but thrilling, volumes of real, live poetry; previously the poor fellow thought that a University Press was some sort of Ivy League love-in. However, now that the message has gotten through, I reckon he'll swing a deal with somebody and make that September deadline. It might be nice, then, if you could fit the three odes into *Poetry's* pages by—Oh, June '69, say.

Further, deponent saith not.

With all good wishes for a great year in office,

Yours most sincerely, / Harry Brown

Brown debuted in *Poetry* in 1935, when he was sixteen; Harriet Monroe encouraged him, introduced him to writers, and helped get him into Harvard. He later became a novelist and screenwriter (of the original *Ocean's Eleven*, among other scripts). See *Dear Editor*, Chapter XIII. He had two poems in the August 1968 issue; his last appearance, with the three poems mentioned, was in August 1969.

Julia Alvarez to Daryl Hine   *Connecticut College,*
                                                          New London, Conn.,
                                                            17 January 1969

Dear Mr. Hine,
    For some time it was hard to say 'Mr. Hine,' and even harder to write
'Dear Mr. Hine'— You do not remember me, I'm quite sure as one of the
rejected amateurs. You said my poems were too 'personal'—I searched
everywhere for quotes in which poetry was described and defended as personal, I had arguments to confront you with—I had examples to show
you—The first rejection, I guess, is hard—it says what you have been
spending the last four years doing is 'mediocre' or even worse 'personable.'
But as I prepared for that grand assault, I realized it was an escape from con-
fronting my poetry and with a critical eye saying 'this should be improved.'
The more I thought of your small note—the more diplomatic it seemed
and certainly encouraging as all those notes to beginners must be. I always
felt a certain weakness in my poetry and you helped me pinpoint it. So this
letter that perhaps you thought was some self-assertive, self-defensive 'hate
letter'—is to thank you for something you never thought twice about: a
spur into self-examination and criticism—further, no longer is Fame what
I aim for—I write because I MUST, and if by chance or luck what I write
can help another, and I can settle down and be a writer— all well and good.
But even if I must search elsewhere for a profession and leave my writing
on some dusty shelf to be turned to when there is time without hope of
reward or recognition, I still must write— . . .

X. J. Kennedy to Daryl Hine   *Bedford, Mass., 21 March 1969*

Dear Daryl Hine,
    Happy that the review of British books could suit you and *Poetry*. . . .
    Glad, too, to think that my mild lament for meter may have touched a
response in you. Something you said about A. D. Hope struck me as a re-
buke to anarchy, and the example of your own poems has not been lost on
me. The disappearance of meter strikes me as the most interesting fact in
poetry nowadays, and I wonder that so few seem alarmed by it. The new
anthology *31 New American Poets* [edited by Ron Schreiber] in fact, makes
a point of excluding anyone who writes in meter or stanzas. It is a great age
for lazy slugs who'd rather emit than work. Under the illusion of opening
the way to an oral poetry, many have demolished not only meter and rime
in their work, but syntax and deliberate order, with the result that much
poetry nowadays can't be listened to. There is the curious development of
rock song lyrics, but most seem written by mindless creeps. Someday I'll

write a great blast about all this, change my name to Yvor Winters II, and expire amid execrations.

That's good news that Elizabeth Jennings is writing poems again and that you have some of them.

Sincerely, / X. J. Kennedy

Kennedy reviewed nine books, including collections by Jennings, Kingsley Amis, Edwin Morgan, and Ruth Fainlight. *Poetry* presented five poems by Jennings in May 1969; she also appeared in 1971, 1973, and 1977.

Charles Wright to Daryl Hine   *Venice, Italy, 12 April 1969*

Dear Mr Hine:

Cannot tell you how happy your letter of 8 April has made me. After so many years of knocking on that particular door! The poems that you took, with one exception, constitute the work that I have done since being in Venice and, with only 2 exceptions, form a section of my book manuscript. So you were right in thinking that they were something of a series, albeit loose. I have no quibble with the way you have arranged them—it looks fine to me. I hasten to send you copies of 2 of the poems as I am not sure if you have these versions or previous ones. If you have no major objections, I would prefer you use the ones I enclose as they will appear as such in the book. As you can see from the form I send back, the book [*Grave of the Right Hand*, his first collection] is to come out in Spring of 1970 (which means Feb/Mar, I guess, with Wesleyan). I hope this doesn't push you too much to get the poems out before the book appears. I am not unamenable to reviewing. I have shunned it in the past, but would be quite happy to do it for *Poetry*. In fact, feel almost duty bound. I would prefer to work with books of poems.

Again, such a nice day you have given me today. And, again, I hope you can see your way to use the revisions I enclose.

All best wishes, / Charles Wright

Wright never in fact reviewed for *Poetry*, but Hine accepted every poem he sent; Hine also wrote a glowing recommendation for promotion at the University of California, Irvine, where Wright taught 1966–1983.

F. D. Reeve to Daryl Hine   *Higganum, Conn., 27 April 1969*

Dear Mr. Hine:

I've done something crazy, crazy. As you'll see if you ever turn this page.

It seemed a way to pull these half-dozen poets together. I tried to give most attention to Mr Lucie-Smith [*Towards Silence*], who seemed to me the most accomplished and interesting of the group. I hope no one, including them, will mind that some of their lines are printed and punctuated somewhat differently from the original. Images not in quotes try to come close to the several poets' own.

Having gone through the reviews in a few back issues of *Poetry*, I suddenly thought you might like this. If you think it's pretentious or badly done or just a nuisance, please say so. If you want to make changes do. If you want the review in prose, let's.

Sincerely, / F. D. Reeve

Reeve wrote his reviews of Edward Lucie-Smith and four other British authors (October 1969) completely in couplets. His Verse Chronicle begins: "Handsome though the print and paper be, / The thoughts that float too often are lost at sea, / While weighty matters on the waters whirl / 'Through the public lavatories of the world.'"

Daryl Hine to F. D. Reeve   *Chicago, 12 May 1969*

Dear Mr. Reeve,

Not at all: I have always loved didactic and critical verse, and your review is a very pleasant addition to the all too small corpus of such works. On the first delighted reading I was a trifle perturbed by some of the liberties you take with metre and rhyme, but I found this inexplicably acceptable on later readings, when I think I had learned not to expect an eighteenth-century correctness in a very idiosyncratic twentieth-century parody. Am I right in thinking that the discords are, as in some of Stravinsky's music, intentional? Anyway, the poem is a delight, and as I should like to do away with our dreary prose section anyway, it will fit very nicely (as I think you guessed) into my editorial scheme.

Sincerely, / Daryl Hine
Visiting Editor

W. H. Auden to Daryl Hine   *Kirchstetten, Austria, 18 July 1969*

Dear Daryl,

I am so pleased that you were able to take some of Chester's poems. It has been an enormous boost to his morale.

Is the enclosed 'reactionary' piece of interest to *Poetry*?

Yours ever / Wystan

Chester Kallman was Auden's longtime companion; five of his poems were printed in the December 1969 issue. He had also contributed five poems to the April 1954 issue, during

Karl Shapiro's tenure. Auden is referring to his "Doggerel of a Senior Citizen," which appeared in the same 1969 number.

Howard Nemerov to Daryl Hine   *Brewster, Mass., 24 July 1969*

Dear Mr. Hine,

Thank you for inviting me to contribute; owing in part to some differences of opinion with the late regime I haven't published anything in *Poetry* for some dozen years; and now, alas, I've no new poems to give you, for I am not writing poetry just now.

Nor would I ordinarily review the stuff; I thought I'd made all the enemies I needed by age forty. But by coincidence I am going to start my students at Washington University off on Naked Poetry this Fall so I may have one or two things to say about it of a hopefully helpful nature. If you will send the book to me speedily at the above address I'll be glad to give it a try.

For your records, by the way, I am no longer at Bennington. My permanent address of employ is Brandeis University, but I shall be a visiting professor at Washington University during the coming year . . .

With best wishes, / Howard Nemerov

Daryl Hine to Howard Nemerov   *Chicago, 14 October 1969*

Dear Mr Nemerov,

Thank you for your *Naked Poetry* review, which I loved and with which I wholeheartedly agree. You had this reader, at least, cheering inaudibly by the last page. A rare manifestation, I believe, these days. Case in point was the offensive Ginsberg puff in July [a rave review by Bill Berkson of *Planet News*]. You wouldn't believe the amount of correspondence, revision, fuss & bother involved, only to issue, as so many of these struggles do, in worse than pyrrhic victory. I ought to print a little disclaimer somewhere: Not responsible for reviewers' opinions, taste, or syntax. Though I do try to tidy up the last when, all too often, it needs it, I have, so far, held back from interference in the mysterious working of the critical, or uncritical, mind. Perhaps I take the principled impartiality and noninterference of this magazine too literally; I have a certain weakness for traditions, even bad ones. Soon, however, if my reviewers, with the rarest exceptions, like your own, keep serving up these unpalatable raves, I may resort to the only revenge left me, in the Notes on Contributors: "Mr X is a student (friend, lover, debtor) of Mr Y." Oh well.

I wish that I could persuade you to write more often for *Poetry*—both prose and verse.

Best wishes, / Daryl Hine

Sandra McPherson to Daryl Hine   *[n.p.], 27 October 1969*

Dear Daryl Hine,

Thank you for the acceptance and thank you for the request to do a review. However, I think I am going to make it a rule for myself never to do
reviews. Writing them contributes to one's pocketbook, not to one's psychic health. I once wrote a review on Brother Antoninus [William Ever-
son], who in his book was obviously having enough problems with women
without me adding to them. . . .

Best Wishes, / Sandra McPherson

Paul Carroll to Daryl Hine   *Chicago, 11 November 1969*

Dear Daryl,

Will you contribute a poem to an auction held to raise money for the 8
defendants in the Chicago conspiracy trial? The auction is Abbie Hoffman's
idea. All of the money raised will be given to the conspiracy Defense Fund.
Apparently the defendants are in desperate need of funds with which to continue their defense. The auction will take place on December 4th in the Lo
Guidice Gallery, 201 East Ontario Street, Chicago. Works by painters and
sculptors from all over the country will also be auctioned. Nora Smith, a
member of the committee of Chicago citizens which is arranging the auction and the one who asked me to try to get poems, suggests that the poems
contributed be signed and, if possible, hand-written on good paper and that
you state what you think should be the minimum price your poem should
command. If you plan to contribute a poem, send it by Thanksgiving to: Mrs.
Farwell Smith, 1234 North State Street, Chicago 60610. Hello!

Cordially, / Paul

For their parts as leaders of demonstrations at the Democratic Convention in Chicago in August 1968, Hoffman and Jerry Rubin, along with Tom Hayden, Bobby Seale, Dave Dellinger,
and three others were indicted for conspiracy and inciting a riot, and became known as the
Chicago Eight when they came to trial in March 1969. (See Chapter IV, sec. 2.) The trial was
drawn out for months, during which Hoffman, Rubin, and Seale provoked Judge Julius Hoffman, violated decorum repeatedly, and were fined for contempt. Although acquitted of conspiracy, most of the defendants were fined and sentenced to five years imprisonment for inciting to riot, in February 1970. The convictions were reversed on appeal, in November 1972,
because of bias by Judge Hoffman. The contempt charges were also overturned.

Karl Shapiro to Daryl Hine   *Davis, Calif., 5 December 1969*

Dear Daryl Hine,

. . . My thanks for the poem ["Elegiacs"] in the Rago Memorial issue. I
thought you did a marvelous job and paid Henry a great and deserved

compliment. And I have meant to congratulate you on the editorship. It is a glorious and weird job, as I am sure you know. Anyway I think back on it as one of the most exciting times of my life. . .

Cordially, / Karl

Daryl Hine to Stephen Dobyns   *Chicago, 17 December 1969*

Dear Mr. Dobyns,

Your review, entitled *Five Poets*, has been exercising my editorial attention. It is too long, not merely for our requirements, but for its own good. It is, I'm afraid, frequently repetitious, redundant, verbose and, all too often, irrelevant: autobiography is not criticism. On the other hand, it is also often perceptive, pointed, and even witty. Accordingly, I have cut it, by about a third, and have also done what I could with the split infinitives, dangling prepositions, and your odd coordinate conjunctions, a practice that, though recommended somewhere by Ezra Pound, can be overdone. You will understand that it would be tedious to detail and explain every change I have felt it desirable to make. If you agree, in principle, to this editorial despotism, you will see its effects on your essay, eventually, in proof; if you cannot wait, we could send you a Xerox of the piece including my penciled corrections. And if the whole thing seems an outrage against free expression, not to say grammatical license, you may of course withdraw your submission—though I should hate to lose the best parts of your review.

Sincerely, / Daryl Hine

A review by Dobyns entitled "Five Poets" (on David Bromige, Greg Kuzma, Marge Piercy, James Tate, and David Wagoner) appeared in March 1971. It is not clear whether the books are those referred to in this letter.

Daryl Hine to Juliet Rago   *Chicago, 29 December 1969*

Dear Juliet,

I am enclosing a cheque [for $250] for a prize awarded by the National Endowment for the Arts and The American Literary Anthology, for several poems published in *Poetry* under Henry's editorship. Had he lived, he would have accepted this award, and while I have had to accept it on behalf of the magazine, it is only right that I should pass it on to you now.

With best wishes, / Daryl

Jack Litewka to Daryl Hine   *New York City, 16 January 1970*

Dear Mr. Hine:

Here is poem. A perfect poem, which doesn't make it a favorite of mine (but more of that later) [are you already saying "Oh no, not another one of these letters"—you're right if you are]. It has a precedent in form. But not in content.

I've given up sending you (the general corporate "you" as in *Poetry* magazine) rich, textured, brilliant poems that, admittedly have flaws (minor) because, apparently, only flawless names can be trusted with minor flaws.

So here it is. Short sweet and capable of being read in one sitting without coffee.

I sound bitter. Really only angry. And frustrated (mustn't forget the time's paradigm). Because I know *Poetry* is doing as good a job as they can.

And the cover is changing. Is Pegasus enjoying the pastured life? And I do buy the issues, and enjoy them if I can find a poem to latch onto (has the quality of material you've been receiving gone down hill in the last 8 months?).

So, the last effort before I establish a competitive magazine and start slandering yours, and begin a devilish little sycophantic editorial board that will support the buttocks of close friends. Alas, alas. Has the decade really closed?

love and kisses / jack litewka

Hine had changed the cover design, replacing Juliet Rago's Pegasus with line drawings and other artwork.

Daryl Hine to P— G—   *Chicago, 3 February 1970*

Dear P— G—:

I am not at all interested in automatic writing: if by Shelley, he automatically seems to have deteriorated on the Other Side. You might try the *Journal of Psychic Research*, or *Psychology Today*, or *TriQuarterly*, which has odd interests. Please note the correct spelling of my name.

Daryl Hine

Unsuccessful with earlier submissions, the author had written to "Darrell Hines" from Michigan in January after sending two more poems from a long series she said were "from *automatic writing* by the poet Shelley" (and Blake, "though not in his old style"). She offered to send thermocopies to show the drawings that accompanied them; she also requested suggestions for other places to which she might submit them.

Jack Litewka to Daryl Hine   *New York City, 25 February 1970*

Dear Mr. Hine:

What do you mean "there are hundreds of places (I) could publish this poem?" (It's an insidious statement!)

Of course there are 100s of places I could publish it. But I want to help the culturally deprived.

May Deus be with you and all his knights.

Case closed.

jack litewka

Litewka was never published in *Poetry*.

Bill Berkson to Editors   *[New York City], 28 February 1970*

[*Written on the back of a subscription blank*]

Dear Sirs,

I have not been receiving any subscription copies for some time now. However, I have seen the last few issues and they are priceless. Who would subscribe to such a horrible magazine? Shit! Not I.

Sincerely, / Bill Berkson

Berkson, a poet and art critic, was associated with the New York "school" of poets; with Joe LeSeur, he edited *Homage to Frank O'Hara* in 1978. See Hine's letter to Nemerov concerning Berkson's review of Ginsberg, 14 October 1969, above.

David Curry to Daryl Hine   *Apple, Springfield, Ill., 17 April 1970*

Dear Mr. Hine:

Howard Nemerov's review of the NAKED POETRY anthology in your April issue is hard to take. I can only assume that you were hoping for an unfavorable review when you assigned the book to him. Rather like asking Agnew to do a report on a peace demonstration.

To my mind, it's one of the best anthologies of contemporary American poetry. I agree that the editors should not have included their own work, and I think that Nemerov is justified in finding the introduction over-stated and dispensable. Other than that, his only objection seems to be that most of the poetry is aside from the English tradition. Is there any good reason to regard that as a criticism rather than a simple, accurate observation? Is Nemerov unable to read poetry unless it's written within set metrics—and, if so, are we supposed to consider this inability an achievement?

He quotes a four-line poem, IN A TRAIN, by Robert Bly and just asks us to accept that it's bad. He doesn't say why. I've loved that poem since the first time I read it in Bly's SILENCE IN THE SNOWY FIELDS, and I can't cooperate. I'm not a part of the in-group to whom Nemerov is confident that he's speaking, and he hasn't bothered to step out and explain the rules so that I can play along. From what Nemerov says in the rest of his review, I guess I'm supposed to dismiss Bly's poem because it isn't metrical. In an inept and misplaced parody near the end of the review, Nemerov changes Bly's Missoula, Montana to Liverfluke Falls, Idaho. Why? Beyond the lack of meter, does he also dislike the plainness of detail? Is Missoula, Montana an unworthy thing for poetry? Would he have been happier with Babylonia? Should it have been dressed up with a couple of fine modifiers, preferably alliterated? . . .

The tradition to which Nemerov is so attached has always emphasized language over life, and most of the poets in this anthology prefer to reverse that. This reversal has a great deal to do with what has been happening in recent American poetry. A review of NAKED POETRY might have considered this reversal closely, but Nemerov was hardly the man to do it.

The old poets in the volume have grown and broken new ground during their lifetimes. Several began in the English tradition but didn't mistake it for the world. They are represented by their most recent work, and Nemerov, who hasn't done much growing, naturally resents this. He'd have preferred, as he says, the Robert Lowell whose "originality and energy and strangeness were earlier exhibited by his handling of English heroic line in complex rhymed stanzas." His love is clearly for the English heroic line and not the originality and energy.

"Why go naked if you aren't beautiful?" he asks. Indeed. And now we know why one man clothes himself in couplets. The beauty of the anthology remains open to be seen.

Yours, / David Curry, Editor

Vice President Spiro Agnew was noted for the alliteration in his demagogic speeches, as when he called anti-war demonstrators "nattering nabobs of negativism."

Harry Ford to Daryl Hine   *Atheneum Publishers, New York City,*
23 April 1970

Dear Daryl:

I was really most unpleasantly taken aback by the silly and ill-tempered review of [L. E.] Sissman's new book [*Scattered Returns*] when I got around to really reading the current issue of your magazine last night. I think Sissman has been overpraised by people like Tony Hecht and Howard Moss (though God knows you can see their reason for doing so since a little lightheadedness and accurate nostalgia is worth a lot these days); it's true too that Sissman leaves himself open to the kind of criticism that your reviewer brings to bear, but the pretentious snotty one-sidedness is really not to be borne.

Yours, / Harry

Ford was Hine's editor.

Daryl Hine to Harry Ford   *Chicago, 27 April 1970*

Dear Harry,

I'm sorry you felt you had to tell me of your distress over S. M. L. Aronson's review of L. E. Sissman. I agree that it is an ill-natured, offensive piece of slick journalism which I oughtn't to have permitted in the magazine; and I think, too, that it is grossly unfair to Sissman's real worth. I suppose I published it in part just to demonstrate the principle of editorial impartiality; to balance the witty and wise Nemerov review (ending as it did with a call for clothed couplets), with which I did agree, by something that (I fondly imaged) nobody could think I had any sympathy for. . . . Having allowed Aronson to persuade me that he review Sissman (for whom he had expressed a great deal of enthusiasm beforehand), I had, I thought, to accept, and print, the consequences, however frivolous. Needless to say, he will not be reviewing for me in future. . . . I print most of the prose that I do print with pained reluctance (Nemerov was a striking exception), but unlike Reed Whittemore, I do print it, and regard it as the least valuable element in the magazine, and am sorry to think that it outweighs in interest everything else that I have been trying to do in *Poetry*. Reviewing remains an overwhelming and incurable source of anxiety, I must admit.

                                                   Yours, / Daryl

Harry Ford to Daryl Hine   *Atheneum Publishers, New York City,*
                                                   29 April 1970

Dear Daryl:

To employ a fashionable phrase, I must say you over-reacted to my letter about the Sissman review. I thought I had made it clear to you in the past that I think you're doing a smashing job in editing your magazine. I also have to say that I never confuse the opinions of editors and contributors, and that I couldn't agree more that the prose is the least important aspect of the magazine. *But* you must also agree that even on that basis it's enormously influential among people who really care about poetry (outside of the *Times Book Review* what could be more important?) and an irresponsible review in your pages means a hundred times more than it would mean anyplace else. That this should only have happened once since you've taken over is a miracle, so be comforted accordingly. But I do hope you wouldn't have wanted me to be silent feeling the way I did.

                                                   Yrs, / Harry

Howard Nemerov to Daryl Hine　　　　　　*St. Louis, Mo., 3 May 1970*

Dear Daryl,

(with your agreement, I think we might go on to front names)—Thanks for your letter and the things you sent therewith. . . .

As for Mr Curry's letter [complaining about H.N.'s review of *Naked Poetry*, April issue], O Dear. I did try as hard as could be not to be self-righteous about things. . . . [sic] But I guess my complaint wd be that these chaps seem never to allow that their sort of poesy might also be the proper subject of a squinty and jaundiced look. And he's got that usual obsession about meter (concerning which I said almost nothing): "I guess I am supposed to dismiss Bly's poem because it's not metrical." Reminds me of a remark I canceled out of the review: "the first remark of the first American poet to land on the moon will not be in iambic pentameter, but will probably be about it." . . .

I did think the Aronson piece was a bit hard on poor old Ed [Sissman]. But I have a sneaky sense that poor old Ed overdid it last time out, and that Aronson may simply have been right in the essential point, thought the truth he tells doth lack some gentleness, if not the time to tell it in. Ah well, the life of an editor is hard beyond the line of duty.

All best, / Howard

Diane Wakoski to Daryl Hine　　　　　　*New York City, 27 May 1970*

Dear Daryl,

High praises for Aronson's roast of Sissman. Well deserved. And carried off with more finesse than I've seen in critical writing in a long time. . . .

Diane Wakoski in the
early seventies.

I've been going through a very troubled time, suffering an odd sort of paranoia on the subject of grants, awards, publications, etc. A feeling that the establishment is "out to get me." Of course this is not true. But I suppose it is a natural feeling (exaggerated in my case) that one might have if he has written for 15 years, published for 10, produced 6 large collections of poems, published 12 books, and knows that whether or not he's one of the important poets of the century, at least he writes well and uniquely and speaks for an important segment of the literate population, and still he cannot get reviewed (I mentioned before that POETRY perhaps through lack of organization and not a desire to ignore me has never reviewed one of my books), cannot get grants, never receives awards—he knows something is wrong.

However I'll be 33 this year (the year, in Christian mythology, to be crucified), and I feel that 1970 is the beginning of my second decade as a poet. What was appropriate for a young unpublished immature writer, is no longer appropriate for the middle-aged. I feel that one of the things I can do to exorcise some of my demons and perhaps straighten out some of my own thinking, would be to occasionally write about other writers who interest me (either who make me angry as Sissman did Aronson, or who seem to be very important and exciting poets, as I think Jerome Rothenberg is). I will never "review" books, not being a critic. But I am a clear thinker, a poet with strong tastes and a rational mind for talking about my tastes. . . .

Daryl Hine to Diane Wakoski   *Chicago, 19 June 1970*

Dear Diane,

I'm glad that you found something to like in *Poetry*, even if it was only a pot roast of poor old Ed., and I know that Steve A. was gratified by your appreciation, and as he is now back in NYC (having left *Playboy*) perhaps you will meet. He's very bright & funny, and not quite as unkind in person as in print. . . .

I don't think your paranoia about Success is well founded at all; I seem to see your name everywhere, and in lights. And so many people drop it nowadays. I guess it is natural to feel neglected, particularly at our age (I'm told that the thirties are tough—too old for prodigy & too young for eminence) but I think it's unbecoming to complain. That's not what you're writing for, or is it? If it is, there are quicker, easier ways to notoriety & fortune, believe it or not. About reviews of your books: I don't know about Henry, but I've sent out those that have appeared since I've been here (& that's easier said than done, as your postcard will prove): one was so badly reviewed that I killed it in proof—a kindness, believe me; another is forthcoming (don't ask me by whom or when) & a third—*Magellanic Clouds*— was the subject of a letter to a reviewer this morning. I have a terrible time getting reviewers (in other words), nobody can write prose, and most of those who might, as you must know from your personal acquaintance, are hopelessly irresponsible.

I'm leaving on Saturday for several weeks, but someone here will send you the review books on request.

Sincerely, / Daryl Hine

Erica Jong to Daryl Hine   *New York City, 10 August 1970*

Dear Mr. Hine,

I just returned from a short vacation and found your welcome letter. Steven Aronson is not the editor on my book [*Fruits & Vegetables*, 1971]; Aaron Asher is—but Steven was one of the people who was enthusiastic about it when it circulated through Holt's offices. After I read your note,

Erica Jong about the time of her first publication in the magazine, 1971.

I began to think that the name Steven Aronson sounded familiar and it suddenly occurred to me that it was he who wrote that wickedly funny review of Sissman. (The sort of hatchet review all writers must have nightmares about—though in Sissman's case, I thought the hatchet not wholly undeserved). I said hello to Steven a few minutes ago when I called another editor at Holt. I will probably be introduced to him there next week.

I'm glad you want those four poems and publishing them in February would be perfect. I'll let you know if the book publication gets delayed; at this point early March looks pretty certain. Please publish the poems under Erica Jong since the book (and everything hereafter) will be under Erica Jong. One compelling reason for this is to avoid tiresome identification with Auden's phantom wife and Thomas Mann's late daughter [Erika] (to whom I'm not now and have never been related). I have published something like 18 poems under Erica Mann so perhaps that name might be mentioned (somehow) in the biographical note. Or perhaps three names could be used in the biographical note (but *not* on the poems—since three names sound stuffy to me). . . .

Lately I've been working on a prose fantasy (fiction) to be called, perhaps, "The Man Who Murdered Poets" and on another collection of poems and on changes in this first collection.

I think the title of the book will be *Fruits & Vegetables* but that could change.

Best wishes, / Erica Jong

Auden married Erika Mann, an actress and author (1905–1969), in 1935, to help her escape
Nazi Germany.

Richard Howard to Daryl Hine   *New York City, 30 September 1970*

Dearest Daryl,

   . . . Am I right in thinking that John Hollander, who was to review
Harold Bloom's book on Yeats has withdrawn his review from you? If so,
may I "do" the book, which I have almost finished reading? . . . the Bloom
book, to which I have a very nuanced response, really calls for some handling, some manipulating even. Let me know.

   Not only the world news has been bad: on the very day of the Pulitzer
[Prize announcements; R.H.'s *Untitled Subjects* won the award for poetry]
Ted [actually Theo, a friend] was arrested on a charge of "criminal mischief"
for throwing, at five a.m. Monday, a garbage can through a plate-glass window of Tad's Steak House (really rather an aristocratic folly, I suppose), and
his behavior in court so eschewed ordinariness that he was sent to the prison
ward at the Bellevue Psychiatric Hospital. It took me a whole week to get
him out of there, my lawyer and his doctor and myself all working, pleading
and pushing hard . . . including a day, yesterday, in court when the entire
thing fell through, almost, because Bellevue refused to discharge him, saying
that his clothes had become "infested" because they had been mixed up with
other clothes, and he could not leave until they came back from the laun-
dry. This while we were waiting for him to appear at court. Well, all the
problems were met if not solved, and he is out, and with no criminal or felo-
nious record, but life, with its pressures on the inside and the outside matching and meeting as they do or will, life sometimes appears to conspire to take
the sweetness out of what should be one's little triumphs. . . .

Hollander did in fact review Harold Bloom's *Yeats* in the October issue; he found it "profound, startling, and sometimes difficult." He concluded: "Anyone studying or teaching
modern poetry will be using this book for decades. And Yeats aside, anyone interested in sophisticated treatments of the relation of art to life will need to start again with its opening
chapters."

Thomas Dillingham to Daryl Hine   *Cambridge, Mass.,*
                                               [November? 1970]

Dear Mr. Hine,

   Is it too much to hope that you paid Louis Zukofsky for the "review" of
"A" 13-21 in your November, 1970 issue, and not Aram Saroyan? I suppose
we can always be grateful to read even snippets of Zukofsky, but that

doesn't detract from my feeling that Saroyan is a pretentious and affected
fraud and the publication of his "work" by any but a vanity press a case of
editorial absent-mindedness. We are all familiar with the feeling that a work
is so good one can do no better than to quote it but in that case you could
have simply referred the reader to your back issues, or the book itself, and
used the space freed for some new poetry—or perhaps you might simply
have included some empty pages as an ample commentary on the quality
of Aram Saroyan's mind—original to the point of vacuity.

Sincerely, / Tom Dillingham

Saroyan's review consisted entirely of quotations from the several sections of the poem.

Seamus Heaney to Daryl Hine   *Berkeley, Calif., 3 February 1971*

Dear Mr Hine,

I venture to submit some poems to *Poetry* for a number of reasons. I'm
at UC, Berkeley for the year so I might as well make a bid for an American magazine of note; I've just seen that wise review [by Robert B. Shaw
of Heaney's *Door into the Dark*] you carried in the November issue. . . .

However, this is not (or not meant to be) an ingratiating letter: the poems are pretty rooted in an Irish world and I'll understand completely if
they're not your kind of work.

Good luck with *Poetry*. Your editorship is showing them all right!

Sincerely, / Seamus Heaney

Heaney first appeared in *Poetry* with "Gifts of Rain" and "May" in February 1972.

Ogden Nash to Daryl Hine   *[Baltimore, Md.], 24 February 1971*

Dear Mr. Hine,

I am happy to accept your invitation to display my trivia on November
13 or November 20. I have pretty well given up public talks or readings after 15 years on the national circuit that almost wrecked my health, but this
sounds like a most attractive occasion. I have had luncheon and dinner in
London with Betjeman, once as John, then as Sir John. He is a delightful
man, and I look forward to seeing him again. I also think the fee [$1,000]
a generous one.

I shall of course bring my wife, and ask you to make hotel reservations
for us. I suggest that you prod my memory some time in October. . . . I
don't fly, but believe there is still a train from Boston to Chicago.

Yours sincerely, / Ogden Nash

P. S. I'd like to know how long you'd like me to read.

Hine had invited Nash on 22 February; replying on 3 March, Hine told him that thirty to forty minutes would be fine, and that the Auditorium Theatre (one of the largest in Chicago) would be the venue.

Robert Pinsky to Daryl Hine   *London, England, 11 March 1971*

Dear Daryl Hine,

Sorry. An hour or two after sending my end-of-strike greetings, revisions, American postage, etc., I got your note. And though I still haven't deciphered one line, it's clear enough that you have kept the two (better) poems that I'd forgotten about and sent back the two others, which I turn out to have revised much less than I had thought.

As that Pandora's Box of auxiliary tenses indicates, the only hope is to write this second note right away.

I'm here for a year—last August until next August—and have run into Jerry [Jerome] McGann a few times. This house is one of those boxy suburban villas deplored by Victorian writers, and stands on the corner of Narcissus Road, which accords well with all of this self-regarding revision of poems, corrections of letters. The other streets around all have more normal English names like Agamemnon and Sumatra.

Thanks a lot for taking the poems.

Best, / Robert Pinsky

Many complained that Hine's tiny hand was hard to read. The street address of the house was on Pandora Road, in Camden. Pinsky had four poems printed in September.

Stephen Dobyns to Daryl Hine   *Wilmington, Del., 28 April 1971*

Dear Daryl Hine:

My first book of poems, *Concurring Beasts*, will be published by Atheneum this winter. I would be grateful if you would assign the copyrights of mine which appeared in *Poetry* over to me. . . .

I have left my job at *The Detroit News* and will be boarding a Yugoslavian freighter called Klek in a week's time bound for Tangiers. Probably I'll return in late fall. I shan't be working, however, and plan just to travel around this country for a while. Klek doesn't sound like a very seaworthy name. The 3,000 word contract sent with the ticket warns me that the company is not responsible, along with everything else, for "barantry and shafting."

Sincerely, / Stephen Dobyns

Peter Stitt to Daryl Hine   *[n.p.], 10 May 1971*

Dear Mr. Hine,

Let me apologize for this messy assortment of papers of different colors and textures. My wife has had the typewriter tied up for a long time, and will have. I was lucky to get five minutes to type the "Elegy . . ." . . .

I wrote "Peter Stitt's Poems About Poetry" when Jim [Wright] was here, April 17. He read it and said, "Peter Viereck once said to Roethke, 'I want to be a mad poet.' Roethke replied, 'Peter, you've got to be a poet first.'"

I would like some day to write a review for *Poetry*. I could send you a copy of my Wright review if you would like to see it. I did a series of seven or eight reviews of contemporary poetry for *Minnesota Review*.

I hope you like these, Thanks in any case for reading them.

Sincerely, / Peter Stitt

Stitt had his first critique in *Poetry* in 1980 and became a frequent reviewer.

Mrs. Ogden Nash to Daryl Hine   *Baltimore, Md., 13 May 1971*

Dear Mr. Hine,

I have put off answering your letter, hoping against hope, but yesterday the doctors told us definitely that there was no hope for Ogden's life. So this is the final answer to all your thoughtful inquiries. Thank you.

Yours sincerely, / Frances L. Nash

Nash died 19 May. In a draft of a condolence letter to Mrs. Nash on the same day, Hine said he still planned to put on a program to honor him "as the most accomplished writer of verse in this country, indeed if not in the language, and the one who has surely given more plea-sure to more people than any other living poet."

Erica Jong to Daryl Hine   *New York City, 30 May 1971*

Dear Mr. Hine:

Thanks for your cooking poem which has amused me greatly. In some way, I'm reminded of the opening of Fielding's *Tom Jones*. The writing/cooking metaphor has a long and venerable history and will go on, I think, because it's a genuine analogy arising from the unconscious. Eating and writing, as you knew from my book [*Fruits & Vegetables*, 1971], are never very far apart in my mind. I especially liked your "lower East Side Sioux" (rhymed with "procreative goo"), and "literary Yiddishkeit" (rhymed with appetite), and "the velvet underground" (rhymed with "sleeping around"). I'm also fond of the word "PoBiz." I have a friend who calls certain poets "poeticians."

I confess to being somewhat relieved that you're not publishing my N.Y. poets parody. Perhaps I ought to be as outspoken as other people with worse taste, but basically, I'm a coward. Perhaps the parody comes across as personalized aggression, but, in fact, I know none of the Bowery kids (as I think of them) personally. It's just their "poetry" which arouses my aggression—and their silly publicity antics. I don't know Anne Waldman at all. She might be charming, but her poetry would still infuriate me because it's a travesty of everything I care about in writing. For me, this has little to do with metrics. I think bad poets (like the Bowery crew) would still be bad poets even if they wrote in recognizable meters. What makes them bad poets is their lack of imagination and their banality, and meter is no antidote for that. (Think of Nahum Tate and Robert Southey!)

I spent my college and graduate school years writing sonnets and sestinas and even produced two full-scale mock-epics while I was at Columbia studying Augustan lit. (and loving Swift's unprintable poems and Pope's Horatian Epistles above all). When I won my first poetry prize in college it was for a poem called "TO JAMES BOSWELL IN LONDON." After all those years traveling with a rhyming dictionary and thinking of myself as an updated version of Lady Mary Wortley Montagu, I'm delighted to be free to devise my own forms and my own rhythms. But I'm no proselytizer for free verse, or for any other poetic formula. I'm convinced that every good poet finds his own way, and that any way worth following is necessarily lonely. I could never understand why poets (who are supposed to be individuals above all) insist on banding together in groups as if they were Mafiosi. It's this group-grope aspect of modern poetry which depresses me most.

I think we probably agree in hating any sort of formula for writing. The Bowery formula and the Kayak-surrealist formula end up being equally unimaginative. Berryman's dream songs were only good until they became an institution and then they deteriorated into self-parodies, I think. I don't want all poets to sound alike or to embrace the same aesthetic, and I scarcely understand why they always seem to be drawing up sides for some poetic third world war. On my way up to Buffalo and Cortland to read two weeks ago, I read Margaret Atwood, Irving Feldman and Neruda. I'd hate to think of a poetic climate in which all three of them, in all their differentness, could not exist, or could not be published. . . .

I'm glad you like my (shocking) pink book and I hope it can be reviewed before too long.

Best to you, / Erica Jong

Fruits & Vegetables was reviewed, by Alan Williamson, in February 1972.

Susan Fromberg Schaeffer to Daryl Hine   *Brooklyn, N.Y., 7 June 1971*

Dear Mr. Hine:

I just got your standard rejection slip with a note in red asking that no carbons, zeroxes [sic], photographs, or plaster of paris impressions be submitted to your magazine.

While I am flattered that, after three years, someone else noticed that zeroxed copies of poems were being submitted by me, I can only hope that your policy of originals is not one you intend to inflexibly maintain.

It is *my* policy never to send out originals, although I am aware that the policies of the writers count for nothing. Do you have any idea how many English magazines confiscate my manuscripts and fill the manila envelope with advertising for themselves? How the *New York Quarterly* has been sitting, like a great wet chicken, on poems "for further consideration" that I'll be lucky if I ever see again; how many editors have kept poems from my TOADPOEMS to "read to the children" although they're not sure they intend to publish them? How many magazines have accepted poems over two years ago which have never seen the light of day?

I am a Professor at Brooklyn College, a frenetic and very understaffed school where I do not have or want the luxury of teaching creative writing. I also have a house to run—I see no reason to sit at the typewriter like Rapunzel, weaving the same poem out of the same straw, or like some demented Penelope, stitching the same damn thing up over and over again.

I, for one, *love* my zerox machine; when something happens to it, I am absolutely bereaved.

Furthermore, and perhaps most important, your policy will most certainly not prevent duplicate submissions. I have a great many friends who are unemployed poets and when they get nervous, like nothing better than to sit around and re-type and resubmit their poems. Further, I cannot say I think they are at all wrong to do so. I do not intentionally submit duplicate copies of poems to magazines, but I am not infallible, and if I don't have a record of a poem as submitted, I will type it up again and send it out. I'm not even sure a policy of deliberate duplicate submission requires defense after the behavior of editors I've come across in the last few years. I don't know about other poets, but for me it's not an unusual occurrence to get in the mail two copies of a magazine I assume are specimen copies and find two poems of mine printed therein—two poems the magazine had never told me they accepted. Who in their right mind can keep track of things like this which occur two years or more after the actual submission takes place. I got a copy of Scopcraft with a poem in it I wrote so long ago it took me some time to realize I had written it.

I'm sure at POETRY you get a daily avalanche of poems, but that's the breaks of fame. I get over 100 papers a week to grade, and am followed around by students whose ingenious attempts to ferret me out would qualify them for the CIA. I *could* set up all kinds of onerous requirements which would make their lives harder and mine easier, but I have not up to now thought that a good plan.

I understand that it is your magazine, and you will do as you please, but I would like you to know how one disgruntled submitter and subscriber feels about little red notes about originals.

Best, / Susan Fromberg Schaeffer

Schaeffer made her first appearance in *Poetry* with two poems in the April 1972 issue.

Gary Snyder to Daryl Hine　　　　*Nevada City, Calif., 28 June 1971*

Dear Daryl Hine,

Submitting this poem.

I enjoyed your Heroicks in New American & Canadian poetry—I once got a long poem in heroic couplets accepted as a paper, in graduate school (anthropology). Nothing better to be didactic in.

Regards, / Gary Snyder

David C. Yates to Daryl Hine　　　　*New Braunfels, Tex., 2 July 1971*

Dear Mr. Hine:

Thomas Wentworth Higginson became a goat of literary history because he could not recognize brilliance when it tried to slap him in the face. Your rejection of my three poems—"The Wall: It Needs Repairing," "How Your Smile Went," and "I Love You and the Typewriter Is Still"—unfortunately, places you in his category.

Sincerely, / David C. Yates

P.S. You may ridicule the above message, but it would be wise to place this letter on permanent file—for posterity's sake.

Colonel Higginson corresponded with Emily Dickinson for several years but dissuaded her from publishing her poems. After her death, he and Dickinson's sister printed her poems—after "correcting" them heavily. Yates taught journalism at Southwest Texas State University, San Marcos, and in 1976 founded *Cedar Rock*, which he edited until his death in 1985.

W. H. Auden to Daryl Hine　　　　*New York City, 16 November 1971*

Dear Daryl:

Much looking forward to my visit [at Poetry Day]. I'm counting on you to procure me the necessary tickets for the journey, as I am very bad about that sort of thing.

Braziller are publishing Chester Kallman's new book, *The Sense of Occasion*, on December 13th. I think it is first-rate. I hope you will be able to review it for *Poetry*.

Yours ever, / Wystan

Poetry Day that year was held 3 December, a memorial tribute to Ogden Nash, the poet originally scheduled. Since "one reader will bore," Auden suggested Phyllis McGinley, John Updike, and Ira Gershwin be asked, as well. In the end, he read alone, before a smaller gathering of invited guests at the Arts Club. At the request of associate editor Michael Mesic, Auden wrote a poem especially for the occasion, "Ode to the Medieval Poets," printed in the November issue. Auden inquired again on 16 July 1972: "*When* is *Poetry* going to review Chester Kallman's *The Sense of Occasion*? It's damned good." The book had been reviewed by Mesic in the April 1972 issue.

Paul Carroll to Daryl Hine   *Chicago, 16 November 1971*

Dear Daryl,

Thanks for your note about the Guggenheim. Naturally, I understand your position and I want to wish you the best of luck with your own application for a fellowship.

I've resigned as Editor-in-chief of Big Table Books. As a result, I'm free of any editorial commitment. I'll appreciate it, Daryl, if you'd keep me in mind should you ever need someone to step in and fill in as visiting editor or, indeed, as editor, should you decide to move on to something else, as I remember you saying you were thinking about doing a year or so ago.

Best of luck with the Auden evening [Poetry Day]. I regret that I can't afford to attend this year; but thanks for sending me the invitation.

Cordially, / Paul

Geoffrey Grigson to Daryl Hine   *Swindon, Wiltshire, England,*
                                                     29 November 1971

Dear Daryl Hine,

You were going away, so I didn't reply at once. To have that prize [Union League Civic and Arts Poetry Prize from *Poetry*] was unexpected, entirely, and pleasant, entirely; and though I shouldn't say it, the poems (the second group) did read rather well when *Poetry* arrived. Which surprised me. I read my poems in print as a rule and am indifferent, and critical in a dull way, pushing aside the Olympian idea that poems (in manuscript) ought to be in store for five years before they are traveling in type.

Feeling better for these dollars, I shall send off 100 or so poems to Macmillan's next week—and I think I shall settle down to a crossbred between a book and pamphlet *About Poetry*, or *About Poems* if I cannot think of a better title.

Isn't every prize (except the one given to oneself) ridiculous? Our prize commissars have been in session awarding £5000 to a novelist so limp and damp that he disintegrates if you pick him up, and £1000 to a pamphlet of verse which is certainly of prize pretension, *Mercian Hymns*, by Geoffrey Hill, another professional prize-winner.

All the same it is a very blue and proper day here, and we've just been flown to Dijon and back for a lunch & a dinner at Saulieu in the snow; and have returned with enough *croissants* for 4 breakfasts; or five if greed is restrained. . . .

Yours, / Geoffrey Grigson

Charles Wright to Daryl Hine　　　　*Irvine, Calif., 29 November 1971*

Dear Mr Hine—

Here are 3 new poems I hope you might like. They are the newest things I have done and, perhaps for that reason, I am very fond of them. At the risk of self-indulgence, I would like to say something about them, especially the longer one. Dog Creek is about memory and its distortions—in this case the memory I have of a small government town I lived in at age 6 in North Carolina. In the 1st part I try to write the poem lyrically, song-like (if that's not too pretentious for this day and age). In the second part I try to tackle it imagistically. In the third part I begin to do it geographically and then admit it can't be done and comment to that effect. And also to a larger effect in the last stanza. Anyway that's why the parts are parts, why they have a somewhat different tack each time, and the why of the parenthetical ending and why the poem never comes to an "ending." Negatives is about sitting outside a dark house under the full moon—everything is reversals, especially the mythic allusions in the last stanza, where one remembers instead of forgets by crossing the River. Fever Toy is about compulsion, any compulsion. In this case I did have suicide in mind. Sorry to go on so long, but I like the poems so much I wanted to make sure you had a handle on them. I feel that all I have said is in the poems, but I admit that it might take some ferreting. Anyhow, I hope it's worth the trouble. That little book of mine I mentioned month ago is finally coming out in Dec. I have asked them to send you a copy. All best to you, and excuse my rambling, please—

Charles Wright

Hine accepted all three, including "Dog Creek Mainline"; in 1972 eight of Wright's poems were printed over four issues. They were reprinted in his collection, *Hard Freight* (1974).

Philip Booth to Daryl Hine   *Syracuse, N.Y., 27 January 1972*

Dear Daryl Hine,

Stevens is, as you say, "naturally inimitable." I mean no mere imitation in the poems I'm enclosing for consideration; I mean only to pay my debts quickly and openly. They are due. . . .

I never copied anybody's whole book, much less *The Auroras*. But I did, damn it, trade in three of those early, separate Knopf volumes, in order to be able to get *The Rock* section of *The Collected Poems*, when it finally came out. I ought to be shot at sunrise.

All best, / Philip Booth

In his review of Stevens's *The Palm at the End of the Mind* (edited by Holly Stevens) in December 1971, Hine recalled that when he was fifteen he copied out the entire *Auroras* in the Vancouver public library, since he could not afford the book. He remarked that "there is no other then-living poet for whom I would have gone to such trouble, wherein the tedium of transcription was perpetually transformed into delight."

Todd Gitlin to The Editors   *San Jose, Calif., 15 February 1972*

Dear Editors,

I understand that you have printed, or are about to print, a review of my anthology, CAMPFIRES OF RESISTANCE: POETRY FROM THE MOVEMENT. I would appreciate your letting me know in which issue it appears, so I may find a new mirror.

Sincerely, / Todd Gitlin

In his October 1973 review of the collection, William Pitt Root found the collection uneven (many contributors were not really poets) and said several of the poems already sounded dated. President of SDS in the early sixties, Gitlin became a noted sociologist and professor at Columbia whose studies of American culture and mass media include *The Whole World Is Watching* (1980) and *The Sixties: Years of Hope, Days of Rage* (1993).

Daryl Hine to James Atlas   *Chicago, 6 March [1972]*

Dear James,

This time, I prefer your verse. The essay, though 99% o.k., is marred by a certain sloppiness—dangling participles in page 5 . . . and one or two howlers: Henry James, who died in 1916, cannot be included with Pound and Eliot among expatriates of the 'twenties and 'thirties (note apostrophes); I have substituted Hemingway. Also, there is only one living poet in English now who can, like Bishop, be decorously referred to by his last name only, and he isn't (David) Shapiro: there are three Shapiros, alone, on the judges' list for the National Book Awards this year. . . . But those are minor matters: this essay was easier to read and copyedit than your last two efforts, though I can't suppress a wish that I'd been your freshman English teacher. . . . I am not merely disgusted by sloppy grammatical construction, but puzzled by it, as I would be by a cyclist who constantly fell off his machine: what does he think he is doing?

Your vagaries in this respect would constitute one reason that I could not consider offering you a position at *Poetry*. In my attempt to say this more delicately, I seem to have left you with a more grievous error still: it never occurred to me that you were aiming at the editorship, which isn't really in my gift. In any case, there is a queue ahead of you, including Paul Carroll, who has, unbidden, also offered his services. No, in my "kind & patient" way, I was trying to tell you that there is *no* position for you at *Poetry*. Michael [Mesic] was uniquely qualified for his role here by his relationship—all right, discipleship—to me . . . I am much better suited by his replacement, an intelligent, cultivated, mature, and attractive woman with enough literary savvy and no poetic pushiness [Rob Colby Allen, who first appeared on the masthead in April 1972]. But thank you, as we say in various letters, for thinking of *Poetry*.

I hope the above does not unduly distress you. I am learning that kindness and patience are a waste of time when they only lead to misunderstanding and impertinence. Most important: you are too well qualified in other areas for the job I might (God forbid) have to offer. . . .

Please do not answer this, but presently let me see some poems and, when you feel up to another review, let me know.

As ever, / Daryl

Atlas had his first review in *Poetry* in March 1969; he worked as an intern in the office in the summer of 1969, and Hine wrote him a recommendation for a Rhodes Scholarship in 1970, when he was a student at Harvard. Atlas's review of J. V. Cunningham, David Shapiro, Ford Madox Ford, and H. Phelps Putnam, titled "Old Wines, New Bottles, Old Bottles, New Wines," appeared in the January 1973 issue.

CHAPTER VI

The Seventies

1. The War Issue

With no end in sight and ever present in the news, the costly conflict abroad continued to trouble the national conscience and roil the body politic. Despite his promise as the 1968 Republican candidate to bring "an honorable end to the war in Vietnam," Richard Nixon as president demonstrated this pledge had no more validity than his campaign slogan that he would "Bring us together." Nixon had further claimed to have a "secret plan" for ending the war. In fact he escalated it, significantly, with secret bombings in March and then the invasion (styled an "incursion") of Cambodia in April 1970. Protests against the Cambodian operations erupted, and on May 4, the fourth day of large demonstrations at Kent State University in Ohio, four students were killed and nine wounded by inexperienced National Guard troops called in to maintain order. A widely distributed photograph of a girl kneeling beside the dead body of a student became an indelible image that further reinforced popular sentiment against the war.

Peace negotiations in Paris, which had been unsatisfactory and intermittent, finally ended in stalemate in 1971. Thus the conflict was prolonged during Nixon's first term, and during the four years an additional twenty thousand U.S. soldiers were killed. Anger and frustration over the protracted war continued to seethe at home and abroad. Matters came to a boil once more following the so-called Easter Offensive, which began 30 March 1972, when large contingents of Communist forces swept across the demilitarized zone and deep into South Vietnam, in an attempt to take Saigon and bring down the U.S.-supported government. The armies from the North were ultimately unsuccessful, but the attacks and counterattacks wrought huge damage from bombing and inflicted enormous casualties on both sides.

In a dramatic television broadcast on May 8, Nixon announced to the nation that he had ordered the blockade of shipping to North Vietnam through the mining of Haiphong harbor and all other North Vietnamese ports. A few days later, as a gesture, however futile, of disgust with the latest carnage and disapproval toward the new "strategy," Hine began to prepare a special issue of *Poetry* "Against the War," scheduled for September 1972. On May 11th the editor mailed out a form letter to two hundred poets soliciting contributions "protesting the acceleration of the undeclared Indo-Chinese War." "I am not an American citizen," he said, "but this is not an American issue. It is of global importance." In closing, he wrote: "Poetry is a matter of life and death."

With its striking cover—black type impressed on solid black paper—the issue aroused much commentary. From the large number of responses to his letter, Hine chose twenty-seven submissions for the special edition, including poems by Richard Hugo, David Ignatow, William Stafford, Philip Levine, James Schuyler, Geoffrey Hartman, Maxine Kumin, Geoffrey Grigson, Denise Levertov, Alan Dugan, Josephine Jacobsen, May Swenson, C. K. Williams, and Charles Wright. In the prose section Hine also printed messages from several poets who regretted that they had nothing to offer for the issue or had received word too late to write a piece. Babette Deutsch's note read: "Unhappily, the magnitude of what one poet calls the obscenity strikes me dumb." Michael Hamburger said he had tried to write something, but had "come to feel that protest poems as such are such a dubious or questionable medium—because they aren't even read by the people whom one wants to affect." Basil Bunting, who could always be depended upon for a cranky opinion, asserted:

> There's not a soul who cares two pence what I or any other poet thinks about the war, Nixon, Wallace, marijuana, pills, oil spills, detergent advertisements or the fog from Gary. We are experts on nothing but arrangements and patterns of vowels and consonants, and every time we shout about something else we increase the contempt the public has for us. We are entitled to the same voice as anybody else with a vote, no more. To claim more is arrogant.
>
> So I won't be contributing to your special issue.

Of the many other letters that Hine chose not to print, a few of the more pointed are presented below. Of particular interest is the response from the Australian poet James McAuley to his involuntary inclusion in the issue (which Hine published in part later, following his complaint), as well as the tart missive from a reader in Canada, Robert Beum.

Alan Dugan to Daryl Hine   *New York City, 11 May 1972*

Dear Daryl Hine:

I support your action although I'm doubtful about its political usefulness: I've spent too much time reading & writing poems against the

unconstitutional genocidal U.S. intervention in Southeast Asia to be anything else than cynical about an action such as yours. Nevertheless, I guess,
one should go on, so I send you a manuscript poem ["Stentor and Mourn-
ing"] which I recited at Goddard College on Armed Forces Day. Some of
the revisions were suggested by the students. I'm sorry I'm not being more
professional: see my first sentence above. I'm glad you're doing it.

Best regards, / Alan Dugan

Cid Corman to Daryl Hine   *Utano, Japan, 15 May 1972*

Dear Daryl,
    There is no way for me to answer you except by playing you back on
yourself and wishfully thinking you will HEAR.
    In any case, nothing to return, but I would appreciate a clear rejection—
if you find your own words unacceptable. It is always interesting to see how
far courage goes in this world—especially when it makes a point of declaring itself.

yours always, / Cid Corman

Corman's "poem" consisted of the sentences in Hine's form letter broken into "verse." Hine
scribbled on the letter: "No reply, ever." The editor did, however, write a response, which
was not mailed: "I sent out 200 letters such as the one which roused your paranoid irritation. I do not like being addressed by my first name by fools & madmen unknown to me
personally. Shove it."

James Schuyler to Daryl Hine   *Southampton, N.Y., 19 May 1972*

Dear Daryl Hine,
    Here is a poem ["May, 1972"] for you to use if you wish.
    I'm sorry it's not more positive. I mean, overtly anti-"escalation". But I
tried it that way and it didn't work.
    But if this seems merely another "war is bad" poem to you, and you
would rather not use it, I will perfectly understand.
    I applaud your undertaking.

Best regards, / James Schuyler

Richard Hugo to Daryl Hine   *Missoula, Mont., [n.d., 1972]*

Dear Daryl Hine:
    Thanks for your letter. As you know I haven't written much in the "pub-
lic arena," not that I've anything against it. Just that every time I tried the
poems came out so awful. But I've been writing somewhat differently lately
and so am sending this along. It may not be quite what you want, and

there's an even better chance it isn't good enough. After 100 years of writing, rejections means little.

Regardless of this poem ["On Hearing a New Escalation"] and its fate, I wish you and *Poetry* and your special anti-war issue all success.

Regards, / Dick Hugo

Charles Wright to Daryl Hine   *Irvine, Calif., 23 May 1972*

Dear Mr Hine—

I hope you are still going forward with the Special Issue on the War. And I hope you will like this small, but deeply-felt, poem on the subject well enough to include it. I wish I had more, but after so many years one can hardly bear to think about the subject any longer and remain even faintly rational. I'm glad you're doing an issue on the thing.

Best, / Charles Wright

Wright's "Victory Garden" was printed as the last poem in the issue.

C. K. Williams to Daryl Hine   *Philadelphia, Pa., 24 May 1972*

Dear Daryl Hine,

Unfortunately, all of the war poems I have (and there are, Lord knows, a lot of them) just came out in my new book [*I Am the Bitter Name*, published in February].

All I can offer right now are these versions from the Sanskrit, from Mayura—they're free versions; this war is what I had in mind.

I'm really glad you're doing a war issue. Everyone seems to be so used-up about it. Conned. The feeling that it can't go on, can't go on, but it does. I've been reading all spring all over the place: even the kids don't seem to want to know about it anymore.

Good luck, / Charlie

Williams's five-line translation from the Sanskrit, "Claws," was printed in the issue.

W. D. Ehrhart to Daryl Hine   *Perkasie, Pa., 2 June 1972*

Dear Mr. Hine,

It has been brought to my attention by Mr. Daniel Hoffman that you are planning to do an issue dealing with the Vietnam travesty. Acting on his suggestion and with apologies for my unsolicited contribution, I submit for your perusal this small collection of war poetry which comes out of my experiences in that war. I served there with the U.S. Marine Corps from February 1967 to March 1968 (Sergeant; Purple Heart, Navy Combat Action

Ribbon). While a few of my war poems were printed in *Winning Hearts and Minds* (1st Casualty Press, 1972), all of these enclosed are yet unpublished. I shall be pleased if you find any of them acceptable for your purposes. . . .

Sincerely yours, / William D. Ehrhart

The submission was not accepted. Besides poems, Ehrhart published several memoirs, including *Vietnam-Perkasie: A Combat Marine Memoir* and *Busted: A Vietnam Veteran in Nixon's America*; a collection of essays, *The Madness of It*; and *Ordinary Lives: Platoon 1005 and the Vietnam War*.

John F. Nims to Daryl Hine   *Lake Bluff, Ill., 1 July 1972*

Dear Daryl,

I think your first-appearance retrospective [October 1972, the 60th Anniversary] sounds great. And am pleased and flattered to be included ["Parting: 1940"]. 1940 that was? Of course, I was only six at the time, but even so . . . [sic] How can I tell people I had a poem published 32 years ago? "What have you done since?" they'll say, coldly. I really think the issue is a good idea, though, and will probably be a "collector's item." Should be interesting for what it shows about changing tastes, etc.

I'm sorry I didn't write about your invitation to offer something for the Indo-China War issue. Another very good idea. I didn't answer, and probably can't have a submission in time, because I'm trapped in my own microcosm, or mini-cosm. I think I told you I'm doing a sort of introduction to poetry [*Western Wind*], which was due over a year ago, and then due in Jan., and then in March, and then promised for May—but still not finished. . . . I should finish a first version in two or three weeks, and if the fire from heaven should strike, and a great voice bid me take quill in hand and smite the oppressor—well, I'll let you know. . . .

Did Rutgers ever send you a copy of *Sappho to Valéry*? I mean *you* personally, not just a review copy (because you told me you got that). I still have a few, and would be glad to send you one, if you want a large heavy book. I'm afraid it's been a disaster; expect Rutgers to declare bankruptcy any day now. The perfect example of The Book Nobody Wants. And I can see why—wouldn't buy it myself. A nice book to write, but I'd never want to read it. . . .

All the best, / John

May Swenson to Daryl Hine   *Sea Cliff, N.Y., 6 July 1972*

Dear Daryl:

I'm sorry my reply is so late, but thanks for your May 11th letter inviting poems for your anti-war issue.

The enclosed ["July 4th"] just got written, and while it's about watching fireworks on Independence Day it's also about America's imperialist greed, our blind appetite for power, our delight in violence.

I think your idea for a special issue is great.

Best, / May

James McAuley to Daryl Hine   *The University of Tasmania,*
                                       Hobart, Tasmania, Australia,
                                       13 September 1972

Dear Mr Hine,

I was somewhat disconcerted to find that my poem 'Winter Drive' ended up in an issue called 'Poetry Against the War.' I am not in the least 'against the war' in any relevant sense; and the dismay the poem expresses is *partly* caused by the culturally, socially and politically irrational and destructive activities of anti-war energumens [people possessed by evil spirits] in recent years.

I don't want to embarrass you by demanding you publish the above paragraph; but I wish you'd told me that you were putting my poem to a political use.

Yours sincerely, / James McAuley

The letter was printed, without the second paragraph, in the December 1972 issue.

Philip Levine to Daryl Hine   *[Fresno, Calif.], 2 October 1972*

Dear Daryl,

Thank you so much for your note. And of course for the award [the Frank O'Hara Prize], which I accept with real pride. And for the money, which is nice because it's time, as you know. Of all the *Poetry* awards it's the best to me because O'Hara was such a fine poet at his best.

I thought the War issue was fine. Some of those letters were really something: "Let's not dirty the fine old name of *poesy* with all this life & death stuff . . ." Beautiful Richard Hugo poem ["On Hearing a New Escalation"].

Thanks again, yours, / Phil

Levine mocks a remark from Eleanor Ross Taylor printed in the Correspondence section, in which she states that "any 'poem' on the subject of de-escalation in Vietnam or elsewhere descends to journalism from the lofty tone I would wish for *Poetry* magazine." He may also be alluding to Marya Zaturenska Gregory's comment: "Poetry can be a matter of life and death. . . . real poetry is hard to write and is rarely written to order. Let's leave platform verse to Yevtuchenko."

Robert Beum to Daryl Hine   *Charlottetown, P.E.I., Canada,*
                                                      13 October 1972

Dear Mr. Hine:

   The September issue of *Poetry* contains exactly one readable original poem: James McAuley's "Winter Drive." The rest of the original poems are just what one would expect from so naive an enterprise as the soliciting of occasional poems on the subject of the Indo-China War: the clichés of liberal and leftist anti-war posturings and hysterias. Will the Left never learn that humanitarian feelings, no matter how fervent, just can't be made to do the work of logic and prudence?

   Some readers of *Poetry* who pride themselves on "awareness" may not be aware of certain paradoxes inherent in this particular manifestation of humanitarian folly. One of them is that in all this alluvium of general righteousness a particular right has been washed away: the good poem by McAuley, which I was privileged to read before it was published in *Poetry*, has been placed in a context which makes it seem like one more contribution to the anti-war spate. The effect is to mislead readers and distort McAuley's intention: the poem becomes a narrower and more ephemeral thing than it is. The Australian master's subject is the (more and more) fallen world, not Indo-China 1972. By implication, also, the inclusion of the poem in the September issue creates the impression that McAuley is aligned sociopolitically with the crowd of shrill "humanitarians" *à gauche*. The truth is that McAuley has the courage of independence and has written devastating critiques of such folks. In the name of peace and justice, *Poetry* has been a little unjust and declared war against a bit of truth.

   Other ironies abound. The people who write and approve such strident moralizings as fill the September *Poetry* are very often the same people who object (not always pacifically) to poets like Herbert, Bridges, and Patmore— and McAuley! —on the ground of "didacticism." And the paradox deepens: characteristically, these voluble anti-war militants are philosophical relativists. Truth, for them, is epiphenomenal and subjective; yet the forces of Saigon and Washington are absolutely corrupt and are to be pursued with absolute wrath. For that matter, history may well see a curiosity in the ostentatious self-righteousness of these people who in verifiable fact supported the overthrow of [South Vietnam President Ngo Dinh] Diem and other actions (under a Democratic administration in Washington, by the way) that committed us to continuing involvement in Indo-China.

   To some extent, singling out the war plays up to fashion and on that account alone is a morally dubious exercise. Worse, singling it out seems to tell us what we never expected to hear from the muses: that physical and political security, the mere preservation of life and a semblance of order, is a lofty, or even the highest, good. In the broadest sense, poetry—which includes truth and innocence—is what makes life worth living; and is worth dying for. Aeschylus and Shakespeare believed that, and Rilke and Pasternak and Solzhenitsyn have believed it.

Suffering, in any case, goes on, terrible suffering: families and hearts and careers are riven in (and by) affluent and technological peace as well as in war; and the long Pax Romana meant long slavery and separation for millions. And in a society as cold and spoiled and fragmented as ours, it seems delusive and diversionary to play up the war so much. In the modern context, can peace—or rather "peace"—be so promising?

No man of good will delights in this war or in the human suffering of any war. But political peace has never been with us for very long and in any case is less dependable than true personal peace—without which political peace is certain to be both fraudulent and temporary. The peace we need to rediscover and reaffirm isn't the peace of the United Nations or the protest mobs, but the peace illuminated for us by Confucius, Christ, and the Buddha. Through its humbling and refining discipline of careful perception and craftsmanship, and through its achievement of imaginative unity and harmonized statement and aesthetic experience, poetry—genuine poetry—has something to contribute here. In fact, real poetic vision is the opposite of, and a chief bulwark against, that politicization of all experience which has been our ruin in this century. I, for one, regret in my heart, not just in my politics, *Poetry*'s descent from poetic to political vision.

I hope you will print this letter if only for the sake of my dear friend James McAuley, who may well be too much of a gentle man to protest *Poetry*'s disservice to him.

Sincerely, / Robert Beum

Beum's letter was not printed. When Diem and his regime became increasingly repressive, many Buddhist monks demonstrated. In June 1963 one monk set himself on fire in protest and burned to death; six others later followed his example. Hundreds of monks were then arrested and several were killed in raids on pagodas. After students demonstrated at Saigon University in August, some four thousand were jailed and the school was closed. The Kennedy administration did not approve of these actions and permitted a military coup in November, during which Diem and Ngo Dinh Nhu, his brother and chief adviser, were assassinated. General Duong Van Minh then took over the South Vietnamese government.

Anne Winters to Daryl Hine   *Charlottesville, Va., 29 October 1972*

Dear Daryl,

I'm sending you my three most recent efforts, with hopes that you may like them for *Poetry*. . . .

I want to say that I liked the issue against the war. It gave me a surprising sense of—easement of some kind, to see it in its black cover & even just hold it. I'm working for [anti-war presidential candidate Senator George] McGovern, but can't say I get any hopeful feelings from *that*—it's rather discouraging, telephone voting surveys in this remote county, as you can imagine. All our best, and we hope things are going well with you.

Anne

Associate editor Rob Allen sent McGovern a copy of the special issue.

2. Peace, Political Backlash, and Poetic Turf Wars

On 7 November 1972, Richard Nixon won reelection by one of the largest landslides in American history: 60.7 percent of the popular vote to George McGovern's 38 percent. Nixon carried forty-nine states while McGovern won only Massachusetts and the District of Columbia. Nixon was sworn in for his second term on 20 January 1973. (In keeping with the new "imperial presidency," the balls and other celebrations for the inauguration were the most expensive to date, costing some $4 million.) Three days later Nixon signed a cease-fire agreement and declared "peace with honor" in Vietnam.

Less than nine months later, on 10 October 1973, Spiro Agnew, his bombastic, opposition-baiting vice president, was forced to resign because of charges of graft and corruption (mainly taking kickbacks from contractors) going back to his days as a Baltimore official and governor of Maryland. He was accused of receiving illegal payments even while vice president—and accepting cash-filled envelopes in the basement of the White House. (Agnew eventually pleaded no contest to charges of tax fraud, for not reporting the bribes as income to the IRS; he was fined $10,000 and given three years' probation.) He was replaced by Gerald R. Ford, who became president when Nixon resigned on 9 August 1974, the first president ever to do so. He had little choice, after the House recommended articles of impeachment on charges of corruption, abuse of power, and obstruction of justice in the wake of the Watergate scandal.

After ten years of turmoil, peace or at least a cessation of hostilities in Southeast Asia had finally arrived; in the United States, relative tranquility returned. But the corrosive effects on the national psyche of the dispiriting decade were not easily repaired, given the extent of the damage: the quagmire of the seemingly unstoppable war and the polarizing protests and violent demonstrations it provoked; profound social unrest over inequality culminating in race riots in well over a hundred cities; the obstinate, unpopular foreign policy of two Democratic administrations and the attempted subversion of state agencies and gross criminality of the Republican regime that followed. In the face of the debacle of Vietnam, the image of the much-vaunted Pentagon leadership was tarnished, the idea of U.S. military prowess and invincibility no longer tenable. Old notions of Authority in general were seriously, perhaps permanently, undermined, while faith in Tradition and civic institutions was called into question and severely eroded.

Set in motion amid this national disillusionment were the several social revolutions and liberation movements that brought about the transformations that would characterize the following decades' freer, more fluid, if far more fragmented, American culture. That volatility and diversity became abundantly evident in contemporary poetry, at least superficially. By the late sixties the long-held authority of the New Criticism in the study and practice of poetry, and literature generally, was crumbling, angrily rejected or simply ignored.

Ironically, while the old academic strictures on form and technique were loosened, more and more poets of the younger generation were finding permanent homes within the confines of the Academy—not primarily as scholars and teachers of literature, however, but as instructors in creative writing. Poets and fiction writers had previously been tolerated in English departments if they held advanced degrees in literature and were scholars qualified to conduct standard courses as well as workshops; now the workshops and classes in creative writing were becoming major attractions among departmental offerings. "Certified" with M.F.A.'s, but frequently less well educated, this new generation of poet-professors championed a range of styles and voices that would not have been admitted into the curriculum before the seventies.

Paradoxically, some of these "liberated" author-instructors became far more intolerant, and certainly ruder, than the supposedly oppressive, authoritarian, "patriarchic" professors of the old school whom they were gradually replacing. The sharp contrasts between their supposedly open-minded philosophy and free-form approach to composition and their increasingly doctrinaire aesthetics and exclusionary attitudes could be striking, though the would-be arbiters seemed oblivious to their self-contradictions. The new autocrats of the seminar table seemed to want to control all poetic territory, as if worried they might lose "market share" to writers who chose to write in traditional modes or even in individual styles that differed from their own, which they disparaged.

Because it persisted in presenting all types of verse, conventional as well as experimental, *Poetry* came in for a good deal of opprobrium in the seventies from anti-formalists and others who believed that literary tradition was constricting and the rich stores of *topoi* and techniques conveyed in the poetic heritage were irrelevant to or somehow impinged on their own ideas and practice. Some of the most extreme and personal attacks on the magazine and its current editor appeared in the tabloid *American Poetry Review.* In a boldly stated but poorly argued article in the September/October 1973 issue, Robert Bly directed his scorn mainly at academic poetry, the old New Criticism, and Harold Bloom's theory of *The Anxiety of Influence.* But toward the end of his screed, Bly appended a nasty barb about Daryl Hine, throwing in a dig at Hine's associate editor (and former student) Michael Mesic to boot. In an amazing slam he claimed: "Hine has managed to Nixonize *Poetry* magazine, to make it irrelevant, narrow, and sullen." How Hine had "Nixonized" it—or even what that term could possibly mean when applied to poetry—Bly did not explain. While recognizing the illustrious past—when the magazine "published all schools, plus the loners, letting them mingle, giving them all respect"—and singling out Rago's tenure for special praise, Bly asserted further: "Hine, who has a rudimentary academic sensibility, and is a sort of architectural student of the infantile, has filled it with third rate iambic regressives, masquerading as grown-ups. . . . Having failed to educate himself away from his prejudices . . . he cannot see the non-traditional poets clearly either, and provides samples of 'free verse,' with no sense of its quality."

With similar disdain, in a column in the next issue of *APR* (November/December 1973) aptly titled "Knock Knock," Donald Hall opined: "The magazine has become the temple of mediocrity." Like Bly, Hall lauded its past decades, when "*Poetry* was the ecumenical meeting-place of American poets, where new poets met old ones, and where you felt like putting in regular appearances, just to show people you were still around." After listing a number of greats who once graced the magazine's pages, Hall concluded: "Now a flossied-up ghost of *Poetry* walks once a month, rarely printing even one good poem, or one sharp piece of criticism. A good young editor could turn things around in a hurry."

Donald Hall, a frequent contributor to and sometime critic of *Poetry*, in the sixties.

Hall's own last appearance in *Poetry* had been in November 1968. So perhaps in the intervening years he had not read the magazine very carefully and thus missed several "good poems" that Hine had printed since, including large groups by Ammons, Ashbery, and Atwood; Auden's "Ode to the Medieval Poets"; several by *APR*'s own editor, Stephen Berg, as well as Robert Bly; a score by Marvin Bell and a dozen each by Turner Cassity and Stephen Dobyns; clusters by James Dickey and Louise Glück. Further, Thom Gunn, Andrei Codrescu, Geoffrey Grigson, Marilyn Hacker, Robert Hass, Seamus Heaney, Anthony Hecht, William Heyen, Daniel Hoffman, John Hollander, and Richard Howard contributed often to the mix during these years.

Poetry also printed new work by Richard Hugo, Josephine Jacobsen, Mark Jarman, Elizabeth Jennings, Erica Jong, Donald Justice, Shirley Kauffman, Kenneth Koch, Maxine Kumin, Stanley Kunitz, and Greg Kuzma. Likewise well represented were Levertov and Levine; (Jay) MacPherson, Matthews, McAuley, McMichael, and (Sandra) McPherson, as well as Meredith, Merrill, and Merwin; Nemerov and Nims; O'Hara and Orlen; Pinsky and Plath; Raab, Reeve, Rexroth, and Rutsala. Among the many S's, one could find Sandy, Sarton, Schmidt, Schuyler, Seidman, Shapiro (David and Karl), Shelton, Shore, Silkin, Simic, Spacks, Spivack, Stafford, Stanton, Steele, Strand, Swenson. Completing the catalogue were Allen Tate, James Tate, D. M. Thomas, Charles Tomlinson, Mona Van Duyn, David Wagoner, Diane Wakoski, C. K. Williams, Anne Winters, Charles Wright, and Louis Zukofsky.

In sum, given the range of accomplished authors and the diversity of styles their contributions to *Poetry* represent, it is difficult to see, for all the grousing of Bly and Hall, what grievous errors or omissions Hine made in his selections. Strong editors are not simply pollsters who measure popularity ratings before filling their journals; rather, they are expected to exercise judgment and make choices based on knowledge, taste, and discernment developed by long study and comparison. *Poetry* in this period might better have been praised for exhibiting courage for continuing, despite the disparagement of partisans, to defend artists of solid accomplishment, and publishing works based on criteria that transcended mere personality, laudable sentiments, or fashions of the moment.

In any case, in the months following these attacks, Hine presented Ashbery's "Self-Portrait in a Convex Mirror," one of the signal achievements of the decade (and the title poem of a collection that eventually won the Pulitzer Prize, National Book Award, and National Book Critics Award in 1976), Hollander's "Reflections on Espionage," large portions of Pinsky's "Essay on Psychiatrists" and Koch's "The Art of Love," and Charles Wright's "Skins," as well as a special issue, edited by Daniel Weissbort (July 1974), devoted to dissident Russian poets, who had to distribute their work secretly, through the *samizdat* system, since it was virtually impossible for them to publish in their own country under the *diktats* of the Soviet commissars and compliant censors in the Writers' Union.

3. Correspondence 1972–1975

Several poets wrote supporting Hine's editorial decisions and expressing pungent disapproval of the attacks by Bly and Hall; unfortunately, most of their letters are too fiercely outspoken to allow publication. Many other writers conveyed objections pointedly, but more politely, to the more typical matters of magazine content and procedure that displeased them. Particularly amusing are the ironic letters from an increasingly frustrated Susan Fromberg Schaeffer protesting *Poetry*'s long-held policy of demanding original typescripts for submissions.

Older correspondents send reminiscences of Harriet Monroe while several promising young writers—including J. D. McClatchy, Edmund White, and Dana Gioia—write to introduce themselves. Charles Wright goes into detail about the structure of "Skins." John Ashbery discusses a reprint of "Self-Portrait in a Convex Mirror," first published in *Poetry* in August 1974. And Hine and the critic William H. Pritchard disagree about and gingerly debate the merits of Ashbery's work.

Susan Fromberg Schaeffer to Daryl Hine   *Brooklyn, N.Y.,*
                                                             1 November 1972

Dear Daryl Hine,

Originals! Originals! What goes on there—Braille freaks, running their fingers over the typed indentations in the paper? I give up. Do you think you could please stagger through the carbon [drawing of prostrate stick figure] of *The Red White and Blue Poems: In Commemoration of the Improbable Cease Fire*? Please? *I* am a carbon copy of my former self. A typewriter around one's neck is no laughing matter.

                                   Best, / Susan Fromberg Schaeffer

Gervaise Guth to the Editors   *Merced High School, Merced, Calif.,*
                                                       22 November 1972

Gentlemen:

Merced High School Library has been a subscriber to *Poetry* for many years. Teachers and librarians in secondary schools have always considered it to be a suitable publication for adolescent and young adult reading.

However, your October 1972 issue was not fit for student reading because of one poem ["Bawdry Embraced"] by Ted Hughes on pages 12-14. Inclusion of such poems in an otherwise acceptable collection of twentieth century poetry destroys the usefulness of the entire periodical.

If you want to publish "dirty" poetry, why not do so in a separate issue? Sincerely yours,

(Mrs.) Gervaise Guth
Librarian

All the poems in the special issue, celebrating the sixtieth anniversary, represented the contributors' first appearances in the magazine; Hughes's facetious sixty-eight-line poem contains several vernacular terms for body parts and functions; it was first printed in August 1956.

Susan Fromberg Schaeffer to Daryl Hine　　　　　*Brooklyn, N.Y.,*
18 January 1973

Dear Daryl Hine,

Here are some more magnificently typed original legible originals with indentations in the pages you can feel from the other side. It *is* always nice to know you're appreciated.

I did send you a poem called *The First Madam*, I hope? . . .

We just went to Vermont to look at some snow. It is obsolete in New York.

Best, / Susan Fromberg Schaeffer

John F. Nims to Daryl Hine　　　　　*Lake Bluff, Ill., 1 February 1973*

Dear Daryl:

I don't think I ever told you that I'm very pleased that POETRY can use some of the short poem-type creations. Very pleased. POETRY still seems to me about the best place to "show" a poem, as the late editor liked to say. Which once moved yrs. trooly to quill:

> This poet doesn't print his art, he "shows" 'er.
> Somebody tell him quick, it's indecent exposure.

My very first sentence, with its unintended ambiguity, suggests a way to deal with books one doesn't want to read:

"Dear Miss Emma Lynn Tweeter: I don't think I ever told you what a real delight your *Wingbeats in the Gloaming* was to me! Sincerely yrs., etc." . . .

That intro. to poetry I've been working on (*Western Wind: An Introduction to Poetry*) now exists in a MS. of 1600 pages. It has to be cut to something like 480 in the next couple of months. Half of my favorite poems have to be thrown out, or laid gently aside, and my deathless expository prose butchered. It's like saying to a 160-pound man, "You ought to slim down a little—say to about 48 pounds."

Best wishes, / John

[P.S.] For whatever it means: *Sappho to Valéry* sold nine (9) copies during a 6-month period last year. Enormous royalties!

Marya Zaturenska to Daryl Hine   Palisades, N.Y.,
                                                        21 February 1973

Dear Mr. Hine:

I have at last plucked up courage to send you some new poems. I do so hope that some of them will interest you. I should of course prefer a group, for "Poetry" means a lot to me, I've contributed to it, since I was a girl in my teens.

Do you know that someone in England, from the University of Leeds, is doing a biography of Harriet Monroe, really a wonderful project if done well. She was a remarkable person and when young and beautiful was admired by both Whistler & Henry James! But she told us that she found James stuffy (very middle western that), but adored Whistler. Remember that the latter's father had some connection with Fort Dearborn before it became Chicago. And the architect of the first skyscraper was her brother-in-law [John Wellborn Root]. And she guided Oscar Wilde around Chicago when he visited it & her anecdotes about it were very amusing, etc etc.

I do so wish you had reviewed Horace Gregory's autobiography [*The House on Jefferson Street*, 1971], it had so much to say about *Poetry* & Harriet. . . . I've started a new collection of my poems for a small book—some of the poems I've sent you will appear in it, if I can ever complete it.

Sincerely, / Marya Z. Gregory

A Russian immigrant, Marya Zaturenska first appeared in *Poetry* in April 1920 at age seventeen; Monroe befriended her, wrote letters of recommendation, and gave her a summer job in the office. It is not clear what biographer she is referring to. But Daniel J. Cahill's *Harriet Monroe* (Twayne Publishers) appeared in 1973; Cahill took his Ph.D. at Iowa. D.H. accepted four poems, printed in September 1973, her last work in *Poetry*; she died in 1982. *The Diaries of Marya Zaturenska, 1938–1944* and her *New Selected Poems* were both issued in 2001.

Turner Cassity to Daryl Hine   Atlanta, Ga., *24 February 1973*

Dear Mr. Hine,

I am glad to report that my long-deferred collection, still entitled *Steeplejacks in Babel*, will appear in May or June of this year from David R. Godine, Publishers, of Boston. They also want to bring out *Scenes from Alexan-*

der Raymond as a chap-book, whatever that may be. I suppose it is invidious to bite the hand that feeds one, but the fact is, the hand is not going to
feed one: they do beautiful printing and don't know beans about selling
books. Well, it's their money, not mine. . . .

Returning from a Canadian vacation in July, I stopped off in Gardiner,
Maine, E. A. Robinson's home town. It suggests now, and may have suggested then, H. P. Lovecraft more than E.A.R., but makes it immediately
apparent why the Robinson brothers took to drink. Still, for a Southerner
it was rather comforting. It reminded one there was a time, decades before
William Faulkner, when it was New England that had all the nuts locked
away in upstairs rooms.

Meanwhile, a prosperous New Year to you and to *Poetry*.

Best regards, / Turner Cassity

Edmund White to Daryl Hine   *New York City, 27 August 1973*

Dear Mr. Hine:

I feel as though I know you; I've heard Jimmy Merrill, Howard Moss and
David Kalstone speak of you so often.

I'm sending you a review I did ages ago of Howard Moss's *Selected Poems*. I did the review for the Sunday NY *Times*, but they never printed it—
first because they thought it too enthusiastic, then later, after Howard won
the NBA and they'd decided enthusiasm was in order, because it was too
late. Naturally, it is even later now, but Howard asked me to send it to you
anyway, just in case you might find room for it. You might have another
objection—I'm not a poet or a poetry critic but rather a novelist; I don't
know your policy on that score.

In any event, thanks for looking this over. I look forward to meeting you
(incidentally, I was thrilled to hear you'd just taken two poems written by
a friend of mine, Alfred Corn).

Sincerely, / Edmund White

Kalstone had been assigned the Moss review two years earlier; though he also found it too
"enthusiastic," Hine accepted White's three-and-one-half-page article ("Midas' Touch"), and
it was printed in the March 1974 issue. White begins: "Even his first published poems were
already so technically adept that an early reader might have wondered where such diamonds
could go."

Ed Orr to Daryl Hine   *Peoria, Ill., 10 November 1973*

Dear Daryl Hine:

In the September/October '73 issue of The *American Poetry Review*,
Robert Bly has made a villainous attack on *Poetry*, *you* and all so represented

["On the New New Critics"]. You have "managed to Nixonize *Poetry*," "made it irrelevant, narrow, and sullen." You have "a rudimentary academic sensibility," are "a sort of architectural student of the infantile," fill your magazine with "third rate iambic regressives."

On behalf of yourself, *Poetry* and your writers (those published in *Poetry*), I think you should answer this misinformed, bigoted, and sophomoric attack. Don't underestimate his influence, which is considerable.

Yours with all due respect, / Ed Orr

Daryl Hine to Ed Orr   Chicago, [mid-November 1973]

Dear Mr. Orr:

Thank you for your concern on the behalf of *Poetry* over Robert Bly's latest bit of savagery. I see no way in which one can reply with dignity to this sort of criticism, and feel in any case that being attacked by the mad dog of modern verse places us, inevitably, in the best company. But it is grand to hear from those, like yourself, who don't agree with these rabid ravings.

Sincerely yours, / Daryl Hine

Philip Levine to Daryl Hine   Fresno, Calif., 28 November 1973

Dear Daryl,

I'd appreciate it very much if you'd consider these poems for publication in *Poetry*. They are the work of a young Chicano poet who lives & works here in Fresno & who has come to me recently for advice. I think he has an incredible talent and a powerful & enduring need to write. The stuff pours from him. I believe he's going to be one hell of a poet.

Yours, / Phil Levine

Levine enclosed work by Gary Soto. Hine accepted part of "The Elements of San Joaquin" (May 1974), which became the title poem of Soto's first book (1977), and *Poetry* printed him frequently thereafter.

J. D. McClatchy to Daryl Hine   [New Haven, Conn.], 29 January 1974

Dear Daryl Hine:

Last month, as I was about to leave for the MLA (like too many others, to find a job), my friend Jimmy Merrill gave me your phone number and suggested we get together. Aside from a shy, natural reluctance to intrude, I was so stunned by the Palmer House grotesqueries that I never did call.

Jimmy wanted me to show you a recent poem of mine about therapy called "The Pleasures of Ruins" [October 1974] which he liked enormously and thought you would too. I don't know about that, but I thought I may as well send it along to you. And since therapy is supposed to teach us to gather our small strengths together, I'm also enclosing a few other pieces, each rather different from the other. A can of worms, but of course I hope you'll like them all.

I hope too that the next time I'm in Chicago I won't be surrounded by 9,000 prima donnish types which this time forced me to stay in my room with a bottle of Johnnie Walker and 7 cheap thrillers, and that I'll have the chance to meet you then. Till then, all best wishes. . . .

J. D. McClatchy

Geoffrey Grigson to Daryl Hine   *Swindon, Wiltshire, England,*
17 February 1974

Dear Daryl Hine,

My wife says you said, Why not send some more poems in the spring? I am sure you said nothing of the kind. But I might as well send this batch for your consideration since poems accumulate, and we are both emerging from the winter coma of work, i.e. books. The poem I like best is *Angles and Circles* [December 1974].

I expect there was more said in America than England about Wystan Auden's death. We had dinner with him not so very long before, & we weren't surprised altogether. My generation is getting thin. No MacNeice, no Auden, no Cameron—and no successors!

Yours, / Geoffrey Grigson

Auden considered his Oxford classmate Norman Cameron (1905–1953) the best poet of their generation. Cameron was also a close friend of Robert Graves and Dylan Thomas. His *Collected Poems* were edited by L. Warren Hope, who also published a biography. In his last days Auden was invited back to Oxford and lived in a cottage at his old college, Christ Church. He died, of heart failure, in Vienna on 29 September 1973, and is buried in Kirchstetten, Austria, his longtime summer residence. Chester Kallman died in Athens two years later.

Charles Wright to Daryl Hine   *Irvine, Calif., 11 March 1974*

Dear Mr Hine—

I hope you might like, and use, the enclosed poem. It ["Skins," December 1974] is my most ambitious thing to date, I think. I know it is rather

long, but not so long as it looks. Which is to say that it obviously doesn't
have to take 20 pages—they can just as easily go one after the other, however you could fit them in. As for the form of the thing, it is constructed
like a ladder: 10 up and 10 back down, the movement being from Point A
to Point A. At the risk of over-explanation, a notation for each section
would go as follows: 1, Situation; 2, Gran Schema; 3, Existentialism; 4, Mor-
tality of universe; 5, Religion(s); 6, Metamorphosis; 7-10, 4 elements; 11-14,
Primitive magic, Necromancy, Witchcraft, and the retreat from same; 15 is
a recitative; 16-19 are the 4 elements again and 20 is back to the situation.
Anyhow, I hope you like it enough to find room for it in the magazine, and
all best wishes, as always—

Charles Wright

James Atlas to Daryl Hine   *Concord, Mass., 24 April [1974]*

Dear Daryl:

It was very good of you to write as you did; I appreciated your concil-
iatory tone, which was perhaps more than I deserved. I have not felt easy,
over the last year, about the suspension of our friendship. I trust you will
look on my outbursts as those of a young man.

The review of [Richard Howard's] *Preferences* was originally written for
The New Republic, which accounts for the rather journalistic pose. I found
that writing for such journals, *The Nation* and *The New Republic*, trained me
to compose in a more supple, less clotted style; and yet the editor there was
not in sympathy with my views in this case. As I think back over the reviews I wrote for *Poetry*, I realize that your criticisms were, for the most
part, just; it is only recently, writing full-time, that I have come to possess a
more lucid style. I would like to write for you again, and in the "higher"
style your pages allow.

I have been extremely busy these last few months, and I have several
other essays promised; moreover, I have a contract now with Farrar, Straus
& Giroux to write the biography of Delmore Schwartz. However, if you
would consent to a leisurely pace, I would be glad to take on some books.
Since I will be away in June, it wouldn't be until July (or even later) that I
could promise a review. If this is all right with you, could you send me a
list of books from which to choose?

I will be in Chicago toward the end of June, and it would be good to
see you then, if you're in town.

Best wishes, / James

Atlas's review was printed in October 1974. He also did a group review in 1975 and reviewed
Auden's *Thank You, Fog: Last Poems* in June 1975.

John Ashbery to Daryl Hine   *New York City, 18 June 1974*

Dear Daryl,

Art in America would like to reprint my Selbstbildnis poem ["Self-Portrait in a Convex Mirror"] in their January issue. Is this all right? I thought I should check with you before they proceed further as they are planning to get a color reproduction of the Parmigianino to go with it. (A similar thing happened when my poem "Fragment" was reprinted with illustrations in *Harper's Bazaar* after it had appeared in *Poetry*.) Incidentally it was a great pleasure to see it set up in type and I am eagerly looking forward to seeing it in the magazine [August 1974].

John Ashbery at the time of the first publication of "Self-Portrait in a Convex Mirror" in *Poetry* in 1974.

Another thing: on the updated autobiographical fiche I returned to you I think I said I would be teaching English at Brooklyn College starting in September; would you kindly amend this to teaching "in the creative writing program" (without inverted commas, though)? This because I would like to reveal my presence there to potential students. Thanks, and my best to you.

Sincerely, / John

Francesco Parmigianino's *Self-Portrait in a Convex-Mirror* (c. 1524) hangs in the Kunsthistorisches Museum, Vienna. Concerning the *Harper's* mix-up, see Ashbery's letter to Rago of 24 October 1968, above.

Howard Nemerov to Daryl Hine   *St. Louis, Mo., 9 October 1974*

Dear Daryl,

Good to hear all goes well with you too. Of course it delights me that you should respond so quickly and so favorably. So here are three more which Howard [Moss, poetry editor at *The New Yorker*] has not only turned down but—in collusion w the Post Office—lost (though of course I'd prefer to think he was jealous), and I'll keep sending you the

new book an ear and a finger at a time, like a kidnap victim, till you cry
Hold, Enough. . . .

I suppose I should suggest formally that you oughtn't to burden yourself
with more of the forty-odd pieces coming your way than you can comfort-
ably handle in a year, which is about when I'd expect Chicago to have them
out in book form. In fact, if you are acquainted with Allen Fitchen at the Press,
you might find it easier all 'round to look at his copy and just let me know
which if any poems you'd especially like; save a lot of postage and fiddle.

Meant to say last time that you might please renew my subscription if it's
run out. At least, I don't seem to have seen the magazine in rather a time.

Best, as always, / Howard

The New Yorker had right of first refusal for Nemerov's work. In December, Hine presented
a glowing report on his book to the University of Chicago Press as an outside reviewer, chosen by Fitchen, a senior editor.

John C. Hansen to the Editor   *Paullina, Ia., [1975]*

To the editor, Poetry:

I am 82. It has been a long time since I last wrote to the editor of Poetry. More than sixty years.

At that time Harriet Monroe was the editor. I had been a subscriber for
three years and I had written in to cancel my subscription. I said that I was
a farm boy living in a backward and forgotten corner of NW Iowa. That I
was trying to broaden myself. I had studied the verse in each issue in search
of that beauty of expression and depth of thought that I felt must be hidden in each verse. Else why were they published. But I decided that with
the exception of two numbers they were all pitched at a level above my
limited intelligence. . . .

Monroe's Answer[:]

"I hate to lose you as a subscriber. They are all too few and hard to come
by. I want to say this, Mr. Hansen, you are expecting too much from my little magazine. One masterpiece a year would be a wonderful record."

Then she asked for a list of my favorite poets both ancient and modern.
I listed among others Swinburne and Arnold, Masefield and E. E Cummings. At this she gave me up in despair[:] "Swinburne to Arnold, Masefield to Cummings. How could anyone hope to please a taste that ran to
such extremes."

I have long owed this warm and talented editor an apology. Harriet—
wherever you are, I'm sorry.

Yes I write verse (see sample) but not the kind you dare publish.

John C. Hansen

Linda Pastan to Daryl Hine   *Potomac, Md., [March 1975]*

Dear Mr. Hine,

I have been sending a group of poems to *Poetry* once a year since I was so advised by J.V. Cunningham, back in graduate school. And I am not being sarcastic when I say that I was encouraged, last month, to receive my first personal word from *Poetry* . . . a "sorry" written in pencil. (Well, only a little sarcastic . . .)

Maybe you will find something here you like enough to publish. Maybe twice a year is better than once.

Many thanks, / Linda Pastan

Pastan first appeared in *Poetry* with two poems in January 1977. She eventually published over 80 poems in the magazine by the time she was awarded the Ruth Lilly Prize in 2003.

William Pritchard to Daryl Hine   *Amherst, Mass., 14 May 1975*

Dear Daryl Hine,

Yes, do send along the Ashbery since by itself I wouldn't have made much of the Vermont notebook business. I think (incidentally) that Ashbery has been mainly puffed rather than criticized, and I am far from being Harold Bloomianly [sic] convinced that he is the legitimate successor to Emerson etc. I take him a good deal less seriously. So if you can accept what will probably be some carping, do sent it along. All the other books arrived, including "Scars Make Your Body More Interesting" (was it?) which of course turns out to be prose-poetry.

Best wishes, / Bill Pritchard

Pritchard gave *Self-Portrait with a Convex Mirror* a very negative review; see Hine letter of 25 July. The following year the book won the National Book Award, the National Book Critics Circle Award, and the Pulitzer Prize.

Howard Nemerov to Daryl Hine   *St. Louis, Mo., 28 May 1975*

Dear Daryl,

Having little or no imagination, I have to wait and see, so it wasn't till this morning, doing the proofs herewith returned, that I was really overwhelmed by the magnitude of what you are doing for me and my book, and by your magnanimity in doing it. Why, you've practically impressed me with myself, and I shall go about feeling like a poet all day long. . . .

Your arrangement of the poems is striking and apt. I trust you won't mind that their arrangement in the book is different, as it would have to be to accommodate as many more poems again. . . .

Have a good summer!

Best, as always, / Howard

The August 1975 issue was devoted entirely to thirty-seven of Nemerov's poems, including the often anthologized "Boy with Book of Knowledge" and his essay "Thirteen Ways of Looking at a Skylark." The selection comprised the title poem and half the contents of Nemerov's ninth collection, *The Western Approaches: Poems 1973–75*, published the following month.

Daryl Hine to William Pritchard   *Chicago, 25 July 1975*

Dear Bill Pritchard,

I don't care for the American practice of calling people whom one has never met by their first names, however well one may feel one knows them by their work, so beg to compromise on this old BBC usage, like the Russian patronymic.

In a continuous ozone alert I haven't been going down to the office, but brought your review home to read, which I have done with pleasure, with the partial exception of the concluding pages on Ashbery, which I find quite unacceptable, dismissive and, frankly, bitchy: neither John nor Harold is a close personal friend of mine, but I do feel that the one's verse and the other's criticism deserve greater consideration than this. Of course, as a Romantic, Bloom exaggerates, sometimes grotesquely: but as you know, I published many of Ashbery's poems in *Poetry*, and for once feel that the inconsistency of a review that is not merely hostile but a snub would be too great. Besides, I just don't agree, and am tired of publishing views with which I radically differ, at least when they seem to me, as in this case, hasty and ill-considered: and when I also know the critic to be capable of so much more. So, I wish you would consider spelling out your objection to the latest Ashbery as a separate, substantial piece; or, if you have no interest in prolonging the tedium, allowing me to give the books to a more patient critic (not H.B.), of which there seem to be no dearth.

Apart from that, the piece is excellent: I particularly enjoyed your treatment of Rich and Atwood, also personal friends, but ones whose work causes me infinite and increasing ennui: in a clerihew: "Margaret Atwood / If she shat would / Wipe her ass / With leaves of grass." I also like your remarks on L. Glück, whose texture I have much admired: and generally sympathize with the tenor of the rest of the review. Actually, and between us, I feel some of what you do about J.A., but also greatly enjoy and admire just the quality you found to blame: the "just words". What else, no one has ever been able to tell me, is poetry?

Sincerely yours, / Daryl

William Pritchard to Daryl Hine   *Amherst, Mass., 11 August 1975*

Dear Daryl Hine,

Just returned from a week away. I can hardly claim total amazement at the Ashbery rejection since I think I imagined your possible uneasiness with it in the covering note I sent. Ordinarily I take the strict B. H. Haggin line: a reviewer's review should not be tampered with, emasculated or what have you because the editor happens not to agree with one or more of the judgments. But you make the case for not taking it about as well as can be made. I can imagine and have experienced shifty and more authoritarian ways of accomplishing what you did with scruple and point. So O.K., too much of the back-of-the-hand to Ashbery in two little (2-plus pages) and maybe even (though I hate it to be called) "bitchy." On the other hand.

I have now read two reviews of *Self-Portrait*, an admiring rave by David Kalstone in the *T.L.S.*, an admiring rave by John Malcolm Brinnin in yesterday's *Times BK Review*. In both cases [it] seems to me they come down to saying It's All Words, after which they add Wow! Whereas I say something less ecstatic. I'm pretty much convinced that A's poetry is bullet-proof, that you can't get at it by trying to follow along, paraphrase, demonstrate "transitions," admire variegated tones etc etc. And that reviewers from Bloom on down tend to substitute ecstasy. But I guess I substituted denigration.

Question now is whether you'd like me to pursue this in a separate review of Ashbery which takes up Bloom's essay as well as current reviews of the new book. I think maybe I could get at something interesting about the language of review-criticism, 1975, along with maybe bringing out more positively what Ashbery *does* (as well as doesn't) do.

But maybe you don't want that much of me in *Poetry* and maybe you've got somebody in mind to do this instead. If so say the word and I'll send the books back; otherwise I'd appreciate taking another crack.

In appreciation of the Margaret Atwood effort, have you heard this Philip Toynbee one?

> There's no use in talking to Toynbee
> To pay him back in his own coin; he'd
> See nothing amiss
> In talking such piss:
> But how would a kick in the groin be?

Supposed to have originated with [Kingsley] Amis.

Best wishes, / Bill

P.S. Of course I know that poetry is "just words." I am trying to say why I appreciate the just words, say, of Philip Larkin, and why they make me want something more than Ashbery provides. I guess I just don't want the substantial self dissolved into brilliant bits. But this is just nostalgic, or reactionary? . . .

D.H. wrote 9 September, declining Pritchard's offer: "I do feel anything like an attack would seem peculiar if not schizoid in our pages," since *Poetry* had printed so many of the poems collected in *Self-Portrait*. Richard Howard reviewed it in the March 1976 issue.

4. Troubling Times and Another Resignation

After nearly two decades of relative prosperity, *Poetry* again began to exhibit symptoms of financial ills ahead. Housed in a converted apartment on the first floor of an old brownstone, the offices were now crammed with books and fast running out of work space. Because of the Near North Side location, rent was high ($340 per month) and certain to rise. The lease had a three-month eviction clause, and there was fear the bank that owned the building might exercise its option at any time. In 1974 the board proposed finding more permanent quarters and even considered buying a building, perhaps a townhouse. But with the top bid for an "acceptable site" limited to $155,000 the chances of finding such a space, at least in the vicinity, were slim. There was also brief mention of raising capital funds. A trustee proposed that an anthology of work from *Poetry* be compiled, with the rather optimistic hope that the book would provide additional revenue. The recent subscription rate increase had helped, but only for a short while because of rising costs for postage. It was suggested the magazine be more actively marketed to libraries; at the time only about 5,000 subscribed.

In 1974 total circulation held steady at about 8,000 copies a month, but by 1975 sales began to slip. Over the next several years, annual subscriptions and newsstand sales gradually declined, from 7,556 in 1975 and 7,513 in 1976 to 7,192 in 1977; by the end of 1978, distribution sank below 7,000 (6,993 to be exact) for the first time in a decade. These declines came, in part, because federal appropriations begun in 1966 to underwrite school library purchases of literary journals were ended. Revenue from the Poetry Day readings partially offset publication costs. In 1974 the appearance of Mona Van Duyn and Howard Nemerov, just after publication of the special issue devoted to his work, netted about $7,300; the 1975 Poetry Day reading by Stephen Spender raised some $9,200. But Karl Shapiro's program the next year produced less than $5,000 after expenses, while James Merrill's brought just a little over $6,000 in 1977. This downward trajectory did not augur well, and given the time and costs involved in putting on the reading and the dinner, some wondered if economies might not be made, including scaling back the dinner.

In any case, other sources of revenue had to be found. Hine negotiated a new contract with the Lilly Library at Indiana University to purchase the *Poetry* papers. The Library had ended an earlier arrangement in 1968, after acquiring the correspondence and business files from 1961 through 1967. The Lilly agreed to a price of $2,500 for the files of each year from 1968 through 1977, and would pay for them as they were sent from the magazine, two years' worth at a time, over the next five years—checks very gratefully received.

In 1975, Joseph Wiley, associate editor since the beginning of Rago's tenure, informed Hine that he wished to resign since he had received a sabbatical from his high school teaching job. Wiley had served faithfully as first reader of manuscripts for twenty-five years; more remarkable, he had worked the entire time without pay. In the late spring of 1976, Michael Mesic, who as associate editor since 1970 had served in several capacities including production manager, also decided to quit.

Hine approached me about assuming his position in May. I had written articles on various poets and done some reviewing for *Poetry* as well as attended a few magazine events, but, as I pointed out, I had limited experience editing, apart from my own writing. I also reminded Hine that my field was not contemporary poetry. (I had taken a Ph.D. three years earlier at Chicago, specializing in Restoration and eighteenth-century drama and English comedy, and had begun teaching in 1969.) Hine assured me that I had the qualifications he was looking for, and so in June I joined the staff as associate editor, on a part-time basis. Besides serving as first reader of manuscripts, I handled magazine production and, gradually, publicity and fund-raising chores. The review section and other back-of-the-book responsibilities were eventually added to the list.

By fall the job was taking up full-time hours. Hine had begun work on *The POETRY Anthology, 1912–1977* some months earlier, but had not made much progress. He asked me to join him on the project as co-editor, and I agreed. Since publication was scheduled for fall 1978—and there were 130 volumes to survey and make selections from—the book consumed every available free moment. Further, to increase income in 1976 the board had proposed establishing an Associates program, in which supporters who gave donations at various levels became members of the Modern Poetry Association and received subscriptions, tickets to readings, a newsletter, and other benefits. (One such, the discount poetry book club, was soon abandoned.)

Despite the additional staff effort required to start up and run the Associates program, and the extra pressures with the fast-approaching deadline for the anthology, regular editorial work on the monthly issues proceeded as usual. Among the highlights of these years were the first appearances of Ashbery's "Syringa," "Fantasia on 'The Nut-Brown Maid,'" and "The Ice-Cream Wars"; several selections from Hollander's series of "Spectral Emanations"; and "O," the opening of James Merrill's *Mirabell: Books of Number*, the second part of what became his mammoth trilogy, *The Changing Light at Sandover*.

During 1976 and 1977, *Poetry* also published posthumously a dozen pieces by Frank O'Hara (including "Poem" ["Green things are flowers"], "The Mike Goldberg Variations," "Intermezzo," and "Maurice Ravel") and nine by Ezra Pound. Groups were also offered by Alfred Corn, William Logan, Sandra McPherson, Michael Ryan, John N. Morris, and Donald Revell. Among the diverse other contributors were Larry Rubin, Reg Saner, Grace Schulman, David R. Slavitt, Dave Smith, Gary Soto, Ann Stanford, David Wagoner, Diane Wakoski, Chris Wallace-Crabbe, J. P. Ward, Michael Waters, Patrick White, and Anne Winters. The stable of reviewers included a similarly wide spectrum of poet-critics, among them: Dick Allen, Jonathan Galassi, Sandra M. Gilbert, Ben Howard, Richard Howard, William Logan, John Matthias, J. D. McClatchy, Robert B. Shaw, and Jon Silkin.

Extra-editorial activities began to consume ever-increasing amounts of time as money problems persisted. We were successful in winning a $2,000 challenge grant from the Coordinating Council of Literary Magazines and another, for $5,000, from the National Endowment for the Arts in 1977, to help raise circulation. Meeting the challenges was a struggle, however, and the prospect of continuing efforts for grants and other solicitations was not attractive to the editor, whose relations with the board had grown strained.

Hine had in fact been unhappy in the position for some time, and not only because of more frequent attacks from critics in recent years. Like Dillon and Carruth, Hine was not temperamentally inclined toward fundraising or publicity campaigns. The additional burdens distracted him more and more from his own poetry and translations, resulting in chronic resentment. Then health problems complicated matters further.

Hine had spoken at various times of his dissatisfaction; then, in mid-June 1977, rather precipitately, he decided to quit. When he told me he intended to submit his resignation immediately, I suggested he wait at least until he had secured another job, perhaps a teaching position, and offered to help him with the search. He said that whether he found other employment or not, he had definitely made up his mind. He contacted John Frederick Nims, who was well familiar with *Poetry*'s operation from his earlier stints on staff, and asked if he would be willing to take on the editorship again.

Nims agreed. He and I first met over a lunch Hine held in his backyard gazebo, during which we considered how the editorial work might be handled during the transition. Recognizing he might wish to assemble his own staff, I told Nims I would of course resign and offered to remain long enough to train my replacement, but he insisted I stay on. Hine then discussed the matter with senior board members, and in mid-July he formally submitted his resignation, to become official at the end of the year.

At its September meeting, the board accepted it, along with Hine's request that his name remain on the masthead as long as the poems and prose he had chosen made up the contents of the magazine. After authorizing a three-year contract with John Nims, the trustees also approved a motion to pay Hine his full salary through June of 1978, in recognition of his "devotion and contribution to POETRY" over his nine years as editor.

4. Correspondence 1975–1977

Susan Fromberg Schaeffer to Daryl Hine   *Brooklyn, N.Y.,*
                                                                      3 January 1976

Dear Daryl Hine,

Your unexpectedly incisive note accompanying my last batch of poems prompts me to write you this undeserving, miserable, humble letter. Quality, not quantity, is what you want. How every little hint helps!

Generosity deserves to be repaid, and I thought you might like to know something of my system for writing poetry, soon to be patented. Every week I try to write 78 poems. Seventy-eight because seven is the number of the days in the week, eight the number following, and seven plus eight equals 15, which is just half the days in some months. Mysticism has little place in this scientific age, I know, but nevertheless it crops up in the blood of some of us, as certain traits did in the Jukes family (the Harpe's family as well, though they are known only to the erudite historian).

While some editors might think, upon receiving a large, lumpish collection of poems that all had been written in one week, I am glad to see that you, at least are astute enough to eschew such thought as: perhaps it took said author this long to type up six months work; or again, perhaps it took said author a great deal of time to reach that much maligned scribe-object, the Xerox machine. Or, perhaps said author is taking advantage of the cheaper postage rate for object sent in bulk. I myself will never, I hope, lead you to believe I have sacrificed the desire for quality by submitting quantity, for I now clearly see the way to guarantee quality of submitted work is to submit one poem at a time for your discerning eye.

With all best wishes for the New Year, and Infinite Joy on my part, for I now know you have not changed with Time, as so many things dreadfully do. I sign myself respectfully,

Susan Fromberg Schaeffer,

knowing you will understand that, since I write so few letters, this is, of course, one of the very finest quality.

Dana Gioia to Daryl Hine   *Stanford, Calif., [spring 1976]*

Dear Mr. Hine,

I am the poetry editor of *Sequoia* as well as a graduate student in international finance at the Stanford School of Business. In the latter capacity I am flying to Chicago at the end of April on a business trip, and I am wondering if during this professional sojourn I might be able to stop by the *Poetry* offices for a visit.

I will not be looking for a job. The reason I am visiting Chicago in the first place is to finalize a position I will be taking this summer. Nor do I have any manuscripts that I want you to publish. I am visiting you out of a sincere and long-standing interest in your magazine.

I have been reading *Poetry* for the last seven years and would like very much to see how it is put together and distributed. The magazine has influenced me very much, even to the point where *Sequoia*'s format borders on plagiarism.

This letter must seem unorthodox at best. I honestly won't make a nuisance of myself if I come. I can't provide much in the way of character references, but, if you chance to talk to Robert Shaw, a friend of mine who is a pretty frequent contributor in your pages, I trust that he'll put in a good word for me.

I hope to hear from you.

Sincerely yours, / Dana Gioia

DC Berry to Daryl Hine   *[n.p.], 1 May 1976*

Daryl:

Swar to Gott!

Can't believe what you boys reject and the abstract bullshit (M[ichael]. Ryan—April issue) you print. You ever heard of poems with hair, skin, lo a navel?

—At least now I'll know my future rejections are for spite. —Aw, c'mon, don't pay me any mind.

Frustrated, / DC Berry

James Atlas to Michael Mesic and Daryl Hine   Cambridge, Mass.,
                                                                14 May 1976

Dear Michael & Daryl:

The occasion of this little note is to inform you of a change of address . . .

I have just written page 400 of my biography of Delmore Schwartz, and as the end draws near, I find myself writing more and more rapidly, ignoring whole years of his life; but who will know the difference?

I heard about you all from Jonathan Galassi who was very impressed with Chicago.

Best, / James

Atlas's *Delmore Schwartz: The Life of an American Poet* appeared in 1977.

Dana Gioia to Joseph Parisi   New Hope, Minn., 8 July 1976

Dear Mr. Parisi,

Thank you for your kind letter [requesting samples of his criticism]. I am sorry that my reply has been so long in coming, but I am working this summer in Minneapolis, and your letter was forwarded to me very slowly via two old addresses. . . .

The reviews I am sending you were quite obviously published in a newspaper. This fact should account for the editorial peculiarities of the copy— e.g. the very short paragraphs and strange subtitles. Please do not hold me accountable for the horrific titles and captions attached to each review. These are the work of an undergraduate editor with a perverse and predictable penchant for "action" titles. Any other stylistic peculiarities are, alas, my own. My reviews were also cut to fit the space available in each issue, and occasionally this resulted in some herculean leaps of logic. . . .

I have begun a career in business and am very happy with my choice, but my major personal interests remain in literature. I would be delighted to join your reviewing staff since it would give me an opportunity to continue writing under the best possible circumstances.

I guess this might be an appropriate place to tell you a bit about myself. I have a solid background in American and European literature. As you can tell from my name, I am of Italian descent, and I know that language in addition to German and French. I also have a decent command of Latin. I would be very happy to review translations from any of these languages, especially German or Italian. In poetry you can judge something of my interests from these reviews. If I can be so bold as to make a suggestion, I would like to say that *Poetry* has been very lax in the past about reviewing recordings of poetry. This subject certainly lacks the glamour for a reviewer that a new book of poetry allows, but it is an important area that deserves some attention. Such a review might be a logical place for me to begin.

I must apologize for answering you at such lengths. I hope some of what I've told you will prove helpful. Once again, I would like to thank you for your interest, and I am waiting your reply with no small amount of anticipation.

Sincerely yours, / Dana Gioia

Gioia's first reviews for *Poetry*, an omnibus article on eight books, appeared in May 1982, his first poem in January 1982.

John F. Nims to Daryl Hine   *Bemidji, Minn., 18 July 1976*

Dear Daryl,

This is just a note on this tasteful stationery [letterhead with a picture of the Common Loon, identified as "Minnesota State Bird"] to say I'm glad you thought "Cardiological" would work out [printed February 1977]. Yes, it's good to be writing some longer things again, after those years of only translations and short-shorts.

I'm up at the writers conference at Bemidji for a few more days. One wonderful man here: John Howard Griffin. The man who had his skin darkened medically to see what it would be like to be a black in the south. He wrote *Black Like Me*. What I didn't know about him is that, though born in Texas, he was educated in France from childhood. Knew many of the poets and other lit. men of the 40's and later. Was a neighbor and close friend of [Pierre] Reverdy, on whom he has written an essay. Also a concert pianist once and a photographer who has "shown," as Henry used to say, his work. Serene and witty though he gets around with effort and seems to be living in constant pain—osteomyelitis brought on—some say—by the medical treatments to darken his skin, which affected the bone marrow. I've rarely met anyone so impressive.

Ramble, ramble.

Anyway, thank you.

All the best, / John

Karl Shapiro to Daryl Hine   *Davis, Calif., 24 November 1976*

Dear Daryl,

Last things first. I am enclosing my plane fare and the Ambassador [Hotel] bill, part of which you will decide. Our thanks for making our visit so smooth and gentle.

This [Poetry Day] reading and visit to POETRY meant a great deal to me. In fact, as you can probably guess, it was a landmark implanted. All those old doors momentarily opened, and so many young faces peering out of venerable masks. I wouldn't have missed it for the world, and I am grateful that I had this opportunity.

And I am glad to have met you. Anything complimentary I can say as an ex-editor has got to sound patronizing, but I'll say this anyhow. I think you have brought a new dignity to the magazine and a style which justifies its continuity. That came out pompous but it's the way I feel. I always love to hear the carping that buzzes around the mention of the magazine; it's never stopped since October 1912 and I hope it never will. . . . I would hate to be editor in this day and age when everybody who is afraid to wear a tie is a poet.—I really read your magazine.

Teri sends her thanks and best wishes with mine. I hope we'll meet again. I'd love to be able to have at least an evening with you. Are you coming to the West Coast to read or lecture? Our Department lies about their money but I think I could get their attention if I mentioned you. And our friend and fellow teacher Sandra Gilbert will certainly feel the same as I do.

Cordially, / Karl

Hine visited the Shapiros and read at the University of California, Davis, in June 1977.

W. D. Snodgrass to Daryl Hine   *Erieville, N.Y., 14 December 1976*

Dear Mr. Hine,

I am enclosing, herewith, a copy of my in-progress cycle of poems, *The Führer Bunker*, for your consideration. . . .

It may be worth noting that the facts and details of the poems are historically accurate on the whole. Bormann's letter, for instance, is made up entirely of quotes or paraphrases of actual letters he wrote his wife. The facts of the Goebbels' poems (e.g., girls' names) are correct. The details of Speer's poems come either from his book or from an interview I had with him. His friend's name (the Dr. who didn't know he was dying, himself, of cancer) was not Paul but Speer *did* compare him to Hitler in the last days. It is, of course, unlikely that Speer would have known all those English texts in the last poem (24 April)—quotes from Milton, Frost and Whitehead. I merely assume that these can stand for comparable German texts—my knowledge of German literature isn't deep enough that I could come up with German texts which would echo richly enough.

Could I ask, please, for a "sudden death" decision on these? I would very much like to place as many of these poems as possible before the book publication. I enclose an S.A.S.E. for the return of my manuscript.

Sincerely, / W. D. Snodgrass

P.S. I see, to my chagrin, that I neglected to mention the publisher, B.O.A. Publication in Brockport, N.Y. They—i.e., Al Poulin—will publish my book jointly with one by a young poet, Barton Sutter, whom I have chosen.

Hine did not accept the submission.

A. R. Ammons to Daryl Hine   *Ithaca, N.Y., 1 March 1977*

Dear Daryl,

It is all way out of the question [coming to Chicago for Poetry Day]. I would love to be there and see you and read for the gathering and help *Poetry* if it I could but I cannot.

I just got the news that for the last reporting period more copies of *Diversifications*, my recent book, were returned than sold! I'm going to start taking lessons on appearing before audiences to see if I can drum up enough sales to keep my publisher going. The Collected, though, is in a fourth small printing and that is sufficient, surely. But I write because it feels like a wonderful thing to do (there is some doubt that it is a wise or valuable thing to do) and I suppose others do approximately likewise.

You honor me far too generously, but I am very grateful.

Sincerely, / Archie

Ammons eventually agreed to read for Poetry Day in 1995. Because of his fear of flying, he and his wife Phyllis drove from Ithaca.

Bill Doxey to Daryl Hine   *[n.p.], 31 March 1977*

Dear Daryl,

These poems will shock you; I hope you will give POETRY readers an opportunity to be shocked also.

What's happened to poetry? Has it become an industry of sorts (perhaps at cottage level)? All this sweetness and light, all these poets published because they are the students of older poets—and sound like watered down versions of them!

If I sound mad it's because I am: both crazy and angry! What we want (I mean both need and lack) is energy, surprise, ASTONISHMENT! Poetry has become an old bitch again—not gone in the teeth, but going through menopause! For Christsakes man, you of all people should realize this— yet issue after issue it's the same old bland stuff—ho-hum—lovely in a teacup and sunny room way. This stuff reminds me of poetry before WWI!

Shit, maybe you'd rather publish this than my stuff—hope you'll be big enough to think about what I say. Of course as editor of the big P you don't have to listen to anyone so this will be a challenge.

My stuff is in the current issue of THE SMALL FARM and has been in CAROLINA QUARTERLY, SOUTHERN REVIEW and others.

Thanks, / Bill Doxey

Doxey was not published in *Poetry*.

Robert B. Shaw to Daryl Hine *New Haven, Conn.,*
24 September 1977

Dear Daryl,

I hope you've had a pleasant summer. Ours was; but too short as always. You must be much involved now with preparing for John Nims's new administration, & your own liberation. Just when does he take over? . . .

Wesleyan are supposed to be sending copies of my book [*Comforting the Wilderness*] imminently. Official publication is in October. I trust you'll be receiving it soon, also.

Lowell's death came as a great shock and as something of a personal sorrow. Over the last few years, especially in the short time when we were colleagues at Harvard, I'd come to feel more for him than the respect due a former teacher. It had just become friendship; I had just begun to call him Cal. I had been so much looking forward to giving him a copy of my book. Now, I wish I had sent him the MS. Fate pulls the rug out from under such plans. I went up for the funeral, a very splendid requiem mass at the Church of the Advent. More the style of *Lord Weary's Castle*, one might think, than of the later work. Yet I felt he would have liked it. I'm glad that he lived to see his own latest book out [*Day by Day*], and to see some good reviews of it. For me, it seems the most interesting collection since *Life Studies*. Some day I'd like to write about the two books, contrasting their treatments of similar (family) material. . . .

Faithfully, / Robt

On his way to a reunion with his former wife Elizabeth Hardwick, Lowell died of a heart attack in the back seat of a cab in New York City on 12 September.

Stephen Yenser to Daryl Hine *Los Angeles, Calif., 20 October 1977*

Dear Daryl,

James [Merrill] tells me that you're planning to resign at the end of the year. Speaking as a reader, I'm very sorry to see you give it up—though I can certainly understand that you must already be sighing with relief and in anticipation of having more time for your own work. One can only hope for the magazine's sake that the next editor has something like your breadth of taste. . . .

Best wishes as ever, / Stephen

CHAPTER VII

John Frederick Nims Redux

1. A Warm Reception for and from
the Once and Future Editor

Word of the Nims appointment had spread far by late summer even without a formal announcement. When he came by the office in the fall and
began soliciting friends for both poems and suggestions, the new editor was
greeted with many letters welcoming him to the chair and decrying Hine's
handling of the job. (In the magazine, the only notice of the changeover
appeared in the terse contributor's note for the departed editor's group of
poems leading the January 1978 number: "Daryl Hine, with this issue, leaves
the Editorship of *Poetry*. He began his tenure as Visiting Editor in October
of 1968 and succeeded Henry Rago in May of 1969.") During Nims's first
months some enthusiastic correspondents professed that already they found
the magazine vastly improved under his hand: curious observations indeed,
since the contents of the entire issues through March (and most of April)
1978 were assembled by Hine—a fact duly noted on the masthead pages,
as he had requested—demonstrating yet again how friendship, individual
biases and perceptions, and especially personal animus, can skew aesthetic
judgments.

John Nims was the most patently learned of *Poetry*'s editors; but in contrast to his similarly well-schooled and multilingual predecessor, Nims's
classical training and erudition were not held against him. Like Hine and
Rago (and Shapiro), Nims was an unabashed (but soft-spoken) intellectual
with a wide cultural background, deeply imbued by the classics of Western
civilization. Nims's knowledge of poetry ancient and modern, particularly
verse forms and metrics, was encyclopedic. This scholarship was evident in
his criticism (collected in *A Local Habitation: Essays on Poetry*, 1985) and his
own well-wrought and, as some objected, occasionally overwrought verses.
But again unlike with Hine, magazine readers and critics did not consider
Nims's sophisticated personal writing style and preference for forms cause
for suspicion. His peers respected him for his original poetry—his third
collection, *Knowledge of the Evening* (1960), was nominated for a National

Book Award—and even more for his translations from several tongues, including the often reprinted *Sappho to Valéry* (first edition, 1971) as well as his renderings of *The Poems of St. John of the Cross* (1959, 1979, 1995), and Euripides' *Andromache* (1959). During his tenure he also published *The Kiss: A Jambalaya* (1982) and edited and heavily annotated *The Harper Anthology of Poetry* (1981). He was probably best known, however, for his widely used textbook, *Western Wind: An Introduction to Poetry* (1974, fourth edition 1999).

Unlike the often acerbic Hine and Shapiro, Nims had an easygoing and shyly humorous manner that could charm even when he made mordant remarks. But for all his invitingly open appearance, Nims was in fact a strict judge of poetry whose tastes were shaped by the Great Tradition and whose aesthetic criteria were based on New Critical principles. In a long letter of 23 April 1978 to Catherine Petroski, who was preparing an article for the *Chicago Tribune*, Nims talked about his plans for the magazine, noting that "probably no editor of *Poetry* has ever gone on record at such length about what he thinks poetry is" as he had in his introduction to *Western Wind*. He dryly observed that it was fair to say that his "conception of poetry [was] not just based on what's read in the coffee houses in Chicago in 1978" but "on the best poetry in seven or eight languages over 2,500 or so years." He added: "I guess I am getting a little bored too with the neo-surrealism (some call it 'Minnesota surrealism'); that is the number 1 fad nowadays with many writers young and not so young . . . reading run-of-the-mill surrealism is like sticking to a diet of pink meringue—after a few days of it one runs screaming for a plain old cheeseburger. Something with *human* appeal." He further observed:

> Another bore nowadays is the "experimental" poetry that imitates the experimenters of the '20's. Sometimes when a young poet says he is "experimental" he means he cannot write a clear, vivid, passionate sentence, and is trying to conceal that fact by his kind of gobbledegook. And a lot of aspirants are scared off by the years of hard work it takes to master the ways of any craft; Pound said that learning to write poetry was a least as hard as learning to play the piano.

Like Pound, Nims was very wary of abstractions and "statements," and advocated concrete images and careful observation.

In a crabbed and sometimes indecipherable hand, Hine was given to penning terse, sharply worded rejection letters. Often, especially in his final years, he (like Shapiro) would say nothing at all when returning manuscripts, a practice that alienated and frequently infuriated senders. In contrast, Nims, like the ever polite Rago, spent a very great deal of time replying to submissions. He may well have surpassed Rago in that department since he routinely tapped out scores of brief but detailed notes a day, with amazing speed, on a manual typewriter, but didn't bother to make copies.

While Rago's rejection letters are the most formal, expansive, and diplomatic left by any of the editors, Nims's are among the most pointed and certainly the funniest in the archives. Even so, not all the recipients of his shrewd and witty comments could have been amused. (Only Isabella Gardner, Shapiro's good friend and associate editor, made bold to tell Nims that his analyses and helpful hints were not appreciated—or necessary, so far as she was concerned.) Having read both the manuscripts and the editor's responses, I can attest that Nims's missives were far more intelligent, well crafted, and entertaining than the poems he sent back with them. Although his genial, even whimsical approach did not remove the sting, it certainly softened the edges of his incisive critiques. And since he was so personable and frequently offered suggestions for improvements, that courtesy only served to encourage rejected authors to send more poems, which they did often by return post.

When he came on board, Nims was thoroughly familiar with *Poetry*'s editorial procedures from his service on the staff twice before. He made his first appearance in *Poetry* in 1940, was soon awarded three of the magazine's most prestigious prizes, and continued to publish in *Poetry* often. Nims had received his B.A. in English and Latin from Notre Dame in 1937 and immediately began teaching in the English department after taking his M.A. there in 1939. While he finished work on his doctorate in comparative literature at the University of Chicago, he volunteered as first reader under his friend Peter DeVries during the dark days during and after the war. He took his degree in 1945, and continued as associate editor to help with poetry manuscripts and the prose section; he also wrote many of the educational supplements the magazine put out between 1947 and 1950. Reluctantly he became a partner in the uneasy trio deciding on poems during Hayden Carruth's brief tenure in 1949.

When he returned as editor-in-chief, Nims had taught literature and writing for almost forty years and had acquaintances throughout the academic and literary world generally. The wealth of good feeling and high personal esteem he brought with him immediately enhanced the profile of the magazine. Between two stints at Notre Dame, ending in 1952, he taught briefly at the University of Toronto then spent most of the fifties in Europe, on a Fulbright and other grants, as a professor in Milan, Florence, and Madrid. He also was a visiting professor at Harvard several times, and at Chicago, Missouri, and Williams College, as well as an instructor at the Breadloaf Writers' Conference 1959–1972. Most of his career was spent at the University of Illinois in Urbana and then in Chicago. (His return to the Chicago Circle campus full time in 1977, after five winters at the University of Florida, was one reason Hine approached him about the position.) Nims's former colleagues around the country and their students were quick to send him work. He particularly welcomed fellow translators Richmond Lattimore, John Ciardi, and Richard Wilbur as well as his friends Brewster Ghiselin, Ernest Sandeen, Lisel Mueller, A. R. Ammons, David Wagoner, Alicia Ostriker, Howard Nemerov, Linda Pastan, Carolyn Kizer, William Stafford, Gerald Stern, and Miller Williams. But whether widely known or emerging, poets of many varieties found a warm reception.

Well-established older writers such as James Dickey, Dannie Abse, Anthony Hecht, James Merrill, William Meredith, Reynolds Price, Donald Hall, Geoffrey Grigson, Ruth Fainlight, Josephine Miles, James Wright, Mac Hammond, James Laughlin, David Ignatow, Robert Penn Warren, and Richard Hugo continued to appear, but less often than in previous decades. Among the younger poets frequently published during Nims's five years were Rita Dove, Mary Karr, Dana Gioia, Gary Soto, Alice Fulton, Albert Goldbarth, Pattiann Rogers, Sandra McPherson, William Matthews, David Bottoms, and Edward Hirsch, to name the more notable.

Other authors who contributed at least half a dozen poems (and often considerably more) include Dick Allen, Philip Appleman, John Ashbery, Margaret Benbow, Laurel Blossom, Edward Brash, T. Alan Broughton, Amy Clampitt, Carl Dennis, William Dickey, John Dickson, Stephen Dobyns, Stephen Dunn, Dave Etter, Brendan Galvin, Sandra M. Gilbert, Marilyn Hacker, Pamela Hadas, James Baker Hall, Daniel Halpern, Charles O. Hartman, William Heyen, Conrad Hilberry, Mary Kinzie, Caroline Knox, Ted Kooser, Philip Levine, Elizabeth Libbey, Robert Long, Thomas Lynch, Archibald MacLeish, Jack Matthews, Linda McCarriston, Heather McHugh, Rennie McQuilkin, Peter Meinke, Robert Morgan, John N. Morris, Diana Ó Hehir, Sharon Olds, Carole Oles, Katha Pollitt, Lawrence Raab, Robert Beverley Ray, Vern Rutsala, Michael Ryan, Ira Sadoff, Stephen Sandy, Reg Saner, Sherod Santos, William Scammell, Philip Schultz, Dave Smith, Barry Spacks, Elizabeth Spires, Timothy Steele, May Swenson, Deborah Tall, Ellen Bryant Voigt, Roger Weingarten, Max Wickert, Robley Wilson Jr., Baron Wormser, and Evan Zimroth.

With the first issue under his complete control, May 1978, Nims changed the cover design, replacing the original line drawings with a uniform format consisting of the Thurber Pegasus followed by the names of contributors and titles of poems and prose pieces, in the style of an academic journal. Several readers objected to the more prosaic cover; one predicted, accurately, that it would adversely affect newsstand sales. A subscriber in Princeton, New Jersey, protested the editor's decision "of dropping the original artwork that made your periodical's cover the most attractive published in this country between October 1969 and March 1978," and added: "If he thinks his news-

Editors Parisi and Nims inspecting galley proofs in the front office
at 1228 North Dearborn in 1978.

stand circulation is a large enough figure that he will sell more copies by
putting the names of the poets on the outside, I have news for him." The
writer, William P. Michaels, advised Nims to take a poll to see what readers
thought and to suggest "an estimated annual contribution per personal subscriber for getting back the artworks." He promised, "I would pay at least
$10 myself." The editor had also wanted to change the design of the page
layouts and reduce the type size for poetry and prose, but he was persuaded
that the original Greer Allen typography was both distinctive and highly
readable. Further format changes became moot, however, since there was no
money available to hire a graphic designer.

2. Another Crisis and Another Move

Nims was well acquainted with financial crises at *Poetry*, both during his
service in the postwar period and in his year as visiting editor in 1960–1961,
when he had to wire Rago in Europe that the magazine was again close to
bankruptcy. But as soon as he took over the chair officially in January 1978,
a novel difficulty arose. The *Reader's Guide to Periodical Literature* decided
that in December it would drop several literary magazines from its listings,
Poetry among them. Since many libraries subscribed only to journals in-
dexed in the *Guide*, the consequences were potentially serious: 60 percent
of subscriptions were then institutional. Nims immediately contacted big
name authors, editors, and other influential literary people he knew, some

150 in all, and asked them to write urging the *Guide* to reconsider its decision. Upon his request, regular readers and librarians also wrote in protest. Although more than a hundred supporters sent letters, the campaign was futile. Within months of *Poetry*'s deletion, the magazine lost hundreds of longtime subscriptions from libraries that failed to renew.

But a downward trend was already apparent. In December 1977, total paid circulation stood at almost 7,200, some 300 fewer monthly copies than in the preceding year. By 1978 the figure was just under 7,000; in 1979 it was fewer than 6,600. The numbers continued to slip, and by 1983, Nims's last year, the magazine reported the total for subscriptions and newsstand sales had dropped to 6,173. There were scant means to regain the lost subscriptions, let alone increase circulation. Not only did the magazine lack a budget for advertising and promotion, it was now having problems meeting the rent. Fortunately the University of Chicago Printing Department granted exceedingly generous grace periods, as it had for years, and refrained from demanding payment, even though the printing bills were now usually six to nine months in arrears.

In February 1978 Studs Terkel, having heard of *Poetry*'s problem with the *Guide*, invited Nims and me to discuss present conditions at the magazine on his popular interview program on WFMT-FM in Chicago. When *The PoETRY Anthology, 1912–1977* was published in September, Terkel again invited us on his show. There was a very great deal of print coverage on the book, including a front-page essay by Irving Howe in the *New York Times Book Review* and an article in *Time*. This extensive (and free) publicity resulted in temporary up-ticks in subscriptions and newsstand sales. These were far outnumbered by the huge influx of submissions: always the case whenever and whatever the media attention for the magazine.

Meanwhile the board considered various ways to deal with the worsening financial situation. One idea, quickly abandoned, was to turn the magazine into a bimonthly or quarterly. A special campaign to boost distribution in schools was also discussed, but there was skepticism whether the costs of discounts would be offset by increased subscriptions. Another proposal was to approach descendants of Harriet Monroe's original guarantors, and corporations they might now head, for support of an endowment. To aid in the campaign I wrote a thirty-page, well-illustrated booklet, "*Poetry*: An American Institution," giving a brief history of the magazine with a list of the first sponsors, a roster of the most famous authors discovered and printed over the decades, and details about our educational programs, prizes, and library. I also began researching potential benefactors through files at the Chicago Donor's Forum. The drive to gather support from the descendants did not materialize, but the brochure and information gathered became useful in later fund-raising ventures.

For the 1978 Poetry Day benefit, the board decided to forgo the usual reading but return to the old format of a black-tie dinner and auction, which had generated large income in the past. Trustee and Newberry Library vice president James Wells agreed to write letters soliciting donations of books, manuscripts, and other materials, with assistance from Robert Rosenthal, head of Special Collections at the University of Chicago's Regenstein Library. At the annual meeting of the board in June, the treasurer predicted that the deficit would mount to over $20,000 by fall; thus, he emphasized, the Poetry Day benefit would have to be a great success not only to cover current expenses but to carry *Poetry* into the next year.

Nims informed the board he would forgo his paycheck over the next months, a generous act that helped ease the cash-flow problem. Meanwhile we scrambled to gather donations to match the challenge grants from the NEA and board chairman J. Patrick Lannan by the 30 June deadline. By mid-June the $5,000 was raised. The Illinois Arts Council recommended only $2,500 on our original $10,000 grant request (the legislature cut the Council's appropriation), but with the help of an anonymous gift of $2,000 and receipts of almost $14,500 from the Poetry Day auction—twice the amount of 1977—the magazine was safely in the black, at least for the time being. Aware that the budget's delicate balance could quickly tip back into the red, and with no space left in the offices to hold the steady inflow of new books, Nims hit upon a solution to both problems.

During the summer he approached friends at the University of Illinois at Chicago Circle (as it was then called) about the possibility of finding quarters for the magazine on the campus. The head of the English department, Jay A. Levine, not only supported the idea but helped negotiate a remarkable arrangement by which the magazine would be provided, without charge, a large corner suite with an adjacent secretary's office for the three-member staff (circulation manager Nadine Cummings, business manager Helen Klaviter, and myself), and a regular faculty office for the editor, in University Hall. In addition, the *Poetry* library, then comprising over 25,000 volumes, would be temporarily placed in storage in the university library's rare books department. (A plan to compile a shelf list of the collection and then make it available for student use was planned but never realized.) A five-year agreement that stipulated no formal affiliation with and no editorial and financial control by the university, and allowed for earlier departure if the Association so desired, was signed on 12 January 1979. The university paid all moving expenses and even provided furniture, and the transfer from North Dearborn Parkway to South Halsted Street was made over two bitterly cold days in mid-February.

Cluttered and quaint, the old quarters fit the stereotype of a fusty, book-lined literary office perfectly, down to the fireplaces and mismatched secondhand furniture. But there was always fear of a fire, and with relief the staff quickly settled into the clean, well-lighted space, which was smaller but more efficient. Residence in the midst of the English department did present new potential problems, however, with the poet-professors, not all of whom were fond of the magazine. With careful diplomacy, Nims advised his poetry-writing colleagues that he would prefer not to consider manuscripts from them; he said this policy would prevent any suspicion of "cronyism" or the appearance that *Poetry* was a "house organ" of the creative writing program. After a submission was returned to Paul Carroll (exactly the sort of instructor Nims had in mind when he devised the rule), the ever-trying author objected to the editor by return mail, and sent copies of his letter to the dean and all the writing program faculty.

This annoyance aside, the transition went smoothly; mail got forwarded, issues came out on time, and our relations with faculty and staff were cordial. At the annual meeting in June 1979, the trustees approved a revision to the bylaws expanding board membership from thirty to thirty-six in hopes of increasing financial support. Richard Wilbur was suggested and approved as the 1979 Poetry Day guest of honor. His well-attended reading was held on 18 November in the auditorium of the First National Bank, which offered the space without charge. The dinner followed at the Mid-Day Club high in the same building, an arrangement that proved so convenient that those locales became the regular venues for most of the benefits in the years to follow.

At several meetings during 1979 various methods for stabilizing finances, building circulation, and increasing publicity were discussed. Additional programs were suggested for attracting new sponsors, including a presentation in Washington, D.C. Pat Lannan approached Illinois senator Charles Percy about this idea, and he mentioned it to friends in Congress and the administration. We were delighted to learn that President Jimmy Carter was an avid poetry fan, as was Rosalyn Carter—so much so, she offered to host a major celebration of American poetry in the White House. Her staff contacted us, and we provided lists of names and addresses for poets, publishers, scholars, and friends across the country. Invitations from Mrs. Carter went out in late November.

On 3 January 1980 several dozen poets, including Karl Shapiro and John Nims, recited their work in the East Room and other parts of the crowded Executive Mansion. (We never learned who chose the readers.) Not all those invited got in on time to hear them, since many had to wait outside in the brisk winter air in a line over a block long, as the Secret Service slowly ran security checks. It was the first such event for poets ever held at the White House, and everyone seemed to have a splendid time, especially during the reception—including the president, who took an hour off from

J.F.N. with Mrs. Carter and Mrs. Mondale at the
White House celebration for American poetry, 3 January 1980.

the crisis that followed the recent Soviet invasion of Afghanistan to greet
the throng assembled on the receiving line in the grand entrance hall.

Over the next days a number of people called to inform the *Poetry* staff
that the *Washington Star* misidentified Robert Hayden, the noted Black
poet, as John F. Nims in the photograph accompanying its story about the
event. Replying to Michael Blumenthal's letter of 12 January commenting
on the newspaper's "usual, erudite caption style," Nims wrote: "Yes, I saw
the Robert Hayden picture with the wrong caption—but only after a
Washington friend I had not seen for 20 years or so long-distanced us to
ask if I really had changed so much."

3. Correspondence 1977–1980

Marvin Bell to John F. Nims   *Iowa City, Ia., 15 November 1977*

Dear John,

By now your ears must be ringing from suggestions for *Poetry*. Here are
more, but only because you asked. . . .

There is no denying the pleasure with which most people react to the news that you will be taking over. I don't fault Daryl for attempting to place his own stamp on the magazine, for trying to prove by example that poetry in rhyme and meter is better than ever, or for searching hard for Auden's offspring. I recognize that one can easily be overwhelmed by the amount of bad so-called "free verse" around now. Daryl tried hard to counteract it. However, the effect was that *Poetry* lost its image of eclecticism (or, as Henry Rago might have preferred it, catholicity). As one person put it, the editor of *Poetry* should not impose his personal taste on the magazine. I don't quite agree with that, but I do hope for an editorial taste more various than that which presented itself through the pages of *Poetry* in recent years. I respect Daryl completely, but I believe that Henry Rago's taste made *Poetry* a more important, and even useful, magazine. I see no reason why free verse cannot be selected for the magazine with the same fierce regard for the formal with which Daryl responded to metered verse....

The reviewing in *Poetry*, with exceptions, has become prejudicial and pretentious. Some of the reviewers are simply not qualified. Others are inhumane. (Sorry to seem to refuse a place for "humanity" under "qualifications"!) I think the reviewing stable should be emptied, more or less. If you ask, I'll name poets who I think can write intelligent, fair and economic reviews. (Compare the tone of the reviews recently to the reviewing tone when the reviews were written by Lowell, J. Wright, Stafford, etc.) I think more books should be reviewed....

I prefer covers with names and titles, such as Rago used, to covers with drawings. I certainly prefer type on the cover to drawings as plainly arty (oxymorons, look out!) as those Daryl has employed. I am opposed to anything that makes people whisper at the mention of "poetry," and starts the pussy willows waving in the background. If there is to be "artwork" on the cover, let it be better. However, I think there are many good reasons for preferring a cover of type, not the least of which, it will help sell the magazine to buyers and help arouse the interest of readers. In its own way, it was a device by which Rago was able to make small announcements, even judgments.

The biographical notes should be fleshed out, and never allowed to become as skimpy as they often have been recently. And the news notes should not present meaningless and arbitrary information about such things as poetry readings. I personally don't care for the changes Daryl made in format. Not everyone thinks about these things. Maybe this is personal taste only. However, I think the longer page is a mistake because: (1) we end up with more white space, with many poems floating; (2) the squarer format more equally accommodates the thin line and the wide line. Moreover, the longer format is simply "wrong." It is too narrow. It neither looks nor handles well. It seems frailer.

I don't like the type either. I feel that there is too much white space be-tween lines. This, of course, is a function of the move to a larger type size. I think the type is a bit too large. I think the leading between lines is much too much. The result, for me, is that it is physically difficult to read the po-ems. . . .

Finally, I think that Poetry Day needs to be rescued. It has become an af-fair of enforced privacy. I remember when it was an Occasion. Rago would send free tickets to those of us who lived within driving distance and had some ongoing relationship to the magazine. The reading would be in a grand hall, downtown, at night. The party would be a bash and there was great tolerance for the crashing of it by serious young poets. The overall event remained elegant, but there was lots of us hoboes around too. And we were welcome. . . . I should add that at this time it seems to me Poetry Day will work best if 2, 3 or 4 readers are presented in one evening. And I think some of those readers should be discovered among my not-so-young gen-eration, that there be a mixture of ages among the readers. . . .

There you have it, as they like to say in London. I've told you what I think, John. Nonetheless, I well know what the problems are, and my re-spect for you does not depend on your agreement or your action in behalf of these suggestions. I wish you a grand success with the magazine, and not too much havoc. Once you are open to submissions of poetry, I will send poems if I have them. Right now, all I have is a virus.

Yours, / Marvin

Nims soon replaced the cover art with a uniform format featuring the Thurber Pegasus and names of contributors with titles of poems and articles. Bell's other recommendations on magazine content and graphic design, as well as Poetry Day, were not followed.

George Starbuck to John F. Nims　　　　*Boston, Mass., 15 December 1977*

Dear John Nims,

Congratulations to POETRY mag!! And a proud, deep, tearful, stricken-dumb salaam, as you leave our ranks on that fatal, fateful mission, to be-come as wretch, as outcast, as champion, as god. . . . But beware: look what happens: by first return post, a readymade Xmas pome [sic]. *Everybody*'ll have 'em. . . .

John F. Nims to Frederick Morgan　　　　*Chicago, 20 January 1978*

Dear Mr. Morgan:

. . . If I had met you in New York, you might have warned me that an editor does a lot besides edit. Since I came into the office two weeks ago,

I have hardly had the time to glance at a single MS. A crisis my very first week! Since you say such kind words about *Poetry*, let me enclose a copy of the letter than explains it. I also wrote about 150 personal notes to accompany it. In my most surrealist moments I would not have dreamed that *Readers' Guide* could be a threat to *Poetry*—but just look!

The letter should have a P.S. We have learned that these publishers are sensitive to letters of remonstrance. Their indexing committee met in New York last week, and, because of some 200 such letters, restored nine of the forty-odd magazines they had dropped. But not *Poetry*. No letters for Pegasus. Maybe now we can get some? . . .

My first impression is that the new poem is perhaps too long for *Poetry*. Not absolutely too long for it would fit in. But too long in comparison to the kind of poems we can generally run. It seemed to me a little diffuse—but this may be a mistaken first impression. More very soon. I'm sorry I've been so slow.

I hope *Hudson Review* [Morgan was founding editor] is not plagued with anything like this.

Sincerely yours, / John F. Nims

John F. Nims to Frederick Morgan   *Chicago, 23 January 1978*

Dear Mr. Morgan:

Over the week-end I did read, and with pleasure, both of your books. And then I read "Century Poem" again, and it seems to me, both in the light of what you are capable of, and of the space we have available, that it is too long for us. Frankly, I don't like it as much as many, many pages of poetry in your books. Maybe it's not echt-Morgan? . . .

The spectrum of poetry and poetry appreciation is of course a wide one, and my guess would be that our tastes do not perfectly coincide. (Why should they? It would be terrible if everybody liked the very same poems.) I guess I lean toward Valéry's kind of strictness. Or Pound's insistence there should not be one extra word. And his insistence that poets should not explain their imagery. And Williams': No ideas but in things. And Garcia Lorca's: The poet is a professor of the five bodily senses.

My (possibly false) impression is that you like a looser, more easily flowing kind of poetry, which is sometimes willing to work away from the concrete in the direction of abstract statement. Great when it works. Of the poems of yours I saw, I much preferred the very concrete memories of your childhood. . . .

I've never forgotten something I think, I *know*, Jules Renard said: One can say of almost all literature that it is *too* long. And that is true of most poems—even some haiku! Some of your poems seem too fallible to me, to have a kind of hazy bituminous quality, which I wish you had compressed to brilliant anthracite. Diamond—if we compress even further—is even nicer. And I suspect that your two books would have been even stronger than they are if you had published only the stronger 50% of the poems. There are some fillers, don't you think?

Maybe it's impertinent of me to write like this, but I think I mean it as a kind of guide to the kind of poem I hope *Poetry* can publish. And it must be terribly hard for you—as an eminent and powerful editor—to get honest reactions to your work. But I do hope, when you have some nice TIGHT poems you really like, that you won't disdain *Poetry*.

Sincerely yours, / John F. Nims

Hugh Kenner to John Nims   *Baltimore, Md., 23 January 1978*

Dear Mr. Nims:

The close of the Hine Era is welcome news, since he dropped me from the staff without a word of explanation and would never so much as answer a letter of mine. Hence my long absence.

As for your welcome invitation: I don't know if you mean to keep the prose section to omnibus reviews, which just now I don't particularly want to do more of. I could polish up and send you a bit of a book-in-progress on The Meaning of Rhyme (subject is just that), but I'll wait till you tell me that the format as you conceive it would accommodate such an item. Please note my current address; I left Santa Barbara in 1973.

And my sincere congratulations on your ascent to what EP once called "Old Harriet's roost." I have always cherished a sentence of his on her: "Harriet was dumb but honest; and honesty is a form of intelligence."

Very cordially, / Hugh Kenner

Kenner's first article in *Poetry* appeared in June 1949, and he was a regular critic during the editorships of Shapiro and Rago. He reviewed more than one hundred books in all; his last article, on Wyndham Lewis, appeared in October 1972. He is best known for his influential study of *The Pound Era* (1971).

John F. Nims to David Wagoner   *Chicago, 27 January 1978*

Dear Dave,

Lately I've reread I think all of your poems. I don't have the *new Collected Poems*. . . . But I do have seven volumes, up to and including the handsomely printed *Travelling Light* (but did their copy editor misspell forms of *yield* not once but three times?)

I went through them again with much pleasure, coming on old friends and making new ones. Lots of poems I've read to students in my writing workshops. You have taken me to visit ospreys and warblers in car engines and camels and garbagemen and Arizona and Mexico and the Hemingway Memorial and a hold-up man and Thor and Beauty and the Beast and snake hunters, and taught me how to stay alive, and meet a bear, and walk in a swamp, and travel light.

I've gone happily along with you in all these ways—but I just can't seem to follow you into Indian country. I can't hear your voice any more. Any of your voices: not the one that sharply relates, as with the osprey nest, or the one that mythologizes richly and with humor, as in Beauty and the Beast, or the one that rather wryly tells me how to deal with dangerous nature.

In these Indian poems, the voice seems to me toneless. As if you were writing in something not your native tongue. As if these were unskilled translations. As if you were trying to forget all you knew about writing. As if you didn't really write these. Worst of all—as if you were an anthropologist.

Maybe (of course) this is my fault. A lot of mythologizing leaves me cold—though Thor and B. and the B. did not. And Graves doesn't. But all this rain-in-the-face stuff does. For me, a drag. I'm sorry, and I'll bet this book of yours will come out and be Highly Acclaimed and win prizes and I'll be left sitting there like old Egg-on-his-Face himself. But unrepentant.

Please, when you finish the anthropology textbook and get back to your *real* voice, will you send *Poetry* something? I hope you can tell from the above that I really like many, many of your poems, and look forward to seeing more authentic Wagoner.

That's good news about your editing the Princeton series. . . . You probably know I'm your fellow editor, in a way? I do for the Lockert Library of Poetry in Translation what you do for the poetry series.

And thanks so much for your letter to the *Readers' Guide* people, a copy of which just came. Hope we can stomp on 'em. . . .

All the best,

Sincerely, / John

[P.S. *in left margin*] Since writing, I came across your poems in the June '77 issue. *Very* nice. I especially like the "Elegy" and the one about cutting down a tree. Hope you'll give us a chance at some like those. The other night my Muse appeared to me and said, "Hey, I got a poem for David Wagoner. Wanna hear? It's called, 'On David Wagoner's Poems' and goes: Many's a beaut'll / Blow your noodle. / All he's done futile / 'S that Kwakutl!" I handed her a rejection slip, tho'.

David Wagoner to John F. Nims   Poetry Northwest, *Seattle, Wash.,*
4 February 1978

Dear John:

You're not the first to express doubts about my Indian enterprise, but you're the funniest. I know I'm taking a chance doing it, but what the hell. On the other hand, some people like them a great deal, and the response at readings has been very good. We'll see.

I want to thank you for the time you took to explain your feelings. My God, I don't think I've ever written a reply of that length (except on a book) in the 12 years I've been bumbling away at it. I'm very grateful. . . .

X. J. Kennedy to John F. Nims   *Bedford, Mass.,*
16 March 1978

Dear John,

Hey, thanks for keeping the two epigrams and the Hart Crane piece. And special thanks for sending the old copy of the epigrams. Yes, by George, you're right—the old versions are lots better, lots livelier. Yer an editor in a million. . . .

On 'A Word from Hart Crane's Ghost'—the word *woman* is right. Hart Crane freaks will recall that Crane leapt to his death after he had begun the first and only heterosexual affair of his career—with Peggy Baird (former Mrs. Malcolm Cowley). She was on the ship he jumped from, and once wrote a memoir of it all. They were going to start a new life in the States, and it wasn't going to be gay. Now my own hunch (not really original) is that the prospect of being hitched to a woman, and the new responsibilities he would take on, loomed too huge for Crane, and helped him into the Gulf. [John] Unterecker goes into this in his biog *Voyager* [1969] (of which I have read only the juicy parts). . . .

Cheers to you and to Bonnie and to *Poetry.*

As ever, / Joe

"On a Well-Dressed Man Much Married," "Jack and Jill," and "A Word from Hart Crane's Ghost" appeared in the June 1978 issue.

John F. Nims to Brian Swann   *Chicago, 17 March 1978*

Dear Mr. Swann,

I guess we're having trouble keeping up with all of your MSS.—especially when you send revised versions of some poems.

Can't we slow up a little? It seems to me—if I may diffidently say so—that you are writing too much. The result—again an "it seems to me"—is a kind of thinness in what you write. It seems to come too easily. I don't suppose we want all poets to be like Philip Larkin, who writes, or at least publishes, about one poem a year. One excellent poem! Maybe we could be more like Auden—who averaged seven, wasn't it?

Anyway, I think editors would take your poems more seriously if you would send them out more selectively: maybe four or five poems you *really* like two or three times a year? To one magazine, I mean—say *Poetry*?

Excuse me if I presume.

All best wishes,

Sincerely yours, / John F. Nims

Philip Larkin to John F. Nims   *Hull, England, 21 March 1978*

Dear Mr. Nims,

Many thanks for your kind letter of 6th March. My memory nowadays does not extend back more than seven days, but I am delighted to hear that you did visit us at Hull, and that you had a good time. Congratulations, too, on your appointment as Editor of *Poetry*, which I believe we do take [at the University of Hull library], but in which, as you correctly surmise, I have never appeared.

I am afraid the only reply I can make is that I write so little—in fact I really doubt if, nowadays, I can claim to write at all—that my poems have to go to angry and resentful British literary editors in justification of craven promises over the years. If I do suddenly re-enter a creative climate and am in a position to offer poems more freely, I will certainly remember your charming letter. But until then this is really all I can say.

Again with many thanks, and please extend my familial greetings to Mrs. Nims.

Yours, sincerely, / Philip Larkin

John F. Nims to Frederick Bock   *Chicago, 22 March 1978*

Dear Fred,

Yeah, I think "Pastoral" is very nice now, and we're glad to have it. You won't mind if we run a footnote on "rout his drouth"? saying something like: In the editor's opinion, this phrase is a Real Toad in the poet's imaginary garden: Watch Out for Warts! Or something tactful, huh?

The others are of course good too, but the Marian Anderson one is ruled out because we just took a poem on Beverley ("Bubbles") Sills, and Rule 1089A says: "Poems on the other arts shall be discouraged, and in no case shall two poems on a single art be accepted in one fiscal year."

"No No in the Library" is ruled out by Rule 19234XZ, which reads: "No poems incorporating the words 'shorn hush bleeds no ichorine day of deft fuss' shall be accepted or *countenanced!*" I'd love to take it, but I'm bound by the rules.

But thanks again for "Pastoral," which just makes it under Rule 1887Q. All the best,

Sincerely, / John

Seven months later Bock asked to withdraw "Pastoral," which was already set in type; the editor obliged. Thanking Nims on 4 November, Bock offered to pay typesetting costs and said he would send a paperback copy of *Edsel,* Karl Shapiro's 1972 novel, for the Poetry Day auction: "It's hard to come by, I hear."

John F. Nims to Stanley Moss   *Chicago, 24 March 1978*

Dear Mr. Moss,

Perhaps my return of your poems should be accompanied by an apology for the limitations of my taste. Perhaps I am just not a proper receptor for the wave length you are working on. All I can say is that these poems do not come across *to me* as successful poems. My failure, maybe.

If I were asked why they do not work for me, and were foolish enough to answer (as it seems I am), I think I would say that the energies which must be in your own thoughts, feelings, perceptions do not make themselves felt in the language, which for me is rather flat and limp. The excitement of poetry has to be in the language as much as in the ideas (Mallarmé: "Poetry, my Dear Degas, is not made out of ideas; it is made out of words.") and I'm afraid I don't find the language of these poems exciting.

Another commonplace: "Poetry ought to be at least as well written as prose" (Pound). I feel that sometimes you may be so much concerned with larger matters that you are indifferent to the quality of the writing. In "The Aristocrats," for example, I am bothered by "fragments of petal," since only hard things, brittle things, can break into "fragments." The notion of a brittle thing breaking is built into the etymology of the word. . . .

Of course such things are trifles, but "trifles make perfection, and perfection is no trifle" (Michelangelo, I guess—I'm boring you with a little anthology of platitudes. Or truisms). Let me give you one more: The difference between the right word and the almost right word is the difference between lightning and a lightning-bug (Mark Twain).

I think you permit too many lightning-bugs to sneak into your poems where lightning is called for. . . .

With all best wishes,

Sincerely yours, / John F. Nims

John F. Nims to Marvin Bell — Chicago, 10 May 1978

Dear Marvin,

Well, first, this is not a rejection. Then, to mollify you further, we just got what I think you will think a very nice review of *your* new book. Group review, intelligent. . . .

Your review. I dunno about this business. I thought I'd just be reading poems here and explaining "AHHHHH!" or "Phooey!" But it's not that simple. All kinds things.

Like your review. Your prose is just fine. But the more experienced staff members here tell me it has too much quotation. I counted up the lines, and yes, there are 181 lines by you, and 192 by the people you're reviewing. A little anthology you want to make? I think it does throw things off balance. . . .

Anyway (my favorite word—very philosophical), would you mind cutting your quotations as you see fit? For our publishing pleasure? That way you can add transitional sentences, if necessary. Delete introductory sentences, which introduce a poem not there any more. All like that.

Please cut the quotes to less than half their present length, and all will be fine. To say about 90 lines, instead of 190?

Furthermore (another phil. word), think how embarrassed you'd be getting paid for so much of other people's work.

Hope this will be O.K. with you. Really sorry about the delay—won't happen again. . . .

Hope all goes well. Is it knee-high yet out there?

Sincerely, / John

John F. Nims to Brendan Galvin — Chicago, 18 June 1978

Dear Brendan Galvin,

Happy to keep "Tautog" and "Stethoscope" [October 1978]. As an old Chicagoan, I'm naturally attracted to any poem beginning "Capone-face." . . .

There are very good things in the others too. I like the way the water moves, halfback-fashion, in the river poem. And the weed poem. And the one about the Pompeian girl. Was it Joseph Conrad who said that after finishing a page one should pick it up and shake off all the loose words? Maybe, just maybe, some of your poems could be tighter? Fewer loose words? Maybe.

Anyway, thank you for sending the poems. And all best wishes.

Sincerely yours, / John F. Nims

John F. Nims to Pamela Hadas   *Chicago, 18 June 1978*

Dear Pamela Hadas,

I like your visit to Leonardo's studio ["Plain Lisa"] and am glad to know it will be in *Poetry* [January 1979]. Lisa's dental problem helps explain her odd smile, all right. Never thought of it that way. She and George Washington. Guess you could put her face under his wig in the Stuart painting, and George's face on the Mona Lisa.

No, I don't remember talking to you about translating Sappho at Bread Loaf. But I don't remember names well, not well enough to attach them to the people they belong to. Do you look like Lisa, or George?

Best wishes,

Sincerely yours, / John F. Nims

Joseph Parisi to John F. Nims   *Chicago, 28 June 1978*

Dear John,

Some more correspondence. . . .

Jim Wells called to say he had talked with the man on the Illinois Arts Council; it doesn't look good. The legislature, in its infinite wisdom as the ripples rush eastward from California, has cut its appropriation to the IAC by $300,000. This means they've given away more money than they had to give. Also, the Council doesn't like us: "more of a monument, etc." Thinks we should model our marketing after the illustrious E[lliott] Anderson of *TriQuarterly*; other remarks of this kind. . . .

Important letters, proofs, and some manuscripts were forwarded to the editor while he was on vacation or teaching out of town. J.P. wrote J.F.N. again on 30 June: "we've moved cash from savings to checking and will tread water for another month."

A. R. Ammons to Joseph Parisi   *Ithaca, N.Y., 29 June 1978*

Dear Joseph Parisi,

"The histories of modern poetry in American and of *Poetry* in America are almost interchangeable, certainly inseparable."

That's supposed to be prose, of course. Not much, but at least it's short, and late enough to leave out! Anyway, have fun, pray for grants, and be cheerful! . . .

Ever, / Archie

As part of a campaign to increase subscriptions, J.P. asked several prominent poets for statements about the magazine to be used in an advertising circular.

Joseph Parisi to A. R. Ammons   *Chicago, 5 July 1978*

Dear Mr. Ammons,

Many thanks for your kind words. And they're not too late; we hope to go to press in a couple weeks. Although we've been somewhat more successful with grants, I'm beginning to wonder if they're worth the trouble. But then it is balm to the social conscience to know we're helping several bureaucrats stay in business. . . .

Meanwhile, as the ripples from California grow to waves as they move eastward, we learn that the Illinois Arts Council has cut its appropriations. This, after they'd allotted the funds. (They weren't a lot, to begin with.)

If we keep on smiling, we're going to be hysterical. But somehow we've always come through. Thanks to friends like you.

All best wishes, / Joe Parisi

Marvin Bell to Joseph Parisi   *Iowa City, Ia., 16 July 1978*

Dear Joe,

Thanks for the Ashbery book and Hollander insert. . . .

I can't promise less quoted matter in future reviews. We may differ about this: I feel that poems should be quoted wholly as much as possible, that excerpts are usually misleading and never prove a critical assertion (because everyone knows how "judicious" excerpting can work), and that reviews should not be occasions for making up critical judgments about history, culture or art—all of which are correct in theory but wrong in any case. I find most of the reviewing today prejudicial or dumb, and I want to help *Poetry* maintain a wise and more loving critical attitude. But don't trust me: even as I reaffirm my basic decisions I stand ready to derive a few general statements from such books as Hollander's, Ashbery's, J. Wright's and Ignatow's. However much material is quoted, I'll try to do right by you.

And I'll get some poems in to you sooner or later. I'm afraid I love to keep tinkering and am reassured just to keep them in drafts.

Yours, / Marvin

The revised reviews appeared in October.

Karl Shapiro to Joseph Parisi   *Davis, Calif., 1 September 1978*

Dear Joe,

Perhaps a strange query. I got the POETRY anthology, which I think fascinating and to me rewarding. A few days after I received it Isabella Gardner called me, quite upset that she was not there. (In fact, I checked the index for that before she called.) She disclaimed, and I believe her, any anthological ambitions but was hurt at this particular exclusion.

Chez moi, I know the stings and arrows of anthologies, as what poet doesn't. Belle was not only my right arm when I was editor but I published her with a sense of having discovered her, and have always had a deep feeling for her poems.

She didn't intend me to "do" anything about this but I thought I would write you—I don't know where Daryl is—and seek a softening word.

Karl Shapiro about the time of the Seventy-fifth Anniversary gala in 1987.

My best to you. I owe John a letter. Soon I'm going to sick (sic?) some poems on POETRY.

Best, / Karl

Joseph Parisi to Karl Shapiro   *Chicago, 8 September 1978*

Dear Karl,

Thank you for writing and letting me know about Belle Gardner. I am distressed and can understand that she was upset not to be in the anthology. I am beginning to realize what dubious enterprises anthologies are, since so many people are bound to be displeased. In the end, both editors of the one in question were dissatisfied, as well. . . .

Belle was in the first version of the anthology, which was considerably longer than the finished book. But the cost accountants at Houghton Mifflin grew faint at the sight of the monumental manuscript and issued orders that it be cut, by one-third or more. We were so irked that we contemplated scrapping the whole project. With heavy hearts and a reluctant blue pencil, we then set about trying to make a new book—the "giants" were cut down to sizes we thought inappropriate considering their over-all contributions to the Magazine (Stevens wound up with only 240 ll., etc.), strong poets had to stand on only one poem, while others (on the *third* revision) whom we favored and thought important got one small poem or none at all. As I said, finally not even the editors were pleased with the book; neither of us cares to compile another.

Now, all this is hardly a comfort, I know, but perhaps it will help explain the curious omissions. The 130 odd volumes of POETRY are too much of a good thing.

Both John and I look forward to seeing your new poems.

All best, / Joe

John F. Nims to Anthony Hecht   *Chicago, 7 September 1978*

Dear Tony,

I think we can make the two changes in your poem [section III of "The Venetian Vespers," October 1978]. Our Associate Editor has to go down to the Press to look at the "repros" ("re-pros"?), whatever they are, and thinks there is still time to tinker. We'll try. . . .

Yes, I guess I was part of the junta that did the editorial work here [in the forties]. . . . I was Visiting Editor all by myself in 1960–61. Many grim things in my past.

The Anthology is—odd? (Burn this letter.) Not exactly my choices always. But interesting. *Time* mag. is supposed to do a piece on it week after next. Mostly about *Poetry*, I guess. I wish we would be flooded with subscriptions, but I'm afraid all we will get is more MSS.

I know how you feel about classes. I go back week after next. Many grim things in my future.

All the best, though, / John

[P.S.] I would have thought that Gabrieli would have had 2 *l*'s. But then there is the Royal Danieli Hotel in Venice . . .

Isabella Gardner to John F. Nims   *Hotel Chelsea, New York City,*
                                                      20 September 1978

Dear John,

Thank you for writing. Yes, of course, I was disappointed at not being represented in the *Poetry Anthology*—although I think astonished & shocked would be more accurate than *disappointed. That* sounds a bit thin and whiney.

I am aware that you had no hand in the compiling. I was pleased indeed to be included in your *Western Wind.* . . .

But, John, you *are* responsible, not for your rejections, but for your exacerbating habit of including homilys [sic] & comments. Every poet can easily contend with a simple rejection slip. The poems of mine you turned down I was able to place elsewhere. As God knows can Jim Wright, Galway Kinnell, David Ray, Marcia Masters, etc., etc.—Roland Flint et al.

I cannot think why you feel it is incumbent on you to instruct poets you reject about the quality of their work. All of us submit what we are *not* ashamed of! I don't honestly think that many poets of those you rejected saying "it's not the best you" are inclined to try again. I, for one, will not. There are other journals, magazines & periodicals.

As always, love to Bonnie,

Sincerely, / Belle

P.S. If you feel *compelled* to write something on a rejection slip—a simple Try us again, *soon*—or, Such & such (a poem) I liked best—But really and truly, black and bluely, lay me down and cut me in twoly—a simple rejection slip is more palatable.

Helen Vendler to John F. Nims   *Boston, Mass., 22 September 1978*

Dear Mr. Nims,

It gave me great pleasure to hear of yr appt as editor of *Poetry*. . . . I have admired yr translations and that idiosyncratic anthology/text *Western Wind*. Somebody—maybe Stanley Elkin—tells me you are also a very nice man, so on all three counts I could scarcely refuse [an invitation to review]. I do have too much to do, like everyone else, but I wd like to take on [I. A.] Richards' *New & Selected Poems*, for a short review.

Yr letter was one of those revelations that there are still writers whose even business letters (as cummings wd have put it) are distinctive. Ms. Odechuck is unforgettable.

Yrs, / Helen Vendler

J.F.N. mentioned that among books recently received was *Poems for the Fancy Free*, by one Anne Odechuck. Nims remarked: "That's a real name, and as ill-omened a one for a poet as I've seen in a long time." Vendler's review of the Richards collection was printed in the April 1979 issue.

John F. Nims to [name withheld]   *Chicago, 28 September 1978*

Dear Mr. M—,

Thanks for your note; it's good to get any kind of feedback from readers and contributors.

I don't remember writing those couple of lines at the bottom of the rejection form, but it's clearly my handwriting, so I did. I wouldn't think either "audacity" or "courage" are relevant words, though. You have to imagine a harried editor with a stack of MS. before him which we have decided to send back, and his job is to stick a rejection form in each one. If he writes anything, even "Sorry," it shows some kind of personal interest. If he takes the half second to write "Sorry" he really *means* he's sorry.

The comment was certainly not meant to be what you call an "insult." I would guess I was talking as much to myself as to you—this is a thing I wonder about. It's not even a comment; it's a question.

I know about the Grecian urn and the antique torso of Apollo and Auden on Breughel—but I still suspect it's true that *most* art about art is bad art. Second-hand. I'm sorry if you think "pedantic" is the proper word for that attitude.

But mostly I want to say that no insult whatsoever was intended, and I'm sorry if you thought it was. I was just wondering. Summoning up all my courage I sign myself, with all best wishes,

Sincerely yours, / John F. Nims

Returning his rejection slip, the irate author had objected to a perceived affront from "the editor who had the audacity to write this insulting little note, but not the courage to sign it"; on the slip J. F. N. had asked him: "Do paintings need poems about them?" The submitter had further opined: "It was against just such pedantry that Monroe and Pound were struggling."

Carolyn Kizer to John F. Nims　　　　　*Williamsport, Pa.,*
12 October 1978

Dear Mr. Mims [sic],

You sent such a nice letter when you took over *Poetry* (THANK GOD), and I promised to send a suitable poem when I had one. I enclose a suitable poem.

(I hope you can ignore this hideous stationery [from the Genetti Lycoming Hotel]. I am On The Road.) As soon as I get home and find my checkbook, I shall re-subscribe. It's such a pity. I have every issue from Vol. 1, No. 1 (my mother appeared in *Poetry* once) up until the late unpleasantness. . . . I would pray that your right arm be strengthened, but I see that it is in fine working order. That splendid poet (and woman), Diana O'Hehir [sic], came over the other day with a 2-page letter of rejection from you, and the poems rejected. She said she would have rather had that letter than to have had the poems accepted. We went over the poems together, and you were right—and so perceptive—on every point. Superb editing. Nobody has done that for a poet since I left *Poetry Northwest*. (And you are even better than me, Pims).

Yours faithfully, / Carolyn Kizer

Diana Ó Hehir to John F. Nims   *Oakland, Calif., 15 October 1978*

Dear Mr. Nims:

Thank you so much for your letter with its beautiful, thorough, and intelligent criticism. Such criticism is really almost better than an outright acceptance—I really mean this—because it gives the writer feedback and something to work on and with. I fully appreciate the time that this kind of response takes. Thank you again.

Enclosed are re-writes of the three poems which you discussed, plus three other poems which I'm submitting for your consideration.

I feel presumptuous saying this, but POETRY seems enormously more exciting since you have become its editor. And since it's the best-known journal in the country, this is good news for the world of poetry . . . and makes me even more astonished by the time and care you take with your responses.

Very best to you, / Diana Ó Hehir

[P.S.] Yes, Ó Hehir is an Irish name, but it's not a version of O'Hare—they're two different names.

John Ciardi to John F. Nims   *Metuchen, N.J., 10 November 1978*

Dear John:

I am overjoyed by your acceptance of that whole group. Generous and over generous. And to teach you a lesson, I am sending one more for you to consider, though (note) with a stamped return envelope. . . .

All's well here. My book of limericks with Isaac Asimov has its Bar Mizvah publishing day next week and has sold out the first printing. Wouldn't it be something if this non-book turned out to make money. As a world measure, Isaac and I split an advance of $5000 for it. Then Norton accepted my new book of poems—and the advance for that was $250. Which is, I hasten to add, generous. But cross check the indices, so to speak.

I have a contract (and a generous advance) for my Browser's Dictionary: Harper and Row: ms. due circa April next, the immediate task being a dreary endlessness of two-finger typing. I am ready to believe I really have learned a smidgeon about word and phrase origins in these last 10 years, and have become obsessive about it. The joys of the harmless drudge. Ah, what we fall to. . . .

Ever fondly, / John

Ciardi and Asimov followed their *Limericks: Too Gross / or Two Dozen Dirty Dozen Stanzas* (1978) with *A Grossary of Limericks* (1981).

John F. Nims to Carolyn Kizer   *Chicago, 1 December 1978*

Dear ~~Carol-Anne Kaiser~~ Carolyn Kizer:

O.K., I promise I'll never again get your name wrong. Carol-Anne is sort of nice, though. Ever thought of spelling it that way?

I like your mean poem about children and animals ["Children," April 1979]. Mean and touching too. You will of course make it up to us if any Fond Mommas cancel their subscriptions? Or any dog lovers? I mean we're accepting it. Hope you're in no great hurry; our issues are pretty well made up until next summer. Any book publication deadline?

I'm glad you know and like Diana Ó Hehir. I don't know her, but I do like her poems. Otherwise I wouldn't have written her about them—we don't do that for everybody. Some new poems of hers came in lately, but I haven't seen them yet. Haven't *read* them yet.

The Gus Genetti Motor Lodge, huh? In Wilkes-Barre? Boy, that's really living.

Best wishes, / John Nims

[P.S.] We have three children, a large collie, and a cat (male) named Phebe. Want any? Take your choice.

John F. Nims to Mona Van Duyn   *Chicago, 12 December 1978*

Dear Mona,

I am very pleased to see your name on the envelope you sent the ballad in, because I've been hoping that we'd have some poetry of yours before too long. I was even about to write and plead.

"Ah," I thought, "here will be one of the Great Poems of our time—one laying bare the mysteries of Life and Death that have long perplexed us weary mortals."

But that's not exactly what I found. This was not the kind of seminal poem I expected. At first I was disappointed. "This is not," I felt, "major Mona. This is more a mere bagatelle, albeit not sans charm." (That's how I talk to myself.)

But then I got to like it. Why not? Why not just tickle the Muse instead of allus [sic] bowing and scraping to her? I think this would be fun to run next summer, say next July or August, when nobody wants to read another "The Waste Land" anyway. Poems to read in hammock by lake.

So O.K., let's take it ["The Ballad of Blossom," August 1979]. On one condition, though. When you next write some more characteristic poems— poems that achieve troo Sublimity—think of POETRY. Send us some serious stuff. O.K.? O.K., it's a deal. . . .

Best wishes and MERRY CHRISTMAS and like that,

Sincerely, / John

Ronald Bottrall to John F. Nims   *Cairo, Egypt, 30 December 1978*

Dear Mr Nims,

Thank you for your letter of 14 December. There is nothing impertinent, outrageous, etc. in it. I hear the same emphasis on image rather than statement from British young men, especially those who go to the Iowa University School of Creative Writing. Are we now in the era of The New Imagists or the era of Mixed Icecream Metaphors?

The trouble is that I am 72 years old and have been publishing poetry for nearly 50 years (ten books and another ready). Some people think I am the best poet writing in the English language, others don't. My early mentors among what we used to call "modern poets" were Pound, Eliot, Laura Riding and Robert Graves, three Americans and one Welshman with German ancestors. I do my best nowadays, I read John Ashbery, Marilyn Hacker and Gjertrud Schnackenberg, but old habits are too strong to break easily. Besides, this "imagery business to the bitter end" (BOTTRALL) would have tragic effects on the sonnets of Shakespeare, Milton and Wordsworth. You would have to cut out last lines such as, "They also serve who only stand and wait." A shockingly crude statement that. Milton must have turned his blind eyes on images. It would have the same tragic effect on the whole of Cavafy's poetry.

Worse still, many of the poems in the POETRY anthology would have to be doctored. Even John Berryman in "Snow Line" pp. 391-2, ends: "It's not a good position I am in. / If I had to do the whole thing over again / I wouldn't." As bad as Milton. Also Marilyn Hacker in "Under the Arc de Triomphe: October 17", p. 485 ends: "I cannot think with whom I spent the day / nor what I thought. I slept and woke alone." Reads like a statement to me. . . .

Now to the poems I sent you. I have rewritten the second half of "Limbo", copy enclosed (sorry I can't change its form) and I agree, exceptionally, that you may omit the last stanza of "Darkling". In case you do not like the new "Limbo", I am including three more poems: (1) "Metamorphosis", which I wrote a few weeks ago. No-one can say that the ending is a statement, at least in the ordinary sense of the word. (2) and (3), about our new flat, are a pair, but "Change of Season" can be published without "Change of Place", if you wish.

All good wishes to you and POETRY (in every sense of the word),

Yours sincerely, / Ronald Bottrall

Nims had written 14 December, asking Bottrall to shorten and otherwise alter the submissions, explaining: "It may well be that I've been too influenced by our modern emphasis on the image rather than the statement—but I felt that some of your poems are perhaps weakened by spelling out, at the end, what the imagery had already implied. Please excuse me if I'm being impertinent, outrageous, etc.—I'm just trying to be 'editorial.'" J.F.N. accepted "Aspects of Darkness"; it was published in April 1979, Bottrall's last appearance in *Poetry*.

Caroline Tate to John F. Nims   *San Cristobal de las Casas,*
                                                   Mexico, [n.d.], 1979

Dear John:

I am sure that I haven't any published manuscripts of Allen's. He married so fast and so often that it is hard to keep up with him. I suggest that you try Helen Tate and Isabella Gardner. I am ashamed to say I have lost Allen's address. . . .

Allen's death was a blessed release from pain. I have had so many notes of condolence that I am bewildered. But I think your plan is fine. Red [Robert Penn] Warren ought to be able to help. He kept in touch with Allen throughout the years.

I am a prisoner of arrhythmic heart. These mountains hem me in. My heart won't allow aeroplane flights, so here I am forced to stay put. My doctor is very stern and very Spanish. The flowers bloom here the year around. After a while you feel that if they had good sense they would stay dormant part of the year. Yes, we had some good times in Italy. If I had my choice I'd live in Rome.

Love to Bonnie and good luck with your venture.

                                                   Caroline

The special issue "In Honor of Allen Tate" in November 1979 included Tate's "The Swimmers," poems by Warren, William Stafford, and others as well as a tribute by Ashley Brown and Tate's essay "Mere Literature and the Lost Traveller." Tate (b. 1899) died in Nashville on 9 February. He and Gardner were married from 1959 to 1969.

Robert Penn Warren to John F. Nims   *Fairfield, Conn.,*
                                                   28 February 1979

Dear John—if I may be so bold:

For years I have been meditating an essay on Allen's poetry, and have made only false starts. So I can't promise more than a false start. I'll be thinking about it. But don't count on it. Right now, recently back from the funeral, I don't really feel like an essay.

But there is a poem, which, good or bad, tells a truth about A.T. It is new, and I might want to do some retouching. Any suggestions welcome. I hope that this pleases you enough to use for the occasion, anyway. I'd like to be represented.

Later on, I'd like to send you some other poems—more in the days work. When you became editor I felt I wanted again to contribute to *Poetry*.

All good fortune!

Sincerely yours, / Red Warren

Warren contributed three poems to the Tate memorial issue (November 1979):"Synonyms," "The Moonlight's Dream," and "Aspen Leaf in Windless World." In his cover letter to the submission on 12 May, he wrote: "Here are four poems on their first trip from home. Be nice to them, they're still shy."

John F. Nims to David Wagoner   *Chicago, 27 March 1979*

Dear David,

Yeah. I like these. And they go together well. Glad you're into bugs instead of Indians. A step up. That's not racist; it's just pro-bug. Bugs have few people to speak up for them. But liberation! . . .

I'm glad you heard from Harold Bloom. I like Harold; we were together at the Bread Loaf School of English two or three summers. I don't always like his criticism, but who does? Burn this letter: first it's Indians, now it's Bloom. I'm not sure Harold likes poetry at all—but he sure does like ideas-in-poetry and influences and derivations and visions and insights. Anyway, he'll help make you immortal, and that's good.

All the best. Finally it's spring in Chicago!

Vernally, / John

Karl Shapiro to John F. Nims   *Davis, Calif., 17 May 1979*

Dear John,

When you became editor you asked if I had anything to send for POETRY. If the situation hasn't changed, I have a new essay called CREATIVE GLUT. It is very much like what you said in the AWP Newsletter just now.

Mine was a lecture, like all my essays, a Faculty Research Center Lecture I was elected to give, to my horror. It took me months of sleepless nights. It's funny too. It would need cutting of local references and so on.

If you are now booked ahead I'll understand.

Love to you both from us both,

Karl

[P.S.] For your five or six poets I got it down to what I call my B-S-K theory, only three poets at any one time. (Byron and you know.) I am hearing compliments for *Poetry* from all around.

In his cover letter of 29 May with the essay, K.S. wrote: "The presentation got a standing ovation although I don't think one person in the Liberal audience agreed with a word of it." It was published in October 1979 and provoked controversy because of its acid remarks about writing programs.

John F. Nims to Marvin Bell   *Chicago, 21 August 1979*

Dear Marvin,

My not writing doesn't mean anything except that yes, I am swamped. Always trying to catch up. Joe thought you were going to phone a week or so ago, which gave me an excuse for not writing.

That's O.K. about the Ashbery and Hollander. The Ashbery has been re-assigned. . . .

Not much lit. news. I hear that ol' Miz Poe's son Edgar is still working on that dumb bird poem. Emily's very busy directing the Amherst Writers' Conference again and publishing *everywhere*. She's so pushy. Publish publish publish. "Can't you ever keep a poem to yourself?" I ask her. "Lissen, Bud, I gotta get it while I can," she tells me. "Fame ain't gonna do me no good dead." And I suppose you know the latest about Walt? Old scamp! Quite a world, the lit. world.

All the best, / John

Elizabeth Bishop to John F. Nims   *Lewis Wharf, Boston, Mass.,*
                                                      6 October 1979

Dear John:

I'm enclosing a slightly changed biographical note [for *The Harper Anthology of Poetry*, published in 1981] . . . [sic] Yours was essentially correct but I felt the *emphasis* was wrong!

Now I'm going to take issue with you—rather violently—about the idea of footnotes . . . [sic] with one or two exceptions (I'll mention them later) I don't think there should be ANY footnotes, for me, that is. You say the book is for college students, and I think anyone who gets as far as college should be able to use a dictionary . . . [sic] If a poem catches a student's interest at all, he or she should damned well be able to look up an unfamiliar word in the dictionary. (I know they don't—or most of them don't—but they should be made to, somehow. The earlier poems you are using of course may require some help—but mine certainly don't.) "Isinglass" is in the dictionary; [THE FISH] so is "gunnel" ("see gunwale"); so is "thwart."

One of my few exceptions is the ESSO-Exxon note to FILLING STATION, because I'm not sure how long ago now that happened, but a good many years. Also, I'd let students figure out—in fact, I TELL them—the cans are arranged to say so–so–so, etc. So I don't think *that* has to be explained. However—most of them might well not know that *so-so-so* was what—or still is in some places—the phrase people use to calm and soothe horses. . . . [sic] All flower names can be looked up, certainly—some students even SEE flowers still although I know only too well that TV has weakened the sense of reality so that very few students see anything the way it is in real life. . . .

Elizabeth Bishop

You can see what a nasty teacher I must be—but I do think students get lazier and lazier & expect to have everything done *for* them. (I suggested buying a small paper-back and almost the whole class whined "Where can I find it?") My best example of this sort of thing is what one rather bright Harvard honors student told me. She told her room-mate or a friend—who had obviously taken my verse writing course—that she was doing her paper with me and the friend said "Oh don't work with *her*! It's awful! She wants you to look words up in the dictionary! It isn't *creative* at all!" In other words, it is better not to know what you're writing or reading. . . .

I hope I haven't offended you—but I think the teaching of lit. now is deplorable—and if you can get any students to *reading* you will have done a noble service.

Affectionately, / Elizabeth

John F. Nims to Paul Carroll   *Chicago, 26 October 1979*

Dear Paul,

Thanks very much for letting us see your new poems. I suppose my first thought is that you, as a well-established poet, do not need *Poetry*. Whereas lots of young poets do. Maybe you've noticed that we've had quite a few "new poets" lately. . . . I feel that my obligation is to them, and I want to save as much space for them as I can. . . .

Also, I'm very leery about publishing poems by friends. This is part of my one-man campaign against cronyism that is such a blight on contemporary poetry. You know, all those little groups that huddle and cuddle, laving one another with warm wet praise. Writing blurbs for one another's book. Print-ing one another's poems. Dedicating and being dedicated to. . . .

I'm doubly leery about printing poems by colleagues, since I don't want it thought that *Poetry* is sort of a house organ. The suggestion has been made by local gossips that the University [of Illinois at Chicago] now owns us. Quite the reverse—and I want us to be absolutely above suspicion in this respect.

So my returning your poem, with thanks, has nothing to do with its merits, but to quite other considerations.

All the best, / John

Paul Carroll to John F. Nims Chicago, 31 October 1979

Dear John,

Thank you for returning my poem, "But What Does It All Mean, In the End, Severn?"

My hope is that the current policy of poetry not to consider work sub-mitted by either an established poet and/or one who is a friend or col-league, will not discourage some writer in the future whom the Depart-ment of English and the Program for Writers would like to invite to join our staff.

I had thought that an editor accepts or rejects a poem based on its merit or lack of it. Apparently, my opinion was a bit simplistic.

All the best, / Paul

Carroll sent copies of this letter to the dean of the college, English department head, and all instructors in the writing program. Despite J.F.N.'s request, Carroll continued to submit mss.

Fred Chappell to John F. Nims Greensboro, N.C., 6 December 1979

Dear John,

I hope you're in health, me lad, and otherwise doing mighty fine also. Want to wish you Happy Holidays! from all of us here. You need to come back & see us sometime soon.

I enclose just exactly the thing you've been looking for, a looooong god-dam poem. This is the first time ever I submitted to *Poetry*, so I thought I'd make it disastrous.

Keep up the damn good work.

Yrs for rum crime and riot,

Fred
ole F.

The poem was returned. On 2 February 1980, Chappell wrote again: "Ha, one rejection don't bother Me, fukit. Just makes me send in More and LONGER poems, what I care?"

Richard Wilbur, guest of honor, with John Nims and
Julia Bartholomay, board president, Poetry Day, 16 November 1979.

John F. Nims to Richard Wilbur   *Chicago, 16 January 1980*

Dear Dick,

Thanks very much for the new translations of Act II, i and ii [of Racine's
Andromache]. They are more exciting than Act I, seems to me. I wish we could
publish both scenes, but I'm afraid we're going to have to content ourselves
with II, ii, which will take 6 pages. This translation issue (April) is bursting at
the seams, so that we may have to omit some already accepted stuff. . . .

Looks like a really good issue. We're waiting now for a review by John
Simon of several recent books of poetry in trans.

The affair at Washington was really fun. The next day one of the Wash.
papers called it "one of the most enjoyable White House parties in recent
memory." Lots of nice (American) wine, good finger food, more old friends
than there was time to talk to—really a super-party. Nice house to throw a
party in. The President spent an hour or so there, though it must have been
one of his worst days in a long time (Afghanistan). He doesn't always come
to such receptions, we were told. Quite a few poets have already written to
tell us they really enjoyed it. No complaints that we know of—once we got
inside, anyway. The list of readers "they" (whoever "they" were) picked out
was odd, since there were plenty of better poets in the audience: Tony
Hecht, Ammons, Ashbery, May Swenson, etc. Otherwise, things were great.
The original idea was to help the magazine (*Poetry*) by getting attention,
subscribers, donors, $$$, etc. We think it helped. . . .

Hi, Charlee! Greetings from Bonnie too to Allen Sundry.

Best, / John

The April issue contained originals with facing translations of Belli, Gozzano, Mandelstam, Marin Sorescu, and sections of Wilbur's *Andromache* and of John Berryman's *Job*. Simon's long, two-part review of translations of twenty European poets was titled "*Traduttore, Traditore* or The Tradition of Traducing." The Soviet invasion of Afghanistan in December 1979 led to Carter's veto of American participation in the 1980 Summer Olympics in Moscow, as well as to the U.S.'s costly military training program for Islamic fundamentalists in Pakistan and Afghanistan, which inadvertently came to aid in the creation of the Taliban.

Marvin Bell to Joseph Parisi   *Iowa City, Ia., 28 January 1980*

Dear Joe,

I see that the form I'm enclosing isn't due back until proofs, but here it is ahead of time. Returning it now gives me a chance to say thank you for your part in the White House reception. I do remember seeing you in the crowd, and greeting you, and then being turned this way and that by others and not seeing you again.

Well, it was a fine occasion. I heard more than one hatchet being unburied. Dorothy and I had a fine time at the White House and in Washington, and I was delighted be a part of it. It was a grand occasion for *Poetry*, too.

Much gratitude.

Sincerely, / Marvin

[P.S.]—Your review of [John Ashbery's] *As We Know,* seen here yesterday, is excellent. Not so easy to have written with insight and sympathy. As you know.

May Swenson to John F. Nims   *Dorland Mountain Arts Colony,*
                                        Temecula, Calif., 28 January 1980

Dear John:

Here are some poems that you invited me to send so long ago. . . .

Too bad I lost sight of you right after the "stage presentation" of poets at The White House. There was such a mob and several people I hoped to greet disappeared into it. (I got to meet and talk to Karl Shapiro, whose work has always interested me—I don't care that he's badmouthed by others these days—and he once gave a book of mine a really keen review in the N.Y. *Times*.) When Rosalyn Carter called for "all the poets" to come to the platform, I had just arrived in that room. (A lot of us had had to inch along in a block-long line outside before being checked through the gates by a very slow and fussy security guard, even though we got there on the dot of 4 p.m.) I had not known of the program of readings, so

when she said "all poets" that
seemed to include me. I was on
the stage by mistake, I then realized, and that partly accounted for
the blurry face that appeared in
the middle of the photo on next
day's *Times* front page. Never
mind. The whole affair was enjoyable. It actually was a thrill to shake
hands with Jimmy. I'm for him,
and have been all along—although
the hawkish posture he's just taken
raises questions. . . . [sic]

I and best friend, Zan Knudson
who writes juvenile novels, are
working here (until April 8th) at a
new and primitive artists' colony
on a mountain between San Diego
and Riverside. It's in a Nature Preserve and has wonderful views,
wild animals, birds. No electricity;

May Swenson in a snapshot sent to
Poetry at the time of her first
appearances in the early fifties.

we light with kerosene, cook with propane, and heat with wood stoves. A
different weather every day. Right now it's gusty and rainy. New poems are
happening. The ones I enclose were begun last winter in Tucson and L.A.—
four of them—the other two, earlier.

When that review of my THINGS TAKING PLACE that Dave Smith wrote
appears [February 1980], would you send me a copy?

With all best wishes, / May

David Wagoner to John F. Nims   Poetry Northwest, *Seattle, Wash.,*
                                              27 February 1980

Dear John:

Thanks for the acceptance. I'll be proud to be in the rejuvenated *Poetry*
again. You're really doing a very good job, keeping the range broad and the
quality high. Congratulations.

Dick Hugo tells me Jim Wright is dying of inoperable cancer. Makes me
feel very low. We were good friends once. The most uncanny memory of
anyone I've ever known, and a first-rate poet. *Timor mortis* [*conturbat me*: the
fear of death (upsets me)]. . . .

Yours, / David

John F. Nims to Amy Clampitt   *Chicago, 8 March 1980*

Dear Amy Clampitt,

Thanks very much for letting us see the poems. The one we like best of all, and would like to keep for *Poetry*, is "Balms" [November 1980]. Very nice!

"Times Square Water Music" is good too, but maybe "a little long for what it does"? I'm always puzzled too by poems that come on double-column pages. Some poets want them printed that way, some are saving paper.

In "De Motus Cordis" [On the Motion of the Heart]: you think the heartbeat is spondaic? Most listeners to it, from the ancient Greeks on, have heard it as iambic. Lub-*dubb*, as the student nurses say. Ka-BOOM, as the TV ad for the heart fund says. If you've got a spondaic heart, you may be in trouble. Walk, don't run, to your doctor.

Sincerely, / John F. Nims

Marvin Bell to John F. Nims & Joseph Parisi   *Iowa City, Ia.,*
24 March 1980

Dear John and Joe,

As you must know, James Wright is apparently dying of cancer. My information has been second-hand from the start. If accurate, however, Wright is hospitalized in NYC and is now given a short time to live—someone reported 2-3 weeks, maybe months, they were unsure. The diagnosis was reported as throat cancer, later amended to cancer of the tongue.

James Wright shortly before
his death in 1980.

I am deeply affected by this, as by his poetry and his vision, and I would certainly ask you to call on me if there is anything ever to be done. I write now, however, only to set you to thinking about whether or not my review should be published now or should be printed with its present title: "That We Keep Them Alive" [June 1980]. That title derives from the review's last sentence. I returned proof a while ago. Perhaps the review is at press or nearing the press? I'll trust your judgment in this. If there is

any question about the meaning or propriety of the title or last sentence of
the review, or about what the effect might be, please hold the piece or revise it. I'm *trying* to see clearly, and it *seems* to me that the title and its source
in the review are still proper, perhaps. More so now. But I must trust you
to decide. . . .

. . . I don't even want to go on thinking about this, beyond realizing that
this unpleasant alert may be useful. Please do what you think best.

Sincerely— / Marvin

James Wright died on 25 March 1980.

Gregory Djanikian to John F. Nims   *[Baltimore, Md.], 27 March 1980*

Dear Mr. Nims,

Enclosed are four poems for your consideration, most of them formal
in nature. It is discouraging to peruse journals these days and to discover
that the contemporary poetic sensibility seems to regard form as anath-
ema, something to be damned and ridiculed, and at best, condescended to.
I don't know why it should be so. For my part, I would much rather see
poetry in a variety of structures, poems in both organic and traditional
forms, the general individuated in a myriad of particulars. I hope there is
not one style of poetry we must all adhere to: we would be the poorer for
it, I think. . . .

It is incomprehensible to me that many young poets today, for all their
brilliance of imagery and their breath-taking leaps of imagination, cannot
find their way through an iambic pentameter line, and would not care to,
reasoning that form and craft prohibits a plurality of styles. What has been
the result? For the most part, a poetry which sounds and looks the same. Is
it not ironic, Mr. Nims, in this great age of irony, that a poem written in
form today and printed in most any journal should suddenly seem con-
spicuous, refreshingly different, and perhaps even dangerous? The pendu-
lum, it seems, may be swinging back. . . .

Thank you for your time.

Cordially, / Gregory Djanikian

Anthony Hecht to John F. Nims   *Rochester, N.Y., 19 August 1980*

Dear John,

I suppose you are established for the summer in some pastoral setting,
evangelizing among the illiterati, the cows, the chickens and the paying
guests. So this [group] is meant light-heartedly to greet you upon your return. I hope you will like it. And I hope that in spite of the fact that it is a

poetic "quartet," nobody will suppose it derives from Mr. Eliot in any way whatever. . . .

Please remember me to Joseph Parisi, whom I met at the presidential reception for poets at the White House—an occasion which current politics make sad in retrospect. But I will not get off on current politics. I shall simply plan to commit a lot of Lamentations to memory. And add, perhaps, that quite possibly the reason Gov. Reagan took so long to name his running mate is that he was searching for someone named Goneril.

With affectionate good wishes, / Tony

"A Love for Four Voices: Homage to Franz Joseph Haydn" was published in April 1981. Ronald Reagan had accepted the Republican nomination for president on 17 July. Hecht is of course playing on the names of the two treacherous daughters in *King Lear*, Goneril and Regan.

CHAPTER VIII

The Early Eighties

1. Hanging On

Enjoyable and glamorous as the White House reception was—it turned out to be about the only bright spot for the magazine in the dismal year of 1980—the outcome of the event was not all that the *Poetry* board had hoped for. From the standpoint of publicity, the poets' day in the national spotlight was a triumph, to be sure. Friends had happy reunions, po-biz was busily conducted, Karl Shapiro held court with reporters in the nearby Jefferson Hotel and was quoted and pictured with other noted authors in the *Washington Post*, the *Washington Star*, and several newspapers across the country. But the celebration did not produce the new friends and potential patrons for the magazine that had been anticipated. As the year progressed, the gloom over *Poetry*'s present problems and future prospects deepened.

Although the idea of approaching wealthy descendants of Harriet Monroe's original guarantors was abandoned—there were not many extant in 1980—the plan of establishing an endowment was not. I was asked to move ahead with production of the booklet "*Poetry*: An American Institution" as part of the new campaign. Ethel Kaplan, who had given an incisive report on the Modern Poetry Association's finances the previous year, was appointed head of the endowment committee and set a twelve- to eighteen-month goal of $250,000. Possessed of a rare combination of common sense and scholarly training (a Ph.D. in Renaissance English literature from Harvard), Kaplan had already demonstrated her personal effectiveness as a fundraiser by obtaining several donations from friends and acquaintances. Then she called on Marshall Field V and, with the promise not to bother him again, came away with a pledge of $5,000. Kaplan also paid a visit to A. N. Pritzker, the patriarch of the family that built the Hyatt hotel chain. Abe Pritzker greeted her with: "And so, what is this going to cost me?" She said a contribution of $1,000 would be deeply appreciated. He promptly wrote out a check in that amount, and told her: "I've never gotten anyone out of my office so cheaply."

At the annual meeting in June, the treasurer reported that losses suffered in the recent stock market decline had reduced the modest reserve fund by $9,000. Regular donations were down too, and meanwhile costs of publication were steadily rising, though not quite at the rate of inflation (at that time 15 percent). Printing bills had not been paid since February, and by October *Poetry*'s past-due account would climb to over $21,000. The board voted to raise the annual subscription rate from $15 to $20. Such increases were always resisted, in part because renewals usually dropped soon afterward, but there was little choice.

In early October, board president Julia Bartholomay sent an urgent letter to the trustees calling an emergency meeting and informing them: "*Poetry*'s financial condition is fast approaching a critical state." There was exactly $987.39 in the checking account. "Clearly, it is imperative, therefore, that Poetry Day be a success," she wrote. After other plans fell through during the summer, I had hastily proposed a change of format for the annual benefit: instead of the customary poetry reading, a musical performance featuring the soprano Ruth Welting singing famous songs with texts by English poets. Welting had performed brilliantly in several Lyric Opera productions and had many fans in the Chicago area, and the hope was she would attract a larger, more diverse audience than the usual poetry crowd. Her recital of "Poetry in Song" on November 22 received an enthusiastic response and brought in $10,000, about $3,000 more than in the preceding year.

At the emergency meeting in late October, I presented a ten-year summary of income and losses, contributions from all sources, circulation numbers, and other data on operations. Among other things, the report showed publication costs over the last decade rose 63 percent, substantially below the rate of the Consumer Price Index. But paid circulation declined almost 20 percent over those ten years, from about 8,200 to 6,500 monthly copies. At the same time annual net loss from publication soared from $9,000 in 1971 to over $45,000 in 1980. Ethel Kaplan reported that the endowment committee was preparing solicitation materials for approaching foundations and corporate donors, and pointed out it was essential to show enthusiastic backing from the board. She noted that persuading corporations to support poetry was difficult—just how hard we would soon discover—since there was little public recognition to be gained for them, compared to the "visibility" they achieved with gifts for health and education or arts groups like the symphony and the opera.

At the next special meeting, in early December, the board reviewed the situation. The trustees were determined to go forward and find more corporate sponsors and increase Associate memberships. To cut expenses, it was decided that the monthly issues would no longer be mailed out in envelopes. Subjecting the magazine to the hazards of the U.S. Post Office unprotected was an unappealing measure, but it would save more than $5,000 a year. (Besides the expense for envelopes, there were the labor costs: stuffing and labeling had to be done by hand.) We then considered a list of foundations we might approach over the new year.

During the fall, John Nims had written privately to a number of poet friends about the impending crisis. Some sent contributions or declined payment for forthcoming work; many others gave suggestions. John Ciardi offered to put on a series of lectures and turn over the fees to the magazine. In the January 1981 issue the editor printed a lengthy article in News Notes that outlined *Poetry*'s current problems and asked for support from readers. Crises had arisen on the eve of every ten-year anniversary, but this appeal was the first such to be printed in the magazine in almost forty years, when George Dillon feared the end was nigh in the middle of World War II. Nims pointed out that postal rates alone had risen 300 percent in the last ten years, and that inflation and widespread cuts in federal aid to education had taken their toll on library subscriptions.

He explained that the cover price had never covered actual production costs, and that those who subscribed not only helped support *Poetry* "but also poetry and poets," since it remained one of very few literary magazines to pay its contributors. He also observed, with marvelous understatement: "we have fewer individual subscribers than the would-be contributors who send us poems for publication." A major problem, he added, was false perceptions: "Our very success has been a source of difficulty. Many feel that so celebrated a magazine, founded nearly 70 years ago, must by now have a firm financial basis consolidated over the years. But this is not so; it has never been so."

In April a special form soliciting contributions was printed in the magazine but generated only modest donations. The editor himself generously took half-pay in April and May while he was teaching in Charleston, though he continued to read manuscripts, edit and proof issues, and handle other business by mail. In May, Ethel Kaplan, who had recently been elected president of the Association, was finally able to send an upbeat letter to trustees. Through increased giving, grants, and Poetry Day receipts, the magazine deficit had been reduced to less than $10,000. Although this meant there was still none of the usual "extra" income from Poetry Day to tide the magazine over into the new year, she said there was reason for optimism. The Prince Charitable Trusts had given $15,000 toward the Endowment Fund, CCLM was offering a matching grant of $2,200, and other proposals were in the works.

At the annual meeting in June, the president reported that, after our discussion of several options with them, the Joyce Foundation had decided to provide a $5,000 matching grant to increase memberships in the Associates program. She also informed the board that David Wagoner had agreed to read for the 1982 Poetry Day program. (As an additional benefit for *Poetry*, Wagoner tried, unsuccessfully, to arrange the premiere in Chicago for *The Escape Artist*, a film adaptation of his novel just completed by Francis Ford Coppola.) Kaplan then announced special plans for 1982 to mark *Poetry*'s seventieth anniversary. Since spring, she and I had met several times with the head of the Chicago Public Library and her staff, who expressed enthusiastic support for an elaborate, city-wide observance of "70 Years of *Poetry* in Chicago"—readings, exhibits, workshops, lectures, poetry contests— to be presented in the library's downtown Cultural Center and branch libraries and (it was hoped) co-sponsored by the Chicago Council on Fine Arts.

Although there was a net loss for 1980–1981 of almost $10,000, the treasurer predicted a balanced budget for the next year, assuming all the grants came through. (Eventually, in 1982, the MacArthur Foundation gave $20,000, the largest award to date.) In the fall of 1981, however, the cash-flow situation still remained precarious. For the first time in decades, contributors' fees had to be reduced, from one dollar to fifty cents a line, for eight months only. But after more than two years of increasingly bleak financial news, at last the crisis seemed over, and it appeared long-term solutions to *Poetry*'s problems were at hand.

Although fund-raising now consumed ever more time, regular editorial work went on, if later into the evenings and weekends. While fund-raising and promotion were far from Nims's favorite activities, he gamely did his part. For me, the strategizing, visits to foundation heads and program officers, and proposal-writing became distractions, or rather diversions: challenges and welcome changes amid the routines of reading (mostly dull) manuscripts, editing prose, and dealing with printers. When we were successful in our appeals, spirits were lifted. But like it or not, we had come to accept the reality faced by all editors before us, except now we responded much more systematically. To preserve this "American Institution" we knew we would have to be on a permanent fund-raising campaign.

2. Correspondence 1980–1983

Despite the extra-literary burdens during this trying period, the editor continues to write his customary detailed notes and witty rejection letters. In correspondence with friends the financial crisis only brings out more of his characteristic good humor. James Dickey, having spent most of recent years writing prose, is delighted by Nims's confidence in his poetry and the printing of a generous selection of poems from his new collection. Nims regales Dickey with a story about John Ciardi and the malaprop-prone Chicago columnist and interviewer Irv Kupcinet. An upcoming review of Anthony Hecht's *The Venetian Vespers* occasions one of the better jokes Nims recounted during his tenure.

Along with his proposal to lecture for *Poetry*, John Ciardi offers other suggestions to help in the current crisis. Poet-farmer James Hearst presents the fee he received for a poem in a recent anthology, along with a bright remark about poets on poetry. Young Gary Soto apologizes for his hasty hand following Nims's inquiry about the imprecise similes in his submissions (which the editor accepts nonetheless). "Ordinary" readers write in with acute observations and no-nonsense suggestions about handling *Poetry*'s money problems, as well as well-argued complaints about the magazine's contents and on the "plight" of the "amateur reader." The translator Kimon Friar writes excitedly from Athens about the special issue on contemporary Greek poetry while the novelist John Gardner discourses at length about classical Welsh verse forms and his own recent forays into poetry.

James Dickey to John F. Nims   *Columbia, S.C., 19 August 1980*

Dear John:

Here are five poems from the new book [*Puella*], which needless to say I hope you will like. The general plan was to try to imagine parts of a young girl's possible experiences, both some real ones and some she undergoes in fantasy, such as the first one about burning up the doll and the house at the same time (and her childhood with them) and the invocation to the crows— or being invoked *by* the crows. . . . I won't preface the poems with a lot of pre-determining palaver but will just let you have a go at them. . . .

One more thing occurs to me. If it were possible to make enough of a flap about all this I might be able to take on a couple of readings up there and go on some of the talk-shows in that area, such as the [Irv] Kupcinet show, the Jim Conway show, Bob Cromie's book program, and maybe a couple of others. I've been on all these, and the results seem to have been good, and if it would help the magazine and the general situation of your efforts both there and elsewhere, I would be glad to do it. Let me know if you think this idea hold possibilities, and I will be guided accordingly.

Yes, your poem ["Cardiological," printed in *Poetry* in 1977] certainly *is* in the Atlanta hospital where John Stone is a cardiologist, and chief of emergency medicine. My youngest son, who is just going into medical school at Emory, where John also teaches, has worked for the past two summers under John in the emergency room at Grady Hospital, which is a gory place,

I can tell you. John himself was responsible for saving my life there about three years ago, when I bit off part of my tongue in an alcoholic-with-drawal seizure, and almost bled to death. He is a very good healer, and quite a good poet, too, don't you think.

I'll close off now, and wait to hear. Meanwhile, my best, as always,

Ever, / Jim

John F. Nims to James Dickey   *Chicago, 2 September 1980*

Dear Jim,

Very pleased to have the poems. Good strong group! I found your description of the new group helpful, and wondered if our readers wouldn't. What would you think of our quoting in the biog. note on you the two or three sentences beginning: "The general plan" . . . ?

The idea of your giving readings up here and going on talk shows seems a good one. We have not, ourselves, been sponsoring any readings except (most years) our annual Poetry Day. (This year we're having Ruth Welting, the opera singer, in a recital of great song-poems: Campion, etc.) But lots of universities around here have them. Kupcinet is still here—though illiterate as ever. Once when he had [Dante translator John] Ciardi on he asked, "Tell me, John, did you really trans-a-late the whole tetterology?" Ciardi was supposed to see him a week or so ago, but Kup's office announced he was "in Hiatus." Ciardi says that's just outside Hyannisport. Anyway, Kup is here. So is Studs Terkel, a good interviewer. And Bob Cromie. I think Jim Conway has left town. But if you'd like to time such a visit with the appearance of the poems and the review, why don't we wait and see when we can run those?

Sure, I know John Stone, from Bread Loaf. I can't say he saved my life, but he saw me through some lousy summer flu up there about 10 years ago. Yes, a good doctor-poet.

But how good to have you back in POETRY, after all these years! Thanks for sending the poems.

All the best, / John

Five poems from *Puella* were published in March 1981, and received the Levinson Prize. See Dickey's letter of 6 November 1981 below.

John F. Nims to Gwen Head   *Chicago, 29 August 1980*

Dear Gwen Head,

Thank you very much for sending your poems, which we read with pleasure. Good things in all of them! I'm really sorry that, although we liked them, they did not quite compel acceptance. We hope though that you'll let us see other work in the future.

It's always dangerous to try to tell, in a letter, why a poem doesn't seem to work. Likely as not I get a letter back saying something like "Listen, stupid, who asked you?"

But I'll take a chance and tell you that these seem to me somewhat overwritten, considering the subjects. That worm, now—well, near the end you say, "Yet still I have not told . . ." as if you knew you were trying to tell everything. Some of the lines after that I liked very much—and I wondered if you should not pick out your six or so strongest lines and call it quits. Maybe the six lines is plenty for this worm? I think I felt the same about the gerbil poem—too long. For a dumb gerbil, anyway. Occasionally images seemed to me hard to believe, as in "The Refrain," in which the ice cubes in a glass tap "like the immaculate small hooves of thirsty deer". Kind of silly? That glassful of deer, I mean. And if they're inside the glass why are they thirsty? More likely these midget deer are drowned.

But of course I may be quite wrong. Excuse me for trying to tell you such things.

With all best wishes,

Sincerely yours, / John F. Nims

John F. Nims to Anthony Hecht   *Chicago, 2 September 1980*

Dear Tony,

First, before I forget, let me say that you sent the poems to our old address. So they were slow getting here. . . . But what a nice surprise! . . . A very nice group. Fun! We're happy to have them. They'll look great in the magazine sometime early next year. Lots of incidental delights in the musical etc. plays on words. I like "Civilization and Its Discothèques" especially. (Just picked up the Freud book for 10 cents at a sidewalk sale.) . . .

It took us a while to arrange a review for *The Venetian Vespers*, but now it's out with a highly recommended reviewer [Vernon Shetley] that Helen Vendler thinks is great. Hope he won't show off at your expense. You can never tell with reviewers. Worse than rattlesnakes. . . .

When the second edition comes out, you might want to add, as a scholarly footnote, this anecdote, just sent me by a learned friend. I summarize; add local color:

Two young people get married after a whirlwind courtship on a cruise. Back in America, they are vacationing at the country house of a friend with a swimming pool. The groom steps out on the diving board, does a gorgeous dive. She looks at him, amazed. "Oh," he explains, "we had such a whirlwind courtship that I didn't have a chance to tell you I was on the

Olympic swimming team." Then she dives in, and does a couple of lengths of the pool in what looks like record-breaking time. General amazement. "Oh," she explains to him, "we had such a whirlwind courtship I didn't have a chance to tell you I was a street-walker in Venice." . . .

All the best. We're really happy to have the poem.

John

Shetley's shrewdly appreciative but not altogether admiring review was printed in February 1981. Among his observations: "Hecht is almost unique among his contemporaries in having an alive, and alert, sense of sin. . . . Hecht's anti-naturalism resembles that of T. S. Eliot, a fear of the harrowing experience of the realm of flesh."

C. M. Jones to John F. Nims   *New York City, 5 September 1980*

Dear Mr. Nims:

Blah blah blah blah blah blah blah blah blah blah blah my first creative work blah blah blah blah blah blah blah blah blah blah blah blah blah blah blah.

Sincerely, / C. M. Jones

David Wagoner to John F. Nims   Poetry Northwest, *Seattle, Wash.,*
1 November 1980

Dear John:

I hope it doesn't seem like cruel and unusual punishment to send you such a large batch of poems—18—at the same time. I thought you might like to have a broader range of choice.

Coppola has finished filming my THE ESCAPE ARTIST, and it will be released via Warner Bros. around next April. I'll be seeing the director's cut in late Nov., preliminary to the music and later editing before the preview version. Went to Hollywood for a cast-crew party (300 people!) and what a bash. Two of the original Dead End Kids—Gabe Dell and Huntz Hall—are in it and Jackie Coogan. I saw about 700 color slides from the film, and it's going to be a visual knockout if nothing else. Caleb Deschanel, the director, was camerman for THE BLACK STALLION and BEING THERE. Everybody has high hopes for it. Ballantine is going to reisssue [the novel] in time with the movie release.

Hope all's well with you and Bonnie. I've just been given the $1000 Sherwood Anderson Award for my newest novel, THE HANGING GARDEN, by the Ohio Library Assn. Whee.

As ever, / David

John Ciardi to John F. Nims   *Duluth, Minn., 14 November 1980*

Dear John:

Your letter and the copies of *Poetry* arrived today: a pleasure to see the poems and to find them in such a good issue. I love being next to MacLeish. What better company?

But I am distressed to hear *Poetry* is in such bad financial straits. For what little it can do, please credit my payment for these poems to your general fund: if the check is already on the way, I will simply rip it up.

Have you ever thought of sponsoring a poetry lecture service? I know that could be a briary road. A lot of would-be's would want to be sponsored by *Poetry* in this way, and those not selected would turn hateful. And who gets how much out of what deal? Etc. Etc.

But there is a lecture platform, it can be lucrative, and why isn't it worth at least a thought? There are also a lot of colleges around Chicago. I don't know how to generalize the idea, but I have made a lot of money on the lecture circuit. Suppose I offered you 5 days in, say, late April and agreed to talk to colleges. I've not had much trouble getting $1,000 a shot. Or if the colleges are close together, take 2 a day for $500 apiece. You pay my expenses and take the lecture fees. I think Studs Terkel could be counted on to announce the appearance as a sort of Poetry Festival sponsored by *Poetry* Magazine. . . . I am sure that some other poets would go along with the idea as a benefit for *Poetry*. Certainly somewhere, if someone knows how to tap them, college lecture-concert people have money that could be tapped. Well. . . .

May flights of generous angels sing thee to thy rest.

Love, / John

John F. Nims to Gary Soto   *Chicago, 29 December 1980*

Dear Gary Soto,

Thanks for sending the poems, which we read with pleasure. . . .

Sometimes your similes seem to me to misfire—and just possibly you have a tendency to have too many "like" and "as" figures? That's better than too few, of course; similes are exciting. Or should be. But in "Walking with Jackie" I don't get your "We grin / like shovels . . ." What shape shovels are those? perhaps you mean "grin widely"? But *shovels* suggests such a definite shape, and suggests flat expanse rather than just width? Or do you mean the curved bottom of the shovel? . . . Or a spade, instead of a shovel, straight across generally? Shovels is confusing, and I think similes fail unless instantly clear. That's what they're for. If a simile puzzles the reader, maybe it's not right? Same thing in "Her": "you hug me like a suitcase". Did you ever hug a suitcase? They're not very huggable, unless they're quite small. That's why they have handles, no? If you'd reverse these, I guess they'd make as much sense to me: "We grin like suitcases . . ." "You hug me like a shovel . . ."

Anyway, we really like the poems [printed July 1981]. Excuse me if I'm wrong about the similes.

All best wishes for 1981.

John F. Nims

Gary Soto to John F. Nims   *Berkeley, Calif., 5 January 1981*

Dear John Frederick Nims,

Thanks for your observations about my similes. Sometimes I do [get] carried away, as you pointed out in the two poems you accepted for publication, but for some strange reason I can't stop it. My hand keeps thinking in unlikely comparisons.

It's a new year, and hopefully the beginning of a new book. I wrote two new poems this past week. What a pace.

Sincerely, / Gary Soto

Gary Soto about the time of his first publications in *Poetry*, 1974.

John F. Nims to Richard Eberhart   *Chicago, 6 January 1981*

Dear Dick,

Sorry about the delay. As you can see from the long news note in the January issue, the staff was distracted from poetry manuscripts during November and December by having to cope with another problem: the financial situation of POETRY in these inflationary times. The cost of postage alone has gone up 300% in the last ten years—which is why our budget-conscious Managing Editor won't let me return poems unaccompanied by a return stamped envelope. I'm afraid other things were neglected while the normally efficient staff tried to think of ways to make up for our deficit. But that news note explains. . . .

The new poems do not seem to be you at your very best, and it's you at your very best we care about. These seem a little—routine? I mean, for you. For a lesser poet, they might be triumphs. But you've done better, lots better. These look a little like the poems a poet writes between crests of inspiration, in part to be ready for those crests when they come. Let's wait for a crest? Meanwhile, all the best to you and Betty for 1981, and from Bonnie too.

John

[P.S.] The plural of the Latin *impetus*, by the way, is not *impeti*. It's a fourth-declension noun, not second declension. Pedantic note.

David Sillars to Poetry   *Morrisville, N.Y., 24 January 1981*

Dear *Poetry*,

I read with sympathy your lament about the financial troubles you're experiencing. (News Notes Jan '81) Although I do not particularly like your magazine I can understand why you are well-satisfied with it. 10,000 poets can't be wrong, right?

Here are two suggestions that, if you are serious about *survival*, you will seriously consider (not that they will be unfamiliar to you):

1) drop the per-line rate—I believe it's a dollar—to 50 cents. (You don't think poets want to publish in "Poetry" for the *money*, do you? And let's face it—you're taking on an unfair and unnecessary burden! No one depends on you for their survival.)

2) Require that any poet who is to be published in "Poetry" be a subscriber. (This *should* not need a long parenthesis—let me only say: this is called "cooperation.")

These suggestions can be implemented together or, allowing time for "public opinion" to reach equilibrium, one at a time, or singly.

Yours in survival, / David R. Sillars

Dudley Duncan to John F. Nims   *Tucson, Ariz., 11 February 1981*

Professor John Frederick Nims
Editor, *Poetry*

Your discussion of finances in the January issue was interesting to me especially because of the statistics given to document the leading position of the magazine. I like statistics, though I think most poets don't. If you have fewer subscribers than would-be contributors, as I am prepared to believe, it seems to me there is a remedy you might reconsider (since I am sure you must have already considered it). Many (how many?) of these would-be contributors must be "creative writers" paid by colleges and universities to teach the writing of poetry. They are certainly in the classic publish-or-perish bind, and well they might be, for if no one wants to publish what they write, how are we to know they are any good at what they profess? You are rendering them a service and, as matters stand, for free. In other disciplines, it is becoming common to charge a fee for reviewing a manuscript, $10 in one discipline I know well. Needless to say, this doesn't begin to pay for the professional time required for a fair review, but it does help with the office costs, and it does make a dent in the number of frivolous submissions. One could, of course, offer to refund the fee upon acceptance, or to supply two free issues of *Poetry* as a token of gratitude to the contributor who is willing to help support the periodical she or he depends upon, or otherwise soften the blow of subjecting art to crassly commercial consideration. But I bet there would be no decline in really worthwhile submissions and that no fledgling Hart Crane would go undiscovered. Even better, if you would make known the fact that you actually read what is submitted, that might do more than anything else to make the insult of a fee easier to bear. One magazine I know of kept a handful of verses six weeks and then returned them with a note that they simply were not looking at anything these days in view of their backlog. Other magazines are just less honest.

We know, don't we, that most poetry is written for poets and read, if at all, by poets? The magazines are rather like feedlots where cattle are fattened for the anthology trade and the university presses. A good look at the social organization of your business might suggest ways of solving its economic problems. What you had on pp. 244–245 of the January issue suggests you have a head for quantitative analysis. I hope you find an effective way out of the present dilemma.

Sincerely, / Dudley Duncan

P.S. Congratulations on the *Harper Anthology*. I'm enjoying it.

Duane Niatum to John F. Nims   *Seattle, Wash., 14 March 1981*

Dear Mr. Nims,

Since I've sent *Poetry* and *The New Yorker* my best poems for over a decade, I'm very unwilling to accept the notion that one day I might "crash through the acceptance barrier" you keep telling me about. Because I've invested a good deal of time submitting poems to *Poetry*, I'd like to make one suggestion. Why not devote two or three issues to poets who have never appeared in *Poetry*, but are clearly as good as many who have? Anyway, I hope you'll at least consider this possibility. The "Big Pens" of American poetry don't need your publication anyway. They've taken the room in all the best mags since they became the "Big Pens." And although I feel you're a far better editor than the one before you, I could still point out junk poems from the last three issues of *Poetry*.

Yet I'm grateful that you've never published your poems in *Poetry*, every other issue, the way [Howard] Moss has done at *The New Yorker*. It seemed only natural that [Robert B.] Shaw in his NY *Times* review of Moss's latest book would mention this fact while also showing how mediocre most of the poems are. Twenty-one of the twenty-seven poems originally appeared in *The New Yorker*. I guess I've said enough. I do respect you, but I'm 43, and have been writing since I was 20, so I feel I've paid my dues. And because I know personally many of the poets you publish, including much of what they've had to say about the art in print, they've proven to me that many of them are about as devoted to the Muse as Warhol is to the origins and evolution of art from antiquity to the present. As Sontag made public in *On Photography*, and Lasch, in *The Culture of Narcissism*, our generation's only resources, for the most part, seem to be the detritus from our consumer culture.

Sincerely, / Duane Niatum

Niatum was not published in *Poetry*.

Joseph Parisi to John F. Nims　　　　　　　　*Chicago, 8 April 1981*

Dear John,

Got your missives and masses of Mss., the authors of which have been duly notified of their acceptance. . . .

Nadine [Cummings, circulation manager and bookkeeper] says the reason your last check was so large is that it was Helen's understanding that you didn't want the half-salary to begin until this month. Speaking of which, we have sent out the little card to contributors requesting donations—if they can manage it (don't know if you got a copy yet). Just in time, too, since we are quite low on cash (i.e., just about broke) at the moment; we're taking money out of Merrill Lynch to tide us over to next month, when things should pick up. We hope.

Ethel [Kaplan] got back safely from England, and we met with the people at the Chicago Public Library and Cultural Center on Monday. They are VERY gung-ho about a celebration for *Poetry*'s 70th Anniversary—we've already got dates tentatively set; they want to involve not only the downtown headquarters but all the branch offices of the Library system; hope to get the city quite actively involved, pennants flying down Mich. Ave., etc. They couldn't have been nicer. A person from the City Arts Council was also in attendance and wants to coordinate things with the city—use of Preston Bradley Hall to begin with. We want to have a month-long celebration, if possible, in October. Many different events throughout the month, culminating with a big sit-down dinner at the Cultural Center. They're anxious to get started, glad we're already planning. We'll meet with them again with more details in the middle of May. . . .

Charleston sounds delightful, and it must be fun with all the friends and acquaintances in the vicinity. It's going to be a let-down, though, coming back to Chi-town—can't remember seeing an azalea here in the longest time (except in the Lincoln Park Conservatory). Happy trails to Greensboro and points elsewhere. . . .

Joe

J.F.N. was teaching in Charleston, South Carolina. The banners did eventually fly along North Michigan Avenue—in November 2002, in celebration of the ninetieth anniversary.

John F. Nims to Poetry *staff*   *Charleston, S.C., 26 April 1981*

Dear Helen/Joe/Nadine:

Some odds and ends. . . .

Next time you send MSS. could you please send some rejection slips (I don't use a lot) and a couple or three of the POETRY pads for notes.

Am back in Charleston. The azaleas have gone, but it's still pretty nice. On the drive back I stopped for an hour or two at Duke and ditto Chapel Hill. The first built, you know, by a millionaire in the 20's, all at once. All the same stone. Also has an old campus. Big chapel, which Aldous Huxley said was best example of neo-Gothic architecture he knew. Sort of impressive, in its phony way. Good stained glass, etc. In fact a good imitation of what we gen. have to go to Europe to see. With some noble Dukes (Carolina brand) carved in modern dress on their tombs. Chapel Hill just a little college town with a big grassy campus. End of cultural report.

How about a Duke interested in poetry who wants to build a POETRY CENTER for us? We could put his statue in it. Or some other millionaire, no kidding, who wants to be eternalized in marble? A POETRY bldg. like the Elks Memorial? A bit more modest.

I can dream, can't I?

Best, / John

Joseph Parisi to John F. Nims   *Chicago, 14 May 1981*

Dear John,

Nadine is sending off another (rather large) bundle of MSS, via 4th class. Hope it arrives before you leave Charleston. Perhaps it would be better if it didn't. The auditor from Arthur Andersen is here, generally getting in the way, but will leave on Friday, just in time to make way for the IRS, whose own auditors will be here bright and early Monday morn. No problem proving we're non-profit.

Speaking of which: we will not be able to pay the poets this month, or for the next few probably. We have just barely scraped by. I've placated the U of C Printing Department, for the time being, with Dec. and Jan. bills paid. Still owe Gaper's [caterers]. And United Letter Service. And another four months' printing bills. *We* will still get paid, though, at least this month. Ethel [Kaplan], Gott sei Dank [thank God], has been going out practically daily, to friends, relatives, anyone who seems a soft touch, and bringing back $200 and $500 checks, which have gotten us through this week and next.

The Northern Trust was quite nasty when Ethel approached them, with E. B. Smith [member of family that founded the bank] in tow, yet. E. B. took the occasion yet again to push for P[aul] Carroll [for Poetry Day reader], and has suggested, also, that R. Mills, Jr. would do if P.C. can't make it. We could scream. The Joyce [Foundation] people, on the second go 'round, were very cordial. I'm doing up a little ($3-5,000) proposal right now, which looks promising. Meanwhile, we're sending out a letter next week to all the Trustees, requesting $100 (or more), immediately, to raise to CCLM matching grant money. Pat Lannan sent his $5,000, [trustee] Alice Arlen's been approached, and the Lilly [special grant of] $5,000 should arrive in June. We may make it, but it looks like it's going to be hand-to-mouth at least till Fall.

We're seeing the Chicago Pub. Library people next Wednesday about *Poetry* Birthday #70 and have been dreaming up any number of nifty ways they can organize activities—and foot the bill. We still have to come up with a lot of bucks for that, but that's another year. . . . David Wagoner wrote saying he talked to the movie people about doing the premiere here, but with not much helpful info. . . .

Also enclosed is a form from Arthur Andersen; they'd like you to sign it and return it, to show we're not crooks. Also enclosed is a copy of Shaw's review, which just arrived this a.m.

Wish we could be more cheery. It's a grey day, cold, rainy. Somehow, though, I think we'll make it. Greetings to Bonnie.

Joe

James Hearst to John F. Nims   *Cedar Falls, Ia., 29 September 1981*

Dear John Nims—

The other day I sold a poem to an anthology for a hundred bucks. You are welcome to the money though I know it is only a drop in the bucket. In the last issue of "Poetry" I liked Robert Morgan's poems and "Extremities" by Linda Pastan. Could we have fewer poems about poems? Unless the poem is a sustained metaphor like Frost's "Gum Gatherer," it isn't very interesting. Surely the human family has other more exciting experiences. I doubt Chekhov ever wrote a short story about writing short stories.

As ever, / Jim Hearst

Bonnie Alexander to John F. Nims   *Amherst, Mass., 21 November, 1981*

Dear Poetry:

Your October 1981 issue contains a review by Sandra M. Gilbert that leaves me speechless. I can scarcely believe my eyes: the same person who devoted an entire chapter of a book (*The Madwoman in the Attic*) to demolishing the poet John Milton on the basis of her dislike of his religion now has this to say: "Reading the work of so talented an artist, one doesn't often question the moral or intellectual assumptions that underlie her view of things: those are, after all, the forces that drive her vision." In other words, when Ai [in *Killing Floor*] writes graphic descriptions of torture, murder, and brutality—more appropriate as scenarios for low-budget movies than poems—no one is supposed to ask where such a glorification of sadism fits into the moral or intellectual scheme of human endeavor. One is supposed to revel in the "energy," no doubt.

Furthermore, Gilbert's remarks suggest that she and [Susan Gubar] her collaborator on *Madwoman* consider Milton neither talented nor an artist. Since they saw fit to "question the moral and intellectual assumptions" that formed the basis of Milton's "view of things"—God forbid that anyone should have "ethics" or "poetics" or "faith"!—he clearly doesn't have the right to the poetic license that "talented," "visionary," "uncanny" Ai is allowed. Gore, yes; God, no. The hypocrisy of this stuns even my agnostic sensibility. I can only hope that in the future *Poetry* will turn to reviewers whose opinions are not so shallow, strange, and trendy as Sandra Gilbert's.

Yours truly, / Bonnie L. Alexander

Stephen Sikora to the Editor   *Albany, Calif., 21 November 1981*

Dear Editor,

Can I interest you in the plight of yet another forgotten and oppressed minority in this country? I refer to the common reader. The amateur reader, that is, people like myself who read widely, some of us omnivorously. We are devoted to no one field of publications (hence this form-letter address to all you editors as a group). Most importantly, we are not professional writers ourselves. If any one thing distinguishes us as a group, in fact, it is that we are only consumers, feeding on the print which you and your writers produce.

Therein, of course, lies the source of our oppression and oblivion. Because we do not write, we have no way to talk back to the public writers. Sure, we scribble spiteful or flattering letters to you editors now and then, but not often. That half of literacy is an unaccustomed and presumptuous practice for us. Most of the words I see in the Letters Columns come instead from professional writers who have been moved to anger or delight by their own treatment at the hands of some other professional. Rarely do common readers venture out of their own specialization as consumers, and when they do, a few knife thrusts from a skilled professional quickly send us scurrying back to our proper station of voicelessness.

The power of the purse gives us some kind of speech, to be sure. To some extent we can hold our own and even turn the tables on you professionals by letting your words gather dust on library shelves or by consigning them to the greater oblivion of the garbage dump. This power we treasure and will not give up lightly. No one except school teachers, perhaps, can make us read what we do not wish to. Yet because we *do* want to read—some of us, in fact, need to read—and often will go to great lengths to find something, anything to feed our minds, this power has its limits. We have to take what you dish out, and more often than not the menu has been selected and the meal prepared by the writers and editors alone, in private consultation among themselves. . . .

My one single suggestion, in fact, for relieving the plight of the forgotten and oppressed minority which I presume to speak for here, concerns letter-writing itself. Amateur readers cannot long survive as specialists in only the consumption of literature. Even now, from both ends of the ranks, our numbers rapidly decline as the most devoted among us head for the bright lights of literary publicity and the least devoted turn to those other lights of the television and movie projector. We who remain must also produce, in one way or another, and I can think of no better way to present than through the writing of personal letters.

To this end, I entreat you to consider the condition of letter-writing in our present literary culture and the ways in which this kind of writing might be cultivated for the sake of us, and for your own sake as well. You need us, after all. The fate of literature and literacy rests to some significant degree in our hands. So, please help us.

Sincerely, / Stephen Sikora

John Gardner to John F. Nims   *New York City, 13 January 1982*

Dear John,

I know nothing is more vulgar, foul, or harmful to the tundra than a novelist's coming on like a poet. But for several reasons I send you these alleged poems anyway. One is that, except for Guy Davenport, you are the only poet I know of who does interesting things with ancient forms, both as translator and inventor, and I think nothing is harder than making a half decent poem in English out of the 27 classical Welsh forms. My father can do them all beautifully, and has been suitably rewarded; but he cheats: he writes in Welsh. Another is that you have regularly rejected the real poems of my wife, L. M. Rosenberg, with gentle criticism that, I admit, is always just, not that it explains why you publish all those mindless and feelingless fools. (Her book has just been rejected by the people who brought us Cynthia McDonald, E. Hirsch, Mazocco, etc., so I'm burning a little.) Another is that I pretty much hate contemporary poetry. I think you know I hate from passionate love. What I've written may not be poetry, but it certainly cuts free of the modern cliché. (I do not hate all modern poetry. I like Carl Dennis. Sometimes Linda Pastan.) Anyway, I think there's a certain advantage in writing in impossibly tight, hard forms. One has to admit at the outset that one is not going to say what one thinks—though one would not send off the poem if in the end it did not say what one thinks. Welsh forms are syllabic, not metrical, and have incredibly complex rules of internal rhyme and alliteration (which is why no Welsh poet has ever caused a revolution or, so far as is known, won his lady). The poems I send you are textbook examples of the old Welsh forms—the first in English, maybe the last. If you like, I will send you the rules of the forms. If you hate the poems, I will take it as a slur against all Welshmen, but not a bad aesthetic judgment.

Well, enough of all that. The best thing that's happened in the latter part of the twentieth century is this: Because I was overworked and bored to tears, I spent several days writing poems in old Welsh forms. My wife Liz read them and smiled with childlike joy, saying, "Thank God there's something you're lousy at!" The next morning she was asked to write a funeral poem for the death of a friend's mother. Almost without knowing she was doing it (not really; but you know how these things go) she wrote a true contemporary poem which happened to be riddled with internal rhyme, crossed alliteration, and the sprung-verse chiming we know in Hopkins and Thomas . . . I cried like a baby, not because the poem was wonderful, though I think it is, but because it showed so clearly how the Welsh poetic world I grew up with is dead, and rightly. Over a period of two thousand years (Tacitus mentions it) we created a form so beautiful it was able to keep a Celtic language alive, and suddenly some Jew (my wife, I mean) takes all the gold in it, and throws out all the iron, in such a way that no honest Welsh poet—certainly not my father, who when he heard Liz's poem, wept uncontrollably, in fact vastly, shamefully—could deny that what happened in that poem was an evolutionary leap. What I've sent you is nothing like that. What I send you is the old forms exactly translated. I would gladly give you short (very short) essays on the forms, making them available to real poets. On the other hand, I could accept without grief— almost without noticing—a printed rejection slip.

I hope you're well and happy and working like crazy. I am,

Yours, / John Gardner

John F. Nims to John Gardner   *Chicago, 15 March 1982*

Dear John,

This is not a "rejection." Read on. I think we can use these poems.

I was wishing I had a little leisure in my life so I could take a couple of weeks off and read up on Welsh poetry. Sounds fascinating; I know nothing about it, except that Hopkins apparently picked up sound patterns from it. I did look the terms up in the *Princeton Encyclopedia of Poetry and Poetics*— not too much help. And I got out of the library Gwyn Williams, *An Introduction to Welsh Poetry*, which did have definitions of all the forms you use. But that's all I have time for now: I'm teaching not only a full schedule at the U. of Illinois here, but also about to start a half-schedule at the U. of Chicago: a workshop in poetry that, with office hours out there, will take up a whole day each week. Worst of all, I have about 500 pages of the copyedited MS. of *Western Wind*, which Random House brought out in 1974. They want a revised version, which I've done—that's what the MS. is, and I have to finish it in the next few weeks.

That's why, for now, I've got to drop Welsh poetry until much later— except for what you tell me about it.

Anyway, I think it would be great if we could have these translations and a brief essay—well, essay is too big a word—on Welsh poetry and on the forms you use. Maybe four or five typed pages? Less? We'd probably run the poems at the end of an issue or POETRY, and then we could follow them immediately with your prose note.

There are signs that the younger writers are getting back to forms— more sonnets are being submitted, more sestinas, for instance—but this is still a pretty formless age in poetry, and I think it would be great to call the attention of our readers to a body of poetry written in tighter forms than anything in English. A lesson to them! I liked Williams' saying, on his last page, that Welsh poetry is *not* "the frenzied and extempore outpouring of long-haired bards . . ." but that "The discipline of Welsh poetry is the strictest in the known world of literature. . . ."

Let's show some of that to the readers of POETRY. I just wish my typing were as disciplined.

Yours, / John F. Nims

Gardner's translations (and prose) were not printed.

3. Seventy Years

Early in 1982 the editor began soliciting work for the seventieth-anniversary issue. Nims had hoped to persuade Peter De Vries to write a memoir about his and his wife Katinka's years on the magazine in the forties, but the former editor demurred, as he later declined to come to Chicago to read at Poetry Day. But Nims did receive excellent work for the special number from, among others, A. R. Ammons, Rita Dove, Anthony Hecht, Daryl Hine, James Merrill, Howard Nemerov, Pattiann Rogers, David Wagoner, and Richard Wilbur. Helen Vendler provided a strong essay on Ammons, and Robert Fitzgerald wrote a particularly touching memoir of his friendships, as a very young man in 1930, with Vachel and Elisabeth Lindsay, Harriet Monroe, and Morton Dauwen Zabel.

J. D. McClatchy closed the issue with "Setting the Hard Tasks," a succinct retrospective on the High Modernism championed by Pound and Monroe, and its aftermath in pale imitations and latter-day "avant-gardes." Noting that "in Modernism's broad wake most contemporary poems still churn," McClatchy wrote:

> Every subject and method have been tried—the absence of both, as well. Cinematic montage and cubist collage and action painting; aleatory music and blues and mantras; brutalism's severed limbs, irony's least finesse, the dream's furthest lair—all are in place. Along with every arrangement and derangement of line, rhythm, metric, texture, tone, voice, narrative, and lyric address. With archeological curiosity, each past-mastered style has been retrieved, imitated, ruffled, or parodied. But experiment has been the standard. . . . Every ideology has found its voice, every cause its dialect. . . . Canons gave way, too. Eliot was the first Censor. His preference for the impacted, polyphonic, allusive, disjunctive held sway until the late 1950's, when the yawp replaced the turn, and Whitman ousted Donne. . . . And meanwhile, the sociology of poetry, its goods and services, was overtaken with consumerism: more poets and more readers, more outlets and readings and workshops, more eye-stabbing, more puffery, more boodle.
>
> And yet, has very much changed after all? Or is "change" merely the factor of a short memory? Surely those who believe, say, that Allen Ginsberg's popularity was unprecedented have never heard of Edna St. Vincent Millay. . . . Can John Ashbery be more confusing than Gertrude Stein? Can those who hail the latest poetoid's breakthrough or breakdown have read at all?

Reflecting on America's native regionalism and "the clamor of clans," McClatchy pointed out that neither of the often-invoked terms "academic" or "avant-garde" meant much anymore. "Few such evaluative terms do, especially in a country with so motley and lenient an aesthetic as ours has become in the last twenty years. What *could* shock or muster these days? Anything goes—as often as not in one ear and out the other."

Plans for the citywide celebration of *Poetry*'s seventieth birthday did not materialize, however, for financial reasons, as usual. But in early spring of 1982 we learned that Princess Grace of Monaco was planning to go on tour in the United States reading her favorite poems, and we hoped we might be able to arrange her appearance in Chicago either for Poetry Day or another special benefit. I wrote to Monaco, received a positive response, and began discussions with her staff to set up the event. Unhappily, on September 13 Princess Grace had a stroke while driving on the narrow road above Monte Carlo, and her car plunged down an embankment; the following day she died from injuries sustained in the crash.

Jacqueline Kennedy Onassis was approached as a possible replacement, on the recommendation of Kimon Friar and others; she eventually declined, as she did all such invitations. But meanwhile, with little time to spare, I asked John Ciardi to read for Poetry Day. I also suggested that we turn the occasion of the seventieth anniversary into a tribute to J. Patrick Lannan, our longtime patron, as well. The dual celebration took place on November 12, with the reading at the Chicago Historical Society and a black-tie dinner at the Racquet Club. Ciardi gave a rousing reading and proved a very amusing master of ceremonies. Lannan was visibly moved by the large show of appreciation, and pledged $10,000 a year for the next five years.

With receipts of more than $11,000, Poetry Day 1982 was among the more successful benefits, and thanks to recent grants from the MacArthur Foundation and NEA, as well as increased contributions from the Associate members, the budget for 1983 was the healthiest in years. In June I proposed that the long-obsolete Index to *Poetry* be updated, and $4,000 was budgeted for the task. The project eventually took fifteen years to complete.

Issues following the special seventieth-anniversary number featured, as usual, a wide mix of well-known and emerging authors, but remain highly readable particularly for contributions from women, best among them Amy Clampitt, Alice Fulton, Mary Karr, Carolyn Kizer, Sharon Olds, Mary Oliver, Linda Pastan, and Pattiann Rogers. Among the more notable works offered by men were poems from Randy Blasing, Thomas Carper, John Ciardi, Stephen Dobyns, Dana Gioia, Albert Goldbarth, Edward Hirsch, Rodney Jones, William Matthews, Dave Smith, Gary Soto, Timothy Steele, and (as always) David Wagoner. In a departure from the usual critical fare in the back of the book, the August 1978 issue featured a lengthy, highly original, and much discussed essay by Frederick Turner and Ernst Pöppel, "The Neural Lyre: Poetic Meter, the Brain, and Time," which has become a classic study on the origin and relation of metrical patterns in verse in the human neurological system. It was the last article that John Nims and I edited together.

4. Correspondence 1982–1983

John F. Nims to Peter De Vries   *Chicago, 11 February 1982*

Dear Pete,

Don't worry. I'm not asking you and Katinka to the White House. Not *this* White House. As maybe you guessed, POETRY had a bad year. Looked for a while as if we might not make it. But then some friends rallied as they say round, and we got some grant assistance, and now we know we'll live through '82 at least, and we hope for much longer.

That means that in October we'll see our Seventieth Anniversary. And we're hoping we can make the October 1982 issue Something Special. Any chance you're between novels and longing to do something bellelettristic? Belelletetristic? I should have looked that up: something belletristic. Something reminiscent about your years at POETRY? How it was then? "POETRY: The De Vries Years"; "POETRY: The 1940's." Or whenever you were most in touch. " POETRY: The Middle Years."

We'd love to have something like that from you. A collectible, as (again) they say. An item. I think I'll ask Karl Shapiro and D. Hine if they'd like to do something like that for their period.

We should have the October pieces by the first of July. You could do it, and then set off the fireworks. Any chance?

I hope all goes well there. Has our hellish winter blown over your way? Chill factors of minus 50, minus 60 several weekends lately. Not like the old days, when snow was warm and snuggly.

Very best to both of you, / John

Peter De Vries to John F. Nims   *Westport, Conn., 27 February 1982*

Dear John:

The trouble is George Dillon said all there was to say about those years in the issue they thought, then, was to be the last. A sort of roundup. They were his years anyway, by no means anything to be called "the Peter De Vries years." I was only a stopgap, a rag stuffing up the chinks here and there, till other more permanent (and suitable) arrangements could be made. So I'd feel a little pompous as well as disingenuous in contributing anything from that point of view. Aggrandizing.

A reminiscence about the eternal need to raise money, renewing our shoestring I used to call it, which took up half of our time and bedeviled all our days, might be amusing, except that the satiric terms required might alienate donor support. Since I got your letter I've been turning the subject over in my mind, but nothing substantial enough for an article seems to come out of it, in addition to the above pause-giver. So the question of being or not being between novels is the least of it. Katinka appears to have even less to say than I, on having your follow-up query passed along to her.

If by your deadline anything does start percolating in the old noggin, enough to free us of Frost's ever-relevant warning against "trying to worry something into shape," why, one or the other of us will surely get back to you.

Meanwhile you have our best wishes, and congratulations on the quality and vitality of your editorship—much needed for the magazine.

What a headache sheer financial survival is! Especially today!

As ever, / Peter

Dillon announced *Poetry*'s imminent demise in the April and May 1942 issues. De Vries is being too modest; his contributions during the war years were substantial. Indeed, without his and his wife Katinka's efforts, the magazine would almost certainly have failed. Dillon gave them explicit credit in another article, "For the Record" (October 1948), printed in tribute after they resigned. See *Dear Editor*, Chapters XIV–XVI, for details of "the De Vries years" of 1943–1946.

Helen Vendler to John F. Nims   *Boston, Mass., 6 March 1982*

Dear John,

I would indeed like to do something for you; other editors have indeed just said, as you did, "How about X?" Mostly I say no, sometimes yes. I regret to say a) that I don't like *anything* by H.D., never have, b) have *no* talent for the general view of anything, so the Clausen topic & the 1912-82 topic don't work for me. I would be delighted to review the new Ammons (*Worldly Hopes*, as I recall) for you, however, if you haven't yet assigned it. I am hooked on him. Or any time there's a new Jorie Graham—she's my favorite among the younger poets. I'd also be willing to write on Linda Gregg or Laura Jensen (I'm doing Amy Clampitt for *Parnassus*). I've just done a long piece on Milosz for *The New Yorker*, venturing into foreign territory only because his poetry seems a new form of genius. If Tranströmer does a new volume, I'd like to write about him once more.

Will these do as suggestions? . . . You have so improved the condition of the magazine since you took over I am surprised you have any time left for poetry, as opposed to *Poetry*. . . .

I'm off to Charlottesville for a week; I'll have 2 springs this year—one there, one here. I do condole with you on your disgusting weather out

there. Once spring comes, though, the cherry trees on the lake will bloom;
I saw them last spring there, & they were lovely.

Yours, / Helen Vendler

Vendler's review of *Worldly Hopes* appeared in October.

John F. Nims to Howard Nemerov   *Chicago, 17 March 1982*

Dear Howard,

Thanks very much for sending us the Gnomic Variations. I like the poem
very much, and we're glad to have it for the Seventieth Anniversary Issue
next October. . . .

Your sand dune photo reminded me of something John Howard Griffin
(The Most Unforgettable Character I Ever Met, as *Reader's Digest* used to
say—marvelous man) told me. He and a friend once thought up the idea
of a new religious order, and had stationery printed for The Little Brothers
of Poverty, or something such. (They applied for a grant for $50,000 to
practice poverty.) John, who was a famous photographer among other
things, once got an invitation to submit a photo to an exhibition of porno-
graphic photos. He used his religious stationery to say that his Abbot didn't
like him to do that kind of thing any more, but that perhaps they could use
the enclosed photo. It was a picture, close-up, of two carrots sort of en-
twined. You couldn't tell they were carrots.

Maybe this awful winter is about over. Bitwene Mersh and Averil nice
things are supposed to happen.

All the best, / John

Concerning Griffin, see also Nims's letter to Hine of 18 July 1976, above.

John F. Nims to James Merrill   *Chicago, 25 March 1982*

Dear JM,

Very pleased to have "The Blue Grotto" and "After the Ball" to bejewel
our 70th Anniversary issue next October. It's coming right along; we're getting some good things for it.

Two years we lived in Italy, and I never did get to that grotto. But I think
I met Gennaro [the boatman in the poem], or his cousins, a few times.
There was that day we came back from San Fruttuoso, that little place near
Portofino one can only get to by boat . . . I really *like* that poem. . . .

I'm glad you liked our FM station [WFMT]. The local weather reports no
doubt made the music even more luxurious. Like that passage in I think

Lucretius about the pleasure of being on the shore and seeing a ship in trouble out on the stormy sea.

All the best, / John

Peter De Vries to John F. Nims   *Westport, Conn., 12 May 1982*

Dear John:

I'm not in good enough shape to take on anything like that [reading at the annual Poetry Day benefit in the fall]. Afflictions of the flesh severally make it too difficult, if not impossible. For openers, I have a bad back with a pinched spinal nerve that prevents my even standing *up* for that length of time, let alone speaking coherently. As for the rest, there's no point in being graphic, but lately it's been the better part of prudence to say no to dais and platform, including most recently an invitation from the Library of Congress.

Talk of after-dinner speeches reminds me of how many I used to make for Dear old Rutgers when I was working for the mag, which probably accounts in no small measure for the scunner I've taken to them. I would have to go to those awful banquets and make responsive talks such as they'd expect in return for a hundred-dollar contribution to *Poetry*, or even in some cases a measly fifty bucks. Horrible! Figure I've earned surcease from same.

I'm sorry we can't participate in the magazine's Seventieth—is it really forty years ago since we celebrated the Thirtieth? Maybe by the Seventy-fifth this will all have cleared up, but right now I can only see six months from now as meaning another half-year's physical decline. You shouldn't have much trouble finding someone younger and sprightlier.

By the way, what makes you think half an hour's light talk entails no preparation? I've always found it takes about a day a minute. But maybe I'm dull.

Good luck, and have fun anyway.

Best, / Peter

Hine also had asked De Vries to be the Poetry Day reader in 1977, for the sixty-fifth anniversary, but he declined, also for reasons of health. He died on 28 September 1993; Katinka De Vries passed away two years earlier.

John F. Nims to Ruth Lilly   *Chicago, 4 June 1982*

Dear Ruth Lilly,

It's a pleasure to have you as a friend of the magazine, and an additional pleasure to see your poems. Thank you very much for sending them; we enjoyed reading each one.

They certainly combine many attractive qualities: sensitivity, with a sense of humor, a knowledge of good poetry and the ability to quote aptly, terseness of expression.

I'm sorry that none quite worked out for us. We do have a tremendous backlog, and even at best can accept only about 1 poem out of every 300 sent us. Difficult odds.

But thank you for the pleasure that the reading of these gave us.

With all best wishes,

Sincerely yours, / John Frederick Nims

Kimon Friar to John F. Nims   *Athens, Greece, 18 November 1982*

Dear John:

. . . You might like to know that when I applied for a National Endowment for the Arts Translators' Grant in order to complete my Greek anthologies, I simply cut out the pages from the November issue of *Poetry*, pasted them on the application, and sent them as examples of the kind of poetry I would be translating. That did it, and I was given a $12,000 grant. So you see that your November issue has twice assisted me. . . .

Have you written Jackie Onassis about taking Princess Grace's place? I had sent her the *Poetry* issue [on postwar Greek poets, November 1981], and yesterday I had a letter from her in which she writes [thanking him and praising his translations, which she said gave her great pleasure].

How's that?!

Ever, / Kimon

Princess Grace of Monaco had agreed to come to Chicago and give a benefit reading for *Poetry* in the fall, but died on 14 September, following a car crash. Mrs. Onassis wrote 12 December, declining the invitation, as she did all such requests.

Mary Karr to John F. Nims   *MacDowell Colony,*
Peterborough, N.H.,
5 December 1982

Dear John,

Your letter was a welcome gift when I returned last night from Las Vegas, from the planet's longest computer convention. My tolerance for things like that is less than my tolerance for reading algebraic code off a computer terminal. Also, with my $20 stake at the crap tables I was able to win $280—my rent supposedly while I'm off salary—but my pocket got picked in the Boston airport: sad movie. Your letter was the only good news, and thanks.

I will keep your boy-scout faith about merit winning out and my manuscript being okay. I have scoured *Coda* and am ready to re-work everything this month and xerox my heart out in January. It's probably wise on your part to make a policy of not reviewing un-published books. Your support of my work, as I've mentioned before, means a great deal.

Forgive the typos in the last batch of poems. You're right about "Hard Knocks," third line from the end, should be "nuns click their beads." As for the other goofs, I take heart in the fact that I still don't spell as badly as Lowell did, am reassured (by excerpts from Ian Hamilton's new biography) about

Mary Karr at the time of her first correspondence in the early eighties.

my chosen path even though I'm clumsy with letters. That's a beautiful book, by the way, if you're making out a Xmas list.

The poems I sent you were spanking new and written during a recent manic episode, so it pleases me you could use them.

Have a good holiday, and thanks again for the long letter and the advice.

Warm wishes, / Mary Karr

Alfred Dorn to John F. Nims   *Flushing, N.Y., 29 January 1983*

Dear Mr. Nims:

I am renewing my subscription to POETRY for two years. My check for $37.00 is enclosed.

As a longtime subscriber to POETRY, I am keeping many issues for future re-reading. I am delighted with the quality of much of the poetry featured in recent issues, especially those poems in which blank verse has been used in an imaginative and artistically valid way. I am glad that the influence of the Beatniks and the Black Mountain school is waning and that we are re-turning to poetry of high artistic standards.

I continue to regard POETRY as the best publication of its kind in America. I look forward to my next issue.

Sincerely yours, / Alfred Dorn

Raymond P. Fischer to John F. Nims   *Wheaton, Ill., 3 March 1983*

Dear Mr. Nims:

This is a belated thank you for your letter of November 23rd. I agree with your criticisms. Thanks for taking the time, and I am doing some polishing and shortening of the poems.

I have several interesting memories of Harriet Monroe and one disappointment. I was invited to a "white tie" dinner in honor of William Butler Yeats. I was about 5 feet, 9 inches tall and weighed about 120 pounds. My older brother's dress suit did not fit. He was 6 feet tall and weighted about 170.

                                        Very truly yours, / Raymond P. Fischer

The famous banquet for Yeats was held at the Cliff Dwellers' Club in 1914; Vachel Lindsay read his poem "The Congo" and made such a spectacular impression that it launched his career. Fischer in a later letter noted that Monroe printed one of his poems, "which she said was not quite up to the standards of POETRY magazine, but was a remarkable achievement for a boy," in the Correspondence column in September 1919. Fischer's "Time" and "An Aged Man Remembers April" were published in the April 1984 issue.

Frederick Turner to John F. Nims and Joseph Parisi   *Kenyon College,*
                                                              Gambier, Ohio,
                                                            23 March 1983

Dear John and Joe,

Please pardon this form of address, but this letter is to both of you, and the alternatives (Messrs. Nims and Parisi; Mr. Nims and Joe) were rather ghastly. I shall consider Joe as having introduced us all.

Many thanks for your generous responses to the essay ["The Neural Lyre," August 1983]. I'm delighted you can use it. Thanks also for your excellent suggestions. I have embodied them in the enclosed corrected copy—perhaps you could send back the old one to avoid confusion. . . .

I'm sending the contributor form on to Ernst Pöppel. He wrote to me recently, suggesting modestly that he shouldn't really be cited as a co-author, as I did the writing and the synthesizing. But it seems to me that his experiments and observations are central to my argument, and I'll concede only that my name should precede his on the title page. . . . I'll divide the honorarium with him.

I read a shorter version of the essay to the Reimers Stiftung group, which is really the most formidable scientific audience I could imagine. . . . I am pleased to report that the response was pretty enthusiastic, and that my science was either endorsed or allowed to pass without criticism. The major critical discussion centered on the question of whether isochrony—the dividing up of events into durations of equal length—could be entirely identified with rhythm. But they agreed that my argument stood whatever the conclusion.

Beside the corrected ms. I enclosed, with some trepidation, my epic poem *The New World*, for your entertainment. I'm told it's quite an easy read once one gets into it a couple of pages. Obviously format and length make it something of a waste of time for magazine editors to read, but you have been so sympathetic to my work I thought I'd try it on you anyway.

With best wishes, and thanks,

Frederick Turner

Ted Kooser to John F. Nims   *Lincoln, Nebr., 11 June 1983*

Dear John Nims:

I can't tell you how much it means to me to have work accepted by PO-ETRY. I'm completely thrilled. Back in 1959 or '60, when I first started to write, I sent you one of my first efforts, and you (you were then [visiting] editor, too) were kind enough to write me a rather lengthy note of rejection with comments. I think that your response, coming at that time, was a great encouragement to me to go on, which I have.

I didn't much like POETRY during the years that Daryl Hine had it, and it's true that I have rarely submitted. I'm delighted that I decided that with you at the helm perhaps my work would have some chance there.

I've been publishing now for nearly twenty years, but have never felt quite so accepted among American poets as your letter has made me feel.

Best from Nebraska,

Ted Kooser

Kooser made his first appearance in *Poetry* with four poems in November 1983. An insurance company executive for many years, Kooser was appointed U.S. Poet Laureate in 2004 and won the Pulitzer Prize in 2005.

CHAPTER IX

Expanding in the Eighties

1. Another Transition

Late one afternoon in June 1983 John Nims invited me into his office. The rest of the staff had left for the day, and we began talking about poetry (as opposed to *Poetry*), a luxury we almost never indulged. Then, matter-of-factly, John told me he wished to resign before the end of the year and said he hoped I would take over for him. Since he had not given any indication before of his intentions, I was truly taken aback. Seeing my reaction, he brought up the fact that he would be seventy in November, and said that the next year he planned to quit teaching as well. He did not say that he was tired of editing, but I could well understand if, after all the work and worry of the preceding five years, he was ready to give up an often thankless job. He did mention that he wanted more time for his own poetry and to finish up new editions of *Western Wind* and *Sappho to Valéry*. I said I was sorry to hear his decision but could appreciate his wanting a change. I added that I had not anticipated being asked to succeed him. Much as I enjoyed my work as associate editor, I never had designs on the top spot and, as I told him, assumed I would find another job when he left.

Apprised of Nims's decision, the executive committee approved a "leave of absence" for the next year, the final one of his contract. Following his recommendation they asked me to take over, with the title of acting editor, and I agreed. Officers and other trustees I had worked with closely on various projects supported me for the job without qualification, as did John Nims, though unlike most previous editors I was not a poet. One longtime trustee, herself a poet, recalled *Poetry*'s many troubled times and dryly observed of its past poet-editors, starting with the minor lyricist Harriet Monroe, that their skills especially as managers and fund-raisers seemed inversely proportional to their talents in verse. But some on the board felt that a poet should occupy Monroe's storied chair and proposed that other such candidates be considered; and so a large search committee was appointed. In September 1983 I assumed full editorial responsibility, began selecting manuscripts and assigning reviews, and saw through the press the final issues Nims had assembled.

As during his first service on the staff, Nims's personal sacrifices made it easier for *Poetry* to weather another period of stringent economy, while his abiding cheer and genial spirit greatly increased goodwill toward the magazine. In the May 1984 issue, News Notes formally confirmed the change in editorship with these observations:

> In the almost six years of his tenure, his taste and judgment have been reflected in issues that have won the praise of poets and critics around the country. What was not immediately evident in these pages, however, was the constant encouragement, very often accompanied by detailed commentary, which he offered to countless poets, particularly aspiring ones, who submitted work to the Magazine. For his great service to *Poetry* and his unfailing kindness, the Board and the Staff offer sincere thanks and join with the authors he aided and his many other friends in wishing him all the best.

After seven years as first reader, five of them handling the prose section as well, and with the experience likewise on the financial and development sides, I was better prepared than most *Poetry* editors when they arrived, in both the literary and business aspects of the operation. But the transition was also made smoother because the backlog of material Nims left allowed me to build up my own acceptances gradually. Like editors before me, I was not taken with all the poets my predecessor had printed frequently, and some authors formerly favored began appearing less frequently. But writers who for whatever reasons had not contributed in years began offering work and were printed again while a great number of eminent authors who got their starts in *Poetry* continued faithfully to give us first looks, often sending title poems from their newest books. From A. R. Ammons (whose many later appearances included "Sumerian Vistas") to "Cowboy Poet" Paul Zarzyski, we tried to represent the range of American poetry during the last decades of the century, with generous samples from foreign writers as well. Besides special numbers devoted to contemporary poets of Great Britain and Australia, we eventually presented double issues in dual-language format featuring recent work in Italian, German, Irish, and French. Regular issues also included translations from Latin, ancient Greek, and classical French drama as well as Spanish, Hebrew, Russian, Japanese, Chinese, Romanian, Polish, Turkish, and other tongues.

Personal taste and critical acumen aside, any editor's success, as judged by the lasting quality of a journal's contents, depends upon luck: the caliber of work being produced at any particular time and the poems that happen to be submitted for publication. It was our good fortune that fairly consistently throughout the eighties and nineties both established and emerging authors sent us highly original, well-crafted, emotionally and intellectually engaging pieces. Stephen Young and I collected some of the most memorable pieces in *The POETRY Anthology 1912–2002*.

Besides Ammons, among the notable poets who appeared after 1983, often with dozens of pieces, were Diane Ackerman, Dick Allen, John Ashbery, Marvin Bell, Randy Blasing, Chana Bloch, Robert Bly, Philip Booth, David Bottoms, Neal Bowers, Hayden Carruth, Raymond Carver, Billy Collins, Carl Dennis, Stephen Dobyns, Rita Dove, Stephen Dunn, Richard Foerster, Brendan Galvin, Sandra M. Gilbert, Allen Ginsberg, Albert Goldbarth, Debora Greger, Eamon Grennan, Susan Hahn, John Hollander, Andrew Hudgins, David Ignatow, Rodney Jones, Mary Karr, Jane Kenyon, John Kinsella, Kenneth Koch, Yusef Komunyakaa, Maxine Kumin, James Laughlin, William Logan, Philip Levine, Sandra McPherson, William Matthews, J. D. McClatchy, Walter McDonald, W. S. Merwin, Lisel Mueller, Sharon Olds, Mary Oliver, Linda Pastan, Reynolds Price, F. D. Reeve, Pattiann Rogers, J. Allyn Rosser, Kay Ryan, Reg Saner, May Sarton, Philip Schultz, Robert B. Shaw, Enid Shomer, Charles Simic, Charlie Smith, Dave Smith, R. T. Smith, Cathy Song, Katharine Soniat, Gary Soto, Roberta Spear, A. E. Stallings, Gerald Stern, Julie Suk, Joyce Sutphen, May Swenson, Leslie Ullman, John Updike, Mona Van Duyn, David Wagoner, Jeanne Murray Walker, Michael Waters, Charles Wright, and Robert Wrigley.

Distinctive poems by these and other accomplished but less frequent contributors each year formed the vital core without which *Poetry* could not have maintained its reputation or pleased its diverse readership. But any editor is equally if not more interested in finding new talents and in promoting promising aspirants, thus fulfilling a principal function of a literary journal. About one-third of the authors we published each year were making first appearances and sometimes their publishing debuts in *Poetry*, many of them students and recent graduates. While the editorial staff tried to be kind to everyone, first readers kept particularly careful eyes on newcomers; and when someone seemed to have potential, we tried to be helpful even though we usually could not keep their early submissions. In many instances, brief notes and then longer letters, often with specific advice, might go back to authors with their poems over a period of years before these "discoveries" saw publication.

In rarer cases, unsolicited pieces met recognition the instant they came over the transom. Among these happy immediate acceptances, and the most notable of the debuts during my first years at Monroe's desk, were Kay Ryan and Billy Collins, both unknown to me when they sent their work from opposite ends of the country. Already near or in their forties, they had received very little recognition as poets, quietly perfecting their craft while working as teachers of basic English courses (not creative writing), Ryan at a community college in the San Francisco Bay area, Collins at CUNY's

Lehman College in the Bronx. After more than twenty years' labor, each became an overnight success in the nineties.

Beginning with the October 1983 issue, I reinstated art on the covers, reproducing contemporary pieces from various galleries as well as earlier works from the Art Institute of Chicago, thanks to Sam Carini, the generous longtime curator of prints and drawings. More substantial editorial changes occurred inside the covers. Since miscellanies lack force and haphazard assortments can pall, I assembled each issue around a central subject or general motif, often with contrasting subtopics. Themes were not chosen in advance, but in the regular course of submissions over many months several distinctive poems would come in that related to the same ideas—love in its many manifestations, death, illness, and Nature, of course, the most often recurring. At any given time various other topics seemed to be "in the air." While arranging the contents of a particular issue, I was often struck by unexpected resemblances in images or parallels in figures of speech as well as contrasting points of view that made for a kind of "conversation" among the various authors. Oftentimes individual poems took on added resonances juxtaposed to or in context with other pieces in an issue. Rather than a hodgepodge, each issue became a small anthology of poems carefully orchestrated (or so it was hoped) with voices in their several registers playing variations on or counterpoint to diverse aspects of the central theme.

With *Poetry*'s finances still far from robust, hope sprang again that additional aid might arise in the East, this time New York City and environs, home to large segments of the magazine's subscribers and contributing authors. In September, as we prepared for Poetry Day 1983 with Stanley Kunitz (one of our best-attended readings), I made inquiries about setting up an event the following year in Manhattan. Henri Cole, then executive director of the Academy of American Poets, was enthusiastic, and when he told the Academy's founder, Marie Bullock, about the project, she insisted they co-sponsor it. Finding an underwriter proved unsuccessful, but the show did go on, on 12 October 1984 at the Guggenheim Museum, with readings by Maxine Kumin, Anthony Hecht, and Gary Soto; Richard Howard was master of ceremonies. The reception at the National Academy of Design was crowded and festive, but the hoped-for new donors did not materialize, proving yet again Peter De Vries's dictum that parties seldom produce patrons.

Two weeks later in Chicago, Stephen Spender was the reader at Poetry Day 1984. Sir Stephen arrived about noon the day of the program, and while caught in traffic from O'Hare we had plenty of time to discuss Auden, Isherwood, Berlin in the thirties, and his translations. A member of the search

Sir Stephen Spender,
the reader for Poetry Day 1984,
at the Arts Club of Chicago.

committee for editor (not an ally, I sensed) invited herself to our late lunch, where the poet told stories of his Oxford days and first meetings with Virginia Woolf and the Bloomsbury Group. I mentioned that although I had read a number of biographies, one point still remained unclear. Did he in fact take his degree? "No, not actually," he replied. Anticipating my next question, he explained: "I never passed the German exam." After lunch the trustee escorted our guest to his hotel. Whether en route she solicited Spender's opinion about the editorship or what he might have said, I do not know; but immediately thereafter her attitude became extremely friendly. The search committee met in December and decided to confirm me as editor with a two-year contract. At their next meeting, in January 1985, the full board approved their recommendation unanimously.

News of the appointment generated a fair of amount of publicity, with stories in the papers and interviews on NPR and Studs Terkel's program on WFMT-FM. Positive press notwithstanding, the financial situation remained shaky, forcing regular dips into reserve funds to pay bills. In June subscription rates had to be raised again, slightly, from $20 to $22. Carolyn Kizer, who had just won the 1985 Pulitzer Prize for Poetry, accepted our invitation to read for Poetry Day in November. Kizer's performance, like Spender's, enjoyed an enthusiastic reception, but each of the events brought in less than $10,000, as did the dual presentation by Raymond Carver and Tess Gallagher in 1986. For years the increasing overhead to produce these benefits diminished their effectiveness as fund-raisers, and it was clear other avenues had to be found to assure reliable cash-flow throughout the year. Increasingly I also felt we needed to present programs with greater depth and to expand *Poetry*'s educational activities and its role in the larger community. If we could combine the goals, so much the better.

Meanwhile the monthly issues appeared on schedule. We also assembled the first of several special issues, an edition devoted to recent poetry from the British Isles, the first such collection in *Poetry* since 1962. With the assistance of Elise Paschen, who was then studying at Oxford, a great amount of material was collected. But most submissions had a flat, enervated quality, to my mind anyway, and despite much labor over two years it seemed we still might not have a sufficient number of engaging poems to fill an issue. Another round of gathering brought fresh pieces, along with a strong essay on the contemporary scene by John Bayley, and the British issue finally came off press in July 1985.

2. Correspondence 1983–1986

Newly appointed editors usually receive large bundles of welcoming letters, many of them fulsome, some of them voicing invidious comparisons, most of them to be taken with several grains of salt. But the excited replies from authors after receipt of their first acceptance forms are obviously genuine in their expressions of delight, as the letters here indicate. Frequent contributors also write of their satisfaction when recent work finds a home in *Poetry*, and a number of authors relate reactions from readers, and other publishers, after poems appear in the magazine. Even warmer letters arrive from award winners immediately after the annual prizes are announced each fall.

Updates on recent literary and personal affairs form the better portion of letters from authors. But among the more amusing missives are those from "ordinary," nonprofessional readers who do not hesitate to send blunt opinions, point out errors and deficiencies, or give other evidence that *Poetry* subscribers scan its pages carefully and take more than a passing interest in the contents each month.

Kay Ryan to Joseph Parisi   *Fairfax, Calif., 19 October 1983*

Dear Mr. Parisi,

I am very happy that you have chosen my poems, "Marianne Moore Announces Lunch" and "The Egyptians," for publication in POETRY [May 1984]. And I am pleased that you found the rest of the group interesting as well. What a world, that has such good news in it! . . .

As I said in my letter accompanying the poems, it has been difficult to find acceptance for the kind of poetry I seem constitutionally fated to write. But with one acceptance like this in my pocket I think I will be able to go on grousing and working for quite a while.

Most sincerely, / Kay Ryan

Kay Ryan at the time of her
Poetry debut, 1984.

Reynolds Price to Joseph Parisi   *Durham, N.C., 27 November 1983*

Dear Mr. Parisi—

On the contrary, I was glad you showed "A Heaven for Elizabeth Rodwell [, My Mother]" to Stephen Spender. He's one of my oldest and best friends above ground.

And I was glad to see "Ambrosia" in the November issue. One of the really nice—and believe me, utterly unusual—things about appearing in PO-ETRY is that *young* people always come up afterwards and say, "I saw your poem in POETRY." The only other magazine I've experienced that has a similar distinction is PLAYBOY. . . .

Let me know if you pass this way.

Sincerely, / Reynolds P.

John F. Nims to Joseph Parisi   *Chicago, 8 May 1984*

Dear Joe,

Just a little note of thanks for the very nice news note you had in the last issue, about my leaving. Just the kind of thing I might have hoped for. Thanks for the thought and care that went into it, and for writing it so well.

I'm glad you said "resigned" instead of "retired"—a word that makes me feel ready for the old folks' home. I am resigning from the University as of June 15th, but only because it seems to have some budgetary advantages. I plan to keep teaching next year, but with the winter quarter off.

One little thing I wonder about: do you still like the idea of using only last names on the cover? I wondered about it when I saw DENNIS DEVLIN on the January cover. Denis (sic) Devlin was a well known Irish poet who died not so long ago that newly discovered poems are not impossible. Then you get things like ANDERSON ANDERSON in the new issue. And so many ambiguities are possible. There are at least three DICKEYs who write poetry—who knows which you'd mean? Not to speak of the HALLs, LONGSs, MOORES, MORGANS, MILLERs—SMITHs? What if some day you accept a poem by Emma Lou ASHBERY? Or just happen to have an issue with poems by Emma Lou, Lisa MERRILL, Rosalie WARREN, Roger HECHT, Nancy NEMEROV, Marquita STRAND, Willie WAGONER? Could that ever be misleading. . . .

Best, / John

Joseph Parisi to Warren Bean   *Chicago, 17 July 1984*

Dear Mr. Bean,

Thank you for your letter. Alas, like Homer, *Poetry* occasionally nods. Despite numerous readings and proofing by the copyeditors, errors do

creep in, to our horror, as in the instances your most careful eye has spot-
ted.

Generally, we do allow the poets a certain amount of liberty, though in
the case of truly egregious mistakes of fact or usage, we try to dissuade
them. In the case of "maize," perhaps *corn* should have been used; but the
generic meaning of the term (any grain) is still not as well known, among
American readers anyway, as it might be. Ignorance on all our parts about
the proper habitations of tigers led to the slip-up in East Africa. For
shame.

We do appreciate your concern, and the time you've taken to set us
straight. We shall try mightily in future not to breach your trust.

Sincerely, / Joseph Parisi

Writing from St. Helena, California, on 12 July, Warren Bean pointed out various errors in
recent issues: "a poet put a tiger in the elephant grass of East Africa" (July 1983); another put
"'maize slaves', and, by implication, maize, in ancient Egypt" (May 1984); and another "put
a 'breech' in a wall" (June 1984). "Do you try to correct your poets before publication; or
do you believe they should be allowed to let Cortes discover the Pacific, so to speak, if they
want to?" he enquired.

Anthony Hecht to Joseph Parisi   *Rochester, N.Y., 31 October 1984*

Dear Joe Parisi

Many thanks for your very kind note about the evening at the Guggenheim [Museum] devoted to *Poetry* Magazine. It was a pleasure to have been
asked to take part, and I enjoyed myself (though at certain moments during the actual performances I was quite put off. Seated as I was, over to one
side, I was able to view the audience, and there was a couple near the front
who seemed to be in animated conversation throughout; or, more accurately, the man, young and bearded, seemed to be lecturing sans intermis-
sion to his girlfriend, who was clearly rapt and unwilling to interrupt. This
annoyed me in behalf of the other poets on the program, and I determined
that when it came my turn I would make a point of not distracting myself
by looking in the direction of that monologuist. Only after I had been
home in Rochester for some days did I get a letter from Sandy McClatchy,
telling me that the couple had been seated just in front of him, that the girl
was deaf and the man had been repeating the poems to her silently, line by
line, so that she could lip-read).

I'm sorry, too, that we didn't have a chance to talk after the reading, but
I was quite tired, having taught two classes that day in Shakespeare and
Yeats, and slipped out stealthily as early as I could. . . .

With best wishes, / Anthony Hecht

Kay Ryan to Joseph Parisi   *Fairfax, Calif., 7 November 1984*

Dear Joseph Parisi,

Thank you for your interest in the poems I sent to you in September. I'm afraid I am rushing you before you've had time to divest yourself of your overstock, but I want to send you some recent poems anyhow. They're easy to return.

And I wanted to tell you more good news that *Poetry* is directly responsible for: Copper Beech Press of Brown University has offered to publish a book of my poems [*Strangely Marked Metal*, 1985]. The editor saw my poems in your pages and asked for a ms. Thank you for the tremendous boost *Poetry* has given me.

I hope things are going well for you and that the mss. tide is down below armpit level by now.

Most sincerely, / Kay Ryan

Jonathan Holden to Joseph Parisi   *Manhattan, Kans.,*
14 December 1984

Dear Joseph Parisi

Thanks for taking the four poems and for the note. You mention my "patience" as if to apologize for having taken too long to report, but actually this was by *far* the fastest response I've ever gotten from POETRY. . . . I must say that from the editorial chores I've occasionally undertaken—judging contests, especially—I don't know how you do it, it takes such stamina, not to mention an endless reserve of . . . would "spiritual generosity" be the word? Much harder than being a psychoanalyst and for rather worse wages. (It was Peter Lorre—the actor—who studied psychoanalysis for a while in Vienna. He quit that study in disgust, saying that psychoanalysis is like trying to "treat a disease" by focusing attention exclusively on "the asshole." The connection between this parable and editing thousands of unsolicited poems I'll let you complete.) . . .

Well, keep up the good work, and take plenty of vitamins to ward off poetic overload.

Yours, / Jonathan

Carl Dennis to Joseph Parisi   *Buffalo, N.Y., 15 January 1985*

Dear Joseph Parisi,

I'm glad you liked "The Greenhouse Effect," one of my favorites, but in a massive housecleaning and revision spree the two other poems you took have been dismantled and put away in my drawer of near misses. I think the end of "Clean Thinking" is strong but the tone is blurred so that the reader is not sure how exactly we are to take it, and the connection with Aunt Esther is by turns too tenuous and too emphatic. The poem seems to creak along and to be finally unconvincing. . . .

One of my New Year's Resolutions, you'll be happy to know, is to hold my poems a few months longer before I send them out. I see the light eventually, but sometimes too late to spare myself the burden of self-rejection when a hard-pressed editor has already given his time to them. I'm sorry for the inconvenience I may have caused you here. If you'd like to publish more than one of my poems, I'd be happy to send you some poems I have at hand which have escaped with their lives from the jaws of revision.

Sincerely, / Carl Dennis

J.P. wrote to "unaccept" the poems on 22 January.

Jim [James W.] Hall to Joseph Parisi   [*Key Largo, Fla.*],
18 *March 1985*

Dear Mr. Parisi:

Well, good gosh. What a thrill to find you're taking four poems for my favorite magazine. . . .

I wanted to let you know that I used the August '84 issue of *Poetry* in a recent Contemporary Poetry class with great success. I just picked it randomly and hadn't even spent an hour looking at it. But after studying it carefully for a week and teaching it for two three-hour sessions, I have to say that there was a unique thematic consistency in the poems of that issue. I mean that it read more like a book of poems than a literary magazine. I'm sure you didn't solicit poems about literary or artistic allusiveness, but you wound up with an issue that wrestled wonderfully with the issue of the poet's role among the community of artists. Sculptors, painters, weavers, etc. The wonderful juxtaposition of Linda Pastan's poem with Sara Teasdale's. Both of them exploring the inside-outside of the artistic creation. That, in fact, was the other consistent feature of these poems. Again and again the issue concerned how art can rise out of the sordid (Mesa's "The Progress").

Maybe I'm rhapsodizing about the obvious. Maybe editors do this all the time, and I've never noticed. Ye gad. Think of it, a wheel! But it sure was news to me. And to make matters more interesting, we found many poems in the *Georgia Review* and *Iowa Review* that dealt with similar concerns. Maybe this is just a period in which a lot of good poets are trying to find their middle C again. Go back to our roots in the history of civilization and place ourselves more firmly. It's about time, I'd say. Things seem mightily adrift to me in the current scene. No great touchstones to measure your own work by. Only a Gerald Stern or a Mary Oliver or Philip Levine to guide you through the fog of mumblers. Lots of mumblers mumbling.

Anyway, I thought you might be interested to know that your editorial work is paying off some odd dividends. I plan to keep using the magazine in class this way. I think it was at least as profitable as reading the several books of poetry we also studied.

Best, / Jim Hall

Albert Goldbarth to Joseph Parisi   *Austin, Tex., 20 March 1985*

Dear Mr. Parisi:

It's not secret that *Poetry* prides itself on, among other things, the quality and frequency of its many asterisked first appearances, and it's no genius-work one needs to see that *Poetry* is honestly open to considering the work of all good newcomers, and not just the work of friends of friends—but it's always especially pleasant when such knowledge become personalized. One longtime and very dear friend of mine, David Clewell, recently had work in *Poetry*—the January issue, I believe. Yesterday another old, close friend, Robert Lietz, called me from Laramie with excitement in his voice to announce he'd just been accepted into *Poetry*'s pages. Of course I don't want this kind of thing to go too far—or what's to become of us staunch, true, sterling, tillers of the field who have been fortunate enough to contribute to *Poetry* a few times already? Leave new room for us, do. But in the meanwhile, let me tip my hat to you for your open door policy, and tell you of my two friends' pleasure in a more direct way than they may have felt it was proper to do on their own.

Best wishes, / Albert Goldbarth

J. D. McClatchy to Joseph Parisi   *New York City, 11 April 1985*

Dear Joe—

My new book of poems—it's called *Stars Principal* (a tag from Hopkins)—is now finished, and Macmillan will be publishing it early next year. Making *those* arrangements has been a bit of a scramble over the last few months, because three publishers wanted to do the book, and I felt like Paris having to pass out the golden apple.

The long poem and centerpiece of the book is "First Steps," which I'm enclosing and ask you to read for the magazine [printed September 1985]. Because of my "special relationship" with *Poetry* I'd like to show it to you above all. And also, of course, you are one of the few editors in a position to print long and knotty poems. As you'll see, this is something different for me—the alternating tones and time-periods. I'd wanted to shift between the autobiographical and the meditative; to juxtapose the same relationship across personal and historical planes. The sexuality has made for problems of tone, but I think I've solved them—and in the process come up with something that hasn't been seen before. Well, I hope you'll see what I mean, and I look forward to your reaction. . . .

All best— / Sandy

Joseph Parisi to J. D. McClatchy   *Chicago, 15 May 1985*

Dear Sandy,

Thanks for your good letter, and for letting us see the poem. I read it when it first arrived, of course, but, as usual, got caught up in the endless paper-shuffling that this glorious position entails. . . .

I think it is a very strong, if very complex, piece of work, and a courageous one, too. I do wish that in several places you weren't so knotty and opaque, though; it doesn't seem necessary to be so, always, to me. But it's yer pome; I hope, I trust the patient reader will persevere and reread.

What a delightful quandary for you to have to choose among publishers for the book. Congratulations, too, on this day of your award from the Academy.

We ourselves are being tributized tomorrow, by the Society of Midland Authors. . . . I hate these things, which always turn out to be more work for the honoree than they're worth. (I see fresh floods of mss. next week; would that they *subscribed*.) It's so awkward, too, to make polite chitchat over the chicken croquettes while trying to remember the sweet nothings one's supposed to utter after the jello mold. . . .

We're doing a Special British Issue next month, which has been a headache from start (two years ago) to finish—this p.m. God, are they a boring lot. We did get a very nice essay, from John Bayley of Oxford, which helps explain why. . . .

Joe

Edward Kleinschmidt [Mayes] to Joseph Parisi   *San Francisco, Calif.,*
                                                         6 June 1985

Dear Mr. Parisi,

I thought I'd let you know that I'm leaving for Italy on June 13th and coming back here on August 8th—in case you're sending galleys. You could send them here until June 29th and my "girlfriend," Frances Mayes, could approve them.

I'm spending three weeks in Rome, working on poetry and my second novel. Frances and I and two friends from Brown [C. D. Wright and Forrest Gander] have rented an old stone farmhouse near Cortona for July. . . .

Hope your summer is wonderful!

Best, / Ed Kleinschmidt

Mayes, also a poet, recounted their experiences restoring a villa in Cortona, Italy, in *Under the Tuscan Sun* (1996), which became a best seller. They married in 1998.

Raymond Carver to Joseph Parisi

Port Angeles, Wash., 2 July 1985

Dear Mr. Parisi:

Raymond Carver,
a favorite contributor, read for Poetry
Day with Tess Gallagher in 1986.

Many thanks for your letter of the 24th. I'm very pleased and happy that you want to use those poems in the magazine.

And thank you in advance for the preview [of a review] for *Booklist*. I'm eager to see it. I was told, by my editor at Random House, that the *Chicago Tribune* has a review scheduled, as do some other papers, but I don't know who is doing it, etc. In any case, I'm made happy that you liked the book and reviewed it favorably. Collins will publish the book in England next January, and my Dutch publisher will bring out an edition a year from this fall. Amazing.

I have a new address out here. Tess and I are going to be spending more and more time out here and needed a larger house. I hope you'll make note of the new address for your contributor's records.

I don't know where the time is going, either. First May, then June disappeared. And it seems like it was only a little while ago that I was 25 years old.

This is with my thanks, again, and every good wish.

Best, / Ray Carver

The accepted poems were "Shiftless," "The Sensitive Girl," "Balsa Wood," and "The Rest," all included in *Where Water Comes Together with Other Water* (1985), the collection J.P. had reviewed. Carver and Tess Gallagher were invited to read for Poetry Day 1986. Carver died in 1988, at age fifty. A group of his last poems was printed as a memorial in the April 1989 issue.

Joseph Parisi to Sandra M. Gilbert   *Chicago, 12 September 1985*

Dear Sandra (if I may),

Many, many thanks for the superb reviews—well worth the little extra wait. . . . You come down rather hard on dear Amy [Clampitt]—but I'm afraid I must agree she has it coming. (She's let me see a few new things, and I fear she's really going off the deep end, or certainly in the wrong direction. I hope the p-r isn't going to her [basically very bright, reasonable] head.) I'm more inclined to see the positives in Ms. [Gjertrud] Schnackenberg, which I think far outweigh the negatives you so rightly (but perhaps too forcibly?) underscore. I'm less enthusiastic about Marilyn [Hacker]; she strikes me as very self-indulgent, and far less "interesting" than Marge [Piercy], despite the latter's obvious stylistic deficiencies. But all your points are well taken. Copy goes to the printers immediately. (Do you think, though, you could get rid of at least one of those "Jewish Lesbian in France"'s—4 times is a *bit* much, *n'est-ce pas?*) . . .

Meanwhile, all best to you. (Is the Princeton move permanent, by the way?)

Joe

Carl Dennis to Joseph Parisi   *Buffalo, N.Y., 13 October 1985*

Dear Joseph Parisi,

Would you be willing to drop "Winter Light"? I just don't think it's good enough anymore and had my records been better and my ear truer I would have written you before you went through the trouble of setting it up in type. I'd be glad to pay for any extra expenses involved. The poem, which once I liked, seems now contrived. The link of the waiter to the student is too fanciful, as is the class on religion, and the search for the lost student somehow plodding, predictable, mechanical.

I can't imagine it very likely, but if you'd like to publish another poem of mine with "Schliemann" (which I like very much) I think that either of the two I'm including here would be fit company.

Sincerely, / Carl Dennis

J.P. replied 21 October that the poem was already in press; it and "Heinrich Schliemann" were published in December 1985. Many other requests to withdraw or revise poems were made and granted in future, without prejudice. Dennis was awarded the Ruth Lilly Poetry Prize in 1999.

Mark Cox to Joseph Parisi   *Somers, Conn., 15 November 1985*

Dear Mr. Parisi,

Thank you for the kind letter and your interest in my work. I'm sure you realize just how much this means to a young poet such as myself. Hell, it's a major accomplishment for established writers. But we aspiring scribblers, ah, we do things like putting a candle on the dog's food. We samba with the ironing board. We break-dance out of our bodies for a good two days. And when we come to, we can honestly believe that one part of the long apprenticeship is over. It's a nice feeling, you know?

At any rate, now it's time to get back to my pencil sharpener, so I'll sign off. Be well. Thanks again.

Sincerely, / Mark

Cox made his first appearance with three poems in the January 1987 issue.

Dana Gioia to Joseph Parisi   *Hastings-on-Hudson, N.Y.,*
                                         22 November 1985

Dear Joe:

I would like to thank you and the other judges for *Poetry*'s 1985 Frederick Bock Award. I was—in equal portions—surprised, delighted, and honored by the prize. It means a great deal to me both because *Poetry* has published so much of my work over the last five years and also because the Frederick Bock Award is the first real literary prize I've ever won (unless one counts the time I took second place in my fourth grade poetry contest for some deathless verses on my guardian angel, but even there I was surpassed by Emmanuel Di Benedetto who, luckily for me, seems to have retired from poetry). . . .

My best wishes to everyone at *Poetry*.

Sincerely yours, / Dana

3. Enlarging the Audience

"To have great poets, there must be great audiences, too."

—*Walt Whitman, "Ventures, on an Old Theme," 1892,
motto on each issue of* POETRY, *1912–1950*

By the mid-eighties poetry factions that had been at odds since the sixties reached, if not cordial agreement, at least a placid state of détente. For members of the younger generation, the late "poetry wars" were ancient history, and most now felt free to express themselves in forms *and* in free verse, without recriminations. Writing programs placed increasing emphasis on traditional modes and craft: technique (unlike talent) being something that creative writing classes can in fact impart. With the growth of M.F.A. programs, more energy was also devoted to professionalism, and principal goals for aspiring poets became the acquisition of degrees, fellowships, prizes, journal appearances, and publication of the first book, ideally as a winner in a prestigious contest.

To succeed, modern career poets, most in willing or reluctant residence in academe, have had to build résumés and follow institutional rules for advancement. Writing instructors necessarily consider their primary audience fellow poet-professors to whom their work is knowingly addressed, though poetry readings are a primary means of gaining name recognition and, of course, selling books. But the audiences at most readings tend to be made up of people with similar interests and backgrounds. As critics from Karl Shapiro in the older generation to Dana Gioia in the new trenchantly argued, the gulf between practitioners and the public was growing ever wider and perhaps permanent, since "serious" poets felt far less need to please the general reader for whom the art used to constitute an important elective activity—a cultural necessity and an enjoyment, like listening to music, visiting museums, "keeping up" with scientific discoveries and current events.

Members of this larger audience, educated but nonspecialist, increasingly were or felt themselves to be neglected, and sometimes wrote to say so. The great divide between poet and public was hardly a new phenomenon. It could in fact be traced back to the complex High Modernism *Poetry* itself had been so instrumental in promoting. In part the magazine's first prominence as a forum for the New Poetry came by accident. Little did Harriet Monroe realize what was soon to come through her Open Door. The founder had stated her goals in very general terms: first, to print longer, more serious, noncommercial types of poems; and second, to build an audience for such work. But *Poetry*'s commingling of cutting-edge pieces that Pound favored, exemplified by "imports" like Imagism, with Monroe's choices from home-grown innovations provoked the earliest quarrels between the founding editor and her foreign correspondent.

With her populist sentiments, Monroe wanted badly to create a "great audience." Pound declared the public be damned and insisted that poetry belonged primarily if not exclusively to those who produced it. To a large extent his elitist attitude prevailed through much of the century and was scarcely limited to poetry. Radical new methods and challenging styles disconcerted readers; indeed, Modernist iconoclasm was deliberately provocative, and succeeded in alienating many lovers of traditional verse all too well. Ever the idealist, Monroe felt the art had nobler import than technique; it had "lofty" goals, and the other function of her journal was to cultivate a larger, more informed public for it. But perceptions made that task complicated: the forbidding aura fostered by cerebral, allusive pieces in the High Modernist mode overshadowed *all* poetry, even though the majority of poems written over the century actually were not "difficult" in content and method or "accessible" only to adepts with advanced degrees.

While many decades on we still wanted to keep *Poetry*'s door open wide to the latest New Poetry, I felt that we should also return to Monroe's other original aim and pursue audience-building more creatively. Instead of preaching to the choir, we needed to go forth, if not to convert, at least to persuade the larger public that contemporary poetry was both understandable and worth knowing about. While continuing to pursue grants to underwrite magazine operations, I tried to identify new sources of revenue that would also allow us to expand *Poetry*'s educational activities, its "mission" to the larger community.

In any case, the reality was that few donors became excited about writing checks to pay for such unglamorous items as postage and printing bills. Programs that supported writers or helped encourage audience awareness and appreciation of their work *did* attract potential donors and arouse their enthusiasm. We had always been fortunate to have a small group of friends willing to underwrite ordinary publication expenses year after year, but it became evident in the eighties that foundations and government agencies were mainly interested in supporting "outreach" programs.

Although they had become far less useful as fund-raisers, the annual Poetry Day readings continued to attract large numbers of people, especially students, who wished to encounter Major Poets in person. But as more original ideas came to mind, I felt we could expand our educational role by producing programs with greater depth. Within a few years, given time for planning and start-up funds, we did in fact create projects with wide appeal that eventually reached a truly national audience. Meanwhile two events gave a boost in that direction as well as a grace period to develop new ideas.

After our major patron J. Patrick Lannan died in 1983, it became uncertain whether his 1982 pledge would be honored by the trust set up in his will. Our claim was eventually settled in 1986. Lannan family members, who contested the will, called with assurances that their new foundation (established following litigation) intended to continue Mr. Lannan's tradition of support. In 1988 it began awarding *Poetry* annual grants of $25,000, and later $30,000, for payments to contributors. This funding not only secured that part of the budget and allowed us to double the rate for poetry to $2 a line but gave us more flexibility to put on programs. The Lannan Foundation provided several additional grants to underwrite special projects as well over the next years.

About this time other, quite unexpected good news arrived, likewise by way of a longtime benefactor. In mid-October 1985 I received a call from a man who identified himself as John Kitchen. He said he was a lawyer in Indianapolis and represented an avid *Poetry* subscriber and contributor. "You may know her as Mrs. Guernsey Van Riper, Jr.," he said. I did indeed recall that unforgettable appellation, and the fact she had sent both poetry submissions and donations for many years. "That was her name when she was married," he explained. "But she is using her maiden name again. It is Ruth Lilly, and she would like to set up a major prize for American poets. Can you help us?"

Kitchen said they would like the prize to be presented as early as the next spring, with the award—initially $25,000, later raised to $50,000, $75,000, and then $100,000—to be given each year and "only to an American citizen." I suggested that restrictions be kept to a minimum; but considering its size, it might be best to present the prize for lifetime achievement rather than for a single book. He agreed, and so the Ruth Lilly Poetry Prize, simply stated, was to be offered to a poet "whose accomplishments warrant extraordinary recognition." He said Ruth Lilly insisted that as editor of *Poetry* I select the winner; I recommended we have two other experienced judges that as chair I would choose each year. Later I outlined a selection process, beginning with nominations supported by written statements and further rounds to narrow candidates to two or three finalists; the panel would then meet to determine the winner. Mr. Kitchen approved the procedure and asked the American Council for the Arts, an "arts advocacy" group in New York, to help with administration and publicity.

As jurors for the inaugural award, I chose Maxine Kumin and David Wagoner. From an initial dozen poets of widely varying styles, we focused on three finalists and, at a meeting in New York, quickly agreed on Adrienne Rich, a poet we believed particularly worthy to be the first recipient. Although long a significant voice in American poetry, Rich had not won the major literary awards, doubtless for her uncompromising stands on political and particularly feminist issues. The inaugural presentation was held 6 June 1986 at the Newberry Library, with a reception that more than one guest described as a "love fest."

By June work had already begun on three new projects: a special issue to celebrate *Poetry*'s seventy-fifth anniversary the next year, a series of public programs to mark the Marianne Moore centenary in May 1987, and preliminary planning for what we hoped would become an original series of radio programs on contemporary American poets. In the spring of 1986, with encouragement from Thomas Phelps at the National Endowment for the Humanities, we had submitted a proposal outlining a month of programs

POETRY

OCTOBER–NOVEMBER 1987 $10.00

Edward Koren cover for the special Seventy-fifth Anniversary edition.

devoted to Moore. In September the NEH awarded us a grant of over $66,000 to produce them. To help reach a larger audience, we asked three libraries to participate. Each mounted exhibitions on Moore from its collections and hosted segments of the project, and did splendid work publicizing the events.

At the University of Chicago on 7 May 1987, the Regenstein Library's large exhibit, "Marianne Moore: Vision into Verse," opened with a lecture by Maxine Kumin, who read her poem "Marianne, My Mother, and Me" (published that month in *Poetry*). On the following two days a conference on Moore attracted surprisingly large attendance at the Newberry Library. There Robert Pinsky's paper centered on the cultural implications of Moore's language, Sandra M. Gilbert considered the poet as a "female female impersonator," Alicia Ostriker placed her in the context of women's poetry, David Bromwich contrasted Moore with Elizabeth Bishop, and John Hollander gave a disquisition on Moore's prosody. Each day's session ended with a panel discussion and spirited exchanges with the audience.

During the rest of May we presented weekly programs at the Chicago Public Library Cultural Center. Patricia Willis, the editor of Moore's *Collected Prose*, spoke on the poet's early career and relation to *Poetry*, followed by Richard Howard with witty reflections on "Moore and the Monkey-Business of Modernity." A very large crowd gathered to hear Amy Clampitt discuss Moore as "an American Original." Ending the series, Grace Schulman, a friend of Moore's from childhood, played recordings of her readings and talked about the influence of Moore and Pound in the making of Modernism. Most of the talks were later published in *Marianne Moore: The Art of a Modernist* (1990).

Letters had already gone out to a large group of contributors soliciting poems for the special Seventy-fifth Anniversary issue of *Poetry*, scheduled for October 1987. I also invited authors to share recollections about their relations with the magazine, particularly at the beginning of their careers. By midsummer poems began streaming into the office, along with scores of fascinating, funny, and often poignant stories, including several memoirs by senior authors about Harriet Monroe's kindness to them in their youth. We then faced an awkward situation: we had far more excellent poems and prose pieces than could fit into the space originally allotted. I inquired whether Ruth Lilly might be willing to underwrite an expanded edition; she and her advisers responded with a $20,000 grant that enabled us to print work by 140 authors. The quadruple-sized Diamond Anniversary Issue featured a whimsical cover drawn especially for the occasion by Edward Koren, along with anecdotes by thirty-four poets. None of their stories had been published before, including John Ashbery's account of discovering himself debuting in *Poetry* in 1945 after a prep school classmate filched a group of his poems and sent them in—under a pseudonym. Some of the letters we could not include in the issue or had to edit severely are printed below.

In the spring of 1987 I had also submitted a proposal to the NEH's media division for a planning grant to produce a thirteen-part series of radio programs on post–World War II American poetry. The germ of what became our most complex and longest-running project arose during discussions in the summer of 1986 with Elizabeth Carlson and James Rutke, veteran writer-producers for public radio. I felt there was a real need for an up-to-date, engaging introduction to and overview of contemporary poetry, and believed that poets themselves usually made the best explicators of their work. They convinced me that radio was an ideal medium for poetry, and a very effective, economical way of reaching a large audience. They offered to lend their technical expertise in producing the programs.

When I spoke with several poets about the idea of using radio, they were not only enthusiastic but also offered to help. David Bromwich gave early counsel. Then Sandra M. Gilbert and J. D. McClatchy, excellent poet-critics both, signed on as principal advisers to the project, and we began to refine lists of potential poets to be featured in the series as well as experts who might consult on specific authors and serve as interviewers. The proposal emphasized that the poets we selected—Ginsberg, Ashbery, Merwin, Rich, among them—were significant as individual artists, and most were also originators of major movements or outstanding representatives of stylistic trends in postwar American poetry. In August 1987 the NEH awarded a $20,000 planning grant to develop a full-blown production proposal, to be delivered within the next six months.

As work began, we faced a new challenge. In late summer of 1986 we were informed that the library at the University of Illinois planned major renovations the next year, and so the *Poetry* collection would have to be removed. In nine years at UICC, we had accumulated thousands of new volumes as well as large quantities of back issues, business records, and correspondence files, to the point our offices were barely passable. Although grateful for the university's generosity, we had to find other quarters, which was not an easy task: given the square footage required just to house the books, rental costs far exceeded our resources. We began to fear we might have to dispose of most of the collection.

Poetry had cordial relations with the Newberry Library dating at least from the early fifties when Stanley Pargellis had provided the magazine free office space, and so we wondered if we might at least arrange for our books to be transferred temporarily to the library, where we hoped they would be accessible to our staff and perhaps to scholars. When board president Patrick

Shaw broached the subject to him, Charles Cullen, the newly appointed librarian of the Newberry, not only immediately agreed to provide housing for the books but offered the magazine quarters in the stack building: his first official act. An architect, Shaw then made drawings for offices and storage space. Remodeling and moving expenses still posed problems, but the MacArthur Foundation awarded a special grant of $25,000 that covered moving charges as well as costs of most of the construction, shelving, and new furniture. (The three desks and chairs were probably the first brand-new pieces *Poetry* ever owned.) A five-year agreement was signed in March 1987; the library asked only nominal amounts for maintenance and utilities. In June the books were transferred and we were ready to set up shop.

Well settled into our new home, we presented the second Lilly Prize, to Philip Levine, then completed preparations for Poetry Day buoyed by refreshing financial news. Thanks to the NEH grants, Ruth Lilly's gift for the special issue, and additional small awards, *Poetry* approached its Diamond Jubilee solidly in the black. At the seventy-fifth-anniversary gala on 30 October, Richard Howard acted as master of ceremonies as former editors Hayden Carruth, Karl Shapiro, and John Nims offered recollections of the more curious incidents and particular crises of their tenures, which from the distance of several decades took on a decidedly humorous cast. Peals of laughter accompanied Nims's deadpan reading of a missive (later printed in *Dear Editor*) that Peter De Vries sent him in March 1944, in the aftermath of three trying days of entertaining the visiting Irish poet Oliver St. John Gogarty. Carruth recalled the near collapse and last-minute reprieve of the magazine during his brief editorship in 1949. In the question period, when an audience member bluntly asked Carruth why he was "fired," he replied he really did not know. The crowd roared after he added: "But then, I didn't know why I was hired, either."

4. Correspondence 1986–1989

Kathleen Norris to Joseph Parisi   *Lemmon, S.D., 24 February 1986*

Hello:

Thanks for your note. I am enclosing five poems I hope you will consider for publication. This is NOT a multiple submission.

They're all from my current manuscript. I've had poems recently in "Agni Review," "Kalliope," "Prairie Schooner," and "Virginia Quarterly Review." My second book of poems, *The Middle of the World*, was published by the University of Pittsburgh in 1981. I never know how much of this stuff to repeat in a cover letter, but I've learned to be wary. I once had poems sent back in a big hurry from a magazine whose editor had asked me to send some work. It turned out a screener had seen my return address and panicked. I must admit that Lemmon, South Dakota doesn't sound promising: but it's better than Blunt, Oral, or Mud Butte. As far as I know there are no poets in any of those towns.

A stamped return envelope is enclosed.

With best wishes, / Kathleen Norris

The submission was returned, but Norris eventually had two poems in the April 1990 issue.

Ernest Sandeen to Joseph Parisi   *South Bend, Ind., 1 May 1986*

Dear Joseph Parisi:

There's not much point in offering you an account of my "credentials," although this is the first time I've addressed you as Editor of *Poetry*. . . .

Since your succession to the Editorship I have applauded your opening up the pages of this venerable magazine to a host of unknown or as yet little known poets.

I am heartened by this chorus of diverse, vigorous young voices, sometimes from unlikely quarters, evidence that composing poems still flourishes, even though "poetry" seems to have fallen below the level of public notice.

The only way I can compete with these young poets is to outflank them. My best strategy is to act my age, trying to show, if I can, that at seventy-seven I have found things to say, important to us all, about the luck of sheer survival, its modest joys and consolations, its sense of loss, its hopes, doubts and fears—things the younger poets may imagine but cannot really experience. . . .

My warmest best wishes for you and for your continuing success as Editor.

Sincerely yours, / Ernest Sandeen

Mary Karr to Joseph Parisi   *Belmont, Mass., 5 May 1986*

Dear Joe:

I'm glad you can use "Pregnancy" but am still semi-stumped for a better title. Rifling the poem for key phrases, I only come up with "Burdens" or "Soft Mask." Titles are tough for me, so if you can suggest something, please do.

As I think I mentioned in my last note, nothing could rival Gilbert's tour de force on *What the Light Was Like*. Nevertheless, I enclose my effort on that and Glück's latest. . . . I'm interested in reviewing other books—Simic's (which, rumor has it, got a brief nod from the Pulitzer committee recently), Kunitz's *Next-to-Last Things*, Gilbert's edition of women's poetry for Norton, Ostriker's *Stealing the Language.* Vendler selected a curious lot for her latest anthology, but the selection is less odd than the fact that it's called *The Harvard Anthology*, which implies that Vendler now IS Harvard, since she selected the work without the benefit of any editorial committee.

Speaking of the great place, I'm hoping to hear this month about a fall teaching job there, a position that would elevate us from poverty to neo-poverty. If that fails, we may need to sell our unborn child. Maybe we could hammer out a discreet and highly metaphorical ad to accompany the poem.

Again, it pleases me that you took something. As usual, I welcome you comments on the criticism as well.

Warm regards, / Mary Karr

The poem was published under the title "Soft Mask" in September 1986.

Carolyn Kizer to Joseph Parisi   *Stanford, Calif., 16 July 1986*

Dear Joe,

Congratulations on picking Adrienne for that munificent prize! No one deserves it more. Is this prize going to go only to women? If not, I would hope that the name of Hayden Carruth be not forgotten. A major poet and critic, and always always poor, every moment of his life, always living in terrible uncertainty about his future. . . .

Best regards to all, / Carolyn Kizer

Ernest Sandeen to Joseph Parisi   *South Bend, Ind., 8 August 1986*

Dear Joseph Parisi:

Your acceptance of four of the eight poems I sent you [printed December 1986] meant a lot to me. But your warmly gracious letter was especially welcome. It assured me that my long association with *Poetry* is still intact. Most of all, however, I'm gratified that poems of mine will appear in a magazine which is now reasserting its traditional leadership in the world of contemporary poetry.

The Ruth Lilly Poetry Prize is a substantial recognition of both the community of poets and of *Poetry*. If the prize was a windfall, I suspect you must have had some influence in steering the wind toward the one still flourishing periodical which holds the unique distinction of having helped to found the whole modernist movement in poetry.

Adrienne Rich whom you, Kumin and Wagoner elected as the first recipient of the Lilly prize will predictably be hailed as an admirable choice by those who sympathize with the Feminist Movement and as a deplorable choice by those who oppose it. In her life experience, passing from conventional wife and mother to "androgyne," and then to Lesbian lover, as well as in her poems which meticulously trace her progression, Rich has been a confessed and vigorous advocate of the feminist cause. However, it is possible to concede that her poems reach down deeply enough into the realities of our common human consciousness and with enough skill of aesthetic sentience to transform her advocacy into what we can all appreciate as authentic poetry. (Whatever that means.) The truth is I'm not wise enough to solve the enigma of the *poete engagé*, an apparently insoluble problem in our day and therefore usually avoided, although in the 18th century it was not even a ponderable question. . . .

Best wishes to you and for your continuing success as editor,

Ernest Sandeen

Adrienne Rich to Joseph Parisi   *Santa Cruz, Calif., 15 December 1986*

Dear Joe,

I'll be delighted to send you some poems for the 75th Anniversary Issue. It sounds like a great project. I'm glad your deadline is May 15, because I'm taking off March and April for poetry and nothing but, and hope to have more new poems by then. I want to stretch the Lilly Prize over a number of years allowing me blocks of time I would ordinarily not have taken. Having it has let me acknowledge to myself how deeply I've wanted to do that. . . .

I'm still trying to absorb David Kalstone's absence. I couldn't go to the memorial for him because I was teaching, and had already taken off a day for Yom Kippur. Jimmy Merrill sent me a lovely color snapshot of him, in Venice. I keep having this odd feeling that he's not so far gone that he couldn't return. Simone Weil said, "The absence of the dead is their way of appearing", and I muse a great deal over that. . . .

Yours, / Adrienne

A Rutgers professor and distinguished critic, Kalstone died in 1986; his books include *Five Temperaments: Elizabeth Bishop, Robert Lowell, James Merrill, Adrienne Rich, John Ashbery* (1977) and *Becoming a Poet: Elizabeth Bishop with Marianne Moore and Robert Lowell* (1989), edited by friends from his draft following his death.

Robert Penn Warren to Joseph Parisi   *Fairfield, Conn.,*
                                                        15 December 1986

Dear Mr. Parisi:

I appreciate your invitation to contribute something to your 75th Anniversary issue of *Poetry*. But—and it is a great "But"—I can't. Since my last book, last year, I have written some poems. But I am not going to publish any of them. They are too much like other poems already in book form. If poems after a book don't grow in the feeling of a sort of fresh start, in some way, I have, for at least 35 years, thrown them away. I did send the best (I thought) of the new ones now to a very friendly publisher, whose judgment I trust, and he replied that he'd like to see more. Well, nobody has. And will never have a chance to do so.

Robert Penn Warren late in his career; he first appeared in *Poetry* in 1932.

All thanks for your invitation now, and to *Poetry* for many things in the past. The magazine has always been of very great interest for me, and 50 odd years ago when I began publishing there I was grateful for the chance to show my wares. Not to mention prize notice there. I know that I am not alone among poets who owe a great debt to *Poetry*, in all ways.

Sincerely, / Robt Penn Warren

May Sarton to Joseph Parisi   *York, Me., 18 December 1986*

Dear Joseph Parisi:

Let me answer part of your letter about the 75th Anniversary of *Poetry* and say something about the momentous event in my life which was when I was 18 (an apprentice at Eva Le Gallienne's Civic Repertory Theatre in N.Y.) and five poems of mine came out under the title *Words On The Wind* in the December 1930 issue. These were the first poems I had ever sold and that marvelous check for $17.00, a fortune for me at that time, was spent at once on the two volumes of Katharine Mansfield's Letters and a book of drawings of Isadora Duncan by a Spanish artist. (That book has disappeared but I still have the KM letters.) But of course it was the recognition that was precious beyond words, and Harriet Monroe's letter of acceptance which my secretary who knows where everything is is trying to find in the files. If she finds it I'll send a xerox along later.

I shall have it in mind to send you one or two new poems by May 15th. At the moment I'm snowed under with mail that must be answered. Also I do not have much as I have been rather ill for most of 1986 and had a stroke in February. But there are one or two poems and I'll try to find something worthy.

Yours very sincerely, / May Sarton

John Ashbery to Joseph Parisi　　　　　*New York City, 12 January 1987*

Dear Joe,

　Many thanks for your letter and copy of the July *Poetry*. Needless to say I liked David Spurr's essay ["Free But Alone," on Ashbery's *Selected Poems*, July 1986] very much and appreciated the seriousness of his attention. I'm enclosing some poems which you are welcome to consider for *Poetry*. I'll also send you before your May deadline the paragraph you request concerning my "relations" with the magazine. This might be an interesting tale since my first appearance in *Poetry* was not under my own name—a so-called friend "borrowed" some of my poems and submitted them himself.

　Best wishes to *Poetry* on its seventy-fifth and to you for the New Year.

John Ashbery

For the full story, see the Seventieth-fifth Anniversary issue (October 1987), p. 203, and *Dear Editor*, p. 362.

James Dickey to Joseph Parisi　　　　　*Columbia, S.C., 16 January 1987*

Dear Mr. Parisi:

　Thank you very much for your invitation to bring out some new poems in *Poetry*. Any poet—American or otherwise—does well to publish in your magazine.

　More than that, I conducted my whole poetic education by means of its issues; the Southwest Pacific war was made possible to me, in terms of survival, only by means of what appeared, month to month, in its pages.

　Well, I won't go on and on, but will hope to hear from you on these particular poems.

Best wishes, / Jim

Maxine Kumin to Joseph Parisi　　　　　*Warner, N.H., 1 February 1987*

Dear Joe:

　I'm sending you the enclosed long poem ["Marianne, My Mother, and Me"] for what will probably be obvious reasons—do you think this is something that might be suitable for the May Moore hootenanny? I've been writing away on it for months now and feel it is more or less finished, tho I've left out lots of lovely bits I had wanted to get in. It occurred to me that I might be able to talk about these omissions and a few other salient points in & around the poem and then simply fill out the hour by reading from Moore. Do you know all the anthologies she isn't in? Ones with Lizette W Reese, etc., like the Untermeyer?

If you would like this poem for the fall issue, you are welcome to it. On the other hand, it may be far too long for your purposes; please just say so, for I have exactly two others (smaller) I can offer instead.

I know you'll give me a frank opinion of the poem. It's hard to tell right now, as it has obsessed me so long. We are having the kind of winter some have been darkly prophesying—but it should make a good maple syrup year, finally. There is some balance between reading M Moore and shoveling.

All best, / Maxine

Reese (1856–1935) was best known for her sonnet "Tears," included in Louis Untermeyer's *Modern American Poetry* (1919). Kumin read her poem, and commented on deletions she made to it, in her talk opening the Marianne Moore exhibit at the University of Chicago's Regenstein Library, 7 May 1987.

Janet Lewis to Joseph Parisi   *[Los Altos, Calif.], 5 February 1987*

Dear Mr. Parisi:

At sixteen my greatest ambition was to have a poem published in *Poetry*. I thought in that case I could call myself a poet. At nineteen I joined The Poetry Club at the University of Chicago. All of us, I believe, longed to sell something to *Poetry*; many of us did achieve publication rather early. The names of Glenway Wescott, Yvor Winters, Maurice Lesemann, Elizabeth Madox Roberts, Pearl Andelson Sherry, Jessica Nelson North, Gladys Campbell come to mind, and there were others such as George Dillon, whom I did not know personally, who were active in the Club and contributors to the magazine before and after my two years at the University. In June 1920, I had my first poems in *Poetry*.

I remember Miss Monroe from days before my time at the University, for she was a friend of my father, and the magazine was on our library table from its first issue. Between my junior and senior years at the University, which would have been 1919, and between the close of school and the departure of my family to the north woods for the summer, Miss Monroe invited me to be office girl at *Poetry*. That was the Cass Street Office. After the first few days of my apprenticeship, Miss Monroe went on holiday, leaving Helen Hoyt in charge as editor, with me as barely qualified assistant. They were a happy and very interesting two weeks, in which I became fond of both women. I remember Miss Monroe, small, dominating, obstinate, acidulous, yet warmly affectionate upon occasion and always reserved.

I remember the pince-nez which dug deep gouges in the sides of her straight nose; the splendid Chinese coats she sometimes wore to parties; the fine carriage of head, the straight back; and the curiously roughened or tight quality or her voice. Though as opinionated young writers we quarreled sometimes with her dicta, she was for all of us encouraging. She made the writing of poetry not only respectable, but admirable, and the publishing of poems an actuality. She introduced us to the Best People, either in print or in person—Wallace Stevens in print, Carl Sandburg in person. There were others also who were extremely kind to the Poetry Club—Robert Morss Lovett, at the University, especially. I remember in the *Poetry* office Eunice Tietjens, and, when I was in Santa Fe, Alice Corbin Henderson. Miss Monroe came to see me in Santa Fe when I was a bed patient. She brought me two enormous dahlias of rich colors, drooping as dahlias do, on their narrow, wilted stems. The last time that I saw her was at the new office in the spring of 1932, when I was on my way with my small daughter to the cabin in the north woods. That same day I saw also that lovely poet and lady, Agnes Lee.

My father remembered Miss Monroe as a "slip of a girl" reading her poem for the opening of the Columbian Exposition, the World's Fair, in Chicago [in 1892]. I felt proud of her for being in the high country of Peru, on a grand adventure, when death interrupted her.

For new work I can offer you only these to chose from or decline. I apologize for going on at such length, and also for neglecting to mention "the other Harriet," Mrs. William Vaughn Moody, whose house and spirit were so capacious and kindly to our young group.

Sincerely yours, / Janet Lewis

See *Dear Editor*, pp. 234–235; Lewis was married to Yvor Winters, who also met H.M. while a student at Chicago.

Kimon Friar to Joseph Parisi   *Athens, Greece, 17 February 1987*

Dear Mr. Parisi:

Your letter of December 1 has just reached me from Greece to San Francisco. . . .

As for an anecdote. Born on an island in the Sea of Marmara, I was brought to Chicago at the age of three, and finally went to high school in Maywood. There I wrote a great deal of poetry, and avidly read every issue of *Poetry*, thinking of it as an unattainable ideal, situated surely not in Chicago but in some land of the heart's desire. In 1929 I went to The Experimental School at the University of Wisconsin and there, with the daring of youth, chose, as my first attempt at translation, *The Bacchae* of Euripides. I not only translated the play in sprung rhythm, but also designed set and costumes, choreographed it and directed the production. The next year, when I came to Chicago to visit my parents, I clutched a Greek copy of *The Bacchae* in my hot little hands and went to visit the *Poetry* office, but I could not find the courage to knock on the door. I went around and around the block for four or five times before I timidly knocked. The door was opened, as I remember, by a thin, short, wizened old lady (it seemed to me) with grey hair who said to me sharply, "Well, well what do you want?" Her manner was so abrupt and disconcerting that I found myself short of breath, unable to answer. She finally hustled me in, sat me in a chair, and curtly told me to be brief, for she had much work to do. Everything I had ever dreamed of the magnanimity of poets, the kindness and understanding, was shattered at that moment, and my eyes brimmed with tears. Harriet Monroe immediately changed attitude. She came up to me, stroked my shoulders tenderly, apologized for speaking so abruptly, and gently began asking me various questions about myself. She kept me for some time, spoke to me kindly, and asked me to visit again.

As I was going out she asked me to sign the books of visitors, and I was greatly moved to see that I was signing my name below the signature of George Dillon, who that year happened to be my favorite poet: I knew *The Boy in the Wind* and *The Flowering Stone* by heart. Later I often visited the offices of *Poetry* when the editors were Karl Shapiro, Henry Rago, and John Frederick Nims, but that visit with Harriet Monroe has been the most vivid in my memory. In 1951 Shapiro published an anthology of my translations from Greek poetry, and thirty years later, in 1981, Nims published another.

Cordially, / Kimon Friar

Philip Levine to Joseph Parisi   *Fresno, Calif., 27 April 1987*

Dear Joe,

Let me thank you again for this honor [the Lilly Prize for 1987]. I'm very moved that the three of you chose me. By the time I get to Chicago all the money will be spent, but that's what it's for, my wife keeps telling me. Actually we own an old farm house that needed lots of work, & we were trying to finance it when this came along, but it still leaves enough to buy me a lot of time for the poems to come.

You were right: the hardest part is keeping my mouth shut, but so far I have a perfect record, & that in spite of the fact I called my mother on her 83rd birthday & said not a word about this. My wife & I celebrated alone, but then we've been doing that for years. . . .

Lilly Prize recipient Philip Levine with his wife Fran at the
award ceremony in 1987; he first appeared in *Poetry* in 1955.

Thanks again. I've got 45 more days of silence, give or take a few. I can
make it. Easy.

Sincerely, / Phil

The other judges were Linda Pastan and Philip Booth. In the first years of the prize, the
winners were not revealed until the end of the chairman's introduction at the ceremony.

Stuart Dybek to Joseph Parisi   *Kalamazoo, Mich., 12 May 1987*

Dear Mr. Parisi:

Thank you for your invitation to submit work for POETRY's 75th Anniversary issue. Enclosed are eight new poems. I also wanted to enclose a
brief anecdote, but, I'm sorry to say, that it needed so much story to go with
it that I came up empty-handed. It had to do with finding out, around my
senior year in high school, that POETRY magazine originated in Chicago. It
would take several pages to adequately explain why this fact came as a momentous revelation. In any case, it triggered a quest: one night a friend of
mine, who was taking classes at the Art Institute, and I rode subway and
buses and walked, reading street signs, and finally located the old building
on N. Dearborn Parkway. We went on several such quests at that time—to
jazz clubs, famous and infamous areas of the city, etc—and this one ended

pretty much as they all did. The lights were out as might be expected at 3 a.m. I don't know what we expected exactly—Roethke planting bulbs in the moonlight, Allen Ginsberg cupping a reefer in the shadows, the ghost of Vachel Lindsay declaiming from the steps. We stood staring at the building for a while. Dialogue probably ran something along the lines of:

"So this POETRY."

"Yep, this is it."

"POETRY, all right."

Having verified its existence, we make our way back to the Douglas Park "B" [El train] and sleep feeling we'd accomplished something.

Hope something in this group of poems interests you. Thank you again for considering my work for this issue, and for your generous words in the past. Very much looking forward to the issue.

Best, / Stuart Dybek

Rita Dove to Joseph Parisi   *Tempe, Ariz., 5 June 1987*

Dear Joe Parisi:

I will be putting on many hats in this letter; but first of all, I want to tell you how delighted I am that "Ars Poetica" and "The Breathing, the Endless News" will appear in the special issue of *Poetry*. Of course if there's squeeze, you can save one of them for a later issue. . . .

Secondly, my chairman has told me that you wrote a supporting letter for my application for promotion—thank you for taking that time out of your busy schedule. I recently learned that my application for promotion to full professor was successful.

And thirdly, today the book review editor at the Chicago *Tribune* phoned me at your suggestion. Unfortunately, I was unable to help her out—I'll be spending most of my sabbatical year in Europe—but I appreciate the recommendation.

I hope we'll meet someday. In the meantime, best of luck with the 75th issue, and all those in between and beyond—

Best, / Rita Dove

Paul Engle to Joseph Parisi   *Iowa City, Ia., 21 June 1987*

Dear Mr. Parisi:

In the summer of 1932 POETRY had a competition for poems expressing the theme of the "Century of Progress" celebration of exhibits, programs, demonstrations about Chicago's past. It was typical of the city, with its important magazine devoted to poetry, that it should think a poem would be the best of the arts to shout the city's presence. Being in New York City as a student at Columbia University, I sensed a lot about Chicago from the vantage point of Broadway and 123rd Street where I lived. My poem won; it was 199 lines long, the limit being 200 lines. I received a sum, $100 or $200, and a request to read it at the Exhibition. I arrived at the offices of POETRY, then on E. Erie Street, and Harriet Monroe took me to lunch at a "Ladies Tea Room." I was the only *man*, but not quite certain about that. In the afternoon we went to a big hall which was just emptying after a Duke Ellington concert. To my delight, it was filled at once. I assumed these were the poetry lovers of the Midwest until I go up to read and found that most had their shoes off and were rubbing sore feet. I properly howled at them. "America Remembers" appeared in POETRY [June 1933] and later in a collection of my poems called AMERICAN SONG (modesty compels me to state that it was fully noticed on the front page of the N.Y. Times Book review).

Afterward Miss Monroe produced a mass of free tickets to rides and shows and we celebrated until we went on the "Skyride," a little car which had wheels rolling along a high wire suspended between two very high metal towers. Half way across it stuck, would go neither forward nor back. A couple of women got scared as the wind down the lake rocked the car and we all looked down at the threatening ground. One seemed about to become hysterical, when Miss Monroe, the tiniest person on the ride, stood up and said in a surprisingly strong voice, "Don't worry, ladies, a *man* will come." We swayed and muttered and thought of our wills. Then a *man* came along the wire, suspended in a sort of breeches buoy. He pounded with a hammer, turned something with a wrench, crept back to the tower. The air glittered with his swearing. Abruptly the car jerked and we rolled into the tower. As we staggered off, Miss Monroe said firmly, "You see, ladies, don't worry. There's always a *man*." I shared their prayer. Later she confided, "I think a little sherry would help." It did.

And when would POETRY like another 199-line poem? I could probably stretch it to 200 lines.

                                                                Paul Engle

Billy Collins to Joseph Parisi   *Bronx, N.Y., 21 July 1987*

Dear Joseph Parisi,

I was delighted to hear that you have accepted three of my poems for *Poetry*. I suppose that on some subconscious level I have been waiting for this piece of news ever since I dared to submit some poems to the magazine at the presumptuous age of nineteen. At that time I received in response a very sweet, encouraging letter from Henry Rago, not encouraging me to submit any more work, mind you, but to continue writing them. Just to have a piece

Opening of draft of H.R.'s reply to J. Patrick Lannan in 1957
concerning the potential of "young Bill Collins":
"there is something genuine behind these poems. . . ."

of stationery with the *Poetry* letterhead was a thrill in those days, something worth carrying around in your wallet as I recall. The poems that I submitted to you (more than twenty years after the Rago letter) constituted my second effort to get the nod from *Poetry*. You can appreciate how especially pleased I was to hear from you about the acceptance.

Yes, two of the three poems —"Winter Syntax" and "Books"—are to appear in *The Apple That Astonished Paris* from the University of Arkansas Press. They are aiming for a March/April 1988 publication date, so I hope there will be no problems in printing the poems before then. It might be safest to slip them into a 1987 issue.

Thank you again for your letter; I am enclosing the forms for the contributors' notes and I look forward to seeing the proofs and the issue itself.

Best, / Billy Collins

The two poems and "A History of Weather," his first contributions, appeared in April 1988.

5. New Developments, and a Disappointment

News coverage of the seventy-fifth anniversary was generous, the special issue sold briskly, and *Poetry* gained more than four hundred new subscribers in the next weeks. But there was little time to enjoy the afterglow of the celebration. Much work needed to be completed on the proposal for the radio project: confirming poets and scholars, composing detailed outlines of program content, drawing up budgets, setting up schedules for recording, scripting, editing, mixing. Since we also had to produce a sample program, we taped two interviews. With almost no funds remaining for fine-editing, music, and other niceties, we finished one demonstration tape only a week before the deadline for submitting the proposal in late March 1988.

In September we were informed that the NEH declined to fund production. We were told that poetry was always a "hard sell" (a fact we were already well aware of) and were hardly consoled to learn that odds of success in the media division were only 1 in 40. Still convinced the project was well worth doing, and considering the effort already expended, we were determined to find other support so we could refine and resubmit the proposal with a polished demo tape. The Prince Charitable Trusts provided $15,000, and we set to work on the revised version and a new program—featuring W. S. Merwin, with a particularly appealing interview and superb readings—which we submitted in March 1989. This time the NEH accepted the proposal and awarded $148,000 to produce the thirteen-part series, which we now officially titled "Poets in Person."

In the fall of 1988, John Kitchen informed us that "in recognition of Mr. Parisi's efforts" in administering her prize, Ruth Lilly would be doubling her annual donation, to $20,000. He then proposed a new project: a "national collegiate poetry convocation" for student poets, featuring readings, seminars, and other events with prominent poets, to be held annually at Indiana University. In further discussions with him and the chair of the English department, I suggested we make the event a fellowship competition. Writing programs nationwide would be asked to nominate their best undergraduate or graduate students, and a group of fifteen would be invited to attend. Five poets of note, including instructors at Indiana, would join me in conducting workshops with the candidates and in selecting the winner. The award would be $15,000, to allow further study, travel, freedom to write: there would be no specific requirements. Kitchen agreed to the plan, and the first fifteen students assembled in Bloomington in June 1989. Like the first recipient, Saskia Hamilton, who edited *The Letters of Robert Lowell* (2005), many Lilly Fellows would go on to earn advanced degrees, publish books of or about poetry, and garner other prestigious awards, among them Davis McCombs (1993), who won a Stegner Fellowship at Stanford and the Yale Younger Poets Award for *Ultima Thule* (1999), and James Kimbrell (1994), who won a Whiting Fellowship and the Kathryn A. Morton Prize for *The Gatehouse Heaven* (1998).

Expanded programming and the new projects brought the magazine financial stability but placed substantial extra burdens on our small staff. Fortunately, in the fall of 1988 Stephen Young offered to help with first reading and other editorial tasks, working part time at first (all the budget then allowed). When Nadine Cummings retired at the end of 1989, after twenty-two years of truly devoted service as subscription manager, I asked Young to join *Poetry* full time as associate editor, and he began to handle various chores on the business side as well. He became adept with computers and soon became our resident guru and the principal reason we were able to take advantage of rapidly developing applications, including desktop publishing, quickly and relatively easily in spite of our very limited means.

In the midst of the annual Poetry Days, prize presentations, public programs, and grant proposals, regular magazine work did continue, of course. Besides the seventy-fifth-anniversary edition, another highlight among the monthly issues was the triple-length, dual-language Italian Issue for October–November 1989. Co-edited with Paolo Cherchi, it featured thirty-three postwar poets, including Montale and Pasolini and several representatives of the younger generation, a number of them recommended by Dana Gioia. Translators included Jonathan Galassi, J. D. McClatchy, John F. Nims, Charles Wright, and Gioia himself. He also organized a launch for the issue, a reading by four of the poets at the Poetry Society of America in New York City on 11 October. The issue later received a great deal of odd if unintended attention. With its striking cover photograph of a Giulio Paolini plaster sculpture of disjointed body parts, the Italian number appeared behind bars in *The Silence of the Lambs*, in the hands of Anthony Hopkins as Hannibal Lecter.

6. Correspondence 1988–1989

Joseph Parisi to James Laughlin   *Chicago, 30 March 1988*

Dear Mr. Laughlin,

Many thanks for your kind words about the Guide [to the PBS television series "Voices & Visions"]. Had I but known what I was getting into . . . rather a rush job, since I was called into the project late in August and they wanted the thing yesterday. I don't think I want to try to condense the life and work of Ezra into 7 pp. again any time soon. I really did enjoy your parts in the series—what a wonderful contrast to the, I fear, rather dreary (and for most viewers I suspect incomprehensible) professors. By the bye, and out of the blue, comes to the office an essay from Robert Coles ["Bringing Poems to Medical School: A Memoir," August 1988], a wonderful piece, part elegy and memoir of [L. E.] Sissman, part meditation on the effect of poetry on the practitioners of medicine. Anyway, we got to chatting about the series and Dr. Williams, in particular, whom, as you know, Dr. Coles tried to keep up with on some of his daily rounds. I thought the WCW part of the series was about the best: the good doctor came back so warmly, so humanly, and so sadly to life.

Most of the reviews I've seen have been glowing. The exception, of course, was a rather nasty (and beside-the-point) piece in *The New Criterion*. Good god, what's a mother to do: people complain that TV never does anything serious or totally ignores poetry, and then when they launch a huge venture like this, it's crab, carp, crab. Would *TNC* prefer the "general public" have no exposure at all—that sure would get them interested in picking up the Moderns. . . .

Truly, / Joe Parisi

Reynolds Price to Joseph Parisi   *Durham, N.C., 20 April 1988*

Dear Joe,

Back in the early days of porno films, DEEP THROAT wasn't shown in Raleigh where my brother Bill lives. Soon though he noticed an ad, announcing its arrival at the Zebulon Art Theatre. Zebulon is a one-stoplight town, a few miles from Raleigh. So Bill and two of his friends jumped at the chance to see the new wonder, so close to home. They'd go that very night. Bill called at once for show times; the manager hemmed for a moment and then said, "Tell you, buddy, we had to turn that 'un *off*—it was too hot for Zebulon."

As you know, I feared "Juncture" [September 1988] was too hot for Zebulon and am delighted to know it's not. (Not that POETRY is a one-stoplight town of course.)

I'll look forward to seeing proof and then the thing itself.

Meanwhile, a gorgeous spring day here; and I'm nearing the end of my 57 Milton term papers. I hope you're having similar luck.

Yours, / Reynolds

Neal Bowers to Joseph Parisi   *Ames, Ia., 30 August 1988*

Dear Joe,

Just after "Stump Speech" came out in the July issue of *Poetry*, I was jogging through the neighborhood when I heard someone yell, "Hey, Neal, I loved your poem in *Poetry*." It was my podiatrist. . . . And within the next couple of weeks, I heard from friends and fellow poets from places as distant as Florida, Tennessee, and Kansas.

I never get this kind of reaction to poems published anywhere else (including *The New Yorker*), but it's typical anytime I have work in *Poetry*. Once, a fellow named Ron Offen [editor of *Free Lunch*] even sent me $10 for what he deemed "the best of the issue" poems and told me to buy myself some beer, which I did.

Whenever poets get together, there are always complaints about the small audience for poetry; and the gripes are not unfounded. But my experience shows that *Poetry* is a magazine that gets read, and not just by poets. . . .

Best regards, / Neal Bowers

May Swenson to Joseph Parisi   *Sea Cliff, N.Y., 2 October 1988*

Dear Joe:

That's disappointing that your good radio proposal can't be funded by the NEH. Short sighted of them! How much better to have *living* poets present their work—than have it handled second hand post mortem by others.

But somehow I expect that all the work you've done on this scheme will still bear fruit—and that it will be carried through in future. I'm certainly willing to go with it any time it can resume. And grateful that you would count me among potential Movers in American Poetry.

Have you had a chance to look at my latest—*In Other Words* (Knopf)? Will someone review it for POETRY? Alice Fulton—who reviews so well?

My best, always, / May

The proposal was resubmitted and accepted the next year. Swenson was among the poets originally chosen for the series; unfortunately she died 4 December 1989, before we could tape her interview. *In Other Words* was reviewed in July 1989 by Linda Gregerson.

Mark Halliday to Joseph Parisi   *[n.p.], 20 February 1989*

Dear Joseph Parisi,

I think it was in 1971 that I sent *Poetry* a poem about a cat. The poem seemed marvelous to me; its great feature was a pun: paws/pause . . . [sic] Since then my style has changed, but has never been quite right for *Poetry*—till now! It is delightful that you accept "A Kind of Reply" [September 1989]. Heartfelt thanks.

Sincerely, / Mark Halliday

Reynolds Price to Joseph Parisi   *Durham, N.C., 2 May 1989*

Dear Joe,

I'm delighted you can use the two heron poems [December 1989]. . . .

By the way, I was enormously moved by Ray Carver's last poems and look forward to seeing the volume. I'd admired but never met him; and then in NY in May '88, there he was for the Institute-Academy induction ceremony. He came hulking up to me with praise for my work, and then he leaned closer to say "We share something else too. I'm fighting cancer." With that, Jim Merrill walked up and Ray drifted off. For once in my life, I made the right gesture—when I got home I wrote him a letter of thanks. He replied at warm length, and was dead in a few days.

Yours, / Reynolds

Carver's four poems appeared in April 1989. He died of lung cancer on 12 August 1988, at age fifty.

Mona Van Duyn to Joseph Parisi   *St. Louis, Mo., 5 June 1989*

Dear Joe,

First of all I want to thank you from the bottom of my heart (and the other judges too) for thinking highly enough of my poetry to give it the Ruth Lilly Prize. It couldn't have come at a time better calculated to lift my spirits, since I've been ill with one thing and another all year, with three hospitalizations, and am still not nervously or physically back to normal.

Mona Van Duyn at the Lilly Prize
presentation in 1989.

I'm really deeply grateful. I'm so sorry we missed Thursday's get-acquainted dinner, which I was looking forward to. Thanks, too, for all the planning—the hotel (which we saw so briefly!) was lovely. Thanks, too, for your words about my poetry quoted in the *Chicago Tribune* today (and ignored by the headline writer!). . . .

Friday was lovely up to & through my reading, but the barrage of picture-taking, interviewing, autographing & greeting friends tired me more than I realized. I got Jarvis and slipped away, got our bag at the hotel, went to the airport and, on standby, caught an earlier flight home. I'm really sorry that I'm in such rotten shape—I really missed half the fun.

I'd love to have a Xerox of your introduction. I couldn't hear some of it because the waitresses were moving about [backstage], getting the lovely lunch together. I'd like very much to have it if you wouldn't mind sending it to me. . . .

Thank you again—for everything.

Warmest wishes, / Mona

Joseph Parisi to Linda Gregerson   *Chicago, 27 July 1989*

Dear Linda,

Many thanks for the Revised Version of the Schuyler [review of *Selected Poems*, February 1990], which I think is just about "there" now. (Indeed, upon each rereading I'm struck anew with admiration: such wisdom with elegance of style so meetly conjoined.) At the risk of being tiresome, I must add, however, that I am still not completely comfortable at one small spot: viz., "ingenious recruitment." I still feel, to repeat our earlier conversation, that given the context in S's work and given the context of today's misapprehensions and ignorance of the general public (esp. right wingers) about supposed homosexual "recruitment"—an absurdity, since while gays do not usually reproduce, they hardly need to "recruit" straight kids, since each generation seems to produce its own quotient of gay offspring—it would be best to find another word here. (*Seduction* doesn't seem quite right either; mainly S just wants to get, you should pardon the expression, laid, and laments the fact, as you point out, that he's no longer "marketable" with the young lovelies he desires.) Otherwise, everything else on p. 11 is wonderful: esp. loved "Sweet love plays hardball." . . .

Thanks for the splendid work—and for your patience.

Very best, / Joe

Linda Gregerson to Joseph Parisi   *Ann Arbor, Mich., 1 August 1989*

Dear Joe:

Never tedious—I'm very grateful for your suggestions. As you know, I think the drabness of mere caution would be sorry tribute to such work as Schuyler's. But I will be grieved indeed if I play into anybody's cultural stereotypes.

I've revised the sentence in question: here are new pages 11 and 12 to substitute for old. Thank you for your good counsel.

All good wishes, / Linda

Stephen Dunn to Joseph Parisi   *Absecon, N.J.,*
                                                       13 September 1989

Dear Joe,

One more small change in "Loves." I was looking over the other poems of mine that you're going to publish with "Loves" and noticed that in "Landscape at the End of the Century" I refer to ants as "those Calvinists." On page seven of "Loves" I call ants "those communists." Now I know that often there's not much difference between Calvinists and communists, but I thought that I'd better change one of them. . . .

So much for important moments in literary history.

All my best, / Stephen

The poems were published in the February 1990 issue.

W. D. Snodgrass to Joseph Parisi   *Newark, Del., 2 October 1989*

Dear Mr. Parisi,

Do please pardon me if I've already sent these translations to you. . . .

The Orlando de Lassus is that piece ["Matona Lovely Maiden"] one hears all sorts of choirs and choruses sing so sweetly every Christmas. But they've no idea what they're singing about. The song is a *tedeschi*, a familiar genre among Italian composers of the period—its aim is to make fun of the German mercenaries who'd been brought to Italy for one war or another and who were still cluttering up the landscape with their lusts, greeds and bad Italian—you also see them in the art of the period (most frequently in Flemish art, but Orlando was a Fleming by birth). So the song is supposedly sung by such a German soldier under the window of an Italian lady; the refrain is the strumming of his guitar. And his inability to distinguish "d" from "t" accounts for the title. . . .

With best wishes, / W. D. Snodgrass

Albert Goldbarth to Joseph Parisi   *[Wichita, Kans., n.d., 1990]*

Dear Joe Parisi:

Just a brief note—not to take you to task for the unfortunate little cartouche of bar coding that's now appearing on the cover of POETRY—but to once again indicate my deep pleasure at not only individual poems in *an* issue but at the way you manage to thematically orchestrate those poems. Okay, so my poem "Sentimental" led, via its "heartwormed puppydogs," to "dog poems" by Carper and Graham—no big deal. But by the time I hit the two *en face* "bee poems" I was encouraged to reread a number of issues randomly selected from the last couple of years—reading them as integrated wholes, not just as compendia of miscellaneous good pieces—and I must say I'm amazed at the careful editorial mosaicwork, and at the singular task you've set yourself.

Best, / Albert

CHAPTER X

New Ventures in the Nineties

1. The Situation Late in the Century

In the last decades of a prolific and perhaps overproductive century, American poetry exhibited signs of maturity, and fatigue. Some eighty years of efforts to "make it new" seemed to have rung all the changes imaginable in styles and methods, and several incomprehensible ones besides. With the passing decades, the many masterworks of enduring freshness left by the early Modernists elicited ever more admiration for their extraordinary creativity. Poets who imitated and borrowed from those originals seldom captured their verve. Still, the glamour of the heady movements of the teens and twenties tempted successive generations to try to replicate them. Most dramatic was the countercultural revolution of the sixties, whose effects on pop culture, education, and the arts were pervasive and linger on, conservative ire notwithstanding.

Since the seventies, would-be iconoclasts have labored under a disadvantage: their dissident forebears, who provoked so much artistic ferment (and frivolity and fatuity), succeeded perhaps too well. In the absence of the accepted standards of yore and with few rules to oppose now that seemingly all is permitted, liberated latter-day avant-gardes lack the creative friction that catalyzed earlier invention. Those who forgot (or never knew) literary history were bound to repeat it, and indeed have done so with tedious regularity. The benighted or simply naive mistakenly believe they are coining brand-new pieces; the equally ill-informed among the public, knowing no better, are easily pleased.

Originality and individuality, the paramount modernist artistic ideals, are always difficult to achieve, a fact that was reconfirmed daily in the masses of unsolicited submissions to *Poetry*, especially the confessional effusions that attempted to be unique "expressions" yet tended to be indistinguishable from one another. But fresher subject matter and perspectives did enlarge American poetry in the wake of countercultural "consciousness raising." Following the success of the various civil rights movements of the sixties and seventies and the growth of ethnic studies programs, many aspiring authors, inspired by the example of separatist black writers, sought and were encouraged to record in poetry (and fiction and memoirs) the history of their own communities and individual experiences as members of minority groups. In most of their writings the Great Tradition of Western art was seen as largely irrelevant if not oppressive, notions encouraged in some college courses and departments. But the primary goals of these authors were to create solidarity with readers of similar backgrounds while they tried to increase positive awareness among the broader public of their distinctive original Native American heritage or gay and lesbian identities or the cultures and traditions of their diverse immigrant ancestors. Earnest and ofter angry, such poetry and prose pieces now seem of greater interest perhaps as social documents than as artistic accomplishments.

These developments aside, and for all the rich poetic repertoire available, the personal lyric has remained the favorite mode by far. And for all the variety of styles and variations on forms in late-twentieth-century American poetry, the core inspiration continues overwhelmingly to be the Romanticism of two centuries earlier, with its emphasis on the self, individual perception and emotional response (though the "powerful feeling" Wordsworth considered essential now has generally turned muted and melancholic), vaguely "mystical" and transcendental longings, idealization of and desire for communion with Nature, idiosyncrasy and antipathy toward conventions as well as distrust of reason, doctrinal rigidity, social constraints, and other ills and (necessary) evils of civilization.

All the same, neo-romantic poetic rebels and political firebrands of the sixties sought and received tenure, and erstwhile radicals eventually became the new Establishment. With reverse logic, in the late eighties and nineties the retrograde Neo-Formalists—a group from the baby-boom generation who "returned" to traditional meter, rhyme, narrative (generally with suburban subjects, mediocre technical skills, and middlebrow sentiments)— self-consciously attempted to generate a movement in opposition to the reigning free-verse orthodoxy but did not succeed in inducing a counter-revolution. In any case, their endeavors were hardly necessary, since the supremely talented formalists among their elders—Hecht, Hollander, Howard, Justice, Meredith, Merrill, Nemerov, Van Duyn, Wilbur—were still composing at the top of their powers.

Happily, they and other longtime contributors continued to send to *Poetry*, including such genuine postwar originals as Ammons, Ashbery, Bly, Koch, Levine, Merwin, Herbert Morris, Rich, Stafford, Stern, C. K. Williams, and Charles Wright. They were joined by scores of distinctive younger and mid-career artists, among them Marvin Bell, Eavan Boland, Neal Bowers, Amy Clampitt, Billy Collins, Carl Dennis, Stephen Dobyns, Rita Dove, Stephen Dunn, Eamon Grennan, Albert Goldbarth, Andrew

Former editor Hayden
Carruth after the
Lilly Prize luncheon at
the Newberry Library,
June 1990.

Hudgins, Jane Kenyon, John Kinsella, Yusef Komunyakaa, William Matthews, Sandra McPherson, J. D. McClatchy, Mary Oliver, Linda Pastan, Pattiann Rogers, J. Allyn Rosser, Kay Ryan, Charles Simic, Gary Soto, A. E. Stallings, Leslie Ullman, and Robert Wrigley.

In the nineties we were able to recognize several more of *Poetry*'s most accomplished contributors through the Lilly Prize, and it was gratifying to offer it to authors who had not until then received the major accolades they deserved, in particular Linda Pastan, Carl Dennis, David Wagoner, and Hayden Carruth, a former editor who (as Carolyn Kizer's letter notes) lived most of his life in extreme hardship and wrote prolifically despite very little recognition. During the selection process in 1994 we could not foresee the prize would prove a godsend to another winner as it had several earlier recipients. When he received the call, Donald Hall said he felt overwhelmed. He explained that his wife Jane Kenyon, also a *Poetry* contributor, had been diagnosed with leukemia, and the funds would enable him to accompany her to Seattle and stay with her while she underwent treatment.

Hall's correspondence traces the progression of her illness and their fluctuating emotions. Kenyon's sequence "Having It Out with Melancholy" (November 1992) elicited more heartfelt thanks from readers than any poem printed in recent decades. With remarkable kindness, Kenyon had the magazine in her thoughts even as the end approached. As she wished, her last poems were printed in *Poetry*, in December 1995, nine months after her death. No one at the Lilly ceremony in June 1997 could know, of course, that William Matthews, the youngest person to receive the prize, would die just six months later, on November 12, one day after his fifty-fifth birthday.

Encouraging new talents remained our primary goal, and thanks to the very tangible help of the Lilly Fellowships we were able to give several promising student poets a step up in their careers, as noted earlier. In 1996 the convocation format of the competition was dropped, so that funds expended on airlines and hotels could be used to provide a second $15,000 fellowship each year. In the magazine itself, virtually every issue in the nineties contained asterisks next to names in the notes on contributors indicating first appearances in *Poetry*. It remained a special pleasure to read letters from recent newcomers telling of requests from other editors to see their work and happy news about acceptances for book publications; a few examples are printed below. Word of rejections outnumbered them, of course, and seldom was bad news as amusingly related as in Alison Stone's report on her travails.

Certainly the strangest story of publishing problems was recounted by Neal Bowers. A frequent contributor, Bowers wrote early in 1992 after discovering the theft of his "Tenth Year Elegy" and other work first published in *Poetry* in September 1990. In the following months he detailed his frustrating attempts to track down the plagiarist, who continued to get stolen poems printed, under pseudonyms, in several journals. The search stretched into years, and as the tale unfolded it became increasingly bizarre, not least for the blasé responses to his plight that Bowers heard from people in publishing.

In another effort to extend our educational programs, in 1992 we began work on a major project we hoped would improve the quality of instruction in modern and contemporary poetry for children. In our contacts with elementary and high school teachers over the years, many told us they would welcome more up-to-date knowledge and practical training. Several admitted their uncertainty in approaching modern American poetry and even their anxiety in trying to teach it because of what they felt was their own inadequate preparation. After discussions with a number of secondary school instructors we had learned were highly gifted in conveying poetry appreciation in the classroom as well as with several distinguished poets we knew to be great teachers, we put together a structure for what we hoped would become annual *Poetry*-sponsored summer teachers' institutes. In three weeks of "total immersion," the teachers would receive intensive courses on modern and post–World War II poetry from scholar-poets, along with practical demonstrations from talented peers in effective, innovative methods for teaching poetry to today's students. During each institute, the teachers would also meet well-known American poets invited to discuss poetic history and techniques, their own work and methods, and the art in general in workshops and more casual settings.

From 1992 to 1994 we approached various private foundations, who expressed initial interest but ultimately decided not to fund a pilot project. When I described our plans to officers at the education division of the National Endowment for the Humanities, they were enthusiastic. Early in 1994 we submitted a fully developed grant proposal, complete with budgets, letters of commitment from teachers and poets, and detailed day-by-day outlines of the class sessions, with sample syllabi and reading lists. While NEH staff and outside advisers whom they asked for reports were highly supportive, certain academic panelists judging the proposal voted it down.

Their main objection: the institutes were "lacking in theory" and "post-modern critical apparatus." Since we believed the last thing that hard-pressed high school teachers needed was more theory, we decided not to waste time revising and resubmitting the proposal, though we continued to hope to find support elsewhere and get the institutes up and running in the future. Meanwhile other projects demanded attention.

In the summer of 1994 *Poetry* operations were seriously upgraded when we installed new computers and software, which improved magazine fulfillment and bookkeeping and made it possible at last to track poetry submissions. We then acquired a scanner, graphic design programs, and training to bring typesetting in-house, saving tens of thousands of dollars in production costs over the next years. With training from our consultant Dean Shavit (who created templates for the *Poetry* page layouts), most of the staff learned to use the typesetting program, which enabled us to make corrections and fine adjustments literally up to the last minute before go-ing to press. Handling queries and exchanging proofs with authors by e-mail speeded up the editorial process immensely. Foreign issues, each typ-ically involving dozens of far-flung poets and translators, usually had taken about two years to assemble but could now be edited and sent to the print-ers in five or six months.

Exploiting the new technology, we put together a special double- or triple-size foreign issue of *Poetry* almost every fall, beginning with the Irish Number in 1995. Co-edited by Chris Agee in Belfast, it presented three dozen poets working in the North, the Irish Republic, and the United States—including Seamus Heaney, Paul Muldoon, Eavan Boland, and seven authors writing in Gaelic—with a witty "Map of Contemporary Irish Po-etry" by Dennis O'Driscoll, who also arranged a reception and reading pro-gram to "launch" the issue in November in Dublin. Jean Kennedy Smith,

Seamus Heaney read for Poetry Day 1996, the largest magazine event since T. S. Eliot's appearance in 1959.

the U.S. ambassador, opened the festivities with an eloquent tribute to *Poetry* at the Writers' Centre on Parnell Square, where most of the poets in the city (and County Kil-dare as well) seemed to be in atten-dance at the reception. Heaney could not be present, but came to Chicago for Poetry Day in Septem-ber 1996, attracting the largest crowd since T. S. Eliot's reading in 1959. After the twelve-hundred-seat auditorium at the Art Institute was filled, more than two hundred people who had waited for hours still stood in line; they were admitted to the nearby Stock Exchange Room, where the poet came and greeted them in person before they watched his reading via closed-circuit TV.

Despite a large press run, the Irish Number quickly sold out and was reprinted, as was the Australian Number in the fall of 1996. Although authors from "the land down under" appeared in *Poetry* regularly, the special issue was the first devoted entirely to their work. The poet, novelist, and editor John Kinsella assembled thirty authors with a remarkably diverse range of styles, concluding with a retrospective on Australian poetry 1940–1980 by John Tranter, and his own essay "Toward a Contemporary Australian Poetics."

On a much more somber note, the special edition for September 1995 was a memorial to James Merrill, who died, at age sixty-eight, on February 6, only a few weeks before release of his valedictory *A Scattering of Salts*. Merrill maintained a special relationship with *Poetry* from his professional debut in 1945, at age nineteen, and over the decades gave the magazine several of his best-known poems. The issue opened with his previously unpublished "Christmas Tree" and included homages delivered at the memorial service at the New York Public Library in May; letters from JM to Stephen Yenser; an elegy by J. D. McClatchy, who arranged the program and advised on the issue; and W. S. Merwin's long "Lament for the Makers."

Much beloved by *Poetry* readers, Merrill was the subject of scores of messages after his death and the publication of the issue. One letter was appropriately eerie: Stephen Yenser wrote in February 1996 to describe an incident involving literally a scattering of salt that might have pleased the epic poet of the supernatural. Besides the legacy of his work, we felt fortunate he left us the recordings—his inimitable readings and witty and rueful reflections on his life and work—made for the "Poets in Person" project. Hearing his voice on tape can be bittersweet, however, as with others in the series: for in little more than a decade Allen Ginsberg, Karl Shapiro, Gwendolyn Brooks, and A. R. Ammons would also be gone.

2. Broadcasting the Word

In choosing the thirteen authors for the radio series, our plan was not only to introduce important poets from several generations but to outline through their work the major movements and stylistic trends in American poetry since World War II. In tracing their careers we also hoped to show how social and cultural changes in the United States since the sixties had affected the practice of poetry, and perhaps provide insights into the creative process itself. Several excellent critics helped prepare program content and acted as interviewers, among them Alice Fulton, J. D. McClatchy, and Helen Vendler. As we expected, the poets themselves proved the most articulate interpreters of their work—once we were able to coordinate crowded calendars, schedule studio time, and get the poet-interviewer pairs before the microphones.

Logistical problems aside, the tapings were the most enjoyable aspect of the project. Each poet was interviewed for about two hours, then spent another hour reading a dozen or more poems. In the course of the freewheeling discussions, the microphones seemed forgotten as the poets talked about their families, childhood experiences, teachers, and other pivotal influences. Most told humorous and touching stories and offered philosophical reflections and pointed observations on writing. Besides illuminating specific passages, they often revealed details about the inspiration or background for key works, including information that had not been published or recorded before. While the series offered firsthand evidence and fresh facts that are genuine contributions to literary history, the individual programs unveiled within their tightly packed half-hours surprisingly intimate portraits of the poets as working artists and perceptive human beings.

Sessions were set up to record two to four poets a week, at intervals spaced over a ten-month period. Gwendolyn Brooks was taped in Chicago, Adrienne Rich and Gary Soto in San Francisco, the rest in New York City—except for A. R. Ammons, whose phobias did not permit him to travel very far from home. So Alice Fulton and I journeyed upstate to Ithaca, New York, where at the appointed hour the poet began to get cold feet and had to be cajoled into the car that took us to a studio. Ammons's interview with his former student went smoothly for forty minutes, until the engineer signaled a time-out to change reels. "Well, that's enough, don't you think?" said the poet. We informed him we still had two hours to go, and literally cornered him. He then discoursed, brilliantly, on his methods and meanings, and uttered a string of remarkable aperçus about art and how it is experienced, in homely analogies such as a football game. Despite his fears, the Ammons program turned out to be one of the most engaging and (as we heard from listeners) popular in the series.

Given the scope of the project and the size of the "cast," there were bound to be awkward moments. When Sharon Olds, Alicia Ostriker, and I showed up for an early Saturday morning taping, the engineer did not. Rescheduling was not an option, so I went into the control booth, cued up a reel, and pushed the Record button. (What the dancing needles on the dials meant was unclear to me; no matter: on playback the sound came out broadcast-quality.) Allen Ginsberg, the last poet to be recorded, arrived fresh from a protest rally and was all fired up after delivering a speech excoriating Senator Jesse Helms—which he now wished to repeat on tape for posterity. I warned that his diatribe would not make it into the finished program, but he insisted. In the interview itself, with Lewis Hyde, he was candid, irreverent, funny, and touching by turns; for the moment it seemed we were back in the sixties. Toward the end of the third hour, Ginsberg brought out his harmonium and began a most unmelodious rendering of some songs. He was so enrapt it would have been heartless to tell him the tape had run out after the seventh bar.

Copies of each set of tapes immediately went to Elizabeth Carlson, who with Jim Rutke made the transcriptions from which I composed the scripts. For audio engineer I engaged Paul Grigonis, a musician who proved a maestro with recorded voices. Although several studio sessions were still scheduled, in February 1990 we began work on the completed reels, a tedious pre-digital process of cutting and splicing tape, assembling the many thousands of pieces per program, recording the introductions and commentary, and finally mixing tracks for the master tapes. (These steps were handled simultaneously as several programs proceeded in different, overlapping stages of development.) Each show required at least forty hours, and often many more, to complete.

Early in 1990 I had commissioned an original theme and incidental music for the series from Roger Bourland, a composer at UCLA with several film scores to his credit. After hearing the first few cassettes he asked to receive tapes as soon as rough-editing was done. He then composed additional music tailored to the poems and commentary in every program—over seventy pieces in all. To further attract programmers at radio stations, Grigonis and I produced five- and eight-and-a-half-minute self-contained "modules" that could be aired separately or in magazine-format shows. We also made fifteen- and thirty-second commercials. By doing most of the work ourselves, we stayed within our tight budget and even saved enough to print an advertising brochure as well as to produce an extra introductory half-hour program: a capsule history of postwar poetry with key quotations from each of the thirteen segments.

Since work on the audio series had to be fitted into evenings and weekends following regular editorial and business duties at *Poetry*, progress was slower than anticipated. The first five tapes were completed in early fall 1990 and mailed to the NEH with an interim report. I also sent a set with a cover letter to National Public Radio in Washington. (Distributing the series would be immeasurably easier if NPR could be persuaded to pick up the series and transmit it to member stations by satellite.) Since I would be in Washington to confer with NEH program officers, I also set up an appointment with Murray Horwitz, then director of cultural programming at NPR. Hoping against hope to convince them to take the series, I marshaled several arguments on the need for such a series and the particular merits of our own. I was not able to use them. Pleasantries exchanged, Horwitz said, "We'd like to air the series next spring. It's the best thing I've heard yet on contemporary poetry." Having expected a hard selling job, I was speechless. Horwitz filled the dead air by asking: "What, you won't take *yes* for an answer?"

Standing afterward in front of NPR headquarters, I felt dazed and elated. Then a sobering thought occurred: eight more programs and dozens of modules would have to be completed within the next six or seven months. (The broadcasts in fact began on 1 July 1991, before the last four programs in the series were polished, so Grigonis and I had to work literally day and night to get them ready by air time.) From NPR I went to my appointment at the NEH, where the media officers seemed even more surprised and pleased than I was by the good news.

Thomas Phelps, who had also listened to the first tapes, came over from the General Programs office to offer congratulations, and a suggestion. Remembering our earlier collaboration on the "Voices & Visions" television series on nineteenth- and early-twentieth-century poetry and the American Library Association's national reading-discussion project based on it (I had served as an adviser), he felt another project using the "Poets in Person" tapes as the centerpiece would be an ideal way to bring the story of American poetry up to the present for nonspecialist audiences. With much production work still to be done, I was not keen on this idea. But on reflection the discussion-group plan seemed a logical extension of what we hoped to accomplish with the audio series. Friends in the Public Programs division at the ALA agreed, and early in 1991 we put together a detailed proposal.

In our cooperative venture, public libraries across the country would be invited to apply for a pilot project in which the "Poets in Person" series would introduce contemporary poetry to their out-of-school patrons. Twenty libraries would be chosen to send their program directors and a local scholar to a two-day training seminar with workshops on setting up their own reading-discussion series. Besides how-to sessions on organizing and attracting audiences to their programs, they would attend classes offering an overview of modern American poetry. The librarian-scholar teams would also receive hands-on experience by participating in two group discussions themselves. Representatives from state library associations and humanities councils would also be invited to attend the training sessions, to help spread information about the project beyond the pilot libraries.

In their series at the individual libraries, local scholars—generally teachers from area colleges, many poets themselves—would select four or more of the audio programs and organize the authors' work around a central topic; at the start of each weekly session they would present short talks to prepare their groups for the heart of the program: open exchange of ideas in response to the poet's work. Besides stipends for the scholar-leaders, we budgeted funds so that each library could acquire volumes of contemporary poetry to enhance their collections. A special *Guide for Library Programmers* was also prepared outlining each step in putting on the poetry project, particularly helpful for small or less experienced libraries. As an extra aid for the groups, I later wrote a companion book for the series, with brief introductions to the poets, texts of the poems, and reading lists. In the fall of 1991, just as the first broadcasts of the "Poets in Person" series were ending, the NEH informed us it was granting almost $212,000 to fund the workshops and materials, and to underwrite the discussion programs in twenty libraries with twenty-nine different sites.

In the spring of 1992 we conducted the first training, in Charleston, South Carolina. Alice Fulton joined me in giving the introductory lectures and demonstration programs. The twenty library teams represented a broad cross section from small rural communities to large metropolitan areas, and were highly enthusiastic. The libraries began presenting their customized "Poets in Person" series in April or May. As the reports came in from directors and discussion-group participants, we were truly touched by the heartfelt responses to the programs that people expressed on evaluation forms. (Several took the time to write lengthy letters as well.) The NEH was equally impressed; so much so that they asked us to submit a proposal to expand the project to thirty more libraries. A few comments typical of the hundreds received from the first groups indicate why the Endowment was persuaded to fund a second round:

"I am truly grateful for this exposure to contemporary poetry—something I wouldn't do on my own . . . but now I'm hooked! Future programs should be publicized as much as possible, so that more people will have the opportunity to attend. Thank you." (Winston-Salem, North Carolina)

"The insights and comments on the poetry were profound and enlightening. I met poets who I did not know existed! This has been a wonderful education. All the sessions were stimulating and enjoyable." (New Orleans, Louisiana)

"Once upon a time I enjoyed poetry, and then I was turned off. . . . I feel comfortable with the new authors and their personal styles of poetry. I feel as if I were 'coming home.'" (Brevard Country, Florida)

"This series had the organized pluses of a college class but, instead of being encrusted with bureaucracy (fulfilling requirements, etc.), it was brimming with interest and excitement . . . the lectures, the poetry itself, and the group discussions were all stimulating, and brought terrific pleasure to me. Thank you to everyone involved. It was a rare gift to find this program." (Takoma Park, Maryland)

"We kept running out of time each evening due to the lively discussion— we could have gone on for another hour." (Salt Lake City, Utah)

One librarian from a rural community in Missouri told us that farmers listened to the tapes on the stereos in the air-conditioned cabins of their combines. The group in Stonington, Connecticut, was thrilled when James Merrill appeared truly in person at their meeting devoted to his work. On a site visit to a county library in Virginia, the program director and I were chatting on the front steps when a band of leather-clad bikers roared up on Harleys. "Don't worry," she said. "They're in the PIP group."

Because of popular demand, a majority of the original pilot libraries later put on second and third series of "Poets in Person" programs on their own, with local funding. Several humanities council members and state librarians wrote us that the series were the most successful public programs ever presented in their states. In the fall of 1993, "PIP" II extended the project to thirty-eight more libraries, representing thirty states. We decided not to approach the NEH again, but program officers contacted us and urged us to submit a third proposal. Thus in 1995 "PIP" III added twenty more library sites, bringing to thirty-nine the number of states where the programs were offered. "PIP" IV followed in 1997, with fifty new libraries participating. An updated and enlarged edition of the *Poets in Person* listener's guide was also published in 1997. Tight economizing allowed us to offer another demonstration of the project at the ALA winter convention in 1998, and a small supplementary grant in 1999 provided funds to support the discussion programs in another fourteen libraries.

Following the pilot projects, the programs eventually spread to hundreds of other public libraries in forty-four states, and so we were able to introduce contemporary poets to truly diverse audiences that would almost certainly not have encountered them otherwise. Funding for the several NEH projects totaled almost $1.3 million. The portions of the grants that underwrote staff salaries and office expenses were the primary reason we were able to balance the budget most of the decade. Further, by increasing awareness of poetry and *Poetry*, the "Poets in Person" projects helped boost magazine circulation. By the latter half of the nineties, subscriptions and newsstand sales had reached between eight thousand and nine thousand and continued to grow as we approached the ninetieth anniversary.

3. Correspondence 1990–1996

Mary Stewart Hammond to Joseph Parisi   *New York City,*
                                                         24 April 1990

Dear Joseph Parisi,

I had a note from Sandy McClatchy yesterday telling me he has accepted "Accepting the Body" for *The Yale Review*. He also tells me you two had lunch and discussed my "experiment"—the testing of an unnamed (herein) poet's theory on simultaneous submissions—and considered playing a joke on me by each sending letters on the same day, accepting the same poem, and watching me squirm, a joke which I surely deserve to have played on me! And I am certainly squirming.

But I was squirming from the time I acted on this nefarious, double-dealing notion to send Sandy an identical batch of poems as those I'd sent to you a week or two earlier to test this "theory." As I said to Sandy in the accompanying note explaining to him what I was doing, "What bothers me is that I didn't think to submit simultaneously at the time I mailed the batch to *Poetry*, so the editor there is not in possession of as much information as you."

I'm glad Sandy told you [of the scheme], which, looking at a copy of my letter to him, clearly I hoped, if you all were in contact, he would do. I cannot abide people who operate out of a hidden agenda with me, so obviously, knowing I was doing that to someone else has not made me very happy with myself these past 8-9 weeks. So, at least you did have a full understanding of the situation after all. I just wish it had come from me.

The useful part of the "experiment" is that, while maybe a lot of people *have* begun to do simultaneous submissions, and certainly far more than the one I told Sandy about have told me I'm crazy not to, and while I commiserate with their reasons for doing so (mainly, many horror stories of places holding poems for 9 to 12 months and *then* returning them, or worse, *not* returning them, which is a long time to have 6-8 poems out of circulation), I've found it's crazier to do something that doesn't square with the high store I set by straight-forwardness. Better to take note of the places that hold poems so long, and don't submit there, than to do something equally unconscionable.

Meanwhile, I can't wait to tell the people who've advised double, triple, quadruple submission about your lunch with Sandy.

Please accept my apologies that our first contact with each other, which began in good faith, slid over into this sleazy territory.

                                        Sincerely, / Mary Stewart Hammond

Joseph Parisi to Mary Stewart Hammond   *Chicago, 24 May 1990*

Dear Mary Stewart Hammond,

Thanks for both your letters, and for giving us a look at the new work. I'm sorry to be so dreadfully late in responding. As you may have heard from Sandy, I've been On the Road a great deal this spring, a spring which also saw a deluge of mss. in these offices.

Given that we usually reply within six to eight weeks, I wouldn't have blamed you for withdrawing the poems to submit them elsewhere. But, yes, simultaneous submissions can be an embarrassment, for both parties; and for publishers, it can prove quite expensive, if one has to tear up an issue that's about to go to press. It's happened a few times since I've been here; and sometimes authors, usually younger, inexperienced ones, have had to write back after receiving our Acceptance notice, to inform us that some-one else (and dare I say it? less desirable) has also taken the poem, and ours is the subsequent and more attractive invitation. . . .

What I would say to impatient authors is that there is really not all that much superior work out there, and any editor worth his or her blue pen-cil eventually (if not as swiftly as the writers wish) recognizes and accepts the treasures that come along. Always better to send where you *really* want to be published first, than allow valuable work to go out and even get placed just anywhere. (And we all know, given the number of "literary" publications these days, eventually almost anything can, and does, get pub-lished.)

Anyhow, I appreciate your giving us a chance, and am grateful you took the time to write your second letter. I hope all continues well with you.

Sincerely, / Joe Parisi

Joseph Parisi to Alfred Corn   *Chicago, 22 May 1990*

Dear Alfred,

I'm sorry that in my latest whirlwind tour of NYC I didn't get a chance to see you. The tapings [for "Poets in Person"] went very well. At least the one with Rita Dove and Helen Vendler did. I have no idea what I'll be able to do with the Ginsberg [interview]. He began the session with a statement against Jesse Helms, and had several other tirades to consume valuable recording time and tape. But along the way, some material was forthcom-ing that might actually be fit for broadcast; that does not include, however, his renditions on the harmonium. Gads. . . . Anyway, it was a relief to have all the taping finally over with. . . .

Susan Hahn to Joseph Parisi   *[Winnetka, Ill., June 1990]*

Dear, dear Joe,

You were there for me from the beginning and that is why I wanted you to know first—the University of Chicago Press is going to publish my book [*Harriet Rubin's Mother's Wooden Hand*, 1991].

With much gratitude and affection,

Susan

Charles Wright to Joseph Parisi   *Charlottesville, Va., 8 August 1990*

Dear Joe—

Many thanks for your warm and lively letter. I had been hoping to be back in touch sooner than this—and via a poem submission. But I've only done one poem since December and someone grabbed that for his first issue as a new editor and that was that. I got more, as they say, cards and letters about the two poems in the January issue ["Mid-Winter Snowfall in the Piazza Dante" and "Reading Lao Tzu Again in the New Year"] than I've had on anything in years. It's obvious that everyone reads *Poetry*. Anyhow, I'm hoping to get a couple of things together so that I can send you something for your perusal in the next few months. Surely I can't go a whole year . . . [sic]

So glad to hear the program [on Wright for the "Poets in Person" series] is shaping up so well. . . .

Charles

Billy Collins to Joseph Parisi   *Somers, N.Y., 20 August 1990*

Dear Joe,

I am enclosing a few poems for your consideration. I was pleased to appear in the handsome August issue. I thought that the juxtaposition of my "The Afterlife" with David Rivard's "C'è Un'Altra Possibilità" worked well to create resonance. An odd coincidence is that I recently wrote a poem about taking piano lessons. My wife bought me a big piano last Christmas and I have been taking lessons in jazz piano. Pretty basic so far but the self-entertainment possibilities are endless. Obviously, I was a little late for your piano sequence.

It has been a slow summer. I have been suffering with Lyme disease brought on by a deer tick. We live in an area with a dense deer population. Only bow and arrow hunting is allowed, so they multiply and increase as they were told to do in the Bible. The poem "Consolation" is a rationalization of our having to cancel a trip to Europe this summer.

But who asked?

Billy

Oh, a big piece of good news: Edward Hirsch selected my manuscript [*Questions About Angels*, 1991] for the National Poetry Series. A good handful of the poems appeared first in *Poetry*.

Joseph Parisi to James Laughlin   *Chicago, 30 October 1990*

Dear Mr. Laughlin,

   Many thanks for your letter, and for your annual contribution to the Magazine. Poetry Day was a grand success again this year, and we were particularly happy to see so many grade and school students at the reading. The kids listened with rapt attention, and the lines they formed to get Gwen Brooks's autograph would have made a rock star envious.

   Forgive me for not responding sooner. I've been bi-coastal most of this and last month, in Washington consulting with the NEH on our radio project and talking with some people at NPR, then in L.A. and S.F. finishing up last details for the incidental music and starting work on the p.r. blitz. Most of the summer's been spent in the studio, cutting tape, recording narrative, and mixing: a nice break from editing mss. I've also come to have a whole new appreciation for the value of a second. . . .

   I hope all continues well with you. It will be wonderful to present the TW [Tennesee Williams] poem. I hope you'll give us another chance to see some new work by yourself one of these days.

                                        All the best, / Joe Parisi

Williams's unpublished poem, "We Have Not Long to Love," was printed in February 1991.

Billy Collins to Joseph Parisi   *Somers, N.Y., 8 November 1990*

Dear Joe,

   First, my thanks for your part in my selection as the Bess Hokin prize winner for this year. . . . Also, I am glad you decided to take my "Consolation . . ." poem. I like that one myself, and I will enjoy seeing it in your pages.

   Lastly, the enclosed. . . . I have received the occasional letter of praise from the odd stranger, but nothing before like this. . . .

[*Enclosure*:]

Oct. 5 1990

Dear Mr. Collins,

   I believe that a poem should be practical, something people can take with them into their everyday lives. Your poem "The Afterlife," printed in the August 1990 issue of Poetry, is such a poem. I took it with me to my father's house after my mother's funeral and passed it around. The gentle humor (which produced some rather hearty guffaws) and simple message of your poem gave us all a different perspective on our confusion and sadness.

Thank you for your poem. It became a part of people's lives in a way most poems never can.

Sincerely, / Leroy Leonard
Denver, CO

Alison Stone to Joseph Parisi   *New York City, 10 January 1991*

Dear Mr. Parisi:

Happy New Year. Here are four new poems that I hope you'll like. I've also sent you a postcard of my work. (If you are looking for words to describe the painting, I don't share your aversion to ones like "wonderful," "fabulous" etc.) The show was an artistic, if not commercial, success. That means I haven't sold a thing but it was held over for at least two more weeks. (It's still up now, so if you're in town . . .)

My chief New Year's resolution is to abandon the starving artist/noble poverty syndrome and achieve a standard of living where I can afford luxuries like subway tokens and tomatoes. Do you know anyone that wants to buy a painting? I was a finalist in another competition, but my manuscript is still unclaimed. Do you know any publishers that want to buy a poetry book?

My second resolution is to be able to do a split with one leg on each of two chairs like Jean Claude Van Damme in "Bloodsport." I suppose if I achieve that I can have

Alison Stone, poet and artist,
at the time of her first publications
in the late eighties.

a career in the movies and the money will take care of itself. Until then, I teach Russians. (It's getting more interesting now that they have learned some other verbs. In the beginning I could use nothing except the verb "to be" in the present tense. Hard to get excited about.) Some day I will write a poem about them and then maybe it will seem worth it.

Best wishes, / Alison Stone

Neal Bowers to Joseph Parisi   *Ames, Ia., 10 July 1991*

Dear Joe,

Got your letter just before taking off for Tennessee and the 25th reunion of my high school class (where I somehow found myself set up as the featured speaker). . . .

You may be interested to know that "Art Thief" [January 1992] was stimulated by a particular theft on the Iowa State University campus. A small sculpture was stolen in the spring of 1990 and hasn't been recovered. When I showed my poem to some folks at the university museums, they decided to pursue a literal form of poetic justice; so they're having the poem cast in bronze and will erect it on the site of the missing sculpture. I'm sure this won't come about until after the poem appears in *Poetry*, which means the university museums will be entering the arena of the bronze reprint. . . .

Yours, / Neal

Robert B. Shaw to Joseph Parisi   *South Hadley, Mass.,*
                                                     15 August 1991

Dear Joe,

Here is the piece on the good gray poet [essay on Howard Nemerov, May 1992]. It was unsettling to hear of his death [5 July] in the midst of writing it; I hope the way I've handled it doesn't come across as unduly personal.

A strange thing happened early in the summer. I have a friend [Marion Miller] in the Art Dept. here [Mount Holyoke College] who was doing a commissioned portrait of Howard N. for Washington University. We were over at her place for dinner and saw the portrait shortly before she finished it. The next week she took it out to St. Louis to show it to Howard; he was in bad shape, but was pleased with the painting. He told her it was what he had been waiting for. He must have died about a week after that. Such events make me feel that I am living in a Hardy novel at times. . . .

All best, / Robt

John Updike to Joseph Parisi   *Beverly Farms, Mass.,*
                                                  16 December 1991

Dear Mr. Parisi:

For years I've been wanting to submit to *Poetry*, but wasn't sure of the address. Karl Shapiro has given me your name, and I hope this reaches you.

A self-addressed envelope is enclosed, with my holiday greetings and best wishes.

John Updike

John Updike to Joseph Parisi   *Beverly Farms, Mass.,*
                                                   11 January 1992

Dear Mr. Parisi:

Delighted to hear it. The dream of a lifetime, come true. I have been going over old papers and there, from the late 50s, was a rejection slip from *Poetry* (amid many others).

Will I be sent proofs?

Best wishes, / John Updike

Three poems were accepted, and published in the July 1992 issue.

Neal Bowers to Joseph Parisi   *Ames, Ia., 17 February 1992*

Dear Joe,

Here's a great irony for you. Read on. Keep "Art Thief" in mind and then read on.

About a month ago, someone phoned me from Santa Monica, CA to say a poem of mine had been plagiarized. Turned out it was "Tenth Year Elegy," from your Sept. '90 issue. The thief, who goes by the name of David Sumner (possibly an alias, I suppose), retitled my poem, rearranged a few of the line breaks, added a couple of words, and published it under his name in the Fall '91 issue of *Mankato Poetry Review*. Just this morning, I discovered that he also published the same poem in the Fall '91 issue of *Poem*.

I've been trying to locate other thefts by Mr. Sumner and have identified one other case of plagiarism by him—a Mark Strand poem titled "Keeping Things Whole," which Sumner retitled and published under his name in the Fall '91 issue of *Half Tones to Jubilee*. Although I suspect that every poem Sumner has published since last summer is, in fact, the property of another writer, I haven't yet identified the rightful owners of all the works he is trying to pass off as his own.

All of this is weird enough, but what really puzzles me is what I

Neal Bowers became a frequent contributor to *Poetry* beginning in 1985.

should and can do about it. I've written to Strand and to all the magazines known to have published work attributed to Sumner. Some of my friends are urging me to take legal action, but I'm unsure where that will lead or how much good it will do. Until now, I hadn't given much thought to pla- giarists, but it's becoming apparent that there isn't any standard or obvious way to expose and stop someone who's stealing other people's work. The problem seems heightened by the fact that what he's stealing is poetry, where money, agents, and publishers are not factors.

Because there's a good possibility the guy's a nut of some kind, I haven't tried to contact him directly, of course. And I guess it's possible he's play- ing a cynical game, trying to see just how much he can get away with be- fore someone cries foul. His "contributor's" notes have grown more plainly fictional of late, asserting that he was born in Belfast and raised in England. . . .

The poem he stole from me was a very personal one, an elegy to my fa- ther in the tenth year following his death; so I feel that my private life has also been invaded and appropriated. I suspect that people whose houses are burgled feel somewhat the same way. . . .

Yours, / Neal

Philip Booth to Joseph Parisi   *Castine, Me., 4 May 1992*

Dear Joe,

In response to my question about a week ago, Stephen Young was kind enough to agree that it might not be inappropriate for you to send a full set of the splendid new tapes ["Poets in Person"] to a considerably courageous blind woman . . . my former student Ruth Kent . . . how she yearns to hear the voices of poets she formerly read but cannot now read at all. . . .

Thanks to our remarkable small-town librarian, Pat Fowler, and the scholar-poet Kathleen Lignell, both of whom you met in Charleston, the five-meeting "Poets in Person" series here was truly wonderful. Pat set the tone, Kathleen lectured with a fine sense of synthesis, I jumped in with analyses when asked (or when, in fact, I was sometimes so excited by group discussion that I couldn't resist). The order was fine: Maxine [Kumin], Gary Soto (Kathleen had grown up in the [San Joaquin] Valley, herself), Adrienne [Rich], Sharon [Olds], and then Archie [Ammons]. That sequence made for incremental learning in ways none of us quite expected, and by the time we'd finished on the *third* snowstorm night out of the five, we had ex-Naval officers, and Little Old Never-Read-Befores, and a farm-poet-couple from forty-some miles to the East, reading and commenting on Archie's work with all-smiles pleasure and truly impressive insight.

So this is a letter of thanks to you, and you all, for doing what you have done. I can't think of any one to whom the whole series will mean more than it will mean to Ruth Kent. She's a woman of intelligence, caring, and still demonstrable courage.

Best, ever, / Philip

Charles Bukowski to Joseph Parisi   *[San Pedro, Calif.], 1 February 1993*

2/1/93 10:31 PM

Hello Joseph Parisi:

I remember, as a very young man, sitting around the L.A. public library reading POETRY, A MAGAZINE OF VERSE. Now, at last, I have joined you. I suppose it was a matter left up to the both of us. Anyhow, I'm glad I got a couple of poems past you...

There's no hurry on the poems. There will not be a book of poetry this year. Instead there will be a publication of my Selected Letters from the 60's.

Form enclosed.

Thank you, the new year is treating me kindly. What I mean is, the words are forming and churning, spinning and flying for me. The older I get, the more this magic madness seems to fall upon me. Very odd, but I'll accept it.

Good things to you.

yes,

Charles Bukowski

p.s.--photo enclosed. photo credit: Linda Bukowski.

Bukowski's "fingernails; nostrils; shoelaces" and "a not so good night in the San Pedro of the world" appeared in the September 1993 issue. His "cold summer" was also printed in July 1994.

Neal Bowers to Joseph Parisi   *Ames, Ia., 7 February 1993*

Dear Joe,

The enclosed poems are all on their maiden voyage. . . .

You'll be interested to know that I'm still pursuing the plagiarist who took two poems of mine and one by Marcia Hurlow ["Praying for Father"] from the Sept. '90 issue of *Poetry*. To date, I know of 14 different journals that have published or accepted plagiarisms of my poems. I've also uncovered plagiarisms of Mark Strand, Sharon Olds, and Bin Ramke. Probably, there are many others that haven't yet come to light. After a year of investigation and legal pursuit of the culprit, I'm about to write an essay on plagiarism from the victim's point of view. To me, the most remarkable aspect of the whole affair has been the reactions of other writers and editors. It's surprising how many people sympathize with the plagiarist, even after conceding that the evidence against him is beyond refutation. Several people have even urged me not to be so upset, "after all, they're only poems." Honest to God. At the very least, such a reaction tells a great deal about how seriously some writers take their own work. More intriguing, though, is what it says about their uneasiness in dealing with acts of literary theft. These are the things I'm eager to write about.

Hadn't meant to get off on that business, but it's on my mind a lot these days. . . .

Yours, / Neal

Neal Bowers to Helen Klaviter   *Ames, Ia., 13 February 1993*

Dear Helen,

I've been meaning since last fall to write to thank you for your kind note about my plagiarism woes. Unfortunately, things haven't improved, as I keep finding my poems plagiarized in journals around the country. . . .

I hired a lawyer to help me find David Sumner (whose real name turns out to be David Jones), but that proved to be of very little help. The biggest change it produced was in my bank account, and I finally had to break off my legal pursuit of Mr. Jones. He is suit-proof because he is virtually destitute, so there's no point in bankrupting myself by trying to take him to court. Consequently, I resolved to be happy if he would sign a statement admitting his plagiarisms and vowing never to represent my poems as his again. He declined. Now I have nothing at all by way of satisfaction in this business. . . .

Of course, Jones himself remains mostly a mystery where motivation is concerned. Figuring out what he gets out of publishing other people's poems under a pseudonym is impossible to do. Lately, he has taken to using another name, Diane Compton; and that transformation makes me wonder how many other fictitious identities he has created for himself to facilitate his thefts. Among the poets I know for certain he has robbed are Mark Strand, Sharon Olds, Marcia Hurlow, and Bin Ramke. Odds argue that there are many others. . . .

Yours, / Neal

Marcia L. Hurlow to Joseph Parisi   *Lexington, Ky., 22 February 1993*

Dear Mr. Parisi

Enclosed are five poems for your consideration in *Poetry*. . . . Readers have sent me letters about every poem of mine that *Poetry* has published, one reason I have greatly appreciated your publishing my work. For example, the last poem you published, "Nuclear Romance" [February 1992] brought a four-page response from a retired professor of physics. . . .

Some months ago, however, I received a less pleasant letter. An editor of another literary magazine had received a set of poems from a man in Oregon. She recognized one poem as being a slightly altered version of "Praying for Father," my sonnet you published a few years ago. I later learned from Neal Bowers that the same man has also sent out altered versions of his poems which had appeared in the same issue of *Poetry*. If *Poetry* is planning any action to stop this plagiarist, I would be happy to help in any way I can. . . .

Sincerely, / Marcia

Joseph Parisi to [name withheld]   *Chicago, 8 March 1993*

Dear Mr. W—,

Forgive my tardiness in responding: after every holiday we're flooded with mss. (writers *never* take a break, of course). . . .

Despite your curious letter, I've read the poems as objectively and carefully as I can, and would like to keep [poem title] for POETRY (although I find "feint and fizz" a bit studied).

While I can appreciate any writer's frustration, I find it difficult to understand your irritation as far as we're concerned. Piqued by your plangent tone, I went back through the volumes, where I discovered that since 1983 (when I took over the editorship) I have presented at least a dozen of your poems; since we receive well over 75,000 of them annually, an average of one a year doesn't seem to me a bad publishing record. Further, we reviewed two of your books; again, since we get 400–600 (at least) per year and can review only 60-70, you haven't done poorly by us. (I seem to recall reviewing your books myself for ALA's *Booklist*, too.) . . .

No, I'm not Mr. Nims; I've done more for you than he did (if you just want to go by the numbers). So what's yer beef?

J. Parisi

Joseph Parisi to William Logan   *Chicago, 22 March 1993*

Dear William,

Thanks for speeding the review of Merwin, Van Duyn, and Ashbery. Both Stephen and I have read the essay with care; I took it home again this weekend to reread.

After considerable thought, I find that I cannot give full assent to publishing the piece. While much of what you say is doubtless true—and has been, in fact, said by others before—I find the general tenor of the piece rather harsh, and to my mind unfairly biased. As always, you write with great wit and elegance, and as I said, many of your points are well taken. But I am very uncomfortable with the meanness of tone, a snideness that seeps through the stylish surface of the prose.

Therefore I regret to have to return the essay. I cannot help wondering if you too, in time, might well regret allowing these words into print.

Please find enclosed our check for $150, in consideration of the time and effort you have expended on the reviews. I'm very sorry this didn't work out.

Sincerely, / Joe

James Kimbrell to Joseph Parisi   *Charlottesville, Va., 27 March 1993*

Dear Mr. Parisi,

Greetings from Charlottesville! I hope this letter and these poems find you well. Things are going nicely here, though I am busier than usual as I am in Rita Dove's workshop and in a forms seminar/workshop with Charles Wright. Also, Mary Oliver just visited here for a week which was absolutely wonderful. She is truly one of the most generous and honest people I have ever known.

I haven't written Mrs. Lilly since October or November but I plan to send her a copy of a chapbook of mine which should be coming out in the next month or so. She has apparently contributed some funding to the Rope Walk Writer's Conference (in New Harmony, Indiana) and they have contracted me to do a reading there in June. I consider Indiana, needless to say, to be one of the luckiest parts of the world. . . .

Sincerely, / Jimmy Kimbrell

Kimbrell had been awarded a Lilly Fellowship in 1992.

Maxine Kumin to Joseph Parisi *Warner, N.H., 6 April 1993*

[*postcard*]
Dear Joe:

Just this to tell you how much I enjoyed your reply to Heartsick in the new TriQ ["Writing at the End of the Century: A Letter"; *TriQuarterly* 86, Winter 1992/93]. A lovely piece! I've been quoting you transcontinentally (4x thru O'Hare since Jan, ugh, but almost done for the year).

And how warming to these old heartcockles to see Jack Jackson, my Princeton student of long ago, opening the Apr issue. Along w. another notable student of mine, Enid Shomer.

Hugs / Maxine

Alison Kolodinsky to Joseph Parisi *Ormond Beach, Fla.,*
14 May 1993

Dear Mr. Parisi:

This is a letter that has been with me since last September. Somehow today I just decided that if I don't write it down, and mail it to you, it will never go away! . . . You published a poem of mine last summer called "Adoption" [June 1992], which, I am happy to tell you, was published in a new anthology. . . .

My birthday last year (late August) was one of the happiest because my husband bought me the top item on my wish list—the whole series of Poets in Person and the book with it. I was so thrilled to have it! . . . I want you to know that I think it was just such a great series. For people like myself, especially, who are in a way beginning their poetry careers.

But now, the real reason I am writing. I also was diagnosed with clinical depression around that same time. . . . I am doing fine, under a wonderful doctor's care. . . . [W]hat I want to get to is this—that at night, *every* night, when I could not rest no matter how exhausted I felt, when everyone else had fallen asleep, I would plug in one of the tapes in my walkman. I assume you have received scores of letters from poets and others telling you how great the series was (is). . . .

People say how poetry reaches out, connects, etc. but for me it was the rope which held me together night after night after night. And I just wanted to say thank you. . . .

Sincerely, / Alison Kolodinsky

David Wagoner to Joseph Parisi   Poetry Northwest,
                                                    Seattle, Wash., 2 June 1993

Dear Joe:

What a generous letter. And what a generous taking of poems. Since New Year's Day, when something wonderfully peculiar happened to my brain and spirit, I've been working more voluminously than ever before in my life and haven't wanted to risk showing the stuff to anybody. . . . Yours is the first editorial eye to land on any, and having you take 11 out of 16! Now I can go on going on. . . .

Charles Wright was a very good choice [for the Lilly Prize]. And $75,000! I wish Maestro Kitchen could make it retroactive to us poor previous winners. . . .

Take care of yourself. And thanks for your (probably) effective testimony in Washington. . . .

Fondly, / David

J.P. testified in June before the House Appropriations Subcommittee, in support of the NEA and NEH.

James Merrill to Joseph Parisi   *Stonington, Conn., 6 October 1993*

Dear Joe—

I'm so very pleased & touched by your review [of his autobiography, *A Different Person*] in the *Tribune*. (And Harry Ford [editor at Knopf] is doing butterfly hops in his office.) The book's reception has kissed me awake from a long slump. Alas the computer I wrote it on has been pronounced brain dead. I should also tell you (I wrote him a note) that James Richardson's essay delighted one. Now: turn your attention to the rest of the world!

Yours, / Jimmy

Richardson reviewed Merrill's *Selected Poems 1946–1985* and *The Changing Light at Sandover* in August 1993.

Jane Kenyon to Joseph Parisi   *Danbury, N.H., 1 November 1993*

Dear Joseph:

What a nice surprise! Really, I am delighted. I was glad too that the melancholy poem turned up in BAP [*Best American Poetry*].

I'm in my usual fall doldrums, and the prize has given something good to think about.

All best, / Jane

Kenyon was awarded *Poetry*'s Frederick Bock Prize for 1993, for "Having It Out with Melancholy" (November 1992).

Douglas Crase to Joseph Parisi   *New York City, 27 January 1994*

Dear Joe,

I could not be happier with the way the Schuyler piece looks in the Jan. *Poetry*. I am tickled, well, pink—and *so much space* you gave me. Of course the *subject* is worth it, but I am grateful that you let me be its agent. Apparently, what I need is for you to call me more often and must *tell* me to write. Parisi: the muse that won't take no for an answer. Thank you.

Truly, / Doug

Crase's review essay on James Schuyler's *Collected Poems* and career, "A Voice Like the Day," ran to fourteen pages.

Richard Kostelanetz to Joseph Parisi   *New York City, 4 May 1994*

[*Typed on Post-it note:*] Here is your courtesy cover letter.
Dear Parisi,

While I appreciate your spirited card about my Cummings prefaces, didn't the top line say that they come from *An Other Cummings*, alternative selection of the master's work that Norton will publish next year. You may not have gotten that far, or wanted to demonstrate that you customarily don't read before the author's name. Don't you find that inability, or unwillingness, to read is a growing editorial problem. Reading-challenged is a generous term.

From time to time I try visual poetry on you, thinking that you'd rather not be classed among reactionary editors who define their philistinism by ignoring the avant-garde. Perhaps my generosity is mistaken.

Cordially yours, / Richard Kostelanetz

Donald Hall to Joseph Parisi   *Danbury, N.H., 9 August 1994*

Dear Joe,

Thank you so much for the photographs, good reminders of a happy occasion [the Lilly Prize ceremony].

We have been back in the hospital twice, one week each, since I saw you in Chicago. The most recent time was Jane's shingles. She is terribly weakened, using a walker much of the time, but we are assured that the debilities are all reversible—shingles, neuropathies from the chemo, and so forth.

Meantime I am trying to get Jane to find me copies of a couple of poems of her own to send you—but she has not had the strength to get up the stairs. I think that she is a little better the last couple of days, and I would predict that I can get them soon. I hope so. Just in time for your autumnal deluge of manuscripts, no doubt.

For that matter, I threaten to send you some of my own things.

Thank you so much for the photographs, which Jane enjoyed as well. Best to you.

Don

Joseph Parisi to Robert B. Shaw　　　　　　　　*Chicago, 23 August 1994*

Dear Robert,

If you were distracted during the composition of the latest essay, it certainly doesn't show. As usual, this is superb work, incisive, sensible, and so readable. . . .

Lapsed Catholic that I am, I find [Geoffrey] Hill's p.o.v. pretty hard to take, and the style simply awful: my throat goes dry as I try to wend my way through his (to my mind) tortured lines. Clampitt, too, I find more and more to be eccentric in the worst sense: the Baroque profusion is just too much; gets me (and I think her) lost in the curlicues. But you give them their due, and then some, and with such grace.

Your mentioning the packing and moving reminds me of when we were moving my grandmother, a woman who never threw *anything* (I mean that) away. We're talking an accumulation of stuff spanning 70-some years. Going through the basement and the closets was archeological, a time trip, as each successive layer revealed segments of the family history. Toward the bottom of one pile we actually unearthed the scooter I had as a 3-year-old; my mother rediscovered the doll she adored in 1919. It was eerie and sad, and oddly comforting.

I hope all's wellest with you. We're now doing composition in-house on the new Mac (our summer project), so you'll probably be seeing proofs sooner than usual. . . .

Very best, / Joe

Donald Hall to Joseph Parisi　　　　　　　　*Danbury, N.H., 26 August 1994*

Dear Joe,

Here are some poems of my own. The top one, as you will see, started after Jane's illness. The others all began earlier, but I have been working them over, during the last seven bad months. I hope there's something you like. "Goggles and Helmet" is one that I read in Chicago.

I have threatened to send you poems by Jane, and I hope to fulfill that threat shortly. The poems are upstairs, in her study, and it is very difficult for her to climb stairs. She uses a walker much of the time, getting about downstairs. Naturally enough, she does not want me rooting around looking for these poems. I believe there are two that are finished. She has several more that are close, but she is not ready—and she is not able to work on them.

All these symptoms are a result of the treatment for the disease, not the disease. All of them are temporary, I have to remind myself of this fact, about a hundred times a day.

No match, so far, for her bone marrow; but Seattle continues to work on the project.

Best to you, / Don

"Goggles" and three other poems were published in February 1995.

Virginia R. Terris to Joseph Parisi   *Freeport, N.Y., 5 September 1994*

Dear Joseph Parisi:

I'm the "scholar" in the Poets in Person [training] program last December in San Diego whose theme was "Re-visioning America" (Ginsberg, Brooks, Rich, Dove, Soto, and as a somewhat last minute addition, Olds). The first meeting (at Brentwood Library, Long Island, NY) was crowded. The succeeding ones were attended by an enthusiastic faithful (still quite a number) who stayed through all five sessions. As an English professor (Adelphi University) who retired eleven years ago, I found the meetings stimulating and fun to prepare for, and hope to hold another series next spring to include poets I didn't this year—if we can dig up funding, and possibly initiate a similar one in my local library, which is in a different county than this spring's. The series was a real contribution to the cultural life of this area. There is a lot of interest in poetry on Long Island but not of this caliber, especially outside of the universities. I found the tapes and the text very helpful as a way of focusing the group's interest and discussions. I didn't have to invent the fork at each meeting. . . .

I am still amazed at the efficiency of the San Diego meetings. How everything turned out just the way you said it would. When we went in, it seemed impossible that we would emerge so organized. But we did. It was the best run conference I've been to, and I've been to many. My only regret was that, with all those swimming pools, I didn't get in any of them. (I went to the zoo instead.) . . .

With best wishes, / Virginia R. Terris

Donald Hall to Joseph Parisi   *Danbury, N.H., 21 September 1994*

Dear Joe,

Here at last are those two poems by Jane that I have been threatening you with. I suspect you will be pleased that I could find them.

I cannot remember for sure what I have told you. We had planned to go to Seattle next Wednesday, for a bone marrow transplant. We had plane reservations, and an apartment in Seattle. Jane's mother Polly was coming with us to pursue her radiation treatment out there. Then last Tuesday morning we discovered that Jane's remission has started to go, so everything has changed. This Wednesday Jane goes back into Dartmouth-Hitchcock, three weeks or so of chemotherapy, attempting to find a second remission. Her mother will start treatment here, staying at our house and being driven to the hospital by friends. I am back in the motel, where you telephoned me in March, in order to stay all day with Jane. It is possible that we will get back to Seattle, same donor, later this autumn. . . .

                                        Best to you, / Don

John and Bonnie Nims to Joseph Parisi, et al.   *Nîmes, France,*
                                                        20 October 1994

[*picture postcard of Roman ruins*]
Dear Joe, Helen, et al.,

While in Provence we thought we might as well found a city & name it after us. The Temple to Diana worked out nicely, & so did the amphitheater (6 Gladiators Killed on Grand Opening!). But the big tower is crumbly already—shoddy workmanship here. We think we'll name the town GINSBERG and build elsewhere. Back to Chicago in a few days.

                                        John & Bonnie

W. S. Merwin to Joseph Parisi   *Haiku, Hawaii, 26 October 1994*

Dear Joe:

You wrote on the day that I flew home after nearly a month away. Thank you for your congratulations, and for the warm and generous way you put them. I learned of the Tanning [Prize] a few days before I left on the last trip, and I'm still trying to believe it. It was given at a reading of all the Academy of American Poets Chancellors in Washington, and the generosity of other poets in the event was a huge part of the pleasure. I was grateful for having been given a few days to prepare something to say, so that I didn't stand up and stammer Gosh.

I'm happy that you can find room for another three poems. I've been honored by the way you've been placing the ones you've taken in the past couple of years. They're all part of the new mss., THE VIXEN, which Harry [Ford, editor at Knopf] has scheduled not so very soon, though, because he doesn't want it crowding TRAVELS and THE RAIN IN THE TREES just now. As you may have gathered, the poems in the new book are more than usually closely related in various ways including the, I suppose one could say, form. But I think you have plenty of time to get these in print before the book is due out.

Computers—I'm an illiterate, and likely to remain one. My father-in-law gave Paula a somewhat obsolete one (I gather) in some kind of desperation, I think. It sat there for months while people sang praises of the things and What They Could Do. After most of the year she took several deep breaths and devoted some days or weeks, I think, to trying to master the instructions—a new language, if language it is. Finally, in triumph she printed out the typed list of the palm species in the ground in the garden here, which I'd given her, having batted it out on my old buckboard here, whose ribbon grows forgetful here and there as you see. Four pages of additional species have been added to my own list in the year since then, but they have not found their way onto an updated printout list yet, nor has anything else. I don't think we're the ideal computerites.

I do appreciate vastly what you have done in setting up the new poems with their long lines. Much better if they don't have to be broken. It was a wonderful trip but what a joy to be home—to the overgrown garden, the (more or less) laid-back Chows, the hope of work (a kind of Promised Land view over the shoulder of a mountain of mail). Warm good wishes to you and Helen and everyone there.

William

Joseph Parisi to Richard Kostelanetz   *Chicago, 26 October 1994*

Dear Mr. Kostelanetz,

I quite understood the intent of your Cummings submission. I do read what reaches me, even the slovenly stuff you insist on sending. But one would have thought you'd have realized by this time what is and is not appropriate for this magazine.

Call me reactionary, if you wish. I prefer to take the long view of literary history, unlike yourself. Why you continue to bother with your puerile exercises (tart them up with the pretentious term "visual poetry" all you like), remains a mystery to me. Apollinaire (among others) did this sort of thing many, many decades ago, and much better. Your copying what is now

a tired, and tiresome, device is hardly "avant-garde." So, it makes me wonder: just who's the one who doesn't read?

By the way, are you really so hard up that you have to use "Post-it"s for
your (carelessly typed—but, hey, they're only words) literary correspondence? Or am I being "reactionary," again, for expecting elementary courtesy in such matters?

Joseph Parisi

Despite this (atypical) testy moment, Kostelanetz continued to submit pieces and J.P. continued to reply.

Neal Bowers to Joseph Parisi   *Ames, Ia., 23 December 1994*

Dear Joe,

. . . Speaking of plagiarism, my story turned up in *The London Times*,
The International Herald-Tribune, and in newspapers in Canada and Australia. I still can't get over the amount of interest journalists took in the
case. Of course, once the NY *Times* did its piece, everybody got in line,
and I even ended up on NPR and on the local public radio station out
here. I've received a ton of fascinating mail, some of it from genuinely
crazy people—like . . . the NYC man who is taking 3-D photos of the
Vatican and sent me the poetry of a young woman who emerged from a
coma after a near-fatal car crash and found she could write poetry. (By
the way, she can't.)

Because of the tremendous interest the story generated, Nancy and I are
working on a book on the case. My job, between now and the middle of
January, is to draft and circulate a prospectus to see if any publishers are interested in the project. All the while, I keep wondering what David Jones
(a k a David Sumner) thinks of all the notoriety he's received and what, if
anything, he may be up to at this very moment. . . .

Yours, / Neal

Bowers's *Word for the Taking: The Hunt for a Plagiarist* was published by Norton in 1996. In
1997 Bowers was approached about a possible movie adaptation of the book, with a script
perhaps by Tony Kushner. After much negotiating about rights, screenplay, and possible
backers for the film, Bowers concluded in a letter to J. P. on 29 July 1997: "But I've heard
this kind of stuff for about 5 months now, and am beginning to believe the chief product of
those Hollywood types is schmooze."

A. R. Ammons to Joseph Parisi   *Ithaca, N.Y., 9 January 1995*

Dear Joe,

I can't tell you how much I appreciate your kind letter. It helped *so
much*.

I got a good report from my stress test, so I may be OK in that respect. I do become awed & scared, though, when I think of showing up before such an audience [Poetry Day]! Also the trip by car is pretty far, but if we're feeling good, we can do that.

Do let me know when the last backing-out date arrives—and meanwhile I'll keep in touch about any change. I have to go to Wake Forest for a celebration of my work (in March), and I don't know how far down or up that will leave me. Being appreciated is, amazingly enough, not what it was supposed to be.

You know I want to come. And physiology permitting I'll be there. But sometimes in the middle of the night, it is only daunting. . . .

Ever— / Archie

Charles Wright to Joseph Parisi   *Charlottesville, Va., 1 February 1995*

Caro Gio—

Right after we talked this afternoon, Holly came home from teaching and I opined to her how guilty I felt about saying no to your kind offer of reviewing Robert's [Pinsky] Dante book [*Inferno*], but how inadequate I felt to the task of talking about Dante, much less a translation of same which I had attempted 2 cantos of, and she said—"Don't be silly. Of course you did the right thing. You can't write criticism. You don't know how." So . . . That's the indeterminate X I forgot to mention when we talked—I guess I don't know how. She's pretty much got it right, I'm afraid—I've never done it, and God knows I'd hate to start with Dott. Alighieri. . . .

Felice febbraio a te. Stàti bon . . .

Charles

Donald Hall to Joseph Parisi   *Danbury, N.H., 28 February 1995*

Dear Joe,

Thanks for your cheques and the notes—for Jane and me.

February 24th, we flew back to New Hampshire! Jane's marrow works well. She does not have chronic Graft Versus Host Disease. She had that disease of the stomach, but steroids helped. Steroids taper off on March 17th, but then there is the six months taper of another deadly drug—deadly, and life-giving! She is very sick, very weak, but she does not

Jane Kenyon in the early nineties.

have leukemia. Things are looking good . . . and it is wonderful to be home.

Alas, Jane's mother died in New Hampshire on January 26th. The grieving was earlier, largely—and it reconstitutes itself as we come home and find the house full of her things, the books she did not finish reading.

But Friday night our dog sang an aria for thirty-eight minutes without taking a breath, and I don't think he was half so happy as Jane and I were.

She is sick, and it will be a long time before she is writing again, but I believe that she will write again!

Best to you, / Don

Albert Goldbarth to Poetry   *Wichita, Kans., 1 April 1995*

Dear POETRY:

I just finished reading through David Barber's review [of A.G.'s *Across the Layers: Poems Old and New*] in your current April issue.

Sheesh. When a guy's subscription is starting to lapse, you sure know how to turn the screws, don't you.

Renewal stuffs enclosed.

Gratefully, / Albert

Donald Hall to Joseph Parisi   *Danbury, N.H., 14 April 1995*

Dear Joe,

Jane's bone marrow transplant took, we came home on February 24 . . . and this week we discovered that the leukemia had returned. Jane will die, fairly soon. I know you care about Jane. All this suffering, over fifteen and a half months, and here we are. Some chemotherapy could delay her death but I think it would only prolong her suffering. So she believes. Jane is doing remarkably well, rather withdrawn but full of love all the same. She stays dry-eyed while I weep. We work together on a new and selected poems that Graywolf will do next year. Not to mention an obituary and a funeral program.

Yours ever, / Don

Anthony Hecht to Joseph Parisi   *Washington, D.C., 10 May 1995*

Dear Joe Parisi:

A few days ago I wrote you saying I didn't expect to have time enough to compose a poem in memory of Jimmy Merrill. I was wrong, and no one is more surprised than I am. I send it to you herewith. . . .

I suspect, as you may too, that my enclosed poem ["For James Merrill: An Adieu"] had its source in Auden's elegy for Yeats about disappearing in the dead of winter. It was in February that Jimmy died, though it was probably nothing like winter in the southwest where he was staying. But it was winter hereabouts, and the Auden line, with the mystery of his evasive word, "disappeared" chimed with your own comment, "It is still hard to believe, harder to accept, that Jimmy is gone."

Sincerely, / Anthony Hecht

Donald Hall to Joseph Parisi   *Danbury, N.H., 11 May 1995*

Dear Joe,

Here are five poems by Jane, unpublished, which will be in her last book from Graywolf (a New and Selected) next year. She wanted you to see them. (We did manage to talk about just about everything, including the magazine editors who would see her posthumous work!) All of these poems were written before she became ill. While she was ill, the only poems that I sent out were the two that you published in the February issue. We lost track of the others. We did not have them in Seattle. Before she died, I was able to assemble all these new and unpublished poems, and go over them with her. No late revisions. She was surprised and pleased at what we found. . . .

Maybe you are still in Europe. Maybe I sent you this program from the funeral before. I am, heaven knows, a chicken with its head cut off.

Best to you, / Don

Jane Kenyon died the morning of 22 April 1995. The five poems were published in December 1995.

Joseph Parisi to Donald Hall   *Chicago, 16 May 1995*

Dear Don,

The news of Jane's death reached me after I returned from Europe, and I was deeply saddened, as well as surprised. The last I had heard, in the lovely letter you sent immediately after your return from Seattle, was that the prognosis was optimistic. Helen told me you had called while I was away, reporting that the doctors had failed, after all.

Even though we were not fortunate enough to have met her in person, all of us here admired her work tremendously and felt we knew her—and in most important ways we did, through that work, esp. the extraordinary "Having It Out with Melancholy"—and we felt a rare sense of intimacy and therefore of loss for her. Our hearts go out to you.

And so I was terribly touched to receive your stunning poem, and immediately after that the wonderful gift of those last poems of Jane's. I can't tell you how much it means to me, and to all of us at the magazine, to know that you both thought of us in those last days and that Jane wanted *Poetry* to have the work.

Talking to people around the country, before and after Jane's death, I have learned how many others felt a personal bond with her, and how profound an effect her lines have had on so many lives. To read these new poems is bittersweet, but having them is also a great comfort, the continuation of a friendship with someone uniquely talented, understanding, and dear.

Joe

Hall sent his poem "Without," which was also published in the December 1995 issue.

Donald Hall to Joseph Parisi   *Danbury, N.H., 23 May 1995*

Dear Joe,

Thanks for the good letter. I'm very pleased that you will do all five of Jane's poems that I sent you—and I think everyone of them is pure gold! She wanted you to see her late poems. We were able to talk about practically everything—even where the unpublished poems would go! They will make a beautiful bunch, in *Poetry*—which had always treated her so well.

The prognosis was optimistic, yes, but we did know that it *could* fail. Without the bone marrow transplant, the leukemia would definitely have killed her. With her Philadelphia chromosome, in half of her cancer cells, chemotherapy could put her into remission but it could not keep her there. She first lost remission in September, which was briefly restored for our trip to Seattle, but by the time they started giving her more chemo—preparatory to the BMT—that remission was already failing. It was an aggressive cell. . . .

The hope, with a BMT, is that a rejection-effect will kill off any residual cancer cells. The new marrow recognizes the whole body as a possible enemy, and it tries to kill off its host liver, kidneys, etcetera. Many people after a BMT die of this rejection-effect, which is called Graft Versus Host Disease. The thing to do is to get just enough GVHD to kill off any remaining cancer cells, but not enough to kill off your liver etcetera.

Jane had some GVHD—but in the event she did not have enough of it. There is no way to control the quantity of this effect. You hope it is not too much; you hope it is not too little.

After completing the one hundred days from the BMT, Jane's odds got much better—perhaps they went from 30/70 to 70/30 . . . but the leukemia came back and she had eleven days.

I suppose I have had between seven and eight hundred letters about Jane. Astonishing. The out-pouring of response—from India and France and England and mostly from the United States—would have astonished her. Obituaries came out all over the country, and the *New Yorker* printed her dates under one poem . . . and hundreds and hundreds of people took time to write me, including of course many people whom neither Jane nor I had ever met. I could wish she had known about it . . . but she did

Donald Hall at Eagle Pond Farm in the late nineties.

know, in the last fifteen months of her illness, that so many people cared so much—and it touched and pleased her. So it all touches and pleases me.

But nothing diminishes the gross *absence* in this house! Twenty years of living in this house together, all day every day. It's terrible.

I'm glad that you would like to do "Without." It's realism, or even nat-uralism. As Jane said when I read it to her, "You've got it."

Thanks for your good letter about Jane, and best wishes to you.

Don

Philip Schultz to Joseph Parisi   *East Hampton, N.Y., 24 May 1995*

Dear Joe:

Well, I've starting writing poetry again . . . [sic] it was mysterious when it stopped & even more so now that it's begun again. I feel as if I should in-troduce myself all over again: Dear Mr. Parisi, you probably don't remem-ber me but I used to contribute verse to your magazine & you thought enough of it to (most gratefully) include it (me) in your lovely 75th An-niversary issue.

Really, I'm introducing myself to myself (the poet to the man & vice versa) but—how are you? So much has changed in my life. I left NYU & started my own school for writing, The Writers Studio, which is doing well, I got married and moved to East Hampton (still work in the city though) and recently saw Lillian Braude & remembered our famous dinner when we all laughed so hard. . . . How is it I lost touch with so many good peo-ple? Well, I'm back and the next time you're in town we should get to-gether. Hope you enjoy these poems. Enjoy the summer.

Sincerely, / Phil

A. R. Ammons to Joseph Parisi   *Ithaca, N.Y., 7 June 1995*

Dear Joe,

My cold's getting better, I think. Actually, it had started before I left Ithaca for Chicago [to receive the Ruth Lilly Prize]. I'm so grateful that the voice failure came late.

How to thank you for the marvelous occasion and experience! —You helped me feel at ease, and I was so reassured just by meeting you that what I had fantasized as a trial became a pleasure.

Your brilliant introduction—really an essay—almost convinced me that I deserved to be mentioned in the company you mentioned! I hope to ponder on it and learn from it. It set the tone for the whole gathering which, by the way, was truly impressive—and, as they say, receptive.

Can I bring you something from Ithaca when I come in September? I'll bring some watercolors to show you. I could use your thoughts about them.

My best to your staff—everyone so friendly and kind. And my special thanks to Mrs. Klaviter for the warmth of her many ministrations.

Phyllis sends greetings & many thanks, too—

Archie

W. S. Merwin to Joseph Parisi   *Haiku, Hawaii, 13 July 1995*

Dear Joe,

I like thinking of you playing hooky anywhere as long as it's fun. . . . And I'm very happy that "Completion" has found a home, a first home. Your letter reached me at the same time as the page proofs of the new mss. . . .

I'm looking forward to the JM [James Merrill memorial] issue, and glad to be in it ["Lament for the Makers," September 1995]. How odd the way things alter, read again now that he is gone. Some things, as they say, spring to *life*, or another life.

Paula is perusing the [Jaime] Sabines translations at the moment. I got through the mss., and we are onto the next phase of that. I'll send you some once I'm reasonably sure they're ok. Though I realize that even if you wanted some it might be hard to get them into print before the public reading in late October in New York. Besides, you've your Irish issue [October 1995] pending for then. Well, however it works.

I'm relishing the months of not having to go anywhere. Spending as much time as I can working, and gardening and reading, and even so having to growl chowishly at the mail which I am in fact neglecting, instead of spending hours every afternoon as my own office drudge, spending only 45 mins. or so, and then bolting to the garden. Otherwise, why live here? (If I have to live as though I were somewhere else. Etc.)

The next trip planned, by the way, is the October one (apart form several here in the islands for a variety of purposes). Late October. No thought of Chicago on that one, but might we meet up in NYC?

Ever, / William

Dennis O'Driscoll to Joseph Parisi   *Dublin, Ireland, 7 August 1995*

Dear Mr Parisi,

Many thanks for your kind letter about my 'Map of Contemporary Irish Poetry' [October–November 1995]. I am very glad to be back in *Poetry* and for your encouraging response to my essay. No doubt, when my piece appears, I will come under fire from all corners of this island—both from those on and off the map! It would be difficult to do justice to all of Ireland's poets and impossible (as well as unhealthy!) to take them as seriously as they take themselves. What I have attempted to do is to write the kind of introductory essay which *I* would be interested in reading about the poetry of some culture which was unfamiliar to me. . . .

The pleasure and honour of being included as an essayist in *Poetry* is all the greater for the fact that I regard your critics as the most discriminating and stylish in America. . . .

Again with many thanks,

Dennis O'Driscoll

A. R. Ammons to Joseph Parisi   *Ithaca, N.Y., 12 October 1995*

Dear Joseph—

As part penance for my failure to do for you all I could have wished [at the Poetry Day dinner], I insist on charging my expenses to my under-endowed chair here. You mustn't worry about it.

I finally this morning got to sit down in the coffee shop in sufficient calm and read your introduction. I couldn't help dropping a tear reading how truly you know what I meant, at least, to do and hope I sometimes did. I couldn't have asked for a context truer to the spirit I would want to represent. The only problem, of course (which I'm not asking you to excuse away), is how could I ever live up to your words. Well,

A. R. Ammons with J.P. at the Newberry Library following the Lilly Prize presentation, June 1995.

it's over now, and I am deeply grateful to you for the opportunity to come out to Chicago & be with you and the others.

Yours ever— / Archie

When Ammons was asked to be Poetry Day speaker, we did not fully appreciate his acrophobia; as in the past, the dinner was scheduled at the Mid-Day Club, on the fifty-seventh floor of the same building (Bank One) that held the auditorium for his reading. Despite his fears, the guest of honor came up to the reception, stayed as long as he could, then descended to terra firma, where he was taken to dinner at a less lofty restaurant.

Joseph Parisi to Neal Bowers   *Chicago, 7 December 1995*

Dear Neal,

Thanks for your very sweet letter. But, really, it's we who should be thanking you; the [Union League] Prize was the least we could do for all the great stuff you've given us, and not just in the past year. Just consider it a down payment for your next jaunt. Glad you were able to get some time away.

Sorry to be tardy in responding. I've been away myself, in Dublin, for a "launch" of our special Irish issue. . . . I wasn't on Irish soil more than an hour before I had four phone calls from people inviting me to lunch, dinner, an opening, sight-seeing, whatever. The reception itself went very well. Dennis O'Driscoll gave a very droll intro to the readings. . . . Big turnout, which, I guess, isn't so unusual there. (Even the cabdrivers are highly literate about poetry in Dublin.) Next day, I was invited to a very amusing lunch with Michael Holroyd, who's just done a book on Augustus John.

Dennis O'D took me on a whirlwind tour of Co. Wicklow and Co. Kildare one afternoon. Saw several 18th-c. manor houses, but I liked best the countryside itself—where all those sheep may and do safely graze—and esp. St. Kevin's impressive redoubt at Glendalough. When I told Billy Collins about that part of the trip in particular, he remarked that, while we think of those monks as such dour, ascetic creatures, actually, considering the lakes and the rest of the splendid scenery, we ought rather to call them sybarites: what an eye they had for prime real estate. . . .

Ever, / Joe

David Bottoms to Joseph Parisi   *Atlanta, Ga., 28 January 1996*

Dear Joe:

Hope you are well and working hard. I'm just back from Columbia, South Carolina, and a little worn out. As you know, my old friend Jim Dickey died last week [19 January]. A very sad thing for me, though we all knew it was coming. He'd been sick for two years. I had a long phone conversation with him a few days before his death, and he told me he didn't think he'd make it through the spring. His lungs were shot and he was on oxygen all the time. We'd planned a visit, but it wasn't to be. At least I got to tell him again how much he meant to me. That's something, I suppose.

If you remember Jim in some way in *Poetry*, and I know you often quote from the poems, you might look at the last few lines of "For the Last Wolverine," where he says "*Lord let me die but not die / out.*" . . .

All best, / David

Stephen Yenser to Joseph Parisi   *Los Angeles, Calif., 20 February 1996*

Dear Joe,

Bless your heart for getting "A Day in the Life" into print so quickly [May 1996]! It's not an easy poem to set, and your people did an excellent job. I've made only a few corrections—and a few emendations.

Do you know Del Kolve? He's a medievalist, now at UCLA, famous in his field, whom JM knew for years. Well, not long ago, he and his friend Larry Luchtel, who have an immaculate house in the Hollywood Hills, had a small dinner party, after which a few of the guests—including Roger Bourland, who wrote the music for the video of "The Changing Light"—were sitting in a bedroom watching that very video. Del moved his foot the wrong way and spilled a glass of red wine on the fine white carpet. They do what they have to do—run to the kitchen, grab the salt, come back and pour it onto the stain. In due time, guests leave, hosts go to bed. The next morning, Larry calls Del in to see what Larry presently takes a picture of: the salt has done its job, except in one area, where a burgundy J remains. On the end table beside the stain—and Larry didn't have to move a thing to take the photo—there's a copy of JM's last volume . . . *A Scattering of Salts*.

All best as always from Lost Angeles.

Yours, / Stephen

Robert Bly to Joseph Parisi   *Minneapolis, Minn., 29 February 1996*

Dear Joseph Parisi,

It was such a delight to me to see poetry of mine again in POETRY magazine, and I like my company very much also in that issue—being there with old friends.

I see in the latest issue that you were kind enough to send my last book of poems out to Ben Howard for review [*Meditations on the Insatiable Soul*, March 1996]. It's a lively review, and very generous overall in the care he took with its disparate energies, and generous in its admiration for "visionary beauty," despite a few moose here and there. The lines he ends with are my favorite lines in the whole book.

I'm sending along a few new poems you might glance at. The ones about my farm life as a boy seem to come out transparent like some of the old SNOWY FIELDS poems—which I first saw printed in POETRY.

With good wishes, / Robert Bly

Billy Collins to Joseph Parisi   *Somers, N.Y., 2 March 1996*

Dear Joe,

Sorry my cow didn't make it through your gate, but I return to the typewriter with renewed determination—the very response to rejection that you dread from many, I'm sure. . . .

Thanks again for nudging the Lannan [Foundation] people in their philanthropic ribs. I am reading out there [at their museum in Marina Del Rey] in the famous Garden on June 16th. I have enough friends in LA to add some pleasure to the po-business. . . .

I'm just after writing a furious letter to Pittsburgh. Through an "oversight" they seemed to have neglected to include my book in any of their advertisements. Plus, they printed only 1200 paper copies of the book, so the print run sold out in ten minutes (as you might imagine) leaving me with no books for over two months. The second printing just came out. I know, I know, we should all have such worries. Speaking of ME, I wonder if anyone will review *The Art of Drowning* for *Poetry*? I wonder.

If you have a weakness for bad news, we've got plenty of that. Next week Diane's father (76) is having his right foot removed . . . [sic] that's right, removed. Diabetes. And my mother (95), it was discovered last week, has a cancerous tumor on her colon. The poor dear had a lymphoma beaten out of her with chemicals about ten years ago and now she faces this. Jesus. Next week we have a consultation with the medicos and decide which of four horrible roads to go down. She is a saintly Catholic, daily communicant most of her life, and since about the age of 85 she has been scratching her head, wondering why she is still here and when the golden chariot will pull up to her condominium.

Stay well, dear Joe.

Billy

M. A. Aird [pseud.?] to The Editor   *Vancouver, B.C., 15 July 1996*

To the Editor:

My mother has told me that if I do not publish in your journal by the end of the year, she will cut me off from the family inheritance. Please—

you must help me. . . . You must understand, my mother loves poetry; she is a very passionate woman. But she never wanted me to be a poet, or even to try to write poetry. She says it is a sacred art that only the wisest people can practice, and that I was never bright enough. She wanted me to be a butcher instead; she said to me, "you have strong hands, strong butcher's hands!" . . . So you must help me by publishing some of my work—anything, even the shortest poem in the tiniest print you have. . . .

My mother is a short, stocky woman with big arms; she is very strong. She made a lot of money shearing sheep . . . a million dollars . . . which she said she would give me when I became a butcher. I told her I wanted to be a poet, and then she told me I had to be published in your magazine to even dream of being a poet. Please—you must help me. If these poems are not good enough, I have more—I will send them all! Please don't let me be cut off.

M. A. Aird

J.P. returned the poems on 22 July 1996, with a note: "I'm afraid that you will have to forgo your 'inheritance,' keep shearing sheep or butchering or whatever, and write poems just for the love of it."

John Updike to Joseph Parisi   *Beverly Farms, Mass., 5 August 1996*

Dear Mr. Parisi:

You seem to be the only person in the United States for whom I can do no wrong as a poet. Thank God you're the editor of *Poetry* magazine. To show my appreciation let me renew my subscription. I really enjoy your exquisitely printed and arranged issues—it took me a while to figure out that one poem led to another, to form a monthly garland. Hold my own poems as long as you need to, keeping in mind that I'm 64 and going on 65. . . .

Best wishes, / John Updike

John Updike became a frequent contributor beginning in 1992.

Joseph Parisi to Dennis O'Driscoll   *Chicago, 10 October 1996*

Dear Dennis,

No, we've not forgotten you. In fact, I called a few times (at home), without success. . . .

P-Day was a grand success, the biggest turnout we've had since T. S. Eliot came back in the '50s. Seamus was brilliant, of course, and people were absolutely spellbound: you could have heard the proverbial pin drop. Tickets had sold out two days after the (very small) ad appeared in the paper; people came rushing over to the office to buy them, fearing (rightly) that it would be sold out. There was a line a block long waiting to get in [to the Art Institute], and we put the "extras" in the old Chicago Stock Exchange room, with a video hookup. I asked Seamus if he'd mind going over to say a few words to the overflow audience before the show, and, dear man, he agreed, and charmed the pants off them. There were 200+ for the reception and dinner afterwards; and again he performed way beyond the call of duty. The Irish Consul, Frank Sheridan, gave a smart, funny speech of intro., and then SH talked for another 20 minutes, to the delight of the assembled. . . . In short, a triumph—thanks to your kind intercession and diplomacy. . . .

Seamus Heaney to Joseph Parisi   *Boston, Mass., 10 October 1996*

[*postcard*]
Dear Joseph—
    Well, why not a Boston card, in this season of mists . . . [sic] Greatly appreciated your note and the copies of the excellent press response. Must tell Valerie Eliot about my Avis ranking . . . I guess she would have been with the Possum on that earlier occasion.
    See you.

                                        Seamus Heaney

Heaney read at Poetry Day on 11 September. Newspaper stories remarked that Heaney drew the largest crowds since T. S. Eliot appeared in 1959. Valerie Eliot did accompany him; see photograph in *Dear Editor*, p. 422.

Martin Galvin to Joseph Parisi   *[n.p.], 23 October 1996*

Dear Joseph Parisi,
    Here I am, back again. Thought I'd harry you with another few poems for the reading, being sort of newly back from Ireland, that fine and furious place. . . .
    I was delighted to see the Australian issue, being as certain as any departed Irishman that some of my kin are part of that holy mix of coppers and so-called criminals. The essays by John Kinsella and John Tranter were both informing and pleasing to the eye. I loved that bit about "the problem of wrong landscape"—compared with Romantic England—that almost muted Australian poets for a while—sounds familiar. Tracy Ryan's ending with "the hollowness that Thomas touched," the just rightness of Wallace-

Crabbe's seeing "the wet suits are all handing up / like dead paratroopers," Kinsella's kangaroo—that child's innocent, up to his defending neck in water and blood against the Roo Dog . . . Wow, all I can say, Wow! . . .

Billy Collins to Joseph Parisi   *Somers, N.Y., 30 December 1996*

Dear Joe,

Just a quick note to wish you a happy New Year. I usually try to stay home on New Year's Eve and read Charles Lamb's great essay on that event (our second birthday, he calls it), but this year we have been lured into a dinner party. I am curious to see how this group of aging revelers will manage to stay up beyond midnight without stimulants.

I see what you mean about that last group of poems. But you have not heard the last of me, Parisi.

And just in case you thought that, like Christianity, *Poetry* had managed to reach into every corner of the world, I am enclosing the enclosed which was passed on to me from Garrison Keillor's office. . . .

Yours, / Billy

[*Enclosure:*]
From: Jeannie.Berres@—.— 15-NOV-1996
To: PHC [Prairie Home Companion]
Subj: Poetry
Dear Garrison,

I am a loyal listener to PHC and have one quick question. While listening a couple weeks ago, you read a poem that moved me to my core. It was entitled Splitting Wood, by Billy Collins. You said it was in the Feb. 96 issue of Poetry Magazine. Well, I have done some extensive searching and the local library here in Wasilla, Alaska, tells me there is no such magazine.

I would love a copy of this poem. If you could give me further guidance as to where I might find this jewel, I'd sure appreciate it.

CHAPTER XI

Fin de siècle

1. Several Steps Forward, with Some Backward Glances

As the end of the century approached, *Poetry* shifted into what became the most active phase in its long history, with more publications and programs, additional special editions of the magazine, and entry into the realm of the Internet. In Chicago, larger crowds than ever turned out for the annual Poetry Day readings each fall as well as for the new programs on a variety of topics—music and poetry, Walt Whitman, twentieth-century classics—that we began presenting at the Newberry Library in the spring. Many who attended were students and other newcomers to the art, who often told us with some surprise as they left the hall that they had not expected poetry programs to be so *entertaining*. Meanwhile, from across the country participants in the ever-expanding "Poets in Person" library groups, now numbering in many thousands, continued to express their enjoyment of and gratitude for the programs, responses that were truly heartening to us—as well as to the beleaguered National Endowment.

In the nineties the Endowment, particularly its Arts division, was under assault by Senator Jesse Helms and other censorious neo-conservatives in the Congress—and its budget was cut—because it funded some controversial projects. (And, incidentally, because attacking the NEA had proven an effective way of whipping up emotions and a cheap method for generating campaign donations and votes for right-wing politicians.) Many in the arts community worried that not only would its appropriations be further slashed but the agency might be eliminated entirely. After making accusations of obscenity, the favorite tactic of the guardians of public morality was to affix the dreaded label of "elite" to anything they and their backers on the right disliked. The "PIP" discussion groups offered abundant evidence that NEH-supported educational projects reached—and were heartily approved by—"ordinary" citizens representing a wide cross section of the U.S. population. By 1997 the project had been hosted by more than 130 libraries from Castine, Maine, to San Ramon, California, and from Brigham City, Utah, to San Antonio, Texas. Several directors wrote to tell us they had to set up programs twice a week because more people signed up than they had anticipated; many organized new series because of continuing demand.

Besides the success of the national outreach plan, another major factor in elevating spirits at *Poetry* was the fact that the nineties were largely free of the money worries that beset the magazine in earlier decades. Income from producing and administering the library programs subsidized staff salaries and overhead while the annual Lannan Foundation grants covered authors' payments. Ruth Lilly's gifts not only sponsored her annual prize and fellowships but defrayed portions of *Poetry*'s operating budget. Additional donations from both these patrons underwrote various Poetry Day speakers' fees, publication of double issues, and other special projects. Increased giving by Associate members helped us keep pace with rising printing and postage costs and other ordinary expenses, as did awards from the Prince Charitable Trusts, whose grants also allowed us to acquire and upgrade computer equipment. Writing scores of proposals and reports was tedious but resulted in steady income, and without the distractions of recurring financial crises it became possible to focus on improving the magazine and its circulation while advancing in new directions.

As so often in the past, *Poetry* continued not only to find funds but to attract the right staff members just when it needed them. In the mid-nineties several bright young people joined the magazine at opportune moments and applied their individual talents to make the diverse new projects realities. Besides energy and willingness to work very hard for low pay, the new assistants exhibited abundant good humor, a necessity given our ludicrously tight office space. Within fewer than 850 square feet were squeezed five and usually six people amid proliferating digital equipment, bulging storage cabinets, and desks piled with ever-growing mounds of paper—submissions, subscription orders, proofs, new and back issues, review books, literary journals, correspondence. Unsolicited manuscripts alone were now running to some eighty thousand poems a year, filling many boxes to overflowing. Considering the close quarters, frictions were surprisingly few; the volume and variety of work insured everyone had more than enough to keep well occupied. Since most members of the staff were trained to cover two or more areas of operations, the relentless cycles ran smoothly: monthly issues came off press on schedule, grant proposals were delivered by deadline, and shows did go on precisely as billed.

We were in the process of revamping magazine production when Drew Swinger called for an interview in 1994, just after graduating from Yale. He volunteered his services and soon became indispensable; within a few months he was hired full time. The first new member of the editorial staff to join since Stephen Young in 1988, he lightened many burdens as a painstaking first reader and production assistant. He was also proficient at

Rita Dove photographed
at Poetry Day 1997.

the computer, so his fine eye for detail was put to further use when we took typesetting in-house. He began by refining some of the magazine fonts, and with our consultant Dean Shavit redesigned *Poetry*'s layout, restoring the original Greer Allen typography and improving the prose sections through the many revisions requested by the editor.

Care for accuracy and organization by all the staff eased production of the now-annual special numbers and the additional public programs. In October 1997 the very ample eighty-fifth-anniversary issue featured new work by eighty-five of *Poetry*'s best-known contributors from around the English-speaking world. Adding to the festive spirit of the birthday celebration, Rita Dove agreed to appear at Poetry Day 1997. Large groups of grammar and high school children from Chicago and the suburbs came, heard, and were beguiled by the Poet Laureate; for most, it was their first experience of a poetry reading. Not only was the Art Institute auditorium packed, as with Seamus Heaney the year before, but receipts from the reception and dinner were even greater than in 1996, in fact the highest in the entire history of the event since its inception in 1955.

Sharon Olds read poems by several
other authors at Poetry Day in 1998.

Sharon Olds also drew a capacity audience for Poetry Day 1998, and with extraordinary generosity she devoted half her program to reading works by *other* poets. Robert Bly, *Poetry*'s onetime nemesis, had begun publishing in the magazine again in recent years and agreed to appear for the benefit in 1999, entertaining a truly diverse crowd at the Chicago Cultural Center, even without his drums. In 2000 Philip Levine, a frequent contributor since his first appearance in *Poetry* forty-five years earlier, delighted many old fans, and made many new ones, with both his poems and his sly asides and humorous commentary.

Reflecting a growing trend in the nineties, the October–November 1999 issue presented long poems and sequences by ten authors, including David Bottoms, Albert Goldbarth, Marilyn Hacker, Yusef Komunyakaa, Linda Pastan, and Charles Wright. Going abroad again, the October–November 1998 double issue was devoted to German poetry, as the tenth anniversary of the fall of the Berlin Wall approached. Gathered from both sides of the reunited country by Joachim Sartorius and Karin Graf, the dual-language edition featured thirty-two poets, with new translations of such classic authors as Brecht, Benn, and Celan and large samples from the most talented of the younger generation, including Gerhard Falkner, Barbara Köhler, and Durs Grünbein. To mark the release of the issue, the Goethe Institute of Chicago sponsored two days of readings and a symposium on translation. The entire press run of twelve thousand copies sold out within weeks and was reprinted. The October–November 2000 issue featured thirty-nine French-speaking poets from around the world, collected by Marilyn Hacker and John Taylor; works by all the authors were represented in the original French with translations *en face*. The Alliance Française of Chicago hosted readings and a reception to launch the edition, which sold briskly in both the United States and France.

Long delayed, a major publishing project at last came to completion in 1997. Work on an updated, accurate *Poetry* index had begun in 1983, when Jayne Marek, then a graduate student, initiated her meticulous inspection of the hundreds of issues since Volume I, Number 1 in October 1912. Everyone naively believed the index would be ready by 1987, in time for the seventy-fifth anniversary. By the mid-nineties the data had passed through four or five generations of computers using as many programs. (By 1995 also, Marek had received her Ph.D., was an English professor, and had published an important book on early literary magazines, *Women Editing Modernism*.) The data she compiled, and was still organizing, now resided in several formats; converting the tens of thousands of items into a single database and transforming that into a legible book seemed insurmountable tasks. Yet hope lingered that, somehow, the index might be published in time for the eighty-fifth anniversary.

As if on cue, in the summer of 1996 Chad Gayle, a young fiction writer and recent M.F.A. graduate from Texas A&M, presented himself at the *Poetry* office and offered to help with clerical chores. We soon discovered he was proficient in all manner of computer work and had even designed websites. With remarkable ingenuity over the next several months he translated, combined, and organized the enormous amount of index material into one database, then devised an efficient format for presenting it in book form. These tasks completed, Drew Swinger then designed an elegant layout for what became an oversize, 832-page volume listing more than 27,000 poems, almost 18,000 reviews, and about 4,200 essays by some 4,700 authors during *Poetry*'s first eight-five years. Checking entries, typesetting, and proofing took more months, but the massive undertaking was finished at last in the fall of 1997.

With a generous grant from the Lannan Foundation, *The POETRY Index 1912–1997* was published under our new imprint, The Poetry Press. The revised and enlarged second edition of the *Poets in Person Listener's Guide*, redesigned and set by Drew Swinger with a striking new cover by Chad Gayle, was also issued by the Press in 1997. While work on both books was in process, Chad also began construction of *Poetry*'s first website. The crisp, straightforward pages he created provided notes on current and recent issues, a history of the magazine, information on the prizes and fellowships, descriptions of the "Poets in Person" projects and materials, and submission guidelines. From the week the site was put up, poetrymagazine.org received thousands of hits daily. (We were surprised to learn that, second only to people with dot-edu addresses, the most frequent visitors were in branches of the U.S. military.) The site was later developed to allow ordering on-line. The Web eventually became a major source of new subscriptions, which generally came from interested parties *Poetry* would probably not otherwise have reached.

Beginning in the fall of 1995 Drew Swinger took a year off to pursue an M.A. in poetry, and returned, degree in hand, in the fall of 1996. As he was leaving, Davis McCombs, a Lilly Fellowship winner in 1993, inquired about a job. He joined *Poetry* and served as an assistant editor for a year. (While poring over manuscripts in the office early in 1996, he received a call informing him he had been awarded a Stegner Fellowship, and in September he departed for Stanford.) Chad Gayle left Chicago in late 1997 but continued to update and enhance the *Poetry* website via the Internet. Hearing about an opening, Damian Rogers, then working in the Newberry Library, applied for the position. (She looked the very image of H.D., *Imagiste*, so perhaps it was inevitable that she would join the magazine.) Besides doing first readings and many other editorial jobs, she helped coordinate the new spring series at the Newberry, with great dispatch.

Variety was the aim of the new programs, which were less formal but perhaps more informative than the Poetry Day presentations. In May 1993, for example, William Matthews, a jazz aficionado as well as a fine poet, gave an engaging talk on poetry and music. In 1996 Walt Whitman was honored in a reading by Galway Kinnell and a lecture by David Reynolds based on his book *Walt Whitman's America*, while the 1997 program was a tribute to Native American Poetry co-sponsored with the Poetry Society of America. As part of the national "Favorite Poem" project in 1999, we mounted a ma-

Readers for the Chicago launch of the Library of America's anthology,
American Poetry: The Twentieth Century, at the Newberry Library, 14 April 2000:
(l. to r.) J.P., Damian Rogers, LOA Publisher Cheryl Hurley, Edward Bailey,
Lucinda Bingham, Brother Charles Fitzsimmons, Judith Valente, Fredda Hyman,
Drew Swinger, Mara Tapp, Thomas Phelps, Peggy Barber, and Nicholas Rudall.

jor production featuring several dozen readers, including grade school students, government officials, media celebrities such as Bill Kurtis, and poetry
lovers from throughout the metropolitan area.

To celebrate the publication in 2000 of the Library of America's monumental two-volume anthology of *American Poetry: The Twentieth Century*, we
organized another large group reading devoted principally to poems from
the collection that were first printed in *Poetry*. Besides recitations—most of
the cast delivered their poems from memory—the program featured several
musical performances as well. The evening would hardly have been complete without a rendering of "Trees" (August 1913); but the alternative
country-rock musician Jeff Tweedy also performed Woody Guthrie's "Vig-
ilante Man," and soprano Kelly Hogan sang "Anything Goes." In October
2000 *Poetry* also hosted a special reading to help launch the LOA's newest
volume, *Longfellow: Poems and Other Writings*, edited by longtime *Poetry* contributor J. D. McClatchy.

For the 1998 spring program at the Newberry, Stephen Young and I presented readings from the feisty Monroe-Pound correspondence along with
several other candid letters from *Poetry*'s most famous early contributors and
more recent authors, drawn from the archives and office files. The reception
to the selections, and to the personalities they revealed, was enthusiastic, and
we were asked to repeat the performance at several other venues. From the
rapt responses to these quasi-dramatic performances (and the frequent laughter), we realized a systematic traversal of the archives was overdue, and an intimate history of *Poetry* might be told through the author-editor exchanges.

What better way to observe the upcoming ninetieth anniversary? In November 1998 we began our investigations of the voluminous records of the first fifty years preserved at the University of Chicago.

What we found in the Regenstein Library far exceeded our expectations, and we began to understand how rich a trove and how large a task lay before us. (Two other attempts to survey the archives and write a history had been made in the sixties, one by Karl Shapiro, and quickly abandoned.) The Special Collections stacks were being remodeled, but the reading room was open four hours a day, time we used with some urgency: we had to complete our research quickly if our "history in letters" was to be published by October 2002. Apprehension turned to high anxiety when we learned that in a few months the entire *Poetry* archive would be inaccessible since it was being shipped off to be microfilmed. Under these pressures we worked rapidly but with due deliberation, using every hour we could spare away from the office. (On the long treks to the Regenstein and back, we corrected proofs or did other magazine work.) The Special Collections librarians were always helpful to us. But with extraordinary kindness when the department was closed temporarily in the spring of 1999, Director Alice Schreyer suggested and arranged an interlibrary loan so that we could continue our work with the files at the Newberry Library—then transported the several boxes from Hyde Park to the North side personally, in her own car.

In the spring of 1999, Stephen and I also made the first of several trips to Indiana University in Bloomington, to begin examining the post-1960 files held in the Lilly Library. Meanwhile it seemed that Fortune again wished to lend a hand. In March 1998, Aaron Fagan, another Newberry employee, had volunteered to do clerical work and eventually was hired as circulation manager. During his time as an assistant in Special Collections, he became well acquainted with the Newberry stacks. When we started work on the history project, he mentioned seeing a suitcase and boxes of documents deposited there by early *Poetry* trustees. Most of the material was uncatalogued. When I called up the items, to my amazement I found the valise and cartons contained unofficial notes from meetings, personal letters between staff members, interoffice memos, photographs, and other long-forgotten documents from the late forties and earlier. From these it was possible to reconstruct, week by week and sometimes day to day, the turbulent months in 1949 when *Poetry* edged toward bankruptcy and narrowly escaped closing. The papers also revealed in detail how Hayden Carruth struggled to control the editorial direction of the magazine, and lost. (The untold story was finally recounted in Chapter XVI of *Dear Editor*.)

While research into the archives progressed, editorial work and educational programs proceeded according to schedule. Special editions were assembled, and the regular monthly issues were compiled from poems winnowed from the now almost ninety thousand submitted annually. In addition to the Poetry Day readings in the fall and the spring programs, the Lilly Prize ceremony was presented each June. Following Gerald Stern (1996) and William Matthews (1997), the awards were given to W. S. Merwin (1998), Maxine Kumin (1999), Carl Dennis (2000), Yusef Komunyakaa (2001), and Lisel Mueller (2002). Linda Pastan was the last of the eighteen poets to be selected during my tenure as chairman.

Maxine Kumin visiting the *Poetry* office before the Lilly Prize ceremony in 1999.

In the late nineties we also began a concerted effort to increase magazine circulation and Associate memberships. Aaron Fagan had already set up a system to generate regular renewal notices as well as acknowledgments to subscribers and donors. He then consolidated several databases, including records of former subscribers, for use in targeted subscription drives. To aid in the venture, we composed a new advertising brochure. These first solicitations helped raise circulation by almost 6 percent. Then, in early 1999, projects manager Helen Klaviter obtained a grant from the Council of Literary Magazines and Presses (CLMP) that provided services of a marketing consultant and technical support for the first large-scale direct-marketing ever conducted by *Poetry*.

Results of the mailings were extraordinary, with response rates to the special offers ranging from nearly 5 percent to more than 6 percent in the several rounds. Between 1999 and 2000, circulation rose by 26 percent. One mailing in April 2000 alone brought in 1,127 new subscribers, the largest single increase in *Poetry*'s history to date (and possibly for any literary journal). Renewal rates ranged from 65 to 76 percent. By December 2000, total monthly circulation, including newsstand sales, reached nearly 11,000 copies, the highest ever. To cover single copy sales and sample requests, the monthly press runs had to be increased to 12,000 copies or more—an unusual

Yusef Komunyakaa at the Lilly Prize presentation in 2001.

achievement, since literary journals (the majority of them quarterlies) generally have circulations of between one thousand and two thousand and rarely beyond five thousand copies. As *Poetry* neared its ninetieth anniversary—itself an unprecedented accomplishment—the budget was secure and the future looked fairly clear. In the fall of 2001, however, the outlook became rather more complicated.

2. Correspondence 1997–2002

No matter the special editorial projects, new public programs and publications, or perusals of archival material, voluminous current correspondence continued to stream into the *Poetry* office and regular business carried on as usual. Amid the flood of missives several surfaced that retain interest, as the samples below indicate. John Nims writes that he is nearing the end of his complete traversal of Michelangelo's poems, and declares: "No more translations ever, I hope." Allen Ginsberg and A. R. Ammons are fondly remembered in anecdotes sent in by admirers shortly after their deaths. The upcoming eighty-fifth anniversary occasions comments from distinguished contributors, including Seamus Heaney and Mary Oliver.

Other longtime correspondents such as Kenneth Koch and Maxine Kumin send graceful messages of thanks while younger poets deliver glad tidings of happy developments following their first appearances in *Poetry*. Carl Dennis wryly reflects on a fine (if belated) offer extended to him after he received the Lilly Prize, while Gary Soto offers an update on his recent career and work with children. More unusual reports come from poetry-writing prison inmates, one grim, the other black-humored. Frustrated frequent submitters enclose plaintive and witty cover letters with their latest contenders for publication.

Philip Levine and the editor compare notes on their impressions of past and recent poetry galas (and occupants) in the White House. A supporter in Vermont engages in droll correspondence about subscribing to *Poetry* and snatching food from the mouths of babes. Another reader sends an incisive critique of the biases of book reviewers and the (perhaps false) distinction between "confessional" and "personal" poetry. Dick Allen sends his reflections on "tragic generations," the old New Criticism, and autobiography in poetry. Robert Bly tells of his and other poets' disappointment at the fiftieth-anniversary ceremony of the National Book Awards.

In the wake of the attacks on 11 September 2001, several letters from *Poetry* authors and readers reflect their shock and lingering dismay, and some writers give their accounts of the horrendous day and the immediate aftermath in New York City. Letters concerning Charles Wright's canceled

Poetry Day reading (scheduled for 13 September) tell of reactions in Chicago and elsewhere to the terrorism. In a happier context, on the eve of the ninetieth anniversary David Wagoner recalls curious episodes from his very brief stint as a reader at *Poetry* in the fifties, Michael Waters shares a story from Broadway with a cautionary message about the rewards of po-

Poetry March 1997 cover by Rockwell Kent.

etry, and Stephen Stepanchev relates a boyhood memory of a visit some seventy years earlier with Harriet Monroe.

Billy Collins to Joseph Parisi   *Somers, N.Y., 23 February 1997*

Dear Joe,

I was very happy to get the bright-looking March issue with that generous spread of my poems. And what a surprise to find that drawing of me on the cover!! The bird landing on my flute—I hardly have to say—was a special sensation. . . .

All best regards to you, Steve, Helen,

Billy

John Brehm to Joseph Parisi   *Brooklyn, N.Y., 3 March 1997*

Dear Joe,

Thanks again for publishing "Postcard from the Heartbreak Hotel" [February 1996]. I got some good responses. Billy Collins and I had a nice exchange about our poems in that issue, *The 1996 Anthology of American Poetry and Magazine of Verse* asked to reprint it, and Texas Tech University Press solicited my manuscript after seeing the poem. . . .

It was great being back at Cornell last Spring semester, especially seeing Archie [Ammons] again. I spent a good deal of time with him. One feels in the presence of genius, an effect which is heightened, and softened a bit, by his farmboy-who-stumbled-into-the-library persona. He's a remarkable character, as I'm sure you must know. Archie complaining about getting old and having to go to the dentist so often: "I used to hate it. Now I'd just as soon sit there as anywhere else." . . .

Hope you're well as always,

All best wishes, / John Brehm

Stuart Mitchner to Joseph Parisi   *Princeton, N.J., 16 April 1997*

Dear Joe Parisi—

I begin to think the poems I sent you back on Dec. 13 have fallen through the cracks or between the lines or maybe out into darkest cyberspace via your new computer system. . . .

Of course like thousands of writers all over the globe I wrote something for Ginsberg the day Ginsberg died [5 April]. Long ago when I worked at the Eighth Street Bookshop in New York, Ted Wilentz brought him upstairs to meet me (I was doing the accounts—it was always fun to send bills to E.E. Cummings!). I was somewhat embarrassed since my first novel had featured parodies of him under the name Alexander Grubb and Ted had showed it to him. Ginsberg was very gracious—if I remember right, he *liked* the parodies.

Best wishes, / Stuart Mitchner

Delisa Mulkey to Joseph Parisi   *Atlanta, Ga., 23 April 1997*

Dear Mr. Parisi:

Tuesday morning, while I was walking the dog, I suddenly noticed that my car was gone. The next few hours were spent trying to find out if it had been stolen from in front of my house or towed because someone in the Druid Hills Community Association was offended by a domestic automobile . . . [sic] It was towed, and the rest of the day was spent trying to get a release from the police station. At the risk of understatement, it was a bad day. But then I picked up the mail.

I've tried writing this letter many times now, but I can't seem to say how excited I am about being accepted into the pages of *Poetry* without sounding (as we say down here) like a doofus. But let me at least say that I sincerely appreciate the recognition and am still in a small state of shock over it (none of this, of course, has stopped me from telling everyone I know about it.) . . .

Anyway, I am returning the proofs and other contributor information and would finally like to thank you for making me, for the first time since high school, squeal with delight.

Sincerely, / Delisa Mulkey

David Bottoms to Joseph Parisi   *Atlanta, Ga., 3 May 1997*

Dear Joe,

I'm delighted that you will use "Bronchitis," "Occurrence in the Big Sky," and "Their Father's Tattoo" in *Poetry* [August 1997]. Will be great to be in your pages again and with some of my favorite poems of the last few years. . . .

Listen, I have a story to tell you. A week or so ago, I was teaching my graduate class in contemporary American poetry. We were heavy into Roethke's "North American Sequence" and about an hour into a 2-1/2 hour class. I'm trying to make some point about the spirit being dammed up or something, and I hear this sort of agitated rumbling and hissing over to my left. Well, I glance over there and this young woman sitting in the front row is turning red. I go on with my lecture then suddenly, in the middle of my sentence, this woman literally shouts out to the whole class, "I had two poems accepted at *Poetry!*" I usually ask my writing students at the beginning of the class if anyone has had any acceptances or rejections, and I'd forgotten that day. She'd held it in for as long as she could! So, when she let the info fly, I stopped class for a minute and went into a history of the magazine and all the folks who've published there. You wouldn't have believed her excitement! Her name is Delisa Mulkey, and she's a very talented young woman. Thanks for giving her some encouragement.

Hope all is well with you. Send word of yourself if you get a chance.

Yours, / David

Mulkey's "A History of Silk" was printed in July 1997 and "First Crush: Sixth-Period Greek Mythology" in February 1998. She also won a Ruth Lilly Poetry Fellowship in 1998.

Mary Oliver to Joseph Parisi   *Bennington, Vt., 5 May 1997*

Dear Joe,

Thank you for the invitation to submit work for consideration for the 85th! Anniversary issue. I enclose three poems, and hope I'm not too late, and of course hope you like something among them. I've been laggard—I very much like it here in Bennington (just finished teaching Poe!), am surrounded by bushels of prose (unfinished, alas!) as I'm going to write an introductory text on metrical poetry [*Rules for the Dance*, 1998]. Too many young readers don't know an iamb from a dirt bike though both make a certain noise. It is all fun. They have given us a house on campus, in an orchard, big enough and quite beautiful. All our books are still in the ocean house so we keep busy any extra time going around Vermont to buy new old ones.

Hope all is well with you, best wishes,

Mary

John F. Nims to Joseph Parisi   *Chicago, 10 June 1997*

Dear Joe,

Excuse me for bothering you once more about Mike L. Angelo. Would you rather consider some of his more famous love sonnets instead of the madrigals I sent before? I've just learned that these sonnets are available. Most are to (or for) Tomasso de Cavalieri. They don't need those footnotes.

Love poems from the early 16th century are terribly old-fashioned. Even though George Steiner did say, in a recent *New Yorker* essay, that Michelangelo's poems were remarkable for their "opaque magnificence." But these aren't opaque. . . .

Thank God I'm now translating my VERY LAST of Mike L.'s some 300 poems. No more translating ever, I hope.

All the best, or, as Dudley Fitts used to close with,

Tutti bestorum, / John

Nims's translation of *The Complete Poems of Michelangelo* was published in 1998. He died suddenly, of a heart attack, on 13 January 1999. A memorial service was held at the Newberry Library on 15 April; a fund was set up by Bonnie Nims and the former editor's friends to endow a prize at *Poetry* in his name.

Seamus Heaney to Joseph Parisi   *Dublin, Ireland, 13 June 1997*

Dear Joe,

Sorry to be so last-minute-y with this. I'm afraid I haven't that much to send and have been waiting to see if anything would come back from elsewhere or if something new might materialize . . . [sic]

What follows could be called a triptych or could be made into a diptych or cut down to a single shot—"A Suit," preferably. It's a playful dialogue with Yeats's "A Coat," although there's no reason for the reader to know that. The "tie" section is a bit of a sport, really, just trying to see how long one could run on two syllables, how far a single foot could go.

Anyhow, see what you think. And don't worry if it won't fit.

Seamus

Heaney's "Three-Piece" was printed in the eighty-fifth anniversary issue, October 1997.

Billy Collins to Joseph Parisi   *Somers, N.Y., 25 October 1997*

Dear Joe,

Thanks for taking "Taking Off Emily Dickinson's Clothes." I wasn't sure you would go for that one, but I'm really glad you did. How can you not like that title! And I don't mind getting the other poem back; it was definitely the "B" side of the submission.

I'm glad Rita Dove Day was a smash. But these blockbuster Poetry Days must be wearing on you. Next year, invite some old lady who lives in a trailer in Idaho. You would make her very happy, and there would only be an audience of 17 people to deal with. No? . . .

Congratulations on the monster 85 issue: a boatful of poets! When can we have our pasta?, our carpaccio?

Yours, / Billy

Attendance at Dove's 1997 Poetry Day reading rivaled that at Seamus Heaney's in 1996, and contributions at the benefit were the highest for any single event in the history of the magazine, more than $79,000.

Stephen T. Booker to Joseph Parisi   *Florida State Prison, Starke, Fla.,*
14 January 1998

Dear J.,

No news happening here, save for it only gets worse. —For my own personal (seemingly permanent) tour of Hell. I go back to court next month
for a new sentencing phase; and although over 20 years after the fact, the
state will be trying its best to get a new jury to recommend death again.

But of course I'm not down to blow your day apart with my madworld
news. Herewith is a piece—that I finally returned to while battling the flu
back in November—that I feel is right the way it's told me that it should
be. And, so, I gotta see if it passes muster with you (Poetry), etc. SASE here,
too. . . .

Will catch you on the rebound, which I hope matches what you've ac-
corded me in the past—like real soon, right—that I gotta appreciate.

Yours, / Stephen

Caroline Finkelstein to Billy Collins c/o Poetry   *Florence, Italy,*
26 January 1998

Dear Billy Collins—

I sure liked your poem "Taking Off Emily Dickinson's Clothes." It's nice
to laugh in American here in the palazzo. I'm looking forward to your
"Taking Off Jorie Graham's Clothes."

Best, / Caroline Finkelstein

Gary Soto to Joseph Parisi   *Berkeley, Calif., 1 April 1998*

Dear Joe:

I'm glad that you liked the poems I sent. . . .

Joe, these last years—since 1990—I have been torn from writing poetry
to writing prose and simple plays, a great hassle in my heart. First, I quit
teaching a couple of years ago and have had to carve out a living. Actually
I have been successful—some sort of book every season. But the drawback
is this: I tend to give my money away. I have established scholarships,
bought land for a park, started a serious collection of Chicano art,
recharged something I did back in the seventies called the Chicano Chap-
book series (we did six little books last year), and now sit on several boards,
which, as you know, demand money from their members. Who would have
guessed it? This tug-and-pull between poetry and other kinds of writing is
just that: a big tug in which my arms now drag on the ground. . . . I just
went down to Santa Ana where four high school students acted out two

scenes from a play of mine. I felt so good about their performances, flawed as they were, that I went out and bought each of them a pair of shoes. . . .

Otherwise, I'm just fine. My wife and I went to London to see some real plays, not this performance garbage, and we just loved it so much that we have decided to make it an annual trip—London for plays and pot pies.

Take care, / Gary

Aerick Johnson to the Editors   *Atlanta, Ga., 7 April 1998*

Dear Editors of *Poetry*,

This is a brief cover letter accompanying my submission to your magazine for the ninety-eighth year. I am submitting from Atlanta, Georgia, and in compliance with the stereotype of Southern writers, I cannot spell or punctuate, construct a complex sentence or—for that matter—a simple one, and unfortunately do not possess the innovative genius of Faulkner which would enable me to use these inhibitive qualities constructively. If this is not too discouraging I will be pleased if you continue.

As a minor personal note I have a few acceptances and a couple of works currently published in minor literary journals. . . . I will be continuing on academically in pursuit of a doctorate in English (where or how, as of yet, I do not know). I also have served in the military for a number of years, both active and reserve. . . .

Sincerely, / Aerick Johnson

Kenneth Koch to Joseph Parisi   *New York City, 21 April 1998*

Dear Joseph Parisi,

Thank you for printing The Seasons [April 1998] and for doing it so beautifully in the magazine. I've never been quite so happy with the way a poem of mine looked.

With best wishes, / Kenneth Koch

Stephen Young to Gil Kaufman   *Chicago, 13 May 1998*

Dear Mr. Kaufman:

I am a fan of Jewel's music, so naturally I was intrigued when my colleague Damian Rogers asked me to look over and comment on the sample poems you sent. After reading these routine, journal-entry expressions of adolescent angst and teen insecurity, I'm afraid I've concluded that enjoying the music is the *only* reason to take an interest in the poems. Like most efforts of their kind, these have a clumsy, but heartfelt, honesty, so it would be cruel to dismiss them entirely. Yet without the force of Jewel's singing voice, the sentiments offered here lose all of their immediate power. If I had to classify her, it would be as an exploited celebrity whose success in one medium automatically creates a market for any work they've done in another (and also, incidentally, for their autographs, possessions, personal effects, even their hair). Though they may make unique memorabilia, no self-respecting critic would argue that John Lennon's drawings have intrinsic value or that Jim Morrison's verses are important additions to the literary canon. Jewel's poems remind me of one reason that personal diaries are often sold with a lock and key.

I am sorry to be so negative. Luckily for the publisher, however, the quality of these poems won't be the sole determinant of how well they sell.

Yours sincerely, / Stephen Young

Philip Levine to Joseph Parisi   *Fresno, Calif., 17 June 1998*

Dear Joe,

The White House thing was better than I expected. I went during the Carter years & was one of the readers. The Carters were pleasant, but the occasion was more formal. And the food was mediocre. And no booze, only wine. And by 9:30 we were all out of the house. I found Bill rather amazing. A Snopes with city charms. . . .

Be well, / Phil

P.S. I'm so glad we gave the award [Lilly Prize] to Bill Matthews last year. Thank God he had a chance to spend some of it. He and Celia [Bellinger, his close friend] went to Europe last summer, Prague & Venice.

As one in a series of "Millennial Evenings," Mrs. Clinton and recent Poets Laureate organized a tribute to American poetry with a gala reading program and large reception at the White House on 22 April 1998. Concerning the poetry celebration at the Carter White House in January 1980, see Chapter VI, section 2.

Joseph Parisi to Philip Levine   *Chicago, 16 July 1998*

Dear Phil,

Many thanks for your letter and for letting us see the new poems. I'm sorry I wasn't on the premises when you called. . . .

It was great seeing you and Franny at the WH: a grand yet unstuffy occasion, and yes, the repast after the show far surpassed the rather puritan offering at the Carter reception. What impressed me was the informality: no lining up (and being pushed along) a receiving line, as with Jimmy and Roz. Quite something to see Bill and Hill just wander into the dining

At the White House reception honoring American poets, 22 April 1998:
(l. to r.) Anthony Hecht, Aviva Dove-Viebahn, J.P., and W. S. Merwin.

room and strike up casual conversations with people. As I was lingering, near the splendid buffet, WJC started to walk past, then saw me, stopped, came over, said hello and chatted—I mean really talked—for a good five minutes. How B & H manage not only to keep their focus but seem actually to be having fun, despite the endless slings and arrows, is cause for wonder. What *sang froid*; what intestinal fortitude. . . .

Ever, / Joe

Peter Heitkamp to the Editor   *Poultney, Vt., 23 February 1999*

Well, Gee Whiz:

I wrote apologizing for not being able to send any more than the sum necessary to renew my subscription, but I notice that in the current issue you continue to list me among associates. Now I feel real dumb, not to mention guilty. Since I would rather feel poor than dumb and guilty, I enclose a check for the amount of the additional contribution.

For the same amount, I could be feeding a child somewhere. This is a well-known problem in the philosophy of values. My current thinking is that by helping to support poetry, I am helping to enrich and strengthen the humanity of a large number of people, who will then be more willing to feed children. How's that for rationalization?

Sincerely, / Peter Heitkamp

Joseph Parisi to Peter Heitkamp   *Chicago, 3 March 1999*

Dear Mr. Heitkamp:

Thank you for your very gracious, and amusing, letter, and for sending the check for $45. Now, however, you've got *me* feeling guilty. I hate to think that this additional contribution might result in food being snatched from the mouths of babes.

To assuage our mutual guilty feelings, what say you to this proposal: suppose we send, in your name, a one-year, free subscription to the school of your choice? That way we can at least feed children's minds. If this seems meet and just, please let us know where the subscription should be mailed.

We appreciate your kindness, and the delicate (dare I say, almost Jesuitically exquisite?) reasoning your thoughtful missive conveys. I hope all continues well with you.

Faithfully, / Joe Parisi

A subscription was sent to the Middletown Springs Elementary School in Vermont.

Craig Arnold to Joseph Parisi   *Salt Lake City, Utah,*
20 March 1999

Dear Mr. Parisi,

It is with great pleasure that I inform you that my poems "Artichoke" and "Hot," which first appeared in the February and July 1997 issues of *Poetry*, respectively, will be featured in my new collection, *Shells*, to be published by Yale University Press this April as Vol. 93 of the Yale Series of Younger Poets. *Poetry*'s first publication of these poems has, of course, been prominently acknowledged in the book's credits.

I'd like to take the opportunity to thank you, again, for encouraging and supporting my writing at its crucial early stages.

Yours, / Craig Arnold

Gwendolyn Brooks to Poetry   *Chicago, May 1999*

[*Note written on bottom of solicitation letter, enclosed with renewal form and check*]
Hi—I think this 6 year subscription will take me to the end of my life. (I won't have to ask myself "Am I paid up? Am I NOT paid up?"

J.P. replied to Brooks on 9 June, and made the renewal a lifetime subscription; he also thanked her for sponsoring the George Kent Prize. Brooks died of cancer 3 December 2000, at age eighty-three.

M. Pat Cason to Joseph Parisi   *Vancouver, Wash., 10 July 1999*

Dear Mr. Parisi:

The review titled "Late Night Music," written by Bill Christophersen (which appeared in the May issue), embodied an attitude which I found bewildering and—what the heck—maybe even sexist.

Mr. Christophersen writes that William Matthews' poetry "although not confessional, was routinely autobiographical" but goes on to list poems based on the poet's several divorces, his father's death, and "personal poems" about adolescent crushes, adult loneliness, and his wife's cancer. He states that Matthews "bared his experiences and feelings" in his poetry.

Yet, this isn't "confessional" poetry?

It's hard for me to imagine why not, unless it's a matter of the poet's (and, perhaps, the reviewer's) gender which justifies the moniker of "autobiographical" (and therefore, presumably more seriously to be reckoned with) as opposed to "confessional."

Many women poets writing today are used to their poems of witness and personal experience—despite considerable craft—being marginalized, or dismissed out of hand, for possessing exactly these qualities that Mr. Christophersen so lauds in the work of William Matthews.

Sincerely, / M. Pat Cason

Joseph Parisi to M. Pat Cason   *Chicago, 11 August 1999*

Dear M. Pat Cason:

Thank you for your good letter of 10 July. . . . Your observations about the (putative) confessional/autobiographical distinction are most perceptive. While I hesitate to drag in the "sexist" label (it's become so overused and tiresome, don't you think?), I wonder if there isn't some gender basis where the line is drawn, as you suggest. But, more to the point, perhaps it's a matter of semantics, and misuse or misapplication of the word *confessional*.

That is, *confession* rightly means the admission of guilt or revelation of faults—one's own. But the bulk of the now four-decades' worth of so-called Confessional poetry (the term was first affixed, by the poet and critic M. L. Rosenthal, to Robert Lowell's *Life Studies*, of 1959) seems to shift the blame away from the speaker—usually to Mother, Father, ex-spouse, those cruel kids/teachers/priests/nuns/whatever the "I" endured in grammar school. Yes, these may be "poems of witness and personal experience," as you say, but their autobiographical content, far from individualizing the poems, often sounds generic, reductive, stereotypical, predictable—the very qualities poetry, it seems to me, might try to avoid. Thus, whether termed "autobiographical" or "confessional," such utterances have gotten a bad reputation—be the authors male or, as you rightly note, mainly female.

I didn't mean to begin a dissertation here, but I did want you to know I appreciate your letter and the thought and care that went into it. Hoping you wouldn't mind, I've taken the liberty of passing your missive on to Mr. Christophersen.

Sincerely, / Joseph Parisi

Peter Heitkamp to Joseph Parisi   *Poultney, Vt., 12 August 1999*

Dear Mr. Parisi:

You may not remember that it was through your generosity and the devious working of your tender conscience that a subscription was sent to the Middletown Springs Elementary School. Here is evidence of its reception. The evidence has a hole in it because it has been on my bulletin board for a long time, but now I am ready to pass it along to you.

I know most of these little guys, and I think it is really unlikely that they will enjoy this subscription or anything else that they have to sit still for.

Thank-you letter to Peter Heitkamp for a *Poetry* subscription, signed by students at the Middletown Springs Elementary School in Vermont.

However, there are older students in that school—not to mention teachers—who are not beyond redemption. They were busy sitting still somewhere else that day.

I, too, thank you for the subscription. . . .

Sincerely, / Peter Heitkamp

F. D. Reeve to Joseph Parisi   *e-mail, 13 August 1999*

Dear Joe,

My thanks for your note and the check. Aren't you speedy. Serving with you and Leslie [Ullman, on the jury for the Lilly Fellowships] was reward itself. So trebly rewarding was the discovery that John Woods's and David Bottoms's students have been 'round before, and that good poets are good teachers in seemingly out-of-the-way places, and their students come up with their own unconventional integrity. . . .

F. D. Reeve, a regular contributor
of verse and criticism,
in a snapshot from the nineties.

An unusual and thoughtful note came from Kevin Meaux, who spoke of his "too oddly religious" poems, which makes me all the more pleased that our final judgment was unanimous and quick. From my point of view, one can't be odd enough about one's religion. I think of Blake, of course. . . .

Meaux was a student at McNeese State University in Louisiana; Maudelle Driskell, the other winner, was a graduate student at Georgia State University in Atlanta. Morri Creech, who also studied at McNeese, and Delisa Mulkey, another GSU student, both received the fellowship in 1997. David Bottoms later told us Driskell and Mulkey were roommates.

Joe-Anne McLaughlin to Joseph Parisi   *Munnsville, N.Y.,*
                                                          18 August 1999

Dear Joe,

It has been a long time, and I am afraid I am again sending you a burdensome batch. These are all the new poems. . . . Sorry, too, that there are so many on dying and death, but they do seem to be piling up on the Other Side. The other day when Hayden was asked if he had heard so-and-so had died, he replied: "No. But I'm not surprised: people are dropping dead all the time." Typical Carruth. We had a small party for him on 3 August, his

78th birthday. If he makes it to eighty, we will rent a hall and have a grand celebration to which we will invite you and Helen and Stephen, even if you cannot use any of my poems.

Meanwhile we are in fine fettle, that is, when you consider all our foul, sybaritic habits. It is the clean-living ones who are dying. So you guys watch out!

Our best to you and your best

Ever, / J.

C. Dale Young to Joseph Parisi   *San Francisco, Calif.,*
                                                    23 August 1999

Dear Joe,

After a truly terrible day at the hospital, you put a grin on my face with your letter. I am so happy you liked "Sotto Voce" enough to take it for PO-ETRY [February 2000]. I have wanted to place a poem in your magazine for as long as I have been writing. I have been reading your magazine since I was 13 years old. Thankfully, I haven't been writing poetry since then; I was only an admirer and never dreamed, as a teenager, I would end up writing poems. . . .

Growing up, I always thought one only found poems in books and that only dead men wrote them. Your magazine was such an eye-opener for me. There were living poets, and they published in magazines. This no doubt sounds silly, but I was only 13. . . .

Faithfully, / C. Dale

Dean Shavit to Poetry *staff*   *Chicago, 23 September 1999*

Dear Joe, Steve, Damian, and Aaron,

I don't think I need to introduce myself. I'd just like to remind you that, with this submission, I'm entitled to one publication per the terms of your repeat submission program. Below, I've included a copy of my re-

POETRY

Repeat Submitter Membership Card
issued 8/4/89 to Dean Shavit
redeem after six submissions

peat submitter card. As you see, it says that six quality submissions are good for one publication. Well, this is it. I've carried this card in my wallet for ten years, and it is worn, chafed, barely legible, and has been washed by accident at least twice. I don't know if it could stand any more wear!

Sincerely, / Dean Shavit

B J Ward to Joseph Parisi and Stephen Young   *Washington, N.J.,*
                                                   15 October 1999

Dear Mr. Parisi and Mr. Young,

So much has happened to me since I was published in the February issue of *Poetry*. I have been offered readings I don't think I ever would have been considered for had it not been for my appearance in your fine journal. The local government's arts council asked me to organize and direct the Warren County Poetry Festival, which I did. It took place on September 18th and featured Stephen Dunn, Sharon Olds, and Gerald Stern. I was so honored to be introducing them to a large rural New Jersey audience, many members of which were from my hometown. You probably receive letters like this all the time, but I wanted to let you know the publication in *Poetry* lent credence to my work in ways I didn't expect, and has brought jobs my way—enough to keep my old Toyota maintained (219,000 miles). It really made a difference. Thank you. . . .

Take care, / B J Ward

Douglas Goetsch to Joseph Parisi   *New York City, 25 October 1999*

Dear Joseph Parisi:

Thank you for being so encouraging in response to my last few submissions. . . .

My first full-length book *Nobody's Hell* (1999, Hanging Loose Press) came out, as all books of poems do, to a rousing burst of silence, followed by longer, sustained silence. Lately I'm being published in *Prairie Schooner*, *Quarterly West* and *Puerto del Sol*. I've also been writing reviews of books by poets, which are getting accepted at an alarmingly higher rate than my poems, but you can change all that . . . [sic].

Thanks for your time.

Sincerely, / Doug

Goetsch appeared in *Poetry* in August 2000.

Robert Bly to Joseph Parisi   *Minneapolis, Minn., 26 November 1999*

Dear Joe,

Thank you for your good letter. . . .

I was invited to a strange literary event recently, a celebration for the 50th annual ceremony of the National Book Awards. There were a thousand people in the ballroom of the Marriott and each plate—except for those who had gotten the award once—cost $1,000. So money was floating around in the room knee-deep. I was sitting with William Meredith and Phil Levine and his wife. C. K. Williams was at a nearby table. He was one of those nominated in the poetry category, and we all wanted him to win.

A certain disappointment settled in early. I remember the days in the Fifties in which Wallace Stevens and Faulkner would get the awards. This time there didn't seem to be much mention of the word "excellence." The five-minute movie the National Book Foundation played about itself was basically about outreach (promising to use the money, I suppose). The MC for the night was Steve Martin. One feels a little tilt toward entertainment. They gave a 50th anniversary gold medal. They could have given it to Eudora Welty or Saul Bellow or Gwendolyn Brooks, but to my astonishment it went to Oprah Winfrey. So that's the sort of night it was. What's the point of a black tie if you're not honoring the great old writers?

The time came for the poetry award this year. Lucille Clifton got up—she was Chair of the committee—and announced that the prize was going to Ai. At our table there were lots of books slamming down and cries of "Wrong! Wrong!" But since there were a thousand people in the room, nobody noticed that. There it is. What can one do?

The passion for words will not go away.

Yours fondly, / Robert

Stephen Young to Allen K. Mears   *Chicago, 9 December 1999*

Dear Allen,

Of course there's a connection between Diane Thiel appearing here in 1999 and her winning the Tor House Prize in 1998: both are the result of her talent. Although it's impossible to ignore prizes and accomplishments completely, they carry no weight in editorial consideration at *Poetry*. If anything, I, as first reader, have higher standards for the highly-laurelled than I do for unheralded newcomers. Discovering a gifted writer is more exciting than affirming one. . . .

All best, / Steve

Joseph Parisi to Mary Oliver   *Chicago, 21 January 2000*

Dear Mary,

Thanks for letting us see the new batch, which I notice was sent the same day I sent my How I Spent My Vacation letter to you.

I've now read the poems, several times, with the greatest interest, as with all you do. Of the group, I particularly liked "Snake's Song" and "The Outcry." But, but . . . again, I found the rhetorical stance in both somewhat off-putting, or just off. "Snake's Song" has some truly wonderful lines, and individual perceptions here are truly arresting. But the anthropomorphic serpent (who, in addition to other human traits, it appears, acquired the sense of hearing) does not quite convince me, for all his beguiling charms. Also, it seems to me his singing goes on rather longer than necessary for conveying the burden of his song. . . . Again, maybe I'm just not the right reader for this sort of approach to nature. In "The Outcry," your use of "ferny bog" and "mossy log" cannot help but remind one of those "bosky dells" and the "finny prey" of a certain, long mercifully dead type of artificial verse. Surely, you don't want to resurrect it? And if you're mocking it, the tone just isn't right for this poem. Or (always a distinct possibility) maybe I just haven't got the point here?

I know you didn't ask for a critique, and certainly don't require my commentary. But I don't want to give the impression I'm rejecting these out of hand. It's just that the approach here, and in others of yours you've been kind enough to show us recently, seems overemotional and forced and at base false. Wouldn't it be more effective aesthetically, and more respectful and laudatory to these nature subjects themselves, to be truer to (and to trust) the "real" facts, and to submit your powerful attention to the complex details of their actual (un-human) existence?

Sorry to go on so. We do appreciate you giving us first look. I hope all continues well.

Ever, / Joe

Mary Oliver to Joseph Parisi   *Bennington, Vt., [February?] 2000*

Dear Joe,

What a good heart you have! I feel so bad giving you this kind of work—but I do want you to know that I appreciate it. I read your rejections . . . [sic] as if they were vitamin pills. Of course I want to send you something slippery and non-rhetorical, and I'll keep sending, though not overwhelming. I don't know what will happen, I do need a new voice because I'm not quick and slippery anymore, those 36-line silk ribbons belonged to another time. I know I can't give up the long lines, but I know too that isn't what you

Mary Oliver near her home in
Provincetown, Massachusetts.

mean. This is true, I think you have improved everything you've not taken, I do consider what you say, and often make changes. Well, we will see. . . .

I look forward to the history book—what a wonderful project!

I think I won't send you work so often as 4-5 times a year, I don't want a Nims brief back. . . . [sic] How sad he is gone, he was so fine and so generous, I am glad I met him anyway. . . .

Mary

Neal Bowers to Joseph Parisi   *Ames, Ia., 3 February 2000*

Dear Joe,

It was good to be in the pages of *Poetry* this month. As you know, there's nowhere else I would rather have my work appear.

Having said that, I wanted to let you know that I am killing the poet within me (or, at the very least, sending him into permanent exile). I can no longer endure being unable to find a publisher for my books. Over the years, two manuscripts have been lost in the dust of time; and I have two more on hand that have made the rounds sufficiently to indicate that no one is interested in them. Meanwhile, I see books almost daily that are inferior to my manuscripts. . . .

I can't be sure at the moment that I will ever write another poem. If I do, I am resolved never again to attempt to publish. Because you've been exceptionally kind to me over the years, I wanted you to know why I'm about to drop from view. I hope we can stay in touch by way of letters and maybe the occasional phone call.

There is no way I can possibly repay your kindness to me over the years, Joe. You can't imagine how many times you've kept me going by taking poems. God bless you, my friend.

Neal

John Brehm to Joseph Parisi   *Brooklyn, N.Y., 5 February 2000*

Dear Joseph Parisi,

Thanks again for publishing the group of four poems last August. One of them, "If Feeling Isn't In It," will appear in an anthology of poems about dogs, *Bark!*, coming out soon from a Little Brown imprint. . . .

Well, I'm officially a New Yorker now: I got mugged. I wasn't hurt—though I very easily might have been—but it's a miserable experience to go through, one that shatters whatever's left of your illusions about safety and solidity. Crime's way down in Manhattan—mainly because no one making less than $100,000 a year can afford to live there—but Brooklyn is still pretty dicey. Does this sort of thing happen much in Chicago?

I hope you're well. By the way, I absolutely loved the poem by Curt Anderson ["Platonic Love"] in the current issue. Hilarious and very smart.

All best wishes, / John Brehm

Davis McCombs to Poetry *staff*   *Mammoth Cave, Ky., 10 May 2000*

Dear Joe, Helen, Steve—

Warren James McCombs (7 lbs.) was born on April 18. He's a wonderful baby but as I told Carolyn last night, he's a little tyrant. How quickly he sized up the situation and subjugated all of us—even the cats.

Things with the book are going incredibly well. I've had big feature stories in both major KY papers and Publishers Weekly called me the best Yale selection in years.

Best— / Davis

McCombs joined *Poetry* as assistant editor in July 1995, after taking his M.F.A. at Virginia. His first book, *Ultima Thule*, won the 1999 Yale Younger Poet Award; it was also a finalist for the 2000 National Book Critics Circle Award.

Maxine Kumin to Joseph Parisi   *Warner, N.H., 30 May 2000*

Dear Joe:

I greatly enjoyed your long, newsy letter, especially the doings in Dear old England . . . I trust you are back from L.A. and perhaps by now you've read the naughty murder mystery [*Quit Monks or Die!*, 2000], as well as, I hope, the memoir [*In the Halo and Beyond: The Anatomy of a Recovery*, 2000]. . . .

The memoir, if you have not read it, was extracted from me by my generous daughter, who got me well started. Carol Smith at Norton flogged me into doing the rest. Every other day she e-mailed me to "make it more personal, make it more intimate, put dialogue in it." It's a book I'm glad to have behind me.

Meanwhile, it is supposed to be spring . . . So we are down to Victor's old lady brood mare, who was our first foal 24 years ago, and my Deuter, who didn't mean to but nearly killed me. We lost our old dog Rilke to acute kidney failure—the dog that Stanley Moss rescued on the West Side highway—and it was a very sad event. Two weeks ago we took in another waif, mostly because he came named Virgil, and he has been a challenge.

I'm afraid Victor has fallen in love with him as he did with Rilke, and so it goes.

Be well, dear Joe, with love

Maxine

In 1998 Kumin was seriously hurt in a riding accident, when her horse panicked and over-turned the carriage. Miraculously, Kumin survived after breaking two vertebrae in her neck (such injuries are usually fatal) but spent many months in rehabilitation, learning to walk again.

David Bottoms to Joseph Parisi   *Atlanta, Ga., 3 June 2000*

Dear Joe,

Sorry you couldn't make the Governor's shindig [inaugurating Bottoms as Poet Laureate of Georgia], but am sending you a party favor. The thing was actually quite high-toned. I must say things have changed in Georgia lately. In the entire capitol building, not one spittoon. Not that I could see, anyway. And Governor Barnes seemed like a genuinely swell guy. Was very generous to me and my family, and he had actually read my books. Go fig-ure. All of this honor stuff is quite nice. I'm suddenly a popular guy in the neighborhood, and people have stopped putting notes in my mailbox about mowing the lawn and weeding the flowerbeds. Now if I could only parlay this into a few more bucks from GSU. I'm about ready to give up the sec-ond job—picking up bottles on the side of the road is a lot harder than it looks. . . .

All best, / David

Philip Levine to Joseph Parisi   *Brooklyn, N.Y., 13 June 2000*

Dear Joe,

You had some great travels [to Cambridge and London] this past spring. I guess we both did. Years ago I read at Cambridge & before the reading had high tea in Milton's rooms. Tasted like tea, alas. I'd have preferred a whiskey & soda. A few days later had lunch at Christ's Church School—which is now in Devon—& one student was wearing Coleridge's old robes & another Hazlitt's. Walking history. . . .

Anything you choose for the *Poetry* anthology I can get for you very rea-sonably. . . . 90 years of *Poetry*! Amazing. I think I first published in the mag-azine 45 years ago. Rago had just taken over, the magazine was skinny & stapled together; it must have been going through hard times.

We go back to Fresno in a week. I'll be glad to escape the heat.

Be well, / Phil

Elise Partridge to Joseph Parisi　　　　*Blaine, Wash., 17 June 2000*

Dear Mr. Parisi,

I was almost the only person in the huge Blaine, Washington, post office the morning I retrieved an envelope with a Chicago postmark. I gasped so loud when I opened it that I startled the one other customer, a total stranger. "Good news!" I yipped, by way of explanation. After he offered his congratulations, I raced to a pay phone at the nearby Chevron station to tell my husband back in Vancouver.

I'm so happy I'll be included in such good company—past, present, and future. Each month I'm grateful for what I find in *Poetry*: you keep publishing poems by a range of writers, without, it seem to me, exclusionary concessions to fads or reputations. I'm also grateful to you for being encouraging these years I've been submitting—not to mention flabbergasted still to be seeing apologies for delays in your response to submissions!

All the best to you and to *Poetry*.

Elise Partridge

Philip Schultz to Joseph Parisi　　　　*East Hampton, N.Y.,*
27 August 2000

Dear Joe,

. . . It's been sixteen years between books and when I started to write again you were the first editor I sent my work to. I could not have been more vulnerable and your warm response was exactly what I needed. I don't know if I would've continued writing without encouragement. You not only published the poems, you gave me a prize. Howard Moss was a good friend and supporter but no one else has taken the interest in my work as you and *Poetry* magazine. . . . My struggle with confidence and faith wore me out and I finally gave up. Then you wrote asking for poems for your 75th anniversary issue and I refused but you insisted. Surely I had *some-thing*, how could I have not one little poem for godsakes! I was shamed into trying and wrote the only poems I wrote in over ten years and you took both (they're in the book, the one for John Cheever and The Answering Machine). I'm attempting to say no one else during these years insisted.

Now all this. All it means is that I've managed to finish a book and some people seem to like it. I'm not kidding myself. Many people will end up not liking it, but I'm writing again. The book [*The Holy Worm of Praise*] will be out in Spring 2002. I will acknowledge you and *Poetry* in the book, if you don't mind.

Cheers, / Phil

Philip Schultz to Joseph Parisi   *East Hampton, N.Y.,*
                                                  29 September 2000

Dear Joe,

God but am I learning about a realm of publishing I knew absolutely nothing about. When I was at Viking I learned my last book had been taken at a party. Someone who knew someone there congratulated me thinking I had to know already. My editor had taken the book before going to another house and no one bothered to notify me. My new editor made a lunch date with me but before we could meet she left to go back to graduate school in social work. This is God's truth: they finally found someone who wanted to 'do' poetry but he had a heart attack and took early retirement. At this point no one there was willing, or brave enough, to take me on and I didn't blame them. Finally, one sturdy soul agreed to edit my book because his assistant once had a class where I was offered in an anthology about manic depressives. I swear I am not nor have I ever been manic depressive and as far as I know I never appeared in any anthology but I didn't argue and both personages agreed to have lunch with me. No one died or suddenly left the room . . . my book was printed, though, oddly enough, it received no reviews. . . . I became depressed enough to consider submitting my work to a certain anthology. This lasted well over a year when one day I received a large manila (not vanilla, as you know, Joe, I can't spell) envelope filled with 32 mostly positive reviews! My editor, who'd gone off to become Stephen King's agent (which made perfect sense since I seemed to be living in one of his stories) simply forgot or neglected to send me my reviews and after he left someone emptied his bottom drawer. . . . [sic]

Now, Drenka Willen [longtime poetry editor at Harcourt] is a remarkable human being, a dream, actually. She's decided to bringing out the book next fall, along with a new collection by Charles Simic. And she wants to handle submitting the remaining poems and arranging readings, appearances, etc. . . .

It's sweet to realize that the first section of my book is almost completely comprised of poems you printed. I think from what I'm hearing it's that section that won such kind attention. Be well,

                                             All best to you, too, / Phil

Carl Dennis to Joseph Parisi   *Buffalo, N.Y., 1 November 2000*

Dear Joseph,

If you ever wonder if getting the Lilly Prize makes any difference in someone's career, I ought to tell you, in suggesting that it does, that I got a letter last week from one of the good grey eminences at Berkeley inviting me to apply for their post of senior poet. Even when I consider all my genius, I have to admit that such an event was not likely before the Prize fell upon me. I'm too old to pull up roots here, so I won't step forward, but the thought they wanted to consider me is quite flattering.

When I'm asked to read at Gore's inauguration, I will let you know. We will split the fee, as per agreement. The poem is ready. And my rejection letter, should Bush win and his handlers ask me, has already been roughed out. So once again I am a man of all seasons.

I hope you have something to be as thankful for on Thanksgiving as does
your grateful friend, / Carl

Dick Allen to Joseph Parisi   *Trumbull, Conn., 11 November 2000*

Dear Joe,

Well, by now I've waited long enough since your last letter to give you a breathing space. . . . I wanted to thank you for sending me the preview of Robert Shaw's essay, "Tragic Generations" [January 2000], about which you were absolutely right in my liking it. . . . Shaw writes, "It is always enticing (and certainly it is less work) to read a poem as if it were a diary entry" and I'm thinking of how I was educated in "The New Criticism" . . . to avoid the "biographical fallacy," the "intentional fallacy," the "affective fallacy," and even the "pathetic fallacy" at all costs. . . .

It seems to me now that many current poets are actually writing poems which depend upon critics committing the biographical fallacy in order to interpret them. Shaw's right in his seeing of how neither Lowell nor Berryman and certainly Bishop didn't expect or want their poems to be evaluated and interpreted almost solely as tethered to their lives. I remember John, at Brown (I was his teaching assistant for a while), insisting on "the deep image" as being the key to his own work. . . . How strange it is that critics like Richard Tillinghast are now having to "defend" Lowell, who had so unquestionably been the poet of his age. Perhaps when critics of the future return to matters of intricate and amazing style, Lowell and Berryman will be resurrected. . . .

The point is that Lowell and Berryman knew the madness and they stayed hunkered down sometimes for weeks beside the madness, watching it, and finally they trapped it in style. Stevens, too, trapped the madness. And Bishop. One's life does not have to be "mad" to do this. . . . Perhaps one of the sorrows of today's poets, re: what Shaw's working to describe, is that we are not suicidal, we live calmer and cranberry-filled lives, but the "public" still expects us to live suicidal lives, unsated yet as they are on such as Sylvia Plath. . . .

I think whoever are the best of us will bide their time and continue to write the best and most crafted poetry we know how—and then the future generations, wanting to know what it was like at this most pivotal of all times in history, with the Millennium and the computer revolution, will turn to our poems and see that we understood and recorded and threw some chains around our mall arcades and superhighway rushes and that our poems themselves were beautiful lives. . . .

Yours, / Dick

George Scarbrough to Joseph Parisi   *Oak Ridge, Tenn.,*
27 November 2000

Dear Joe:
I am delighted at the news of the award [Bess Hokin Prize, $500] and still too surprised to be wholly coherent. A POETRY AWARD WINNER. As much as I liked the three verses of my July publication, I did not allow myself to dream. . . .

The check is so welcome. It's a battle to keep my Blue Cross–Blue Shield health insurance. Only when I've accumulated enough for that and property taxes, not to mention fuel, can I rest easily and begin to consider writing a poem! So you can see how important being in the clear for another year can become.

Unfortunately, I was quite ill during Thanksgiving week. Sickern a dawg, in county patois. God, how the old bones ached. I'm feeling quite chipper this nauseating November morning, so think I'll clean the last leaves off the yard, among other little tasks I really like to do. . . .

With love, / George

Jimmy A. Lerner to Joseph Parisi   *Northern Nevada Correctional Center,*
Carson City, Nev.,
12 December 2000

Dear Mr. Parisi:
Enclosed, for your consideration, are four poems: Deconstructing Lot's Wife, At the Sushi Bar, But Hey—Thanks For The Manna and That Would Be Lenin, Rolling. . . .

Prior to becoming a (reluctant) guest of the Nevada State Prison System, I was a marketing analyst in San Francisco, a cabdriver in New York City and a soldier in Panama. I was born in Brooklyn, New York (circa 1951), received a B.A. from Chapman College and an M.B.A. from Golden Gate University in San Francisco.

When not evading shank thrusts in the chow hall or spurning the inappropriate advances of overly affectionate strangers, I write poetry and prose

in an 8 x 6 cell I share with Mongo (don't ask). My book-length collection
of poems, The Therapy Isn't Working, is now in search of a publisher.

Thank you for your consideration.

Sincerely,

Jimmy Lerner
Inmate #61634

Lerner worked as a self-described "corporate cubicle slave" (marketing director and strate-
gic planning manager for the Pacific Bell company) in San Francisco after obtaining his
M.B.A. Convicted of voluntary manslaughter in 1998, he was released on parole in early
2002. He described his prison experiences in *You Got Nothing Coming: Notes from a Prison
Fish* (2002); his collection of poems, available as an e-book, is titled *It's All Part of the Punishment* (2004).

John Brehm to Joseph Parisi   *26 February 2001*

[*Forwarded e-mail message*]

Subject: Very sad news: Archie Ammons Died This Morning

Archie was my teacher, too. He was an amazing poet and an amazing
man, generous with his time, his knowledge, his friendship. What struck
me most strongly about him was the way he combined a really odd and
original brilliance—and he could absolutely dazzle you with an offhand
remark—with a comic and unpretentious appreciation of himself and the
height to which he'd risen. He grew up on a farm in North Carolina during the Depression. And in his gait, his way of talking, his way of taking
the world, you never forgot that. I remember one time walking by the
graduate library at Cornell with him and Archie saying, mischievously,
"They oughta just shut that thing down and sell hot dogs out of it."

He was a great reader, of course, would quote Chaucer to you or Dante
or Wordsworth without warning. (And he could be acidic about famous
poets he didn't like. He'd read a passage from Stevens and point out all the
weak verbs, "*is, is, is, was, was, was*, like a bunch of fuckin' bees buzzin' around
in there.") But he always seemed connected to a world larger than academia. "The problem with academia," he once told me, "is that everyone is
always explaining things. Nothing is allowed to go uninterpreted. Nothing
is allowed to remain mysterious. There's always this filmy gauze of words
between you and the rest of the world." But he loved Cornell and he was,
I'm sure, the most beloved teacher on that campus. I could go on and on.
There's no poet I would have rather known and learned from than Archie.
We're all lucky, I think, that he left us so much.

This message is one of several reminiscences and discussions circulated among former students and friends of Ammons through a poetry list-serve.

Joseph Parisi to Phyllis Ammons   *Chicago, 5 March 2001*

Dear Phyllis,

Like everyone who had the privilege of knowing him and who love him and his work, we were very shocked and saddened to learn of Archie's death.

Alice Fulton called me in tears shortly after she got the news, and we talked a good long time about what a remarkable man he was, and about what his work and his general attitude toward the world meant for us. I treasure the times, all too brief, that I was able to have with him.

What he gave us in his thoughts and poems have had and will always have an immeasurable impact on our lives. He truly was an inspiration, in every aspect of his life—his generosity of spirit, his intellectual brilliance, above all his warmth and humanity.

Stephen and Helen join me in sending our deepest condolences.

With love, / Joe

Billy Collins to Joseph Parisi   *Somers, N.Y., 13 June 2001*

Dear Joe,

Thanks for your recent happy phone message expressing czarist approval of the work I sent.

I also want to add my voice to the chorus of congratulations (not com-miserations) on your long and distinguished editorship of *Poetry*. Diane and I would have given serious thought to coming to the celebration, were I not getting back from Ireland the night before. However, we will periodically raise wine glasses to you hoping to create no discernible pattern.

From my own selfish perspective, you were the first editor of a first rate magazine to recognize my work, and there is no other editor with whom I can imagine enjoying such a long, amiable, and (*Write* it!) loving relationship.

Bravo, Giuseppe!!!

Billy

Collins had been invited to a party celebrating J.P.'s twenty-fifth anniversary at *Poetry*.

Billy Collins to Joseph Parisi   *Somers, N.Y., 20 June 2001*

Dear Joe,

So glad to be able to share such heady news with you [his selection as U.S. Poet Laureate]. I know the news will delight my real friends and fill the rest with teeth-grinding resentment.

Thanks again for taking the new poems. I sent you two more a few days later just to give you a wider selection. Please don't hesitate to pass on them since you are now holding four.

Trying to get as much paperwork done today as possible as by Friday the phone (and I) will explode.

Fond regards as always.

Billy

Phyllis Ammons to Joseph Parisi   *Ithaca, N.Y., 2 August 2001*

Dear Joe,

How could I not have answered the beautiful letter you wrote me in early March.

As I read it, I am moved almost to tears for your eloquence and for your generosity in sharing with me your thoughts and feelings about Archie.

Archie and I both had such good times with you and *Poetry* and I remember so fondly the walk from our hotel in Chicago to your office and the hospitality and friendship of everyone there.

Please give my regards to Stephen and Helen. And thank you for your call, Joe.

With love, / Phyllis

Turner Cassity to Joseph Parisi   *Decatur, Ga., 20 August 2001*

Dear Joe,

I decided to devote my tax refund to *Poetry* instead of riotous living, for which I am, in any event, too old. I hope others will do the same. Maybe you could make a pitch on your website.

I had a letter from Ohio Univ. Press / Swallow Press asking if I had enough new poems for another volume. Little do they know. So, I have signed a contract for a book of plus-or-minus 45 poems, to appear c. January 2003.

Meanwhile, I may make a nice long visit to Mississippi to watch the vultures gather around the literary remains of Eudora Welty.

Prosperity to *Poetry*, / Turner

Joseph Parisi to Turner Cassity   *Chicago, 11 September 2001*

Dear Turner,

I was so pleased to get your letter—and not just for the incredibly generous contribution enclosed—though we didn't mind receiving that, either. It's terribly kind of you, and we do appreciate it.

It was very good news indeed to learn that you'll have a new volume out. I trust we'll see galleys in due course? Steve and I have been spending every "spare" moment trying to get our own book completed. Finished the first draft of the POETRY history a couple of weeks ago. . . .

Meanwhile, it's been pretty hectic here this summer: we've been pretty well overwhelmed, with more mss. than ever—I guess poets *never* take a vacation—the Lilly Fellowships, Poetry Day prep (Charles Wright will be here on Thursday). . . . It never ends.

But maybe it does. Just heard a news flash about the World Trade Center attacks. Christ, what next? . . .

Joseph Parisi to Charles Wright   *Chicago, 13 September 2001*

Charles Wright first contributed to
Poetry in 1969 and received the
Lilly Prize in 1993.

Dear Charles,

Just a brief note, to thank you again for being *willing* to read for us at Poetry Day. We tried to get the word out about the cancellation through the papers and the radio and TV stations, with some success. The Cultural Center, where you'd have appeared, has cancelled all programs for the week. And I note there are still no planes overhead in Chicago. . . .

Lots of calls today, very kind and understanding, though disappointed. We've been assuring people that we'll try to get you here another time. Almost no one has asked for a refund, by the way, and several people asked to turn tickets into donations or subscriptions. Thought you'd like to see the nice publicity in the *Reader*, just out this a.m. They ran the big picture of their own accord.

So, *caro*, we really miss seeing you and hearing you, but *domani* [tomorrow] is another day. I hope Luke [son] got home safe and sound. Please give my best to Holly, and accept a big hug from

Yours affectionately, / Joe

F. D. Reeve to Joseph Parisi　　　　　*Wilmington, Vt., 16 September 2001*

Dear Joe,

Not only were you good to write at length but to write at all. . . . I hope Charles Wright did get in, and it surely was hairy, and I hope that the day was good despite the very depressed national mood. . . . As you said, poetry best of all can handle this terrible time. . . .

New York is coming out from under the 600,000 tons of broken glass. It's a great city, natch, and will go on. But all the proposals about biometrics and facial surveying and credit card patterning, plus the threat to bomb somebody—anybody?—soon are truly worrisome. How the "war on drugs" swelled the prisons; what will a "war on terrorism" do?

Thanks again for your thoughtful reading and writing. Hi to Steve.

　　　　　　　　　　　　　　　　　　　　　　　　　　　　　Frank

Joseph Parisi to Maxine Kumin　　　　　*Chicago, 28 September 2001*

Dear Maxine,

Many thanks for your lovely missive. . . .

Like everyone else, we've been in a state of depression since the events of September 11th. Only now getting somewhat back to "normal"— though I don't think that condition will ever truly return. I do hope that no one close to you was directly affected. My sister in Switzerland—which is not noted for the warmth and outgoing nature of its citizens—tells me that when she's walking about Basel, if people hear American/English spoken, they come up to say hello, offer condolences, etc. They had a big memorial service, three minutes of silence, bells tolling. Even the French have suddenly discovered a sense of solidarity.

Poetry Day was scheduled for 13 Sept., but of course we had to cancel— first time in 47 years. After the initial sense of disbelief and outrage, we wanted to go forward with the program, feeling that we didn't want to allow the terrorists still more power in disrupting life in a civilized society. And if ever there were a time when poetry was needed, this was it. But it was impossible. Charles Wright was coming in from Dulles, which was shut down like O'Hare. For over a week the skies were clear over Chicago, a rather strange phenomenon and something probably not seen since before WWII.

It's been pretty grim listening to the politicians, TV loudmouths, and saber-rattlers bloviating and revving up the propaganda mills. I fear that the Congress will lurch forward into hastily-conceived legislation that will not really do much to deter terrorism (our guardians at the CIA and FBI don't inspire confidence, as it is), but will further impinge on our civil liberties. All the war talk and metaphors seem severely misplaced, and the grotesque rhetoric is getting alarming. Falwell and Robertson, our own ayatollahs, carrying on about the "will of God"—that's rich. And then, "W" referring to a "crusade"—that should cool things down in the Middle East.

Didn't mean to rant and ramble on. But I did want you to know how good it was to get your letter. I hope all is well with you and yours. This week we're finally getting serious intimations of fall. Mother tells me she has been harvesting the last of the tomatoes, squash, basil, and has been confecting apple sauce and apple pies and apple turnovers and for all I know applejack.

Love, / Joe

Bill Christophersen to Joseph Parisi   *New York City, 1 October 2001*

Dear Mr. Parisi,

Thanks for the acceptance note, and for your kind and very welcome words. Well reasoned and direct—that's, of course, the way I'd like my work to be perceived. . . .

New York is still a nervous and grieving city. A student of mine came down from the 92nd Floor [of a World Trade Center tower]—but hasn't yet returned to class. A friend lived across the street [from the site]. Her building is still uninhabitable. Two days after the event, I was working in the Time-Life Building, and the place was evacuated over a bomb scare. Usually in midtown offices, whole departments will blithely ignore fire alarms and flashing lights. On that day, all it took was one person announcing "They're evacuating the building" and the place emptied in a heartbeat. The thirty stories' descent didn't feel like much at the time. For the following two or three days, my legs were aching and rubbery. What does 92 floors feel like? And of course the physical aspect is the least of it.

I went down to lower Manhattan the other day to—what? look? be humbled? As soon as the subway doors opened at the Brooklyn Bridge [station], there was the smell of smoke. There's a dense, bristling mountain of rubble still smoldering almost three weeks after the collapse. It's maybe eight or ten stories high. City workers a half mile away are all in face masks. In the plexiglass of a bus shelter a few miles uptown are thirty or forty flyers with various people's photos and descriptions and the names of the outfits they worked for and what floor. "Have you seen so-and-so?" Lampposts, walls of building—all full of these Xeroxed search notices cum obits. You can't pass without reading a couple. And each time you do, you fall apart.

Bill Christophersen

Albert Goldbarth to Joseph Parisi   *Wichita, Kans., 12 October 2001*

Dear Joe:

I've come to be bizarrely fascinated by a note you sent me last month, and I enclose a Xerox of it—for your own bizarre fascination, I suppose. In it, you thank me for a chapbook I sent your way, you indicate *Poetry*'s willingness to see new work of mine, etc. etc.—all the usual stuff of a friendly note, except that this one is dated September 10, just twenty-four hours before the world turned mad. Especially ironic is your predication that after the Charles Wright Poetry Day reading "We shall have some semblance of normalcy"—as if any of us will ever have that again. . . .

Submitting one's work for consideration seems some days like a very small, very tangential, human activity. . . .

Hope you're doing well in the midst of all of the craziness. The Vendler consideration of Archie [in the October 2001 issue] was a lovely bit of critical assessment.

Best wishes, / Albert

Dick Allen to Joseph Parisi   *Trumbull, Conn., 1 November 2001*

Dear Joe,

As I forewarned you, I'm sending you new poems a little sooner than usual. . . . But I couldn't resist showing you these. I'd just about completed them before 9/11 and then I couldn't work on anything for over a month. . . .

We all have our 9/11 stories. Lori and I stopped for road construction at Wolf Pass in Colorado's San Luis Mountains, on the way to Durango, when a weeping Mexican-American worker leaned into our car window and told us. We panicked for about two hours, for we were too deep in the mountains for the radio to work, didn't know any real details, and our son always goes into New York on Tuesday mornings. We later learned that they'd canceled his train a half an hour before he would have gone in. If he'd been there, he might have rushed to give aid (he's a Methodist minister) before the collapse. . . . [sic] At U.B. [University of Bridgeport], we lost one graduate student and one of our Business School professors lost two of his sons.

Nothing's the same. I think the most usual reaction might be how we get up feeling right and then in about five or ten minutes we remember 9/11 and it's surrealistic again—as it must in all wars that are at home or touch home this directly. . . .

All my very best to you and yours.

Dick

Stuart Mitchner to Joseph Parisi   *Princeton, N.J.,*
                                                  13 November 2001

Dear Mr. Parisi:

Reading the *Times* last week I was pleased to see you standing up for the principle of unsolicited submissions vs. the anthrax factor. My first unsolicited submission of poetry was the one I sent you some years ago, from which you took five poems, so I have good reason to appreciate your faithfulness to the principle. It's been over a year since I sent you anything; my last poem in *Poetry* was in the May 1999 issue. The poetry I'm enclosing is post–Sept. 11 and it's about my favorite subject, New York, NY.

I'm half-seriously considering sending this from Pennsylvania. Do I dare risk the stigma of a New Jersey postmark?

Best wishes, / Stuart Mitchner

In "We Regret We Are Unable to Open Unsolicited Mail," by Celestine Bohlen, *New York Times*, 8 November 2001, the editors were quoted as saying they were continuing to open envelopes from unknown senders and read their poems, despite the recent deaths from poisoned letters.

David Wagoner, with his wife Robin Seyfried and daughter Alexandra, following the Lilly Prize ceremony in 1991.

David Wagoner to Joseph Parisi   *Seattle, Wash., 16 April 2002*

Dear Joe:

You said I might send some poems for the special edition. Here are four new ones.

Thanks for all the news. I didn't know you were working on a history of *Poetry*. Does it include Oscar Williams chasing Ellen Borden Stevenson through the old office building?

Poetry Northwest may die this spring. I'll know soon.

Cheers, / David

David Wagoner to Joseph Parisi   *Seattle, Wash., [late June] 2002*

Dear Joe:

I'm glad you like the two new poems. As for the Anthology, I have no preferences. Do whatever you want to.

I only heard about Oscar and Ellen through gossip, some of it from Karl Shapiro, and I'm sure it was slanderous exaggeration. Why does nearly everyone use "weasel" when talking about Oscar? Dylan Thomas also did. In the White Horse Tavern one night, he said, "I can't fart without having Oscar Williams come running with a roll of toilet paper."

My favorite spot in the "new" office building of POETRY was the bar in the basement where I sat in on Nelson Algren's poker game in the side room several times. After dignified poetry readings upstairs, some of the literary crowd would drink down there, and Nelson would come slouching out of the card room now and then in a sweaty undershirt to get another highball.

I volunteered to be first reader one time (it must have been the summer of 1954, just before I headed for the U. of Washington), and Karl gleefully handed over a large box of submissions from which I recommended one poem, and he printed it. All I remember is it was about a crematorium and began "Stand to windward of that fire . . . ." So I was once an editor of PO-ETRY for one poem.

Good luck with your multiple projects.

David

Wagoner enclosed a notice that, after forty-three years, *Poetry Northwest* would close with the Spring 2002 issue; he had edited it since 1966. Ellen Borden Stevenson gave the magazine office space in the old Borden family mansion on Lake Shore Drive, which she turned into the 1020 Art Center. She was president of the board in 1953, until a falling out about money resulted in her resigning and asking that *Poetry* vacate her premises. (See Chapter II and *Dear Editor*, Chapter XVII.) When they were packing up to leave, the staff discovered that someone had bored holes in the walls to keep an eye on them.

Michael Waters to Joseph Parisi   *Salisbury, Md., 22 August 2002*

Dear Joseph Parisi:

Please be kind enough to consider these three new poems . . .

Here's a story: last month I attended a performance of "Private Lives" on Broadway and wound up in Alan Rickman's dressing room. (My wife met him in Romania . . .) Also there was a very dapper old guy right out of [Woody Allen's film] *Broadway Danny Rose*, resplendent in a peach suit, show biz to the bone. When Rickman suggested I try screenplays, I joked that I wouldn't know what to do if I started making money from my writing. The old guy asked what I wrote. "Terrific poems," Rickman told him. "Well, I write lousy poems," he announced, "and make a bundle of money. Maybe you know this one," and he began to sing, "When I was seventeen, it was a very good year . . . ."

He turned out to be Ervin Drake, b. 1919, and he also wrote "I Believe" ("I believe for every drop of rain that falls, a flower grooooows!") which has sold more than 20 million copies. He owns a house in Great Neck and a building in Manhattan.

I hope that you find something in this batch worth keeping, and that you send me a bundle of money.

Best regards, / Michael Waters

Joseph Parisi to David Wagoner   *Chicago, 28 August 2002*

Dear David,

Many thanks for your very nice letter, and for giving us carte blanche with your poems for the Anthology. I wish we could have run more: did you know you have printed over 170 poems here over the years? . . .

I had no idea you had been a first reader for *Poetry*. What a madhouse 1020 LSD was. . . . Nelson Algren twitted [Ellen Stevenson] by pinning on her bosom a "Vote for Adlai" button. As you probably know, *Poetry* was thrown out of the mansion. . . .

All best, / Joe

[P.S.] Really distressed that *PNW* is closing. But you've had a very great run. (I suspect you won't miss reading the submissions, though.)

Stephen Stepanchev to Joseph Parisi   *Flushing, N.Y., 7 October 2002*

Dear Joe,

A memory stirred. Your recent work on the past of *Poetry* did it.

I went to elementary school and high school in Chicago, on the near north side (I lived on Clybourn Avenue). My high school was the Robert

A. Waller High School. I was on the staff of the school paper, *Yellow and Blue*. I learned to set type and write articles. This was in 1931. I offered to do a piece about *Poetry*, and I was told to go ahead. I went to the office of the magazine at 232 East Erie Street and met Harriet Monroe and her associate, Morton D. Zabel. She was a small woman with dark, piercing eyes and a reassuring manner. We talked about Hart Crane, and I confessed that I found reading him difficult. Miss Monroe said, turning to Mr. Zabel, "A boy his age would find him difficult, wouldn't he?!" And Zabel said, "Read him slowly, a little at a time." Then we turned to the submissions Miss Monroe was receiving in the mail. "Do you find the manuscripts interesting?" I asked. She got up and found a batch of newly arrived poems and gave them to me to read. I read them and said, "These poets should look more closely at the objects they are describing." And she said, "Well, I wish you would tell them that." I left soon after that and wrote up the interview and it was published in *Yellow and Blue*. That was my first and only meeting with the woman who founded *Poetry*. I corresponded with her after that, and she accepted two of my poems before she died in 1936. Zabel accepted two more, and so four of my poems appeared in the February, 1937, issue of the magazine.

Affectionately, / Stephen

CHAPTER XII

The Aftermath:
Well-Wishing and Other Reactions

1. Breaking the News

Reflecting on the long-term impact of Ruth Lilly's gift, Billy Collins was quoted as saying on the evening of the announcement that he was certain when the news broke it would "draw a lot of good attention to the magazine and poetry itself." For weeks after the first *Chicago Tribune* story on 17 November 2002, journalists and broadcasters continued to call demanding further details, still more interviews, the staff's response to various news stories and editorials, and information about our future plans. Meanwhile, business of all kinds increased and mail sacks grew heavier with congratulations, submissions, subscriptions, and especially solicitations and requests for aid. Eventually stretching into three months and more, the media attention and attendant distractions went far beyond anything we had imagined—and dreaded.

Almost as amazing as the reactions to the bequest, however, was the fact that we had managed to keep the gift a secret for over a year. Word of the startling reversal in *Poetry*'s fortunes had first arrived thirteen months earlier. After a week exchanging voice-mail messages, I received a call one Friday evening in late October 2001 from an attorney named David Baker, who said he was with the Chicago firm of McDermott Will & Emery. He suggested I sit down before he gave me some news that would affect *Poetry* magazine. Then he came straight to the point and informed me that he was in charge of restructuring our friend Ruth Lilly's estate, and we were among the major beneficiaries.

Baker explained a few aspects of the complex plan he was now in the final stages of developing, and noted that the bequest would begin during Mrs. Lilly's lifetime and perhaps as soon as a year. Under its several provisions, he said *Poetry* would eventually receive no less than $100 million and probably $150 million, perhaps more—so many factors were involved it was impossible to tell precisely—but the bequest would be distributed through various trusts over the next twenty to thirty years. I asked him if perhaps he had misplaced a decimal point. He gave me to understand that he had not. He advised retaining a lawyer and said he would call again the following week to set up an appointment to go over the plan in detail. Sometime after we hung up, I found myself still staring at the receiver.

Letting these facts sink in a few minutes more, I brewed a pot of coffee and began calling key board members. Gasps and moments of silence were the first responses to my story. After assurances that, no, I was not joking, I suggested we follow David Baker's advice and engage our own expert in trusts who could review the plan and provide counsel. At our first meeting with the estate lawyers two weeks later, we encountered several impressive piles of documents, each a foot or more high. Certain hefty folders disgorged spread sheets whose accordion pleats opened to stretch three and four feet down the huge granite conference table, laying out dense columns of figures calculated using many sets of variables.

There would be many more meetings with and among attorneys over the next two months before final versions of these thick stacks of Lilly estate papers were approved in Probate Court in Indianapolis—after a day-long hearing involving David Baker, four sets of lawyers representing interested parties, and our single attorney, Richard Campbell—four days before Christmas. Although the plan was finalized in late January 2002, it would be another year before the first installment of the scheduled payments was received.

When I first conveyed the news, I also recommended that word of the bequest be allowed to go no farther than the board and the staff. The last thing we needed at that point was publicity. We would have more than enough work, and headaches, in the coming months without having to contend with intrusive reporters as well. Everyone agreed that the news should be kept confidential as long as possible, or at least until the right moment presented itself. The next year's ninetieth-anniversary celebration seemed a singularly appropriate occasion at which to make the announcement.

Unfortunately, and probably inevitably given the number of people now in the know, word eventually leaked out. In mid-March 2002, I received a call from James Warren, an editor at the *Chicago Tribune*, who asked if what he had heard about a large donation to *Poetry* was true. (He did not reveal how or from whom he obtained the information, and we never did learn the source.) I did not deny the fact, and we set a date to discuss the matter. Over lunch I confirmed what details he knew, corrected some misconceptions, and gave him further background information. Then I asked, or rather entreated, him to keep our secret. It was a very great favor to ask a reporter to hold back such a major scoop, I conceded, but if he would not release the news until after we made the formal announcement at the

Poetry staff at the Newberry Library office, early 2003:
(l. to r.) editor-executive director Joseph Parisi, subscription manager
Martin Duffy, business manager Helen Klaviter, assistant Fred Sasaki,
clerk Adrian Lucia, and senior editor Stephen Young.

ninetieth-anniversary gala in November, we in turn could promise him our
cooperation and the *Tribune* an exclusive on the story. To my surprise and
relief, he accepted the offer.

No other journalists got wind of the windfall, and so we were undis-
tracted over the following months of intense activity. There was no time to
spare. Phones were seldom idle, and more and more business meetings began to fill the calendar: many conferences with attorneys in various legal
specialties, interviews with prospective financial advisers and potential
money managers, and private consultations with several others for practical
advice. Meanwhile, besides keeping up with editorial work—reading thousands of submissions, producing the regular monthly issues, and compiling
a special triple-size ninetieth-anniversary number—Stephen Young and I
were completing last details on the *Dear Editor* history and had begun
choosing poems for *The POETRY Anthology 1912–2002*, the manuscript of
which had to be delivered by early July if the collection was to come off
press in time for the birthday festivities. At the same time we needed to
complete preparations for the two-day gala in Chicago as well for four
other celebrations scheduled around the country.

James Warren did not contact me again about his *Tribune* article until
late October. Since he and I had last spoken in March, preliminary plans
for management of the bequest had been forming, slowly. A revised char-
ter for the magazine's parent, the Modern Poetry Association, had to be
drafted for submission to the State of Illinois, to restructure the charita-

Ninetieth Anniversary banners along Michigan Avenue, October 2002.

ble organization as a private operating foundation. (Because almost all funding would now be coming from one source, the change was required under IRS regulations.) I recommended it be called, simply, The Poetry Foundation, conveying both the magazine's name and the field in general. (One trustee wanted "Modern" inserted, until it was pointed out that the term had a specific meaning in literary history, too limited for the scope of the new organization. The definite article, and no adjective, completed the name: for, surely, there could be no other such foundation.) Paper-work was submitted to the U.S. Trademark and Patent Office to make it official.

As executive director I also drew up and presented to the board detailed outlines and arguments for a number of new public programs, publishing ventures, and educational projects our soon-to-be foundation might undertake. During the hectic summer the books were finished, and arrangements were completed for the several birthday events around the country: Santa Fe in October, Chicago in November, New York City in December, Los Angeles in February 2003, and Atlanta in March. By early October invitations to the Chicago celebration were in the mail, *Dear Editor* and *The* POETRY *Anthology* were in bookstores, and the special ninetieth-anniversary issue was on newsstands and in the hands of subscribers.

Large blue-and-white banners heralding *Poetry*'s historic occasion and featuring portraits of its most famous poets fluttered from lampposts along North Michigan Avenue as I walked over to the Tribune Tower to meet again with Jim Warren. At lunch we discussed the latest developments and further information for his story. He later made follow-up phone calls, but did not visit our office, to check facts. The *Tribune* sent a photographer over a few days later. While he took pictures of the staff in our cramped two-room quarters on level 2A of the Newberry's stack building, radio station WBEZ, as if on cue, began to air an interview about *Poetry*'s anniversary we had taped earlier in the week.

2. Kudos and Criticism

After the front-page story in the *Tribune* on 17 November came the deluge of early reports in the media, followed by a second wave of commentaries and accounts from many perspectives. Over the next weeks, various news articles outlined the extent of Ruth Lilly's largesse. Under the title "Heiress Plans Charity Spree," the *Indianapolis Business Journal*, in its 25 November–1 December 2002 issue, surveyed court papers and summarized Mrs. Lilly's longtime philanthropy, and found that in Indianapolis alone she had contributed "more than $125 million to a wide range of causes, many related to education, medicine and the arts." The reporter was at pains to show that a large proportion of Mrs. Lilly's estimated one-billion-dollar estate would continue to support local charities. Besides the gift to "the perennially penniless magazine *Poetry*," he noted, her new estate plan would provide the Lilly Endowment, founded by her family and based in Indianapolis, with $100 million or more. Eventually a Ruth Lilly Philanthropic Foundation, to be set up after her death and funded with an endowment of $200 million, would "concentrate its giving in Indiana."

Most of the vast commentary across the country was positive, even glowing. The great majority of ordinary citizens seemed happy to celebrate *Poetry*'s great good luck, and the dozens of letters we received from regular readers of the magazine all conveyed unalloyed pleasure, as the small selection below indicates. But among such an enormous number of reader responses, newspaper columns, magazine essays, and web articles, there were bound to be negative opinions and reservations voiced. Perhaps not surprisingly, various poets and literary editors expressed the most ambivalence and grave misgivings. The self-described "opinionated" literary Web log *The Literary Saloon* wondered on 20 November if such a large amount of money at one little magazine, "certainly prestigious and esteemed" though it was, might not have a "distorting effect" on the literary marketplace: "No one in

S.Y. and J.P., under the original *Poetry* sign, the day before the
Ninetieth Anniversary celebrations, 14 November 2002,
printed with the *Chicago Tribune* article on the Lilly request.

the poetry business can compete with this—no publishers, no other organizations, nobody." Even so, the writer admitted it was "hard to begrudge the people at *Poetry* the money," and concluded: "It's been a worthwhile magazine for many of its nine decades; one hopes the money doesn't ruin it."

In his *New York Times* "Making Books" column for November 21, Martin Arnold noted that poets were "a quirky lot" who considered "connecting money to poetry was somehow unpoetic." Arnold printed a range of responses elicited from poets often printed in *Poetry*, among them Alice Fulton, who said she was "almost scared" when she learned of the donation, since she "had come to believe that marginalization let poetry do what it wants to do." Reconsidering the matter, she thought the money might make poetry seem "a positive thing to people" and empower writers. Rita Dove explained it was "a myth that if one receives money for writing, it's corrupting"—a myth writers "have consoled themselves with." She added, "I can't think of anyone more deserving of money than Poetry magazine, which has remained refreshingly honest over the years, hasn't gone for trends." Arnold cited poetry editors at major New York publishing houses who felt the bequest would draw more media attention, and "more review attention," and thus "help create a larger readership." But John Ashbery doubted "all that money was going to turn America into a country of passionate poetry readers."

More negative stories emerged on both coasts. "In a world of poets, not readers," the second article about the bequest to be published in the *Los Angeles Times*, on November 23, Media columnist Tim Rutten traced *Poetry*'s illustrious history, praised its recent special issues, and concluded that the magazine's "high standards" "probably made it a good choice to become the Getty [Museum] of little magazines." But he hastened to point out the vast discrepancy between the size of the general population and the number of poetry readers. (*Poetry*'s circulation was small, but the magazine still sold over ten times the thousand-copy average of the seventeen hundred U.S. publications that print poetry, he reported, using figures from the Academy of American Poets.) Rutten also mentioned the often-cited laments about the shrinking poetry audience, Joseph Epstein's "Who Killed Poetry" (1988) and Dana Gioia's "Can Poetry Matter?" (1991). But in the end the reporter seemed not overly concerned about mere quantity of consumption, agreeing with Berkeley publisher Malcolm Margolin's assessment: "There's tremendous joy in writing poetry . . . it's more valuable as an activity than as a commodity."

These matters of scale and popularity—the size of the Lilly gift and the minority status of the art of poetry and its audience in the United States—were of course what initially provoked such startled attention not only from writers and readers but from people not ordinarily interested in literature.

For the so-called man (and woman) in the street, the curious story held only momentary fascination and was soon replaced by other oddities in the news. But for some in the literary and business worlds, the facts rankled and seemed to produce lingering resentment. The same day the *Los Angeles Times* published the Rutten analysis, the *New York Times* printed a letter from a literary editor in San Francisco who admitted he was "green with envy" but felt "a gift of this size to such a small organization is bad philanthropy." Since it would now have to become a foundation, he prophesied, "Sustaining the vision of a venerable little magazine will become an afterthought." He added: "Drowning in cash might seem a dream come true; more likely it will turn out to be a nightmare." (The author, Howard Junker, continues to display the letter on his website, to help solicit contributions to his own journal, *ZYZZYVA*. His note to me is printed below.)

In pleasant contrast, *The New Yorker* took a more whimsical approach. In "Windfalls: A Hundred Million," a "Talk of the Town" piece in the December 2nd issue, Nick Paumgartner noted the "range of reactions (glee, befuddlement, envy, disdain)" that had greeted the bequest. Calling *Poetry* "highly esteemed" and recalling its early history, he found "it remains one of the best venues of verse in the land," adding that its small budget and staff and frugal ways indicated "*Poetry* is not built to squander that kind of money." Yet he entertained some possibilities: providing beautiful new offices and "hairdos for everyone," acquiring thousands of acres in northern Michigan upon which to let "a bunch of poets run wild—a Bohemian Grove for real bohemians," not to mention constructing poetry ships and poetry stadiums. Putting the gift in perspective, he observed that "perhaps it's not so much after all": $100 million would buy only "a half of an F-11 Raptor jet," for example, and about a dozen episodes of "Friends." The theater, ballet, and the visual arts usually get "the big money," he concluded. So why not poetry as well?

By far the severest reactions to the Lilly gift appeared in two publications, both also located in New York City but ordinarily at opposite ends of the political spectrum. *The Wall Street Journal* telegraphed its position in a preview headed "Is Poetry Worth $100 Million?" (26 November). The answer to the rhetorical question was, of course, no. Citing *Poetry*'s circulation of eleven thousand, Eric Gibson submitted that it was not necessarily "a sign of philistinism" for him to find the bequest was "slightly disproportionate." He then waxed indignant: "Just what good is all that money going to do? Or to put it another way, what currently ails poetry that $100 million or more could plausibly ameliorate?"

To buttress his opinion, Gibson cited Dana Gioia's eleven-year-old polemic on American poetry, whose dire state according to the poet-businessman (and future NEA chairman) was attributable to current poetry's narrow range and insular character as the "specialized occupation" of a relatively small "subcul-ture" located mostly in academe. "Ten years on," Gibson asserted, "it's hard to see that anything's changed. Poetry's problem is one of outlook, not re-sources." Apparently unfamiliar with the actual contents of *Poetry* (let alone the "Poets in Person" national library project), Gibson recommended that we try to "reconnect poetry with the everyday life of ordinary citizens." But he cautioned, rather contradictorily: "This doesn't mean teaching courses in contemporary poetry, at least not before reintroducing the classics, and so re-minding students why poetry is at the core of our own and every other nation's literary heritage."

In "Poetry Nation," a piece alternately snide and silly published by *The Village Voice* in late November, the editors permitted Joshua Clover his weak puns (to wit: *Poetry* has standards that "are golden with highlights of green, and likely to be read all over") and even more feeble logic. With approval he quoted the suggestion of the co-editor of "the influential [sic] journal *Chain*" that the Lilly money should have been spread among four hundred poetry magazines. "Wouldn't it be amazing," she exclaimed. Likewise mar-velous (for naiveté) were Clover's own recommendations on how the money should be spent, including: buying and distributing, gratis, a million poetry books a year, offering free medical insurance to "every poet ac-cepted for publication," and lobbying for "pro-education candidates in elections at the national level" (an activity prohibited for tax-exempt or-ganizations by the IRS). In conclusion, the English professor fantasized that *Poetry* could "secede from the Union," buy the Marshall Islands, appoint "their [sic] own poet laureate, who would then meet the U.S. laureate in a battle to the death." Move over, Swift and Pope.

3. Salutations and Solicitations

It is a truth universally acknowledged that a little magazine in possession of a great fortune must be in a want of people to help spend it. In the days immediately following the announcement, while the media besieged us de-manding more information, several real estate concerns barraged us with advertisements for new office space. (The business card the TV cameraman had dropped on my table after the first interview was but an omen of things to come.) Multiple faxes, missives by messenger, FedEx packets, "urgent" letters and phone calls informed us of wondrous availabilities: high-rise suites, industrial buildings, lofts, "vintage" and even "historic" houses, prop-erties old, new, under construction or still on the drawing boards. One caller offered to hand over a factory he wanted to be rid of, if we would pay the back taxes. A kindly older gentleman phoned from Virginia to inquire whether we would like to take over a little-used vacation home on a large tract of wooded acreage, which we might convert into a "writers' retreat."

Nothing could have prepared us, however, for the enormous influx of begging letters, grant proposals, and other solicitations that promptly arrived. The appeals ranged from the highly sophisticated to the semi-literate. Handwritten notes related pathetic tales of personal or family misfortunate—whether genuine or fraudulent, it was impossible to tell—and demanded immediate (and usually quite precisely calculated) cash donations. Various arts groups approached with well-wrought missives requesting underwriting for operating expenses or new and "special" projects—many of them having nothing to do with poetry or literature. A couple of organizations tried to take advantage of well-meaning poets published in *Poetry* by enlisting them to act as liaisons or emissaries to convey their propositions.

Like the storied Little Red Hen, our little journal found the previously indifferent suddenly reappearing, now ready and more than willing to help consume the bread. Some reluctant agencies and organizations that heretofore had evinced little affection for *Poetry* or desire to participate in our educational projects, now informed us of their joy at our pending prosperity. Further, they wished to present us with "opportunities" to "cooperate" in ventures of their own devising. A few veteran grant-writers (who should have known better) hastily drew up proposals, complete with detailed budgets, before inquiring if there were any guidelines, or whether we were even in a position to make grants in the first place. Most dubious among the aid-seekers were the supposedly struggling artists and organizations that, paradoxically, were affluent enough to afford professionally packaged "materials," slickly designed brochures, or expensively produced CDs and videos, to "tell their story." Within a few weeks we received enough of such applications to fill four large boxes to overflowing.

By far the most persistent of our many would-be new friends were the financial consultants, brokerage houses, banks, trust companies, and money-management firms who approached us to tout their services, employing every means imaginable. Our resources to this point had always been modest—the annual budget was by 2002 in the $700,000 range—to the evident dismay of some in the press. But slender purses had forced us to be thrifty, efficient, and otherwise prudent in the management of our affairs; we had learned to stretch a dollar a long way. (The staffs of *Poetry* were quite aware of "multi-tasking" well before the term was invented.) And we did have a few on the board with experience in business and finance. For some months we had been quietly formulating plans, gathering expert counsel, investigating carefully selected firms, and interviewing possible advisers and managers. In short, we were not exactly the economic bumpkins that certain reporters and financial wizards who approached us assumed.

Unbidden, in the first weeks after the announcement eager representatives from all types of financial enterprises, near and far, attempted to ply their wares through phone calls, faxes, and glossy brochures specially delivered. Some made surprise personal appearances at the Newberry Library's front desk and on the doorsteps of unamused board members. At *Poetry* we had no receptionist as such (and in all my years as editor and executive director, I never had a personal assistant), so whoever on our five-person staff was free at the moment answered the phone. Now I hesitated to pick up a receiver before learning who was on the line.

One devious salesman, from a large financial services company in Boston, got through by telling our skeptical longtime managing editor that he was an old college classmate. The name did not sound familiar, but I took the call. Of course, I didn't know the smooth talker from Sinbad. He tried to laugh off his ruse. When he started to launch into his pitch, I brought him up short with a question: "Since the very first thing you did when you contacted us was lie, what makes you think we would trust you with our funds?"

We did accept an invitation to discuss their services from another major investment company that was perhaps too eager to acquire our account. Following research into their operations and commendations from trusted advisers, we were well aware of the firm's reputation (we would not have gone to the meeting otherwise), but the division chief still felt compelled to try to impress us by discoursing at great length about his company's "special resources" and "unique management style." (The opulent surroundings—a thickly carpeted labyrinth of marble and burled-wood paneling, fronted by model-quality receptionists amid high-end corporate art, antiques, and orchids—had already given some indications of their style, and made one wonder how much of their clients' "resources" were required for the rent and upkeep.) When he asked his assistant to set up the PowerPoint display and prefaced his presentation by saying, "We have fourteen rules we live by," I abbreviated the session by pointing out that Moses had needed only ten.

4. Correspondence 2002–2003

Amid the continuing torrent of news stories and commentaries, many subscribers, scores of contributing poets, and several readers previously unknown to us sent congratulatory cards, warm notes, and thoughtful letters expressing their delight on hearing that *Poetry* particularly, after such long and generous service in the field, had received such a gift. Several people offered advice. In letters too lengthy to print here, two consultants listed detailed recommendations and even offered to share their professional expertise in management and planning—free of charge.

As the small selection of messages below indicates, editors of other poetry journals, sharing an understanding of the realities of literary publishing, are particularly generous in their good wishes. But a number of people also temper their congratulations by stating their concerns about the future of the organization. Several writers present useful as well as playful suggestions. In the great tradition of American tall tales, one ironic author takes the occasion to rib the magazine about its windfall and pull a prank with a mock epistle of relentless woe.

Others write of their enjoyment of the *Dear Editor* chronicle and the dramatic gallops through *Poetry's* history in the ninetieth-anniversary programs. After the celebration in New York City, the widow of a much-loved poet relates her surprise and delight on hearing one of his early letters read from the stage of the 92nd Street Y. When one of America's most famous novelists is moved to write a long poem in response to the special anniversary issue, the editors find themselves in an awkward position, as the editor-in-chief explains in returning the submission. The Mayor of Chicago sends official greetings and congratulations on behalf of the city always happy to

On stage at the Ninetieth Anniversary celebration hosted by the 92nd Street Y in New York City: J.P., narrator, with Diane Ackerman, Galway Kinnell, Linda Gregerson, and Charles Wright; on screen: Edna St. Vincent Millay.

claim *Poetry* for its own, if not to help it, over its long and impecunious career. But eventually the correspondence returns somewhat to normal, though in their cover letters hopeful contributors usually add kind words about the recent change of fortune as preface to their submissions.

For richer or poorer, the mutually essential bonds between poets and *Poetry* and their readers remained unchanged it seemed as the magazine moved on into another decade.

Sara Van Winkle to Joseph Parisi & Stephen Young   e-mail, 15 *November 2002*

Dear Sirs:

I attended last evening's Poetry Day at St. James Cathedral, and being one of those hopelessly geeky persons who loves to attend performances prepared, I read your fantastic book "Dear Editor" in advance. This is to thank you for two of the most enjoyable and energizing experiences I have had in a very long time. . . .

It is unfortunate that so many readers, students in particular, such as myself in the 70s, tend to think great works of literature akin to stone tablets, handed down in pristine, revelatory glory from the muses on high to the authors, who in turn are blemishless conduits, divinely chosen and empowered. . . . This notion as improbably funny as it is dangerously dumb and discouraging is happily shattered by *wonderful* things such as . . . your book, and with grace, good humor, and unassailable precision. . . .

I hope your wonderful book finds its way into the hands of every lit student in this country, and that it brings them all as much revelation, pleasure and fresh air as it did, and does, me. . . . I came down from Milwaukee for the event, and it was worth every second of the five-and-a-half hour round trip driving time. . . . And while I would have come for Billy Collins alone (God, what a treat), I have to say that what really made the thing special, was your approach, as enlivened by *fabulous* reading, Michael Nowak and Linda Gregerson especially. . . .

Again, thank you very much indeed.

Very truly yours, / Sara Van Winkle

Michael Mesic to Poetry *Staff*   *Evanston, Ill., 19 November 2002*

Dear Joe and staff,

What a wonderful and surprising piece of news. Congratulations! And best wishes from a former staffer [associate editor, 1970-1976] who is thrilled to see your perseverance rewarded in such a dramatic way. I'm sure you will find extraordinary ways to use these resources to further the cause of Aunt Harriet for years to come.

Sincerely, / Michael

Gary Soto to Joseph Parisi   *Berkeley, Calif., 19 November 2002*

Dear Joseph,

I woke this morning to discover the world was tearing itself apart but also putting itself back together. Of course, I'm speaking about the marvelous news about the recent endowment. How lucky we all are! My first inclination was to ask if we can make the increase of payment per line retroactive for work published in the past. This is bad form, though. I'm beside myself with happiness. *Hijole!* Congratulations. . . .

Take care, / Gary

Robert B. Shaw to Joseph Parisi   *South Hadley, Mass.,*
20 November 2002

Dear Joe,

At last, some good news in the New York *Times!*

I thought I would write to congratulate *Poetry* on this stroke (or should I say avalanche) of good fortune. This seems an unprecedented case of Virtue Rewarded, and it is pleasant to think of the Lilly fund being put to good use in furthering civilization for long years to come. Ruth Lilly may prove to have done more for poetry than Maecenus, Lady Gregory, and Princess Marie von Thurn und Taxis-Hohenlohe all put together.

I thought the project for high school teachers mentioned in the article seems a particularly good idea. . . .

Best wishes to all of you. I hope you can take a few days off just to enjoy all this.

Faithfully, / Robt

Clyde P. Watkins to Joseph Parisi   *Oak Park, Ill., 20 November 2002*

Dear Joe,

I was going to send you a lyrical letter telling you how wonderful I feel about the news of Ruth Lilly's magnificent commitment, but Eric Zorn probably did it better than I could have [in his *Chicago Tribune* column].

Let me say this, however. I don't believe that I have ever felt happier about a gift, large or small, to a not-for-profit institution. It's because it has happened for all the right reasons, and it can make so many of the right things happen.

CHICAGO

TUESDAY

NOVEMBER 19, 2002

Eric Zorn

Kind rejection keeps Poetry's meter running

Going out of his way to be kind to beginning and second-rate poets was not in Joe Parisi's job description.

He was a front-line editor, a screener of unsolicited verse for Chicago-based Poetry magazine and charged with helping to find 300 or so publishable nuggets of gold each year amid the gravel of approximately 50,000 submissions.

Rejecting the sincere and heartfelt efforts of aspiring writers was a numbingly regular part of his duties when he came to work for the magazine as associate editor in the mid-1970s. Yet every day, he said, he would write "many, many, many" little notes to send back to some of those whose work wasn't up to the magazine's high standards. Sometimes he jotted a few words on the bottom of the form rejection slip, and sometimes he typed a separate brief letter, always encouraging or grateful.

His predecessors all the way back to the magazine's founding in 1912 had employed this personal touch, and his successors (he became the editor in 1984) have employed it as well.

> **'I just wrote her a few nice words.'**
>
> —Joe Parisi, Poetry editor

"We obviously can't write notes to everyone," said Parisi. "But especially when they're a little bit better than the norm, we want them to feel that someone did read their stuff and did appreciate that they sent it."

The woman he knew by her married name of Mrs. Guernsey Van Riper Jr. was, in fact, the last surviving great-grandchild of the founder of the huge pharmaceutical firm Eli Lilly and Co.

"Once in a while," Parisi added, "what goes around comes around."

We usually hear that expression when doom strikes the wicked. So it's refreshing to hear it in the context of benevolence rewarded; a small but important good deed, done with no thought of gain, repaid years later a millionfold. Make that up to 150 millionfold.

One moral of the story might be that you should always be considerate of others because you never know who might actually be an heir to staggering wealth inclined to toss some of the boodle your direction.

Remember, our folk traditions caution us that the hideous beggar is occasionally a prince, princess or other desirable person wearing a disguise to test our hearts. Those who respond with generosity and compassion live happily ever after in palaces of gold.

But that's a mercenary and, when it comes down to it, inefficient way of dealing with others.

After all, for every Joe Parisi there are hundreds of thousands of good Samaritans, altruists and other thoughtful souls who'll never see an extra dime for their troubles.

For cash return, being gracious is generally a lousy investment.

The real moral of the story lies here:

An old saying has it that the truest measure of a person's character is how he treats those to whom he doesn't have to give respect. Restaurant servers, for example. Housekeepers. Store clerks. Underlings. Toll-takers. Ushers and attendants. Or, in Parisi's case, the hopeful but as yet insufficiently talented poets who clog his magazine's mailbox with now 90,000 offerings a year.

The friendly word. The scribbled line of encouragement. The soft-net landing for the ego that has dared to inch out onto the high wire and then fallen off.

For years, countless would-be poets took their measure of Joe Parisi and other first readers at Poetry when they opened their self-addressed, stamped envelopes to find an upbeat note along with their rejected work. The effort made them feel just that much better about themselves, about the editors, about the magazine.

To pass the meaningful tests of character. To own the well-earned regard of others.

The real reward came long ago. The fabulous riches today are just a bonus.

You have adhered to the mission of the magazine and the principles that have guided you all along, yet you have been kind. Who knows how many other dear friends are out there, waiting to reward you? You deserve this.

And so does Poetry (the magazine and the art form!). It will be thrilling to see what you will be able to accomplish from now on. In my cynical world [fund-raising and development consulting] we call this a transforming gift, but in your case it is really true. Not many people in your general role ever get a chance to experience what you are now experiencing, and certainly no one associated with a small organization representing so much rich potential.

It does my heart good to see this happen, Joe. It's the way things ought to happen, and it will sustain me—and probably a lot of other people who toil in the world of not-for-profit and philanthropic work—for the rest of my days. . . .

With warmest regards, / Clyde

Samuel Hazo to Joseph Parisi   *International Poetry Forum,*
                                Pittsburgh, Pa., 22 November 2002

Dear Joseph Parisi:

Like everyone else I was totally overwhelmed by Ruth Lilly's grant of $100,000,000 to the magazine. That says much about Mrs. Lilly's magnanimity, but it says even more about the trust and confidence she has in your leadership. People do not give money (that kind of money) to those who do not deserve it. You deserve as much credit as she does, and I send you my sincerest compliments and congratulations.

Sincerely, / Samuel Hazo
President/Director

David Bottoms to Joseph Parisi   *Atlanta, Ga., 25 November 2002*

Dear Joe,

Silly me. Sent you a poem a while back—"Shooting Rats in the Afterlife"—and fear now that I didn't put enough postage on the return envelope. . . .

Hope you and all the folks up there are faring well. We struggle along down here, but sorry to say that these last few months haven't been the best. Did I tell you that my mother fell a while back and broke her hip and both arms? 93 years old. Bedridden now, of course, and must have private nurses, the whole nine yards. . . . And hers, of course, is the generation without insurance. It was one of those rare August ice storms that hit us down here with

Longtime contributor David Bottoms,
photographed in the early eighties.

absolutely no warning. You're out checking the mailbox and suddenly a wind blows up, a cloud blows over, and the whole yard is a sheet of ice. Impossible for an old person to get back to the house, especially one weakened by so many years of poverty and deprivation. But we're holding up, struggling on, even though Kelly's law practice dried up entirely this summer. Seems like people finally saw the light, learned to practice the golden rule, and stopped suing each other. She's working the late shift now at a local 7-Eleven, which doesn't bring in much, and I'm afraid if things get any worse, she'll take to the streets.

Not to worry though. I've started a small garden in the back yard, just a few vegetables, but this has helped. I'm just hoping they don't foreclose on the house before I can get in the spring crop. But if that happens, we have a friend (what would we do without them?) who has an old school bus he's converted into a camper. He's willing to let us have that for a very reasonable price. No running water or showers, of course, but I figure we can just take it out on the interstate and park it at a rest stop. Also, in a few years Rachel will be old enough to get a job at McDonald's. Anyway, not to worry about us. We'll make out. And besides, there's really nothing to be done. Well, unless . . . Unless, of course, you happen to know someone who might be willing to make a small loan to a decent and God-fearing family. Nothing large really. I think three or four hundred thousand would get us back on our feet. Anyway, what will happen will happen, and one certainly hates to air this kind of struggle and heartache to his friends. I can sound too much like whining and put a strain on relationships.

On the other hand, as they say, what are friends for? Listen, a horrible thought just occurred to me. I hope you don't think my telling you all of this has anything to do with my learning of *Poetry*'s outstanding endowment from Ms. Ruth Lilly! Please forgive that thought! I know a person with a heart as good as yours couldn't possible be such a cynic.

Listen, super congrats on the Lilly thing. What a wonderful coup! Looking forward to seeing you in the spring. If we're still in the house, maybe you could help with the garden?

All best, / David

On 3 December, Bottoms wrote: "Am so sorry to have alarmed you guys with my prank epistle. I feel a little like Orson Welles [in the "War of the Worlds" dramatization] on the morning after Halloween, 1938. But at least my letter wasn't broadcast over the radio and, fortunately, nobody jumped out a window."

Howard Junker to Joseph Parisi   ZYZZYVA, *San Francisco,*
25 November 2002

Dear Joe:

I hope my dire predictions don't come true: Godspeed.

Best regards,

Yours, / Howard Junker
Editor

In a letter printed in the *New York Times* 23 November, Junker asserted the bequest was "bad philanthropy" and predicted, "Sustaining the vision of a venerable little magazine will become an afterthought."

J. D. McClatchy to Joseph Parisi   *New York City, 5 December 2002*

Dear Joe—

I finally laid my hands on a copy of your book of letters, and raced through it. Fascinating! I suppose you've had to deal with worse cases than Pound or Dahlberg, but I hope not too often. Eek! Like you, I know too well the editor's job not to sympathize with the squirming temporizer. In any case, your introductions are splendid, and the whole book is truly a potted history of poetry—and a series of exceptionally vivid portraits.

I was sorry to see on p. 454 that I didn't make it into the list of Daryl's first-timers, but then I remember Jimmy Merrill telling me that when he was at the Gotham Book Mart during the Sitwell visit, and the famous group photograph was about to be taken, he was asked to step into the next room, out of camera range. . . .

Sandy

Maria Terrone to Joseph Parisi   *Jackson Heights, N.Y.,*
12 December 2002

Dear Joe:

Now that we've met, I feel I can take the liberty of using your first name—perhaps emboldened by knowing that so many of *Poetry*'s writers were far from formal in their editorial correspondence!

It was a pleasure for me to greet you in person at the "Dear Editor" event in New York this week. I've wanted to meet you ever since you accepted "Madame Curie" and "Drifts"—my very first submission to *Poetry*—back in 1997 [February, published in May]. But how could I have known that you're not only an editor, but also an actor! You played the role of Ezra Pound and the other writers so well. . . .

Hearing that you may eventually produce *Dear Editor, Part II*, I suspect that your many poet-contributors in the audience will, from now on, take extra care in crafting witty little missives to you.

But I write *this* little missive to say how happy I was to meet you, to offer congratulations on *Poetry*'s 90th anniversary and to say how glad I am about the magazine's financial windfall.

I hope you have a wonderful Christmas and New Year.

Best wishes, / Maria Terrone

Annie Wright to Joseph Parisi   *New York City, 13 December 2002*

Dear Mr. Parisi,

Only the large crowd of fans, bowed down under armloads of books for you to sign, kept me from introducing myself and congratulating you in person on the splendid program at the 92nd Y. I felt it might be hours before I could meet you so gave up the idea and went home. I am so sorry. I trust you'll be in New York another time and perhaps we could meet then.

Some time in the 50's I bought a copy of *Poetry*, my first venture into that type of journal. I was intrigued by my purchase but I'm afraid many of the poems were well over my head. It took James Wright to help me understand and truly appreciate both poetry and your magazine.

I truly loved the program and was thrilled and touched to hear that wild letter by James [describing *Hamlet*, as rendered in Classics Comics, which he read as a boy]. It came as a lovely surprise. Galway [Kinnell] says "Arghhhh-hhh" quite differently than James once did, but both versions are delightful.

Best wishes and holiday greetings,

Annie Wright

See *Dear Editor*, p. 440.

Richard M. Daley to Joseph Parisi   *Office of the Mayor, Chicago,*
                                              27 December 2002

Dear Mr. Parisi:

As Mayor and on behalf of the Chicago Department of Cultural Affairs, I would like to extend my sincere congratulations to you for the most generous donation you received from Ruth Lilly.

As one of our country's leading literary publications, *Poetry* has show-cased the considerable talent of many well-known and emerging poets alike. Their words, as well as the verse of future poets your magazine inspires, entertain and uplift countless readers around the world.

Congratulations again, and I am certain that your excellent stewardship of this donation and of the magazine will continue with much success.

Best wishes, / Richard M. Daley
Mayor

Robert Parham to Joseph Parisi   Southern Poetry Review,
Savannah, Ga., 28 December 2002

Dear Mr. Parisi:

That I have taken so long to write about the astounding good fortune that comes to you and *Poetry* via Ms. Lilly shocks me, but I trust you have had so many more important congratulations that this one can humbly follow. Since Ms. Lilly has long been a supporter of great consequence, I think all of us poets know very well it has been your presence at *Poetry* that was both the connection and the conductor that allowed all this to happen, indeed encouraged it. Bravo!

Let me end this here, else worse metaphors might follow. Simply know my delight and that of others who may not have written re the bequest and how deserved it most surely is.

Sincerely, / Robert Parham

John Montague to Joseph Parisi   *Nice, France, [December 2002]*

Dear Joe:

I have been meaning to write to you for some time, to offer my congratulations. Destiny seems to have decided that you should preside over the extension of *Poetry* and as far as I am concerned, you are the ideal man for the job.

I can't resist offering a few suggestions which you can treat with the scorn they may deserve. You could enlarge the magazine a little so that you can print longer poems which I, for one, no longer send for fear of usurping the space of others, especially younger writers.

Then you could restore, and increase, the list of Prizes, which give a hint of gambling or racetrack effect which I, as an Irishman, can find amusing, although I do see the bad side. Oliver Goldsmith said, "Writers are like racehorses; they should be fed but not fattened."

They should also not be pitted against each other! I'll plague you with a few (longer) poems but later; just now I want to congratulate you all at *Poetry*: good news, especially from America, is welcome these days. I have formed an association, the AAIP, or Association of Ancient Irish Poets (of which I am the only member so far) to make this a more formal salutation.

Yours affectionately, / John Montague

Bill Sweeney to Joseph Parisi   *New York City,*
[n.d., December? 2002]

Dear Joseph Parisi,
    Please find enclosed "Another Love Song" for your consideration.
    Congratulations on your recent bequest from the estate of Ruth Lilly. As the recipient of one of your remarkably generous and useful rejection letters (as well as, gratefully, one of your equally gracious acceptance letters) I was not at all surprised to hear that your rejection of some of her poems still resonated with her many years later. I hope the opportunities that the money brings to *Poetry* do not take you away from editing. . . .
    My two-year-old announced that he has decided to dress up "as himself" for Halloween this fall. I've decided to try to follow his example as closely as I can.

Sincerely yours, / Bill Sweeney

Joseph Parisi to Norman Mailer   *Chicago, 3 January 2003*

Dear Mr. Mailer,
    Forgive the tardiness of this response to the poem you faxed us on 14 November. As I explained to your marvelous assistant Judith McNally, ordinarily we would have replied within days. But your missive had the ill luck of arriving on the eve of our 90th Anniversary celebration, and just before the news of *Poetry*'s radical change of fortune broke upon the world. Things haven't been the same since, as we have come to understand the true meaning of media frenzy—and why celebrities want to punch out the paparazzi. You, of course, know all too well the ravenous habits of the Fourth Estate. We're only now starting to recover from the relentless attention, and distraction.
    So profuse apologies. Both Steve Young and I have read and reread "On Reading *Poetry* Magazine's 90th Anniversary Issue," with considerable interest (and no little amusement). Certainly it's the most original response to that number that we've received. But, as I said to Ms. McNally, the poem puts me rather in a spot. Much as I like what you've said here (though, for-

give me, I do think the poem might be twice as strong it if were half as long), I don't think we can run a piece that's so self-referential (to the magazine, I mean).

We don't do a "Letters to the Editor" column, but I had thought for a while there that we might run it in the back of the book, along with some of the other responses to the 90th Ann. issue. We've received an awful lot of letters, so uniformly positive and flattering that it would almost make me blush . . . . But the wiser (or perhaps just more cautious) Superegotistical editorial portion of the psyche says, Don't do it. After all the publicity *Poetry*'s been getting of late from newspapers, TV, radio and other "outlets" here and abroad, it might appear that we were adding to the din, blowing our own horn (by proxy), and that would be most unseemly—as our "friends" in the media would be the very first to point out.

So here I am, in the incredible position of having to decline work from Norman Mailer, for godsakes. I hope you won't think me a complete idiot or, worse, a total ingrate. I really was thrilled to receive the poem, and to know that you have read the issue with such care, and reacted so strongly and deeply to some of the selections that you felt a need to respond yourself *in poetry*.

All best, / Joe Parisi

John Updike to Joseph Parisi   *Beverly Farms, Mass., 6 January 2003*

Dear Mr. Parisi:

Two sonnets, to go with the two longer poems I sent you last month. May I presume to ask that the stamped return envelope I sent with them do also for the return of these, if it comes to that? I was delighted to see that your January issue in no way reflected the immense legacy which has recently come your way. I am not alone among *Poetry* admirers in hoping that affluence will not change you.

Happy New Year, / John Updike

Both "Chambered Nautilus" and "Tools" were accepted, and printed in June 2003. Updike had also written 26 November to say *Poetry* "ranks up there with *Scientific American* for instant consultation. It is much the most inviting magazine of its kind, and I love the secret story you weave each month with the unstated connections between the poems. . . ."

Jim Reiss to Joseph Parisi   *Oxford, Ohio, 8 January 2003*

Dear Joe Parisi:

This is to remind you that if you don't find a place for those poems of Jim's very soon, you gotta return 'em to him. There are four of them, "Cecilia

Products," "Mexico Minus You," "Paintable Lady," and "Yippee for the *Demos*," stunning things, all. You are committing a bitter and presumptuous folly in thus long keeping them from the world. If you don't look out I'll just tell the world all about it, and then where will you be?

Lovingly, / Jim Reiss

Reiss is echoing Edna St. Vincent Millay's facetious letters to Harriet Monroe concerning the fate of her submissions; see *Dear Editor*, pp. 1 and 241–42.

Robert Pinsky to Joseph Parisi   *Cambridge, Mass., 14 February 2003*

Dear Joe,

I hope the storm of attention has abated enough that some thoughts I have about money and poetry may be acceptable. If they are unwelcome, excuse me. But I know you are taking your time to think this through properly—and here come my views.

Mainly, I want to refute those who scoff at assigning resources for poetry, compared to social needs. The distinction is false. Poetry is part of our society, and fills important social needs.

There is a great need for what is called "outreach" in foundation jargon. In prison education programs in hospitals and nursing homes, in all sorts of institutions, poetry already has great importance and could use support. Many school libraries and public libraries lack adequate budget for poetry books, magazines, and programs.

American education is said to be in poor condition, partly for lack of gifted and devoted teachers: every year graduates of creative writing programs begin looking for teaching jobs, at many different levels, for which they sometimes find they lack the credentials.

Often, those students have graduated from MFA programs and undergraduate creative programs on a campus where there is a School of Education. But the creative writing people and the education school people, sometimes, have not even met. Until recently, I have not heard of them co-operating with one another. But they have a lot to offer one another, and by co-operating they can bring a lot to American schools.

These few areas I've tried to sketch are only examples, and possibly you are way ahead of me in this direction. I think there are enough prizes and awards; I applaud you for thinking about the opportunity to do something useful as carefully, and as imaginatively, as possible.

And forgive me please if this is unnecessary!

Best wishes, / Robert

Mary Oliver to Joseph Parisi   *Provincetown, Mass.,*
                                                    20 February 2003

Dear Joe—

Your news, of the gift to *Poetry*, is so wonderful, and will make real differences in what you can do—and it must be said—should be said—that such things don't happen randomly, but within context—you are that context. I think, if you had not been captain of the ship, it would have remained a dream. Therefore, along with elation, I want to send you my thanks.

All love, / Mary

P.S. I've got a few poems to send soon—as probably so do 3 million other people these days!

Michael York to Joseph Parisi   *Los Angeles, Calif., 14 March 2003*

Dear Joseph:

Many thanks for your letter. Believe me, the pleasure was entirely mine—I loved our afternoon of literary delights at the Getty. And thank you again for the wonderful books that have already provided hours of pleasure.

This is also to say that I would very much welcome the prospect of working for, and with, you again. . . .

Sincerely, / Michael

York portrayed several letter writers at the ninetieth-anniversary celebration co-sponsored with the Poetry Society of America at the J. Paul Getty Museum in Los Angeles on 16 February. Blythe Danner, Dana Delaney, and Paul Blackthorne also acted on the program.

Joseph Parisi to John Updike   *Chicago, 31 March 2003*

Dear Mr. Updike,

Thanks for your letter. Let's keep [the title] "Chambered Nautilus": I like the echo. I'm enclosing copies of the *Americana* [*and Other Poems*] review [February 2002].

By the way, I meant to mention in my last how much I admired your *Harper's* article/intro to the Shapiro Selected. Extremely astute, both the appreciation and the selection. It's hard to know why Shapiro's reputation took such a dive in his later years, and has had such a hard time recovering. Partly, I suppose, because he kept changing (not always for the better) and was not easily pigeon-holed. Mainly, though, I guess because he bit so many hands that fed him.

As I said in *Dear Editor*, he seemed bent on appearing the outsider, despite his many laurels from the Establishment. . . . Anyway, I hope your good words will help "rehabilitate" him.

All best, / Joe Parisi

Alison Stone to Joseph Parisi   *New York City, 31 March 2003*

Dear Joseph Parisi:

I hope this letter finds you well. I am writing to let you know that, after fifteen years of being a finalist in various contests, my book has won the Many Mountains Moving Award and will be published in 2004. I want to thank you again, because your acceptance of my early poems for *Poetry* was essential to my career on many levels—by exposing my work to anthology editors and critics such as Helen Vendler, and, more importantly, by giving me the confidence to persevere during this decade and a half of "always a bridesmaid." . . .

Through the years, I've had many poets whom I respect give me feedback, much of it conflicting. Most of them wanted me to revise the early poems, which I did. But after hearing your opinion of the revision, I went back to all the original versions of poems you had published and compared them to the revised ones. In every case I felt that the versions you published had more cohesiveness and integrity. They may lack the subtlety and maturity of my recent work, but trying to rework old poems into a newer voice left an unsatisfying hodgepodge. So the published book will include all the poems you published in their original forms.

Again, I thank you for the help and support you and *Poetry* have given me over the years.

Best wishes, / Alison Stone

John Updike to Joseph Parisi   *Beverly Farms, Mass., 5 April 2003*

Dear Mr. Parisi:

Thanks for your pleasant letter. I feel I should explain that the *Harper's* piece is a somewhat cut version, and very oddly billed as a review when in truth it is the introduction to the Library of America volume [of Shapiro's selected poems]. I got out *Dear Editor* and read your pages on Shapiro; they added to my knowledge, and to what he says in *The Younger Son*, or is it *Reports of My Death*. Yes, he does seem to have been a difficult fellow to handle, though in our brief acquaintance he was very sweet to me, and very soft-spoken, in perhaps Baltimore fashion. His widow, Sophie Wilkins, continues in her late 80s to write spirited letters and guard his flame. Don't answer this card; you have much else to do.

Best, / John Updike

Kay Ryan to Joseph Parisi   *Fairfax, Calif., 29 April 2003*

Dear Joe,

Here is the corrected proof of "The Niagara River" ("River" constitutes a great portion of the poem's amusement value).

I just got the May '03 *Poetry* with "Home to Roost" in it. I got a kick out of your little run of dog poems followed by a flock of bird poems. You are a naughty editor.

Thanks for your good letter of March 24. I'm sorry I couldn't make the Chicago festivities for *Poetry*'s birthday. It would have been a memorable—and terrifying—event to impersonate Miss Monroe [on the program]. I shudder to think.

Well "The Niagara River" is the last of the group of poems to be published [July 2003], so I guess it's time to tart up a few new ones to send your way, what do you say?

All best of course, / Kay

Joseph Parisi to Robert Pinsky   *Chicago, 5 May 2003*

Dear Robert,

Thanks for your thoughtful letter. I'm sorry to be late in responding. It's been a whirlwind around here since the Big News broke in November. We now know what they mean by "media frenzy." . . .

I read your thoughts with great interest. It is extremely unfortunate that there's not much communication between Schools of Ed. and MFA programs, and I don't know what the solution is. I suspect a great many creative writers would feel most uncomfortable with the curricula of Ed. Schools, which tend to be on the dull side, or so I'm told. And given the bureaucracies (and textbook adoption policies) in most school districts, it's not easy to effect change.

My own thoughts have been running in the direction of trying to set up Teachers' Institutes, 2- to 3-week "total immersion" seminars that would give junior and senior high school teachers a crash course in contemporary poetry, with a chance to meet good poets face to face, and work with skilled teachers of poetry and poetry appreciation. But haven't gotten far with plans, since there's so much else to do right now. . . .

All best, / Joe

Philip Levine to Joseph Parisi   *Fresno, Calif., 7 July 2003*

Dear Joe,

Now that *Poetry* is the richest publication in Christendom & maybe in history, what the hell are you going to do? In truth I don't envy you. That is so much money it carries with it so many burdens. You could become another Foundation with a staff the size of the Academy Awards & 150 sycophants waiting at the gates. And in the meantime poetry and *Poetry* are forgotten. I hope it works out. And the magazine can remain the magazine. PSA & the Academy already do all those things that are useful & inessential & there are granting agencies all over the place & prizes galore. Hell, the Lilly Prize is already huge. You should certainly spruce up your offices & give your loyal assistants a raise. And have an annual feast. . . .

You be well, & don't pinch pennies.

Phil

[P.S.] Buy a huge fountain pen. [Guggenheim Foundation president] Joel Conarroe had one on his desk—a Mont Blanc—the size of a baseball bat. Pelikan makes a better one. I can get you a deal!

Joseph Parisi to Billy Collins   *Chicago, 14 July 2003*

Dear Billy,

So good hearing your voice yesterday. Thanks for the inside scoop on the P.L. [the selection of Louise Glück as the new Poet Laureate] (which I am keeping in the deep freeze). And thanks for the new poems ("The Teacher" is esp. wonderful). . . . As I mentioned, I finished putting together Sept, my last issue, just before going off to Rotterdam. . . .

Billy Collins at home with "the hound," 2002.

Still a bit strange being in the new space (and *space* is the operative word here), a luxury quite new to us, and one we're having no trouble getting accustomed to. Also windows. Now if the new computer system would just get deloused. . . .

Laying down the blue pencil and green eyeshade is still more of a concept than an emotionally processed reality at this point; too busy, anyway, to linger on it. But I do remember, vividly and often, my delight on that afternoon when I came upon your first submissions. And I just want to tell you that being able to print your work has

J. P. at his desk shortly before departure from the
Newberry Library, June 2003. He resigned as editor
and executive director the following month.

been the greatest privilege—and joy—of my two decades in the editor's
chair. For the many great poems, and especially for all the kindness you've
shown me these many years, I'll always be grateful.

Joe

Billy Collins to Joseph Parisi   *Somers, N.Y., 28 July 2003*

Dear Joe,

If there was room on the walls I might frame that letter from you. How
kind your words were about my role in your editorship. I will never forget
my first acceptance at the magazine even though ever subsequent acceptance provided the same great thrill. . . .

Just back from 13 days in Southampton. All quite glam, including dinner
with Mel Brooks and Anne Bancroft and a lunch (luncheon rather) at the
pond side home of Jean Kennedy Smith, the youngest of the Kennedy
children. My lunch partner? Lauren Bacall. No jive.

Ready to return to taking out the garbage and feeding the hound.

Congratulations on your amazing tenure as editor. Just got your penulti-
mate issue in the mail. Can't believe I won't be aiming poems at your desk.

X O

Billy

Copyrights and Permissions

May Swenson: Permission of the Literary Estate of May Swenson.

Caroline Tate: Published with permission of the Princeton University Library.

Virginia R. Terris: Permission of the author.

Maria Terrone: Permission of the author.

Frederick Turner: Permission of the author.

John Updike: Permission of the author.

Mona Van Duyn: Permission of the Estate of Mona Van Duyn.

Sara Van Winkle: Permission of the author.

Helen Vendler: Permission of the author.

David Wagoner: Permission of the author.

Diane Wakoski: Permission of the author.

BJ Ward: Permission of the author.

Robert Penn Warren: Copyright © 1979, 1986 by Robert Penn Warren. Reprinted by permission of William Morris Agency, LLC on behalf of the Author.

Michael Waters: Permission of the author.

Clyde P. Watkins: Permission of the author.

Robert Watson: Permission of the author.

Edmund White: Permission of the author.

C. K. Williams: Permission of the author.

Florence Williams: Letter by Florence H. Williams Copyright © 2006 by the Estates of William Eric Williams and Paul H. Williams; used by permission of the heirs of Florence H. Williams.

Anne Winters: Permission of the author.

Larry Woiwode: Permission of Neil Olson, Donadio & Olson.

Annie Wright: Permission of Mrs. James Wright.

Charles Wright: Permission of the author.

David C. Yates: Permission of JoAnn Yates.

Stephen Yenser: Permission of the author.

Michael York: Permission of the author.

Stephen Young: Permission of the author.

C. Dale Young: Permission of the author.

Marya Zaturenska: Permission of Patrick Bolton Gregory.

Illustration Credits

Chicago Tribune: Articles (and photographs): 17 November 2002, pp. 1 and 20, by James Warren (reproduced on p. 6, and photograph by Chuck Berman, p. 381); 19 November 2002, by Eric Zorn (p. 390); and editorial, 23 November 2002 (p. 21): Reprinted with permission of the *Chicago Tribune*; copyright 2002, Chicago Tribune Company. All rights reserved.

New York Times: Editorial, 20 November 2002 (reproduced on p. 10): Copyright 2002 by The New York Times Co. Reprinted with permission.

Photograph of Gerard Malanga and Andy Warhol at The Factory, 11 June 1963 (p. 68), by Edward Wallowitch; reproduction courtesy John Wallowitch. Demonstration at Lincoln Memorial (p. 81) and March on the Pentagon (p. 82), 21 October 1967, by Elliott Landy, used by permission. Photograph of 90th Anniversary reading at 92nd Street Y, New York City, 9 December 2002 (p. 387), by Nancy Crampton, used by permission.

Unless otherwise noted, all remaining photographs and illustrations are taken from the office archives of *Poetry* Magazine and used by kind permission of The Poetry Foundation. Photo credits:

P. 4: Harriet Monroe (John Young Photographers); p. 5: Cast at the Chicago 90th Anniversary program, 14 November 2002 (Robert Murphy); p. 18: Amy Lowell (Bachrach Studios); p. 37: Henry Rago in the *Poetry* office (photo by Bob Wilson; copyright ©2006 and reprinted by permission of Christina Rago); p. 37: Robert Creeley and Bobbie Hall (Robert Mueller); p. 42: T. S. Eliot (Angus McBean); p. 50: Randall Jarrell (Ted Russell); p. 59: Allen Ginsberg, William Burroughs, and Philip Whalen (Courtesy Pamela Sanderson, Naropa Institute); p. 68 Andy Warhol and Gerard Malanga (Edward Wallowitch; used by permission of John Wallowitch); p. 70: Rod Padgett letter-drawing (by and used courtesy of the author); p. 81: Antiwar demonstration at the Lincoln Memorial and p. 82: Protestors at the Pentagon, 21 October 1967 (Elliott Landy, used by permission); p. 97: Robert Bly (Douglas Hall); p. 113: Daryl Hine (Sam Todes).

Index

A NOTE ON THE EDITORS

Joseph Parisi joined *Poetry* as associate editor in 1976 and was its editor-in-chief from 1983 to 2003, the longest tenure after that of *Poetry*'s founder, Harriet Monroe. He also served as executive director of the magazine's parent organization, the Modern Poetry Association (now the Poetry Foundation). His most recent books are *100 Essential Modern Poems* and, as co-editor with Stephen Young, *Dear Editor: A History of* POETRY *in Letters (1912–1962)* and *The* POETRY *Anthology, 1912–2002.* Mr. Parisi was born in Duluth, Minnesota, and received a Ph.D. in English from the University of Chicago. He was awarded a Guggenheim fellowship in 2000 and was elected a by-fellow of Churchill College, Cambridge, in 2002. He lives in Chicago.

Stephen Young began as an assistant at *Poetry* in 1988 and served as senior editor until 2003, when he was appointed program director of the Poetry Foundation. He attended Dartmouth College, where he held a Raible Scholarship, and did graduate work at the University of Chicago. In 2000 he received an Everett Helm Visiting Fellowship for work on *Dear Editor: A History of* POETRY *in Letters.*